# Interactive Media
# and Society

# Interactive Media and Society

Corinne M. Dalelio

LEXINGTON BOOKS
*Lanham • Boulder • New York • London*

Published by Lexington Books
An imprint of The Rowman & Littlefield Publishing Group, Inc.
4501 Forbes Boulevard, Suite 200, Lanham, Maryland 20706
www.rowman.com

86-90 Paul Street, London EC2A 4NE, United Kingdom

British Library Cataloguing in Publication Information Available

**Library of Congress Cataloging-in-Publication Data**

Names: Dalelio, Corinne M., 1979– author.
Title: Interactive media and society / Corinne M. Dalelio.
Description: Lanham : Lexington Books, [2022] | Includes bibliographical references and index. | Summary: "Drawing on the academic literature and real-world examples, this book details the impacts of interactive media in various sectors of American society. The aim is to provide the reader with a set of applicable principles and practical tips for understanding and navigating these changes, now and into the future"—Provided by publisher.
Identifiers: LCCN 2022007797 (print) | LCCN 2022007798 (ebook) | ISBN 9781793633002 (cloth) | ISBN 9781793633019 (epub) | ISBN 9781793633026 (paper)
Subjects: LCSH: Interactive multimedia—United States. | Multimedia systems—United States. | Internet—Social aspects—United States.
Classification: LCC QA76.9.I58 D35 2022 (print) | LCC QA76.9.I58 (ebook) | DDC 006.7—dc23/eng/20220331
LC record available at https://lccn.loc.gov/2022007797
LC ebook record available at https://lccn.loc.gov/2022007798

*For my three guys, covering me always with
your support, love, and protection*

# Contents

# List of Figures

# Preface

This book is based on an undergraduate-level college class of the same title that I have developed over the last decade. In that time, I have found that students and experts alike have a tendency to give a great deal of agency to technology, as if it were an unstoppable force with which we simply cannot reckon. But whether they articulate this "Force" as coming from the light side or the dark side, it is rare to find a view that identifies the line delineating the potentialities embedded within these tools from our actual uses of them. Yet the reality is that, while interactive media have created the context for plenty of new possibilities and new problems for us humans, without us they would have done nothing at all. When we regard these tools as having agency, we diminish our own, both limiting our ability to envision new horizons and exacerbating our susceptibility to technology's traps. Hence throughout my own scholarship and teaching, my goal has been to continually challenge the assumptions of both technological determinism and technological solutionism by focusing on the interacting elements of the evolving socio-cultural and technological systems. As I have struggled to find a single text that offers a balanced, comprehensive, straightforward articulation of interactive media's impacts on our society while also providing the reader with a strong sense of their own role in the complex web of consequences and solutions, I decided to write my own.

I finally sat down to work on this manuscript in February of 2020, and it took me over a year to complete. This time frame, one may recognize, happens to overlap with the "unprecedented" and "historic" era in America that includes not only the coronavirus pandemic, but also heightened social unrest due to the murder of George Floyd, and the aftermath of the 2020 presidential election. As I wrote the pages that follow, events arose on a near weekly basis that challenged my core thesis. The idea that we can approach interactive media with both agency and balance was consistently confronted in a time when it seemed impossible to achieve either.

The COVID-19 shutdown has been extremely revelatory with respect to what happens when social interaction occurs almost entirely through online spaces. Without regular access to a living, breathing community of humans, the dehumanizing, polarizing, and radicalizing effects of interactive media have been thrown into high relief in our individual lives and in the public arena. Yet these tools have also been integral during this difficult and isolating time, helping us to connect with one another even though we could not be together in person, so that we could bond over our shared experiences with all their joys and suffering, maintain our social ties, and continue to work together toward promoting human progress. If there was ever a time that technology would have brought about a utopic vision of society or taken us into an irreversible dystopia, this would have been it. Yet here we are, a bit worse for the wear perhaps, but still finding silver linings, recognizing our failures, learning from our experiences, and continuing to persist in our search for productive ways forward together. I cannot say whether or not I have successfully met the challenge that I had set out for myself with this manuscript, but I do believe that the context in which I was writing has helped to sharpen, deepen, and clarify my understanding of the complicated and ever-evolving relationship between humanity and technology. My hope is that I offer something here that will help educators, students, and practitioners to recognize both the opportunities and the pitfalls that interactive media present, as I feel now more than ever that more conscientious engagement with them is needed.

The chapters that make up the text that follows unfold in two different ways. First, their topical themes generally reflect an ordering that first lays out the foundational principles driving the interactive media space (chapters 1–4) and then unpacks these principles in detail by exploring them in various contexts and circumstances (chapters 5–14). Second, they build upon one another in an almost chronological way that reflects the history of our understanding of these tools since they were first introduced into our world, beginning with our first major surprises about the powerful potential that they held for supporting human flourishing, and followed up on with our collective realization that there was, indeed, just as much potential for them to be used as tools of oppression.

Each chapter opens with a story, summing up in a narrative way a real-world case example that reflects and demonstrates many of the concepts and themes that will be addressed throughout the chapter. The perspectives laid out in these chapters are based on an incorporation of a variety of scholarly and theoretical approaches that have been applied, with all of their synergies and tensions, to understand these tools and their impacts on society. The goal of each chapter is to provide a clear and digestible understanding of the current state of knowledge, synthesizing these perspectives in a way that provides a balanced and agentic path through which we can navigate the confusing, chaotic, and constantly upended relationship that we have with the media through which we communicate.

In the first two chapters, I outline the core underpinnings of what makes interactive media different from any media and communication technologies that we had before, and the resultingly unexpected outcomes that they have had on the media ecosystem within which we operate. In chapters 3 and 4, I focus on the "networked" outcomes of these tools, and the ways in which they have allowed us to connect and interact with one another in larger, more informal, and more distributed ways. Chapters 5 and 6 focus on how our uses of these media have influenced culture due to broadened public participation in creative and civic media spaces, and the resulting implications for both everyday people and the media industries. Chapter 7 details what collaboration looks like in these interactive spaces, leading into chapter 8, which focuses specifically on the impacts they have had on the most demanding of collaborative outcomes, collective action. Chapter 9 covers the ways in which changing relationships forged between empowered consumers and responding brands have complicated models of production and marketing, which is reflected in the media industry in particular in chapters 10 and 11. Chapters 12 and 13 focus on the negative consequences of living so much of our communicative lives through media spaces privately owned by technology and media corporations, and chapter 14 provides a productive path forward for society by delineating the many roles each of us can play in its direction.

# Acknowledgments

I would like to express my sincerest gratitude to everyone who provided me with feedback, editing, and assistance on chapters and versions of this manuscript, including the anonymous peer reviewer, as well as: my brother (and supremely talented writer) Mike Dalelio; my departmental colleague Dr. Jeffrey Ranta; my "first reader" and graduate assistant, Dahlia DeHaan; my graduate student (and hardworking journalist) Hannah Strong Oskin; and my graduate assistants, Elizabeth Mottola and Francesco Migliano. Thank you as well to my brother Dennis Dalelio for his insights and feedback, and of course for providing the amazing cover art. I would also like to acknowledge and express my thanks to the following experts for indulging me on Twitter about specific concepts and ideas discussed in the book: Jeff Kosseff, Matt Blaze, Daphne Keller, Larry Sanger, Elliot Harmon, Julian Sanchez, Dan Gillmor, and Jillian York.

On a personal note, thank you to my parents for always being proud of me. My most heartfelt appreciation goes out to my family, my three guys, who put up with me spending extended amounts of time out in "the cave" during the already abnormal and harried year(s) of Zoom, as well as my occasional bouts of overwhelm. In particular, thank you to my husband, Roland, without whose encouragement in the face of challenge and adversity this book would never have even been attempted. Above all, thank you to God for all these gifts and blessings.

# Chapter 1

# Interactive Media

## INTRODUCTION: SAVE OUR SNAPS?

Some years ago, in my "Interactive Media & Society" class, I explained to my undergraduate students that: (1) everything they do online creates data, and (2) this data is typically stored on the servers that are owned by the company whose site they are using and often on several other servers owned by various cooperative entities.[1] As I spoke, I noticed a young woman in the front row looking increasingly apprehensive. She raised her hand and asked hesitantly, "Is it true that the pictures you send on Snapchat can be saved?" The whole class perked up, awaiting my answer. Even though I knew little about Snapchat at the time, my response was, "I'm sure they can—with interactive media, where there's a will, there's always a way." She and several other students responded by laughing nervously and looking around at each other in surprise.

Snapchat, a photo-sharing app that emerged in 2011, allows users to share what Shein[2] calls "ephemeral data," or data that is shared and then disappears after a predetermined set amount of time (in Snapchat's case, a matter of seconds). Therefore, it is seen as a more "private" way to send messages, and users may feel more comfortable sending photos that contain questionable or sensitive content. For example, in a survey conducted in 2014, Roesner, Gill, and Kohno found that 23.6 percent of users admitted to having sent sexual or pseudo-sexual content via Snapchat.[3] As it turns out, my initial instinct when answering this student's question was correct. Subsequent to the release of Snapchat, third-party apps were developed that could capture and recover Snapchat images, regardless of their "ephemeral" disappearing act. In fact, in 2015, the Federal Trade Commission (FTC) filed an order against Snapchat in which it was determined that they had indeed misled their users about the degree of privacy protections for these vanishing messages.[4]

1

Young people today are often called *digital natives* because they grew up with new digital media technologies, and are therefore more familiar with and skilled at using them than previous generations.[5] How, then, could it be that my digitally "native" students didn't even realize that an image lasting ten seconds could be captured, saved, and stored, in unwanted or unintended ways? As it turns out, digital natives, while very good at adopting and using new technologies, are not as good at thinking critically about the tools themselves and their uses of them.[6] In fact, because of their "native" status, they may be even more susceptible to the potential negative outcomes of these tools.[7] While young people today have the skill sets to use new media, they do not fully understand the fundamentals of what they are, how they operate, or how they can interact with each other.[8]

Meanwhile, the research on *digital literacy*, or one's ability to use and understand digital media, shows that educational programs typically have a strong focus on skill-building, training students how to use new media in meaningful ways.[9] While this training is certainly of great usefulness and importance to students, learning how to use these media does not necessarily provide students with an analytical approach to their use.[10] More thoughtful engagement is needed. As Gillmor explains, "learning how to snap a photo with a mobile phone is useful, but it's just as important to know all the possibilities of what you can do with that picture and to understand how it fits into a larger media ecosystem."[11] In addition, while these programs frequently teach students how to think critically about the information received in the digital realm,[12] critical thinking around the tools themselves, as well as the ways in which students are regularly using them, has been largely left unaddressed.[13]

One thing I have found that can help students to achieve a more critical understanding of these (no longer) "new" media is a framework of their unique design features[14] that can applied to evaluate their uses and impacts.[15] At its core, design is how we make sense of communication.[16] When we communicate, we naturally "devise strategies and practices to engage meaning, action and coherence."[17] When we communicate through media, many of these strategies and practices are embedded in the design of the tool itself, which both shapes, and is shaped by, its use.[18] As I will argue in the following sections, while computer-based media technologies do vary widely in purpose, function, and use, there is at least one fundamental design principle that they have in common (that they are interactive), and three that most share (that they are digital, networked, and databased). Because the specific design of an interactive medium can both constrain communication and afford new communicative possibilities,[19] exploring common design principles can help us to think about how they may be both broadly construed and individually understood.

## WHAT'S IN A NAME?

Since this book is entitled "Interactive Media and Society," let us begin by first identifying what, exactly, it is that we are talking about. *Interactive media* may be defined as:

> the collection of communication resources and tools made available via computer networks, mobile technologies, electronic devices, and the Internet, that have emerged in recent decades and enabled broader public participation in society, culture, and commerce.

These include web-based media, social media, software editing tools, feedback tools, video games and their consoles, mobile devices, apps, wearable media, and many others, including those yet to be innovated. While these tools have been referred to as "new media," "emerging media," "digital media," among other varied classifications, it could be argued that the litany of names we use to describe these media confuses and dilutes the heuristic value of each. The term "interactive media" is the most apt umbrella term, because it speaks to the one element of these media that most accurately separates them from that which came before.

In 2001, Manovich argued against the use of "interactive" for the very reason I am going to argue for it: because it is a term that is redundant with computer usage.[20] The present-day notion of "interactive" simply means responsive to some input or command,[21] which is a fundamental design characteristic of all computer-based systems.[22] Manovich's argument against this term made sense in 2001, when virtually all interactive media were made available solely through a computer, but that is no longer the case. This interactive capability is present in an increasing number of devices and "smart objects" today—not just computers, but phones, televisions, video game systems, watches, and car systems that essentially *are* computers. If the projections of the futurists and technology companies are correct, this *Internet of Things (IoT)* will only continue to evolve, and soon most consumers will also regularly access these media through such "devices" as countertops and kitchen appliances.[23] Despite this variability in form, interactivity is the one feature that links all of these media together, and it is the feature that is least likely to change.

Further, the term "interactivity" itself is one that has been defined in numerous ways, in various disciplines, with multiple origins in academic literature.[24] It first emerged with respect to communication in reference to the feedback that receivers of a message give to its sender(s), but more attention began to be given to the term as the first computers and cell phones came on the scene in the 1970s and 1980s.[25] As these devices and other interactive media, like remote-controlled television, video games, and CD-ROMs hit the mass consumer market, the work of scholars in communication and computer science began to converge, and it became clear that the term was being used to refer to both the social and technical aspects of media.[26] Fornäs et al. point out that the term has been used to describe multiple kinds of interactivity: "social interactivity," which describes media that enable human-to-human social interaction, "technical interactivity," which refers to the human-machine communication already mentioned, or "textual interactivity," which is "the creative and interpretive interaction between humans and texts."[27] Interactive media as I have defined them frequently enable all three of these forms of interactivity. Kiousis additionally added some clarity to the term "interactivity" in 2002 when he conducted an in-depth concept explication, reviewing its multiplicities in the literature. The comprehensive definition at which he ultimately arrived is as follows:

> Interactivity can be defined as the degree to which a communication technology can create a mediated environment in which participants can communicate (one-to-one, one-to-many, and many-to-many), both synchronously and asynchronously, and participate in reciprocal message exchanges. . . . With regard to human users, it additionally refers to their ability to perceive the experience as a simulation of interpersonal communication and increase their awareness of telepresence.[28]

This definition also corresponds well to the definition of interactive media opening this section, as it speaks to the centrality of communication and participation to interactivity, as well as the use of mediating technology. Perhaps because rather than in spite of the polysemic nature of the term, it is the most appropriate to use to describe media that are extremely varied in form and function, enable multiple kinds of uses, and operate in unending ways, as each definition of interactivity speaks to the nature of these media in some way. Now that I have established a label and working definition of the types of media I am discussing here, I will explain the rest of this design framework, which begins with a discussion of the social and cultural protocols of media in general, and then moves on to explore these in terms of the three core design features of interactive media specifically.

## MEDIA PROTOCOLS

In his 2006 book, *Convergence Culture*, a seminal work on interactive media, Henry Jenkins presents a useful dual-level model of understanding media, put forth by historian Lisa Gitelman.[29] According to this model, any medium would first be understood at its basic level as "a technology that enables communication" in some way.[30] Each medium, however, also carries with it a second level of "associated 'protocols' or social and cultural practices that have grown up around that technology."[31] These protocols are often features that we assume to be innate to the medium itself, but that is because they have become embedded as norms and standards of the tool, which are so common they become invisible to us.[32] For instance, television is not always live but radio usually is, newspapers provide up-to-date news but not historical facts or entertaining fiction, and telephones generally enable one-on-one conversations, yet none of these things had to be this way. In fact, such *media protocols* are the combined result of how the medium was designed—the forms, resources, and features it makes available—and how we have used it over time (which is not always in keeping with designers' original intentions[33]). In other words, that which users have chosen to adopt, resist, or disrupt in varying ways, and the ways in which they do so, provide feedback mechanisms, which influence the evolution of the medium's protocols.[34]

Gitelman has conceded that defining media according to their protocols is admittedly "muddy."[35] However, this conceptualization can be immensely useful for improving one's digital literacy, because understanding the evolving relationship between a medium's mechanisms of control and our acceptance or subversion of those controls can help us to better understand how we might use it wisely. These protocols can also be thought of as the rules, standards, and habits that we build up around the medium as it gets integrated into our daily lives. For the sake of elucidation and organization, the protocols may be further broken down into three separate but related types: (1) how we receive the content distributed by the medium, or *delivery protocols*, (2) the social and cultural functions of the medium in our lives, or *use protocols*, and (3) what we come to expect from the medium as it delivers content and is used in certain ways, or *demand protocols*. Conceptualizing media according to these "associated protocols" is a helpful way to understand aspects of their uses, outcomes, influences, and effects, while still holding in our minds the unique features, characteristics, and variations of each.[36] With interactive media, however, the massive variability of media forms as compared to prior models significantly complicates the landscape,[37] and a further breakdown of the core design principles underscoring their interactivity, as offered in the next section, can help to provide a foundational understanding of them generally before getting into the specifics of each tool, technology, medium, or app individually.

## DESIGN PRINCIPLES

In the early 2000s, Alexander Galloway employed the term "protocol" to describe the "apparatus of control" that is embedded in interactive media specifically, the programmed processes that regulate and govern everything we do via these tools.[38] This conceptualization of protocol is unique to interactive media, as it is made up of a particularly salient "front-end"—the interface that the user interacts with—and a hidden "back-end"—the code running in the background that instructs everything that happens on the front-end.[39] Conceptualized in this way, the "invisibility" of protocols is literal—not just unnoticed, unrealized, or unknown by users, but in fact unknowable by most of us most of the time, and the barrier that separates the front-end from the back-end is a necessary and formalized feature of the tools themselves.[40] This gives interactive media a special kind of power, entirely rooted in their core design. As Eugene Thacker explains, "the question 'how does it work?' is also the question 'whom does it work for?'"[41]

While the specifics of each tool's back-end structures (in other words, how it works) cannot be fully ascertained without extensive programming knowledge and specialized access, what we can do is clarify the principles that tend to underscore the design of most interactive media, which can then be used as a road map to navigate, evaluate, and think critically about the individual tools as we use them.[42] While interactivity is the one principle that all interactive media have in common, there are three additional "common," or core, design principles that they tend to be built upon, which may be loosely mapped onto Fornäs et al.'s textual, social, and technical forms of interactivity,[43] respectively: *digital, networked,* and *databased.* Each of these design principles also has associated with it certain interrelated media protocols (which develop and evolve at an accelerated pace in the interactive space) for delivery, use, and demand. In the sections that follow, I offer a generalized breakdown of some of the (currently) typical protocols we tend to see for each of these design principles of interactive media. It is important to note, however, that as the tools and devices of interactive media are exceedingly integrated into our everyday existence and subject to constant updating, the protocols evolve at a particularly fast pace.[44] The point of this discussion is to give you a sense of how interactive media have influenced our protocols thus far, as well as to demonstrate how this framework is applied, but the actual protocols themselves are ever subject to change.

## The Digital Design Principle

When media is produced and made available through digital as opposed to analog means, the producer is essentially breaking down and quantifying content.[45] Everything that we see and hear in digital media is actually split into discrete units or samples of information that are sent to our devices, which display them as a continuous whole.[46] Because digital media create and present intangible objects on a screen, they take up far less space, are easier to edit, and can be endlessly replicated in their exact original forms with no loss of quality.[47] As a simple example of how the processes of digital media are different from those of analog, consider the practices of editing, revising, and sharing with five people a manuscript using Google Docs as opposed to working with a physical hard copy. It is monumentally easier to share, change, replicate, and collaborate; the same is true of print, graphic, and audio- and video-based digital media productions. Because of their digital nature, interactive media and the content produced through them are much easier to use, manipulate, edit, rearrange, and share than their analog counterparts.[48] The nature of digital media also means that massive amounts of content can be stored on disks and devices that are increasingly small, compact, and portable.[49]

The protocols associated with the digital design principle have been centered around the idea that interactive media are made more available and more accessible. In delivery, they are low-cost and powerful.[50] The information, ideas, and content produced by interactive media are more easily, and infinitely, replicable and editable as a result of the digital design principle.[51] This results in a convergence of tools, "the formerly distinct media of television, radio, telephone, and mail," where format matters less than mechanism.[52] When digitized, information, ideas, and content exist more as they would in their "natural" state, as thought or energy,[53] but it is also a chaotic and fragmented flow.[54] The digital design principle also means that interactive media can be accessed on multiple devices and platforms, including mobile ones. Interactive media can be taken with us, making them unbound by location.[55]

When media is digital, barriers to production are lowered and more people can participate.[56] Although there is still a pervasive digital divide in terms of access and skills[57] (more on this in later chapters), those of us who use digital media experience a very different kind of relationship to media, and the world, than is possible with other forms.[58] The use protocols of interactive media include editing, creating, accessing, copying, appropriating, and remixing media content.[59] It is no longer just professional media producers who can create quality media, because there is a reduced cost for production, time, effort, and distribution.[60] This has resulted in an "amatuerization" of media production[61] in which the now extremely "active" audience, user community, or consumer base produces an immense quantity of content to an extent that few had ever thought possible.[62] It is also extremely easy and cheap or free to copy, obtain, and access media, which in turn makes it more spreadable[63] and able to reach much larger audiences.[64] Finally, the mobility of media means that we are able to access content more frequently and from wherever we are.[65]

For demand protocols, users of digital media content have begun to expect that it will be easy to edit and manipulate, as well as cheap, accessible, and "for the taking." These are the aspects of interactive media that have made it so difficult to consider in traditional framings of law surrounding intellectual property and copyright.[66] We expect media to be easy for us to access, use, and replicate as we like.[67] We also have begun to expect easy access to others, as it is the new norm for us to be "always on," having a device with us nearly all of the time, sending and receiving information as needed throughout the day.[68]

## The Networked Design Principle

The networked design principle reflects our ability to connect with each other through interactive media. For the first time in history, we have media that allow us to communicate in a many-to-many communication pattern, as opposed to just one-to-many, one-to-one, or, at the most, few-to-few.[69] This reflects the end-to-end or peer-to-peer design of computer networks,[70] which "assures those with a new idea get to sell that new idea, the views of the network owner notwithstanding."[71] In many cases, this creates a more decentralized media structure, eliminating the need for *gatekeepers* or intermediaries filtering the volume of information, ideas, or content that we can access.[72] This many-to-many capability is also the driving principle behind open-source systems, in which everyone can contribute to products.[73]

In terms of use protocols, the networked principle enables social uses such as sharing, group-forming, networking, and collaborating. We express our selves as we share ideas, information, and content, which also helps to spark competition and generate new ideas.[74] We can associate with each other in new ways by forming and joining groups and networks in extremely seamless, simple, and fluid ways.[75] The increased capacity to act and communicate in large groups has also had profound effects on the ways we can collaborate, get things done, and be empowered through online communities and open-source systems.[76] On the negative side, online communities can also support very harmful behavior when people with nefarious intentions use interactive media to find one another, form their own echo chambers,[77] and gang up on others in an effort to silence them.

As the use protocols of interactive media have allowed for these new and unwanted behaviors, the demand protocols emerging from the networked design principle are currently experiencing a significant shift in response, demonstrating the ways in which these sets of protocols are ever-changing and mutually influence one another. Whereas there was once a high demand for information to be unsuppressed and accessible,[78] we are now seeing a demand in some sectors for more control and moderation. The early, libertarian hacker culture that devoted itself to "freeing information" and contributed to the early expectation that information be readily available and unrestricted on the Internet[79] is being replaced with calls for removing unwanted voices, content, and misinformation from the platforms that dominate the culture.[80] As citizens around the world have experienced a significant cultural shift with respect to unprecedented access to unsuppressed information,[81] we are still in the process of working out what we want that to look like.

In other sectors, however, the demand protocol of free and unrestricted content remains. We still tend to expect to be able to distribute and circulate media content however we please, regardless of the original producers' wishes or intellectual property rights.[82] We also might expect media content to be "free," as in without cost, such as through peer-to-peer file sharing.[83] Additionally, the collaborative nature of open-source production is resulting in a lowered expectation for attribution and authorship,[84] and a "blurring of producers and consumers."[85]

Finally, we are increasing our expectations of one another. Combining the networked protocol of connecting with others and the digital protocol of mobility, we know that receivers of our messages have their mobile devices with them, and therefore we expect a more immediate response.[86]

## The Databased Design Principle

When using interactive media, digital information is stored as data, which can be, and frequently is, archived.[87] These databases drive the processes that allow search engines to work and allow various systems to make recommendations to us, show statistics, or identify the most popular content and "trends."[88] It is also this principle that drives the process of hyperlinking and embedding content,[89] as every single display is a stored piece of data, which can then be pointed to with the use of URLs.[90] This design principle has been an imagined component of interactive media since before it was even possible to exist.[91]

The associated delivery protocols of the databased design principle center around this idea of archiving and storage. Most content produced through interactive media is indexed, or at least indexable, meaning that it is searchable through the use of text, keywords, and tags.[92] When archiving is used for the process of networked interaction, it also allows for the possibility of asynchronous communication, producing a "lag" between a given message and its response time.[93] This means that interactive media offer us the ability to communicate not only unbound by place as a result of the digital design principle, but also unbound by time as a result of the databased principle.[94] Messages can be searched, retrieved, and even reactivated at any point in the future.[95] Finally, the ability to store information in databases allows for customized content in delivery, offering recommendations and filtering based on our stored information, preferences, and past usage history, matching with astonishing accuracy "the complexity of our preferences"[96] through auto-mated algorithms.[97]

In use, we are engaging more directly with information by adding our own data points to it. Content and ideas can be organized, curated, amplified, and rated, sometimes consciously through tagging, labeling, downvoting, or upvoting, and sometimes just through use by clicking, viewing, browsing, or purchasing.[98] We are also able to promote things for people, companies, poli-ticians, and so on, as we are consuming because it is so easy to "like," embed, and link content. Thus, in expressing our identities through our preferences, we act as marketing tools for others.[99] But we also often get to provide more feedback and have more of a say through features like reviewing, voting, and commentary.[100] It is easier to organize content, ideas, and knowledge through various interactive media. The ability to communicate asynchronously and archive that communication can slow down social interaction and makes it more explicit, which means we are able to gather and interact in much larger groups than is possible amidst the chaos of live interaction.[101] In addition, we are searching more information more often and at an increased rate.[102] Unfortunately, because so much more data is being shared and collected about us, some use protocols of the databased design principle also leave us vulnerable to identity theft, privacy violations, and surveillance.[103] This data can also be used by companies to track, predict, and even manipulate our behavior.[104]

We have come to expect certain things as a result of the databased design principle. The demand protocols of interactive media include an expectation of comprehensive, searchable content.[105] For example, it is expected that vir-tually any movie will be found on IMDB, any song on Spotify, any research topic of interest on Wikipedia, and that all of this can be easily found with a search engine. We also expect content through interactive media to be easy to link to and allow room for feedback and participation.[106] If there is not an easy "button" for linking, liking, embedding, rating, or commenting, we find our-selves frustrated or surprised.[107] Though not exactly an "expectation," we also post and create our own content with an understanding that it may come back to haunt us at some point in the future.[108] We expect to be able to bring such "receipts" on others if they have committed a perceived wrong in the past.[109]

Considering the interactive media environment as we currently understand it, it can be said that most interactive media at least start out with two or more of these design principles in place, though others may emerge. This framework represents an attempt to solidify the main design principles that we can observe with interactive media thus far. It is not intended to be an argument that these three design principles are all there is or ever will be. In addition, the identified protocols are vulnerable to being squashed or reduced out of existence as new gatekeepers roll in and recentralize, censor, or filter through other design features.[110] For instance, as alluded to previously, the increasingly cloud-based, centralized, and commercialized models of access, storage, and production are currently subsuming the end-to-end model, which is being "replaced by the hierarchical structures of client and server"[111] within dominant technology corporations who have begun to exercise their power to intervene in our communications with one another (more on this in chapter 12).

## CONCLUSION

The design framework of interactive media provided in this chapter is intended to be flexible enough to be used as new tools are developed and emerge by focusing, as Baym has suggested, on "specific capabilities and consequences rather than the media themselves."[112] As we have witnessed the ongoing evolution of interactive media over the past two to three decades and become more societally self-aware of their "capabilities and consequences," both the academic and popular understanding has shifted from one of extreme optimism to one of extreme pessimism. However, as Lindgren argues, the most likely reality "is a pragmatic perspective in between" these two extremes.[113] The fact that so much of our world now exists within interactive media means that every hypothesis and conjecture about their impacts can in some way be found to be correct, in some context or another.[114] Can people find a voice through interactive media? Does interactive media reinforce structural inequalities? Can we use interactive media to find and formulate community? Is it making us antisocial? Has it given us an outlet for cultural expression and creativity? Are we "performing" our lives for likes and follows? Are we broadening our perspectives through the connections we are making? Has our approach toward one another become more divisive and partisan? The answer to all of these questions is yes—somewhere and in some way, but also, not always and everywhere. Thus, any effort to explain succinctly either what interactive media has "done" to us or what it can "solve" for us is probably in some form an oversimplification of a complex and constantly changing set of related problems to which there are no easy answers. Rather than just give up and stop trying, however, the aim of this framework is to offer a simple, design-focused lens for us to better understand, analyze, and explore these tools and their outcomes. It can help to illuminate the ways these tools vary and overlap, how they relate to one another, how they can be used as tools of control, and what they make possible.[115] The design framework as a starting point for a broad conceptualization of interactive media can therefore provide a core basis for understanding what has happened, is happening, or could happen, as well as how we each contribute to those happenings, while acknowledging the complexity of multiple simultaneously and mutually influencing causes and effects. As this core basis is so crucial to conceptualizing the many ways in which interactive media has affected us at a variety of individual, interpersonal, cultural, and societal levels, it sets the stage for the specific contexts and outcomes we will be exploring throughout the remainder of this book.

## NOTES

1. This chapter is based on a previous article by the author entitled "A Design Framework of Interactive Media," published in the *Journal of Digital and Media Literacy*.

2. Shein, "Ephemeral Data," 20–21.

3. Roesner et al., "Sex, Lies, or Kittens?"

4. Osborne, "FTC Finalizes Charges."

5. Prensky, "Digital Natives, Digital Immigrants," 1.

6. Ballono et al., "Young Users," 151; Hobbs, *Digital and Media Literacy*, 32.

7. Aboujaoude, "*Virtually You*," 126–27.

8. Gui and Argentin, "Digital Skills of Internet Natives," 965.

9. Gillmor, *Mediactive*, 24; Warschauer et al., *Supporting Digital Literacy*, 199.

10. Hobbs, *Digital and Media Literacy*, 25.

11. Gillmor, *Mediactive*, 24.

12. Warschauer et al., *Supporting Digital Literacy*, 207–8.

13. boyd, "You Think You Want."

14. The term "design" here is used in terms of technological features and characteristics, not visual aesthetics.

15. Manovich, *Software Takes Command*, 137.

16. Aakhus, "Communication as Design," 112.

17. Aakhus, 113.

18. Poole and DeSanctis. "Understanding the Use," 177.

19. Aakhus, "Communication as Design," 114.

20. Manovich, *The Language of New*, 56.

21. Jenkins, *Convergence Culture*, 137; Miller, *Understanding Digital Culture, 16.*

22. Manovich, "The Language of New," 56.

23. Chui et al., "The Internet of Things"; Kelly, *The Inevitable*, 283.

24. Fornäs et al., "Into Digital Borderlands," 23; Kiousis, "Interactivity," 357.

25. Kiousus, "Interactivity: A Concept Explication," 359.

26. Kiousus, 360–61.

27. Fornäs et al., 23.

28. Kiousus, "Interactivity: A Concept Explication," 379.

29. Jenkins, *Convergence Culture*, 13.

30. Jenkins, 13.

31. Jenkins, 13–14.

32. Couldry and Hepp, *The Mediated Construction,* 32; Gitelman, *Always Already New,* 7.

33. Jemielniak and Przegalinska, *Collaborative Society*, 157, 166.

34. Browning and Stephens, "Giddens' Structuration Theory," 89.

35. Gitelman, *Always Already New*, 7.

36. Couldry and Hepp, *The Mediated Construction*, 52.

37. Grossberg, *Cultural Studies*, 216.

38. Galloway, *Protocol*, 3, 74–75.

39. Galloway, 75.

40. Galloway, 75.

41. Thacker, "Foreword," *xii.*

42. Galloway, *Protocol*, 246.

43. Fornäs et al., 23.

44. Grossberg, *Cultural Studies*, 217.

45. Kittler, *Gramophone, Film, Typewriter*, 1; Manovich, *The Language of New*, 28.

46. Manovich, 49.

47. Barlow, "The Economy of Ideas."

48. Manovich, *The Language of New,* 66–68; Miller, *Understanding Digital Culture,* 15.

49. Miller, 15.

50. Gillmor, *We the Media,* 9; Lessig, *The Future of Ideas*, 72; Mandiberg, *The Social Media Reader*, 1.

51. Manovich, *The Language of New*, 56.

52. Kittler, *Gramophone, Film, Typewriter*, 1.

53. Barlow, "The Economy of Ideas"; Lessig, *The Future of Ideas*, 116; Kelly, *The Inevitable,* 73; Manovich, 56.

54. Grossberg, *Cultural Studies*, 215–17.

55. Baym, *Personal Connections*, 11.

56. Jenkins et al., *Confronting the Challenges*, 7; O'Reilly, "What is Web 2.0?," 47.

57. Baym, *Personal Connections*, 20–21.

58. Jenkins et al., *Spreadable Media*, 40.

59. Jenkins et al., 185.

60. Gillmor, *We the Media*, 153; Lessig, *The Future of Ideas*, 7.

61. Jemielniak and Przegalinska, *Collaborative Society,* 64–65; Shirky, *Here Comes Everybody,* 98.

62. Kelly, "We Are the Web."

63. Jenkins et al., *Spreadable Media,* 3.

64. Baym, *Personal Connections,* 10.

65. Baym, 8.

66. Barlow, "The Economy of Ideas"; Vaidhyanthan, "Open Source as Culture," 29.

67. Manovich, *The Language of New Media,* 35–36.

68. Turkle, *Alone Together,* 171–72.

69. Shirky, *Here Comes Everybody,* 86–87.

70. O'Reilly, "What Is Web 2.0?," 36–37; Miller, *Understanding Digital Culture,* 12–15.

71. Lessig, *The Future of Ideas,* 121.

72. Jenkins, *Convergence Culture,* 241; Baym, *Personal Connections,* 9.

73. Shirky, *Here Comes Everybody,* 239.

74. Hyde et al., "What Is Collaboration Anyway?," 53; Jenkins et al., *Spreadable Media,* 34; Shirky, "Why We Need"; Tapscott and Williams, *Wikinomics,* 94–95.

75. Shirky, *Here Comes Everybody,* 54.

76. Jemielniak and Przegalinska, *Collaborative Society,* 157; Surowiecki, *The Wisdom of Crowds,* 73–74; Tapscott and Williams, *Wikinomics,* 68–69.

77. Shirky, *Here Comes Everybody,* 208.

78. Jemielniak and Przegalinska, *Collaborative Society,* 112; Vaidhyanathan, "Open Source as Culture," 30.

79. Ludlow, "Wikileaks and Hacktivist Culture," 25.

80. Asarch, "Steven Crowder Incites"; Conger et al., "Violence on Capitol Hill"; Edelman, "Stop Saying Facebook"; Mangan, "'Don't Touch Me'"; Marantz, "Free Speech Is Killing Us"; Marantz, "Reddit and the Struggle."

81. Jenkins et al., *Spreadable Media,* 42.; Shirky, *Here Comes Everybody,* 295.

82. Jemielniak and Przegalinska, *Collaborative Society,* 62; Jenkins et al., 16, 184.

83. Jemielniak and Przegalinska, *Collaborative Society,* 64; Jenkins et al., *Spreadable Media,* 16.

84. Davison, "The Language of Internet," 132; Lessig, "Remix: How Creativity," 160.

85. Miller, *Understanding Digital Culture,* 15.

86. Baym, *Personal Connections,* 11; Turkle, *Alone Together,* 176.

87. Baym, 8.

88. Tapscott and Williams, *Wikinomics,* 41–42.

89. Jenkins et al., *Spreadable Media,* 11; Miller, *Understanding Digital Culture,* 21.

90. Kelly, "We Are the Web"; Manovich, *The Language of New Media,* 225.

91. Bush, "As We May Think."

92. Manovich, *The Language of New Media,* 214.

93. Crystal, *Language and the Internet,* 31.

94. Baym, *Personal Connections,* 8.

95. Shirky, *Here Comes Everybody,* 237.

96. Lessig, *The Future of Ideas*, 132.
97. Pariser, *The Filter Bubble, 9.*
98. Hyde et al., "What Is Collaboration Anyway?" 54.
99. Jenkins, *Convergence Culture*, 62–63.
100. Jenkins, 73.
101. Baym, *Personal Connections*, 8.
102. Kelly, "We Are the Web."
103. Andrejevic, "The Work of Being," 237.
104. Tucker, *The Naked Future*, xiv.
105. Lessig, *The Future of Ideas*, 125.
106. Jenkins, *Convergence Culture,* 62–63; Jenkins et al., 154–56.
107. Jenkins et al., *Spreadable Media*, 198.
108. Wesch, "YouTube and You," 24.
109. Hooks, "Cancel Culture: Posthuman Hauntologies," 4.
110. Stadler, "Between Democracy and Spectacle," 249.
111. Lessig, *The Future of Ideas*, 134.
112. Baym, *Personal Connections*, 13.
113. Lindgren, *Digital Media & Society*, 45–46.
114. Poole and DeSanctis, "Understanding the Use," 176.
115. Manovich, *Software Takes Command*, 233–39.

*Chapter 2*

# The Media Convergence Ecosystem

## INTRODUCTION: BABY SHARK ATTACK!

The "Baby Shark Dance" video, uploaded to YouTube by user "Pinkfong! Kids' Songs & Stories," has currently been viewed over 8.2 billion times, meaning it has more views than there are people on the planet.[1] To put that into perspective and because our brains tend to have a hard time understanding really big numbers, eight million seconds is about ninety-three days; eight billion seconds is more than 253 *years*. In other words, eight billion views are *a lot* of views, especially for a video that contains no celebrities, no amazing graphics, and nothing, particularly, of note. There is a massive amount of content for children on YouTube, and this video is not noticeably different from the rest. Yet, it currently sits at the number-one spot in the list of "the most-viewed YouTube videos of all time" according to *Digital Trends*.[2] So what is it about this typical YouTube Kids video, particularly, that made it go so viral? Some answers may be found by tracking its history.

Pinkfong!, a South Korean children's media company, first uploaded the video to YouTube in November 2015.[3] The video is pretty typical of Pinkfong's content, featuring a known "camp song" that has no clearly identifiable owner (think "Itsy Bitsy Spider" and "Old Macdonald"), with adorable kids dancing and simple cartoon graphics. (As an aside, this is a great business model—there are no licensing fees or royalties to pay and the graphics are cheap to produce, so any revenue these videos earn is mostly profit.) According to Pinkfong!, no special promotion was done for this particular video,[4] and it was not a huge standout among their other content. But in the summer of 2017, Korean pop girl bands such as *Red Velvet*, *Girls' Generation*, and *Black Pink* began performing the song live at their concerts, and this kick-started the video's launch into the viral stratosphere.[5] By August 2017, the hashtag #babysharkchallenge began trending among social media users, particularly in Indonesia,[6] and, from there it became a *meme*, in which people spread a cultural phenomenon through imitation.[7] People across Asia started uploading their own videos of themselves doing the Baby Shark Dance to the song, adding their own personal touches. On August 23, the song made it to the broadcast television airwaves when Amanda Cerny, host of the Indonesian version of the *Tonight Show*, joined in on the challenge with her crew.[8] At the same time, subscriptions to YouTube increased 165 percent in this part of the world.[9]

The trend then spread globally, reemerging in the UK a year later, where it was combined with the Drake "In My Feelings" challenge and people began doing the Baby Shark Dance while wearing shark costumes and running alongside moving cars.[10] Once it hit US shores in September 2018, Ellen did her own version,[11] Kylie Jenner got in on it,[12] and James Corden performed a hilarious cover featuring Sophie Turner and Josh Groban on *The Late Late Show*.[13]

While adults might have been participating in this craze somewhat ironically, young children who were exposed to the song couldn't get enough. This was clearly evidenced in an October 2018 video that captured a two-year-old named Zoe desperately trying to get her Amazon Alexa to play the song (and her moment of pure joy and satisfaction when it finally did), which was shared on YouTube by her mother. This video, too, went viral, and Zoe and her family were invited on the *Today Show* one week later.[14] The most recent version of the trend, which just keeps going, is a TikTok version of the challenge involving a remixed and more sophisticated version of the song accompanied by real dance moves performed by talented young people and their avatars.[15] And the evolution continues.

Each step along Baby Shark's path has brought new audiences and more attention to it. Anyone who participated in this meme has likewise gotten increased exposure, which in turn only increases each time someone new participates. It is a self-perpetuating cycle, and the exponential exposure, combined with kids' tendency to want to play it on repeat, has created the perfect storm for this phenomenon, one that no one could have predicted. Pinkfong! has obviously benefited from the increased exposure, but so have the platforms that have hosted this participation—YouTube, Instagram, TikTok, etc. Meanwhile, the original Baby Shark Dance song itself came in at #32 on the Billboard Hot 100 list in January 2019, leaving some music traditionalists to complain, "what hath we wrought?"[16] While there is a certain degree of playfulness in these comments, the "anatomy of a trend" analysis displayed here reveals but one aspect of concern about the way media now circulates. Enabled by interactive media, what gets the most attention in our society today has more to do with engagement than perhaps more deserving measures like importance, quality, or taste.

## MEDIA: THEN AND NOW

With every new medium that has been introduced in the past, there have been hyperbolic claims as to its effects. The VCR was going to destroy the film industry.[17] Radio was going to wreak havoc on record album sales.[18] The phonograph was going to mark the end of interest in playing music and singing, and would ultimately eliminate human vocal cords altogether.[19] Although the introduction of any new technology usually has consequences both good and bad, none of these extreme fears came true. New models and relationships may have been forged and new behaviors adapted to, but human creative instincts and desires still persisted.

So, the question then becomes, is the same true of interactive media today? People sometimes claim we are amidst a "digital revolution," but is this media shift so different from others we've seen in the past? Is interactive media truly something new and unique? Or is this simply just another way to communicate, and all this talk of "revolution" just a bunch of hype? In other words, is interactive media, really, a big deal? Perhaps not, but it must be acknowledged that the current technologies are of a somewhat different order from those of the past. It is not a question of whether a single tool or technology such as the gramophone or VCR will effect change, but in fact a variety of interactive media "species" that have, to a great extent, subsumed and overtaken *all* that came before them.[20] Books, magazines, newspapers, radio, television, film, notepads, cameras, camcorders, phones, board games, letters, billboards, copy machines and fax machines, voice recorders and stenographers, encyclopedias and card catalogs—all of these things and more now exist, at least in some form, as and through interactive media. At a pace never seen before in human history,[21] nearly every form of communication has been reconsidered and reconstrued through an interactive lens, which at the very least complicates our ability to fully understand the consequences of these new species, especially while we are still in the process of their rapid evolution.

Because of the extraordinarily fast pace in which these changes are taking place today, it can be helpful to look backward to a time before we had interactive media available to us in order to understand their impacts thus far. To get my students into this mindset, I often show them a video clip from the *Today Show* circa 1994, a time when just 23 percent of American households had a computer in their home[22] and the Internet itself only contained ten thousand websites.[23] The hosts of the show, including Bryant Gumbel and Katie

Couric, are attempting to understand, as they put it, "what Internet is."[24] It began with confusion over the @ symbol, which they thought might stand for "at," but also possibly "about" or "around." Gumbel, citing that he "wasn't prepared to translate" it, read the email address violence@nbc.ge.com simply as "violence at NBC GE com." The hosts then struggled to explain for their audience what "Internet" is, asking more than asserting. They posited that it is a "computer network," that "you write to . . . like mail" or "an electronic billboard," and sought further clarification from their producers. This clip seems very funny to us now, as we wonder how these people, who spent their daily existence working within the media and information environment of the time, could have been so clueless. But interactive media was so different to what they knew then that few could have truly understood it. What was soon to come like a tsunami barreling into the mediascape was still largely in the hands and minds of the computer programmers and information scientists.

Although the tools and technologies of interactive media have been designed and refined to the point that they are today very user-friendly, seemingly natural, and simple, the reality is that each and every one of us had to learn how to use them, what they are used for, and how to speak about them, during our lifetime. We might have been very young, but we can all probably remember a time when, like Bryant Gumbel, we came across something we couldn't immediately "translate." Maybe it was when we struggled to understand how to use a new social media app that we just downloaded. Maybe it was a time we first came across a new emoji or meme, and missed its intended message. Maybe it was a text-speak acronym that we never saw before and had to look up. We might understand what "wtf," "tfw," and "ftw" stand for now ("what the f**k," "that feeling when," and "for the win," respectively), but it is pretty clear that these could be confusing to someone not yet "in the know." These things, which are so easy for us that we barely notice them now, at one point challenged our cognitive abilities.

We might also recall the first time we truly realized the wonder and power of interactive media. It could have been a time we created something we were really proud of and shared it online, sent a message to a celebrity, or watched something go viral around the world, à la Baby Shark. Or perhaps we lost our phone or Internet access for a time and soon realized just how dependent on it we were. As someone who was a fully grown adult when interactive media made its way into our everyday lives, I can clearly remember the feelings of strangeness first seeing people walk down the street while talking on the phone, amazement upon realizing that I could immediately look up the lyrics to a song or how to soft-boil eggs, and wonder at the seemingly futuristic ability to simply type in an address and be directed, turn-by-turn, right to my destination. While all of these seem commonplace to us now, it is important to understand that they were practically unthinkable before they were made possible by interactive media.

## WHAT TOOK US BY SURPRISE

In 2005, *Wired* magazine founder Kevin Kelly wrote an article entitled "We Are the Web," in which he reflected on the first ten years of the public's use of the Internet, from 1995 until 2005.[25] In it, he explains that, in the earliest days of the Internet's introduction to society, there were many things that media professionals at the time were not expecting to occur. He states:

> Everything media experts knew about audiences—and they knew a lot—confirmed the focus group belief that audiences would never get off their butts and start making their own entertainment. Everyone knew writing and reading were dead; music was too much trouble to make when you could sit back and listen; video production was simply out of reach of amateurs. Blogs and other participant media would never happen, or if they happened they would not draw an audience, or if they drew an audience they would not matter.[26]

In other words, the experts of the day were completely taken by surprise when they realized, first, that people would actually want to do things with these new interactive tools, and, second, that what they did with them would matter. Why would they not have expected this? For starters, they were operating from wrong assumptions. Observing the passive consumer behavior that was typical at the time—watching, reading, listening—they assumed that it matched people's desires. They didn't realize that, in fact, it was merely a result of the structure of the only media that people had access to at the time.[27] Once people could do more, however, they did, in spades. Many surprises, to all of us, came along the way.

### Social Media

One major surprise was that the new forms of media would be not just personal, but also social. With the rise of the "personal computer" (PC) in the mid-1990s, it was largely conceived of as a device that would be used for individual work, to organize files, store music and photographs, read and to write, shop, pay bills, and play games like solitaire. But after the social media explosion in the early 2000s, it quickly became clear that what we had access to were not just tools, but each other. Later, when mobile phone companies first began expanding the capabilities of cell phones, the earliest models were again called "personal digital assistants" (PDAs). But when Apple first released iPods and later iPhones with their app model of customization, we once again learned that if we can go social with our devices, we will. Today, the term *social media* refers to a type of interactive media in which people can gather around shared interests or for the purpose of making connections with one another.[28] The latter are termed *social networking sites* (SNS), where one can create one's own profile and use it to connect, communicate, and share content with others.[29] These concepts seem simple enough, and, with the prevalence of these sites and their integration into our daily existence today, it is hard to believe they were once not only nonexistent, but unimaginable to most people.

## User-Generated Content

Another thing that took us by surprise was that people used interactive media to create and share their own *user-generated content*, or content that is created and distributed by nonprofessionals.[30] The "people formerly known as the audience," as Jay Rosen has described them,[31] went from being consumers to *prosumers*, or people who both consume and produce media, sometimes simultaneously.[32] The realm of content production was expanded to the hands of everyone, and we began to be entertained and informed by not only professionals, but also by each other. This was not anything particularly new, as people have always engaged in play, performance, and creativity (just watch young children playing sometime), but the ability to share this amateur-level creativity publicly is when we started to see that it did, in fact, matter. It may not typically have the polished, flashy, highly trained quality of professional media content, but user-generated content can still garner a vast following and wide reach.

## Gift Economy

It was also a major surprise, especially to people in the media industry, that people would engage in a *gift economy*, giving away their user-generated content for free. The majority of people sharing their own content online make little to no money off of it,[33] and do it more as a labor of love. And yet, online users publish more video content in thirty days than the major broadcast television networks have produced in thirty years,[34] with five hundred hours of video uploaded per minute on YouTube alone.[35] This is more content than any single media corporation could ever even approach funding, and few would have ever thought it financially possible before the existence of the Internet.[36] In addition, user-generated content is, in a way, more sincere than professionally produced content, simply because it is not bought and paid for. As Clay Shirky has put it, "making each other laugh is a different kind of activity from being made to laugh by people paid to make us laugh."[37] Along this same line of thinking, Derek Powazek has proposed that we call it "authentic media" instead of user-generated content.[38]

## Active Audiences

A fourth unexpected behavior was that audiences and consumers would seek ways to be actively involved in the products they consume. Fandom has been the source of a massive amount of user-generated content, as fans prosume their favorite corporate media productions in a variety of "unofficial" ways. But even when they are not creating their own content, *active audiences* often seek and find ways to engage more deeply with the objects of their affection through interactive media, whether that means curating extra information and content, forming communities, or speaking back to companies and producers (publicly) about things they do and do not like. No longer the fringe activities of a small minority, fandom has gone mainstream. This is evidenced by the evolution of Comic-Con from a small annual gathering in San Diego to a major promotional and international venue attended by hundreds of thousands of people.[39] Active audiences "act as if" their activities matter,[40] and media producers have learned, over time, that, in fact, they do.

## Engaged Citizens

Finally, it was not widely understood that citizens might want to be more engaged in public issues and debates, doing more than simply turning on the news to get current events and information.[41] In his 2008 book, *Here Comes Everybody*, Clay Shirky wrote that, for the first time, we live "in a world where being part of a globally interconnected group is the normal case for most citizens."[42] This sounds like a line from a trailer for a 1990s sci-fi film, but it's true. And with the help of interactive media, *engaged citizens* have come out of the woodwork, discussing, critiquing, and disseminating information and news themselves, even outside of the professionalized media structure. Regardless of whether or not they are "experts" on a topic in the traditional sense, everyday people want to have a say in the public sphere, and now they can, sometimes even gaining audiences that match or exceed those of corporate media outlets.[43] Frequently, these efforts to engage large groups of people develop into or merge with activist movements and networks as well.

## MEDIA CONVERGENCE

In discussing the outcomes of these "surprises," it quickly becomes evident that the new behaviors afforded by interactive media have resulted in certain tensions between paid media professionals and those for whom they provide their content and services. The availability and spread of user-generated content and the gift economy may be seen as a threat to the media industry, creating competition for them and resulting in frequent violations of their intellectual property rights.[44] The emergence of active audiences and engaged citizens has created a greater sphere of critique around professional media, calling into question the credibility and quality of their content.[45] The social media companies have been dragged into these tensions as well, as they are held responsible for many of these wrongs having been perpetuated on their platforms, and are getting pressure from all sides to act responsibly to correct them.[46] Many sectors of society today are witnessing corollaries that reflect this clash between what might be seen as the "top-down," expert, and industry-driven modes of communication and those of the more "bottom-up," grassroots variety, as well as the far-reaching consequences of these battles. What has been outlined here is just the tip of the iceberg with respect to these challenges, and many are discussed in further detail in the later chapters of this book.

These changes and challenges are largely the result of multiple media and communication systems converging as interactive media have become more and more prominent in our society. While we had access to very personal, private, and amateur media (such as telephone calls, letters in the mail, home movies, and photo albums) prior to the Internet, we did not typically call these "media," and it was not considered comparable to the corporate media for which we were all an audience. Now personal media can easily merge into public, friends can be audiences or followers, and amateur content can exist alongside professional on the same platforms. These formerly distinct categories of media and communication have blurred, content and information now move along a series of spectrums, and the entire media landscape has changed. When professional media converges with digital media, when amateur media converges with corporate media, when personal media converges with networked media, and so on, it causes significant changes that have far-reaching consequences. No longer a single industry or "media system," the convergence of media has created today what might be called a *media convergence ecosystem*, within which the variety of media "species" serving different needs, functions, and publics have no choice but to interact with one another.[47] This is represented in the graphic below, which shows different types of media systems in a spectrum across the bottom, and the spectrum of

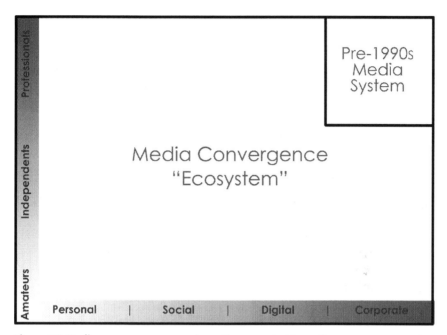

Figure 2.1 **Media convergence ecosystem.** *Figure created by author.*

producers along the side. That which we called "media" in the older system existed inside a much smaller box.

Nearly any media product today moves throughout this map during its lifetime. Baby Shark, for example, was an independently produced digital video when the K-pop girls, who are also professionals within a corporate media system, started covering it at their concerts. When it evolved into a hashtag challenge, it went social, and the videos made in response to it were largely produced by amateurs. When Ellen and other celebrities joined in, it moved back into the corporate media sphere, though with an amateur aesthetic. The video of little Zoe trying to get her Amazon Alexa to play was an example of personal digital media use, but when her mom shared it on YouTube, it became social. When that video went viral and was featured along with the family on *Good Morning America*, it was an amateur production inhabiting a professionally produced and corporate space.

## CONCLUSION

The predictability of the media convergence ecosystem is much lower than the corporate, professional media systems of the past, which had a far narrower range of possibilities. The meteoric rise of Baby Shark, for instance, could not have been predicted. Similarly, in January 2019, when a simple image of a brown egg appeared on Instagram along with the caption, "Let's set a world record together and get the most liked post on Instagram,"[48] who could have imagined that it actually would? A *New York Times* article written about the egg and beginning with the statement, "Please don't expect any of the following to make sense," reflects sentiments typical of professionals working for media corporations who continue to be surprised by amateur and independent productions in the digital and social media systems. After noting, at the time, that "more than 35 million people have liked" the egg post, the author continues:

> Last year's top television show in the United States, "Roseanne," averaged 20 million viewers per week, and about 27 million watched the Oscars. If everyone who liked the photo created a new city, it would be the world's largest by several million. The egg's fans have passed the population of Canada. At that scale, internet frivolity starts to look a little less frivolous.[49]

People in the industry, used to basing decisions on relatively stable indicators like ratings and subscriptions, are still struggling to understand this broader, more complex system, how it aligns with the models they do understand, and what's coming next. But it's not only media professionals who have trouble predicting what the future holds. No one knows for sure what's coming next or how this will all play out, not even those who design, research, or teach interactive media for a living. The multiple interacting media species and systems within this ecosystem increase the volume and complexity of influences on how content circulates. The environment is constantly changing, and the ways the systems relate to one another are always in flux. For this reason, we all continue to be surprised by what happens in the media landscape today.

If not a full-blown revolution, we are certainly in a time of significant change. It is hard to see the forest for the trees when we are living in it, but, like the Baby Shark phenomenon, the trajectory makes more sense through analysis after the fact. In the present, we can see that these tensions exist and that we have not gotten it all figured out yet. We can certainly make projections about where we are headed, but one thing to assuredly expect is the unexpected; the surprises keep on coming. Looking backward, however, we can see that the introduction of interactive media into our society and its unexpected outcomes have led to nearly three decades of confusion, chaos, competition, and conflict within media, as well as many other sectors of society, such as business, government, politics, art, and culture. By focusing on the core dynamics and social principles at the root of these upheavals throughout this book, we will be able to gain insights not only into where we have been, but also where we are now, and where we might be headed.

## NOTES

1. Pinkfong! Kids' Songs & Stories, "Baby Shark Dance | Sing and Dance! | @ Baby Shark Official | PINKFONG Songs for Children," May 12, 2016, Video, 2:16, https://youtu.be/XqZsoesa55w.

2. George, "Most-Viewed YouTube Videos."

3. Ritschel, "'Baby Shark Song.'"

4. Sen, "'Baby Shark.'"

5. BBC, "Baby Shark."

6. Frex, "Baby Shark," Know Your Meme, updated by shevyrolet 2019, https://knowyourmeme.com/memes/baby-shark.

7. Dawkins, *The Selfish Gene*, 192.

8. TonightShowNet, "#Babysharkchallenge With Amanda Cerny," August 23, 2017, Video, 1:00, https://youtu.be/roh2ohRFlsg.

9. Ramirez, "How This 'Baby Shark.'"

10. Ritschel, "'Baby Shark Song.'"

11. TheEllenShow, "Ellen Releases Her Own 'Baby Shark' Video!" September 19, 2018, Video, 2:10, https://youtu.be/WC1sV99hQ2k.

12. Kylie Jenner (@kyliejenner), "maaamaa shark dooo doo doo dooo," Instagram photo, September 5, 2018, https://www.instagram.com/p/BnXXOtjgqBB/.

13. *The Late Late Show with James Corden*, "The Biggest 'Baby Shark' Ever w / Sophie Turner & Josh Groban," September 26, 2018, Video, 6:09, https://youtu.be /8yZSM4_-sgA.

14. *TODAY*, "See 'Baby Shark' Toddler Steal Hearts Once More On TODAY | TODAY," October 30, 2018, Video, 4:37, https://youtu.be/EwpoX4LFTiI.

15. HOW TO PROPERLY, " 🔊 How to properly dance baby shark Challenge Remix - Tiktok Memes compilation 2019," January 19, 2019, Video, 5:10, https://youtu.be/FjCTQGEvZV8.

16. Frex, "Baby Shark," Know Your Meme, updated by shevyrolet 2019, https://knowyourmeme.com/memes/baby-shark.

17. Langenderfer and Cook, "Copyright Policies and Issues," 286.

18. Langenderfer and Cook, 286.

19. Lessig, *Remix*, 25.

20. Manovich, *Software Takes Command*, 233–39.

21. Richards, *The Human Advantage*, 18.

22. Statista Research Department, "Percentage of Households."

23. Karlberg, "The State of Technology."

24. *TODAY* (@TODAYshow), "'What is internet anyway?' Throwing it back to when Katie Couric, Bryant Gumbel and Elizabeth Vargas wondered what the internet was!" Twitter video, June 20, 2019, https://twitter.com/todayshow/status /1141692791736733696.

25. Kelly, "We Are the Web."

26. Kelly, 3.

27. Shirky, *Cognitive Surplus*, 19.

28. Ledbetter, "An Introduction," 1–2.

29. boyd and Ellison, "Social Network Sites," 211; Ellison and boyd, "Sociality," 158.

30. Shirky, *Here Comes Everybody*, 83.

31. Rosen, "The People Formerly Known."

32. Toffler, *The Third Wave.*

33. Fuchs, *Social Media*, 110–11.

34. Lister, "Video Marketing Statistics."

35. Wojcicki, "YouTube at 15."

36. Kelly, "We Are the Web."

37. Shirky, *Cognitive Surplus*, 19–20.

38. Powazek, "Death to User-Generated Content," 97.

39. Chafin, "San Diego Comic-Con"; "About Comic-Con International," accessed January 24, 2021, https://www.comic-con.org/about.

40. Shirky, *Cognitive Surplus*, 21.

41. Gans, *Democracy and the News*, 3–4.

42. Shirky, *Here Comes Everybody*, 24.

43. Tewksbury and Rittenberg, *News on the Internet*, 18.

44. Jenkins, *Convergence Culture*, 198.

45. Lankes, "Trusting the Internet," 113–14.

46. Fuchs, *Social Media*, 257–63.

47. Manovich, *Software Takes Command*, 235.

48. Eugene | #EggGang (@world_record_egg), "Let's set a world record together and get the most liked post on Instagram. Beating the current world record held by Kylie Jenner (18 million)! We got this 👀 #LikeTheEgg #EggSoldiers #EggGang," Instagram photo, January 4, 2019, https://www.instagram.com/p/BsOGulcndj-/.

49. Victor, "An Egg."

## Chapter 3

# Groups and Communities

### INTRODUCTION: CAPTURE THE FLAG

In March 2017, a worldwide game of "Capture the Flag" ensued between the online community found at 4chan.org and their unwilling opponent, actor Shia LaBeouf. Just over two months earlier, after the presidential inauguration of Donald Trump, LaBeouf had begun an art installation with collaborators Nastja Säde Rönkkö and Luke Turner[1] at the Museum of the Moving Image in Queens, New York.[2] The project involved the words "HE WILL NOT DIVIDE US" painted on a wall mounted outside the museum, and an invitation to the public to participate by repeating the words as many times as they wanted to into a camera. As announced on the museum's website, "Open to all, 24 hours a day, seven days a week, the participatory performance will be live-streamed continuously at www.hewillnotdivide.us for four years, or the duration of the presidency."[3] However, the art project did not go exactly as planned.

According to the museum's website, the installation soon became "a flashpoint for violence and was disrupted from its original intent."[4] LaBeouf himself was arrested after being involved in a confrontation at the site that was captured on the livestream.[5] Citing safety concerns, the museum shut down the installation on February 10. Though LaBeouf and his colleagues quickly revived the effort outside the El Ray Theater in Albuquerque, New Mexico, this, too, was taken down in less than a week, after reports of gunshots in the area.[6] Not to be deterred, the art team decided to re-create the project in the form of a livestreamed flag containing the mantra, flying at an undisclosed location, with only the sky seen behind it. Assuming that this would make it impossible for anyone to find, the art project's Twitter account, @HWNDU_livetweet, announced the revived livestream at 10:31 a.m. on March 8, posting, "For the duration of the 4 years a #HEWILLNOTDIVIDEUS flag will be flown at an unknown location."[7] That's when 4chan irreverently took on the challenge.

Members working together in the site's subforum /pol/ (short for "politically incorrect")[8] began scouring the livestream for clues they could use. The hunt involved aligning whatever limited information they could derive, such as daylight, clouds, and ambient noise, with time zones, weather patterns, and known information about natural habitats. Combining this with information collected about LaBeouf's recent whereabouts posted on social media and news sites, the community gathered enough "intel" on the flag to narrow down its likely location to Greenville, Tennessee. Plane contrails were then spotted in the sky and matched with flight paths, and by nightfall, the pattern of the stars gave the community more information about the camera's direction and angle. Using satellite maps, digital editing tools, advanced mathematical calculations, and a volunteer driving around the identified area honking a horn, the users managed to successfully pinpoint the flag's exact location. At 4:36 a.m. on March 10, 2017, the flag was captured. Working together, it took 4chan less than two days to undo LaBeouf's assumed victory.[9]

As ill-intentioned as this 4chan quest was, it still reveals something amazing about the capacity of motivated humans working together, as enabled by interactive media. Like LaBeouf and his team, most people would assume that it would not be possible to track down the location of something based on what little information was revealed in the livestream. The idea that an army of Internet users would be able to pool resources and work together to relentlessly track down and gather information, combining such a wide array of skills and expertise, seemed impossible. To members of online communities like 4chan, however, this was well within the realm of the achievable. Among their many accomplishments, 4chan has identified and caught animal abusers,[10] advanced the field of mathematics by helping to solve a twenty-five-year-old math problem,[11] and even located terrorist training sites in Syria.[12] Similarly, users via social media sites have used their collective power to solve real-world mysteries about genetic diseases,[13] missing persons,[14] and hit-and-run crimes.[15] There is an entire community website dedicated to crime-solving called websleuths.com. The discussion site Reddit has subforums called r/whatisthisthing, where members post and work to identify unknown objects,[16] and r/rbi ("Reddit Bureau of Investigation") with the express intent of solving "real world problems,"[17] among others. Although the outcomes of these efforts are not always positive or successful (such as when the users of Reddit infamously misidentified the Boston marathon bomber[18]), in the networked spaces of interactive media, large groups of people can sometimes work together toward impressive ends.

## MORE IS DIFFERENT

For a moment, let's imagine a situation in which a person is being asked to
state their opinion on a complex issue. Maybe it is their thoughts on abortion or gun control, or a less serious topic, like a recent controversial call in
a game or the latest celebrity scandal. Or perhaps they are asked to consider
whether they think the effects of interactive media on society have been
mostly good or mostly bad. Whatever the topic, giving an answer about their
opinion is likely to be a relatively easy process. They think about it, on their
own, decide how they feel about it, and they're done (figure 3.1a). However,
if they are then asked to discuss this with another person, a conversation
needs to happen, a back-and-forth exchange (figure 3.1b). Maybe the two of
them have the same opinion, and it continues to be relatively easy to determine and express how they feel, but maybe they are diametrically opposed,
and things could get heated. Still, talking to someone else can get people
thinking outside of their own lines a little bit, to consider things they had not
thought of, and maybe, through their talk, the two of them can eventually
come to some level of agreement about this issue.

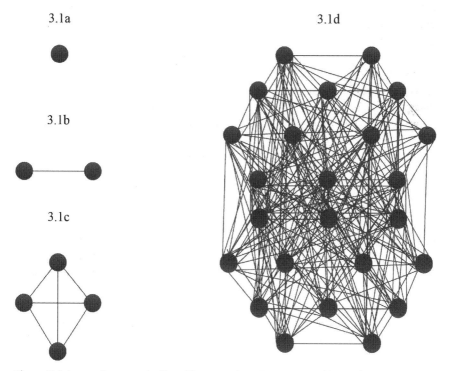

3.1a

3.1b

3.1c

3.1d

**Figure 3.1 Increasing complexity with group size.** *Figure created by author.*

Now, bring in two more people in to the conversation. The odds of all of four people feeling exactly the same way about the issue at the outset are pretty low, and the complexity of the situation increases.[19] Although this group only doubles in size from the previous scenario, the number of connections that needs to be made triples, as each individual has to connect with three others (figure 3.1c).[20] Still, in a group of four, it is possible for everyone to be heard, and the conversation can be that much more productive for expanding horizons on a particular issue for those who keep an open mind. But what if they had this discussion with twenty-five other people? Would each of them make a connection with all of the twenty-four other group members (figure 3.1d)? Would everyone get to be heard? Would they all walk away knowing what each person's nuanced opinion on the matter was? Assuming all twenty-five of them don't have hours of time on their hands and an extremely dedicated spirit to the matter, the answer to all of these questions is no.

In larger groups, communication becomes too complex to manage one-on-one, and new mechanisms need to be implemented.[21] It becomes impossible for every individual to be heard by everyone, so people tend to group together into smaller factions and issues tend to get simplified, often boiled down to just two to three options, or "sides." Leaders might emerge and serve to represent the perspectives and interests of these subfactions, and they will seek information through group-oriented means like soliciting feedback, taking polls, or voting. It is impossible to get total agreement in a group this size, so individuals begin to make compromises and prioritize their causes. This is how larger groups function, such as companies, unions, cities, countries, media outlets, and other types of organizations that involve hundreds or thousands of people communicating and working together.

In an article entitled, "More Is Different," theoretical physicist Phillip Anderson wrote the following about the behavior of elementary particles when they group into large aggregations: "the behavior . . . is not to be understood in terms of a simple extrapolation of the properties of a few particles. Instead, at each level of complexity entirely new properties appear, and the understanding of the new behaviors requires research which I think is as fundamental in its nature as any other."[22] Anderson's principle of "more is different" is true of social systems as well—large and complex groups of people operate very differently from small groups of only a few.[23] And this is true not only in terms of how large groups of people are organized and how they operate, but also with respect to what larger groups of people can, collectively, accomplish.

In the offline world, many of the altered properties and behaviors of large groups result from physical limitations on time, space, and resources—it is simply not materially possible for them to operate as small groups do. These physical constraints are to a large degree lifted, however, when large groups of people are able to assemble virtually. This does not mean that large groups online are able to function as smaller groups would—there are still inherent properties of large groups that exceed our cognitive and social capacities[24]—but it does make them easier to organize and their complexity more manageable.[25] Large groups online have fundamental differences not only due to their size ("more is different"), but also to their nonconcrete nature ("abstracted is different," perhaps). Thus the principles driving their organization, operation, and outcomes reflect yet another category of "groupness," one that we had not seen before the Internet.[26]

## LARGE GROUPS: OFFLINE VERSUS ONLINE

No longer limited to just a few specialized or institutional domains, large groups of people can now organize online around anything and everything, from cats[27] to cancer[28] to Korean cooking.[29] If there is a topic or interest that exists, there is probably a group about it on the Internet. The networked and databased nature of interactive media allows for the circumvention and restructuring of many of the group-oriented mechanisms that would normally be needed for large group communication offline.[30] The capacity for many-to-many communication in online spaces allows for large communicative gatherings that are not inhibited by the limitations of time, space, or energy. This means that online groups have some pretty significant differences from the ways that traditional, offline groups tend to operate. Some of these differences are outlined in the sections below, with respect to the efforts, structures, processes, and conceptualizations of offline versus online groups.

### Effort: Difficult versus Easy

Traditionally, gathering large groups of people has been a complex task, hard to arrange, and difficult to sustain. Organizing people in the real world requires a lot of resources and effort.[31] Certain individuals have to be very motivated in order to make that happen,[32] and typically they need to be compensated in some way for their efforts, or at least have the promise of compensation, which is usually backed by some sort of institutional support.[33] Think of the people who participate in the meetings of Congress, for example, or the UN. Presumably, they are motivated at least in part by their sense of responsibility, but they still get paid to be there. Or imagine a festival or sporting event—people spend a lot of time and effort putting those together, and they are paid by an organization expecting revenue from ticket sales. Even volunteers for nonprofit organizations and activists participating in movements are, traditionally, recruited and organized by at least a small number of people who have dedicated their life's work to the cause and are compensated through the use of fund-raising to support their efforts. Without the assistance of networked technology, it has to be this way in order for someone to put in all that effort, or the organization would quickly break down, and the group would fall apart.[34]

The convenience of online gatherings, however, makes them easier to accomplish.[35] Interactive media sites make it simple for anyone to start a group; it is usually free and takes very little time to just click a few buttons, enter some information, and make it public. Community-oriented sites like Facebook, Reddit, and Meetup already have a built-in userbase that can be tapped into, as well as recommendation and search tools that bring users' attention to the groups. This increases the likelihood of a group's success, but if a large group fails to materialize, no one is losing their livelihood or wasting too many resources, so there is little risk involved in the attempt.[36] Because of the small amount of effort that it takes to start a group and the availability to everyone with Internet access to do so, lots of groups get started and the ones that gain the most interest tend to "stick," gain attention, and grow.[37] This is vastly different from the traditional, offline model of large group formation, and it changes nearly everything about how large groups of people can congregate, participate, and collaborate, at a fundamental level.[38]

## Structure: Hierarchical versus Leaderless

Offline, large groups of people typically take on a centralized, *hierarchical* structure.[39] There are leaders, managers, elites, and gatekeepers in charge of information flow and determining what directions the group will take.[40] Think of how companies are structured, with their organizational charts flowing from the CEO to vice presidents, down to the managers of different branches, and so on. Consider how a government is run, from the president and his or her cabinet members, down through the judicial system or legislative branch to the local operatives representing citizens in the smallest counties and towns. There is always someone at each level to lead, and to take on the perspectives, ideas, and feedback of their constituents, either by addressing them themselves or bringing them up the chain to the next level. Without interactive media, this is the most fair and efficient way we have found to ensure that, to the greatest extent possible, everyone in a large group is accounted for.[41]

Large groups formed through the tools of interactive media, however, are decentralized and frequently referred to as *"leaderless."*[42] Someone can start a group online, but that does not make them *the* leader and, in fact, a well-formed group is likely to continue on even without the originator's continued participation.[43] In addition, because of the end-to-end asynchronous discussion tools used via interactive media, communication typically remains archived and transparent for everyone to see,[44] which means that no one member is necessarily any more "in the know" than any of the others. Anyone who wants to say something can, at any time, and the communication is directly and horizontally delivered to the entire group, peer-to-peer and many-to-many.[45] Because of this, all members can contribute ideas, information, and knowledge to the group as a whole, there are less definable experts and elites, and no one is necessarily given elevated status as an authority, representative, or "manager."[46] As with online group formation itself, ideas are thrown out there, and the ones that seem the most interesting or significant to the greatest number of group members are the ones that tend to "stick."[47]

## Process: Rules versus Norms

Frequently, there are *rules* for communicating in large offline groups. Institutional procedures, policies, and formalities are put into place and expected to be followed. Specific times and places are designated for certain activities and events, such as meetings, elections, sessions, or assemblies. The procedures of these events often follow a certain standardized template, or even documented "rules of order" involving time allotments for speaking (as in a debate on the floor of Congress) and the counting of votes. In companies, employees are expected to communicate to their immediate supervisors or managers and not go over their heads or bypass levels in the hierarchy. Those "in charge" at each level (i.e., managers, chairmen, lieutenants) are additionally assigned the task of maintaining adherence to these communicative policies and procedures. Everyone in the group must adhere to these rules or be penalized, and in some cases may even get expelled from the group altogether if they break them.

Large groups online are not typically like that. Freed from the ties to not only institutions, but also the constraints of time and space, what is allowed in communication is determined more informally through evolving *norms*, which are fluid and constantly contested as members come and go.[48] These norms are understood by the members of these groups, who tend to collectively self-police against "bad" behavior.[49] Some groups may ultimately choose to encode their own set of rules and assign moderators to enforce them, but again, these mechanisms tend to be added or removed in alignment within the group's collective will, and anyone can speak up at any time to express support for or refutation against them.[50] Even the rules of a host platform's "Terms of Use" are subject to change based upon developers' understanding of evolving norms within their site's user base.[51] There are also tools typically in place that allow individual members to flag or block unwanted communications, and this capability is available to everyone.[52] Online, all group members have, at least in principle, equal opportunity to influence how the group's communication is managed, and what is or is not considered acceptable behavior is determined collectively.[53]

## Conceptualization: Organizations versus Communities

We tend to conceptualize large offline groups as *"organizations."* The goal of these groups is to "organize," to "get things done," to direct institutional resources, achieve consensus, and make decisions.[54] The efforts, structures, and processes involved are all designed with some end, achievement, or outcome in mind. Because of the level of effort involved, members have a stake in achieving the outcome, and thus are more likely to be accepting of compromises.[55] They tend to put their trust in authoritative and democratic mechanisms, even as they may subsume the nuance of an individual's specific ideas or preferences.[56]

Meanwhile, large online groups tend to be referred to as *"communities."*[57] This connotes a space in which one can simply exist, live, or be. Although people may gather in an online community because of shared interests, there is often no particular task or goal in mind. People are motivated to participate for the purposes of sharing and support,[58] rather than defined outcomes (even though sometimes things do get accomplished nonetheless). Conversation is key.[59] People find a place to be heard, to share knowledge, perspectives, or experiences, but they do not necessarily feel a need to achieve consensus, conform their opinions, or make collective decisions.[60] As opposed to a hive-mind mentality, online communities tend to be marked by unending debates, discussions, and considerations that reflect dialectical tensions and contradictions,[61] and rife with interdisciplinary and open-ended questions that often aren't fully answered.[62] No one individual member would claim that they fully support everything that is contained within this never-finished and constantly in flux stream of communication. And, because people have little stake in any sort of perceived "outcome," they don't have to. No one is required to accept anything that the group comes to represent if they don't want to.

The term "community," however, can also be somewhat problematic for describing large online groups, as it is a metaphor based on a type of group that exists offline that connotes real space marked by geographical boundaries.[63] Online, "community" is not determined by physical location, but rather by markers of personal interest and identity.[64] Members of online communities find one another because of their interests, preferences, life circumstances, or ideas; thus, people gather *based* on their individuality, not in spite of it.[65] As opposed to an employer or a neighborhood, members of online communities can choose to join or leave at any time with little consequence,[66] and thus they do not feel tied in to group outcomes should things go in a direction they find undesirable.[67] In addition, though online communities typically originate in a single online space, their boundaries can span platforms[68] or they might even move from one platform to another.[69] Thus, despite participants frequently reflecting behaviors and attitudes that might be associated with more traditional understandings of community, such as a sense of familiarity, norms of group identification, and "off-topic" casual communication,[70] the structures and processes are so different from an offline, geographical community that the metaphor often fails to contain the phenomenon in its fullness.[71] The fuzzy, open, and more weakly tied nature of online communities, combined with the ever-shifting landscape of the networked media platforms we use to form them, makes their specific nature and form seemingly impossible to nail down.[72] In fact, Couldry and Hepp argue that some of what we call online "communities" might better be referred to as "collectivities" with a shared orientation on a technological platform but few actual "communal" characteristics, and most large online groups fall somewhere on a spectrum in between community and collectivity.[73] Still, when discussing this phenomenon, we tend to loosely utilize the "community" metaphor as a shortcut to describe generally what we are referring to, while also acknowledging the term's complexity and incompleteness.[74]

## Knowledge Communities

If online communities have no specific boundaries, structures, processes, or goals, it begs the question: why do they matter at all? Isn't this just a bunch of people engaging in insignificant chatter online about nothing of consequence? Whether or not that is the case in some instances, something interesting happens when a group's communication involves the significant sharing of knowledge.[75] All online communities involve some degree of knowledge sharing between their members, but, due to the asynchronous and archived nature of communication, a community in which knowledge sharing is of central significance is, essentially, a searchable knowledge database.[76] This creates the context for what Pierre Lévy has termed *collective intelligence*, where individuals can share, access, and build on one another's knowledge over time.[77] In such a *knowledge community*, where hundreds, thousands, even millions of people pool their collective knowledge in this way, the whole is much larger than the sum of its parts,[78] and it can be quite powerful.[79] Three of the most impressive outcomes of the collective intelligence found in knowledge communities—*diversity*, *collaboration*, and *empowerment*—are detailed in the following sections.

## Diversity

Because they are formed around topics, ideas, and interests instead of geographical locations, knowledge communities can attract people from all walks of life, from all over the world, with a variety of experiences and perspectives.[80] As a whole, such communities capture a view of the world that no one person could achieve.[81] The resulting diversity of viewpoints, information, expertise, and opinions can create an "expert knowledge" out of the community that is actually more all-encompassing and inclusive than what any traditional "expert" could offer.[82] In addition, when people with diverse knowledge sets come together to solve problems, better insights, ideas, and solutions tend to be generated.[83]

As a simple example, let's imagine that a group of five people come together to address the problem of overpollution in a city. What kinds of solutions would a group of five environmental scientists come up with, versus a group that includes, say, an environmental scientist, a city planner, a local schoolteacher, a local business owner, and a community leader? Which group's solutions would be more creative, helpful, and likely to find success? People working within a single sector are typically not privy to the benefits of knowledge domain boundary-crossing,[84] which include the negation of confirmation bias and groupthink and the application of out-of-the-box thinking leading to more innovative, creative, and effective solutions.[85] Likewise, members of 4chan worked to combine knowledge from multiple areas to find LaBeouf's flag—meteorology, aviation, biodiversity, geography, satellite mapping, trigonometry, astronomy, celebrity gossip, digital editing, and local knowledge (and accessibility), among others—to accomplish their capture the flag victory.

## Collaboration

When people in knowledge communities aim their collective intelligence toward some outcome or goal, their activities move beyond simple sharing and communication to collaboration. Finding an answer, solving a problem, and bringing awareness to an issue are just some of the goals knowledge communities can work together to accomplish.[86] When applied to collaboration, the participatory, decentralized, and voluntary nature of online communities extends to influence the fluidity of roles that members can adopt as they contribute.[87] Participation in specific efforts or tasks can be taken on by anyone at any time, on an ad-hoc or as-needed basis, and no one is assigned or relegated to any single duty or specific role.[88] As a result of this flexibility, anyone can ask any question, posit any idea, or offer any tidbit of useful information, which others can pick up and use. Thus, knowledge, insights, and achievements iteratively build upon one another, dovetail, and fit together in unique and unconventional ways.[89]

For example, the 4chan member who noticed the planes' contrails on the livestream might have been different from the one who found the data showing live flight paths, and it was probably a third member who matched up their direction and angle with locations on a map. Even more likely, several members were probably doing each of these activities simultaneously, sharing the results of their work as they went, and adapting their efforts based on what others had shared. Though there is perhaps some redundancy in these processes, the net result is actually more efficient because so many are working on the same or similar tasks at once and from multiple angles. Thus, all of the tasks build upon one another in a relatively short time frame based on the flexibility and adaptability of the communication structures and the lack of rules for work processes in the knowledge community.[90]

## Empowerment

As they say, there is power in numbers, and the sheer size of online communities makes them powerful.[91] In addition to adding diversity of expertise and flexibility to the collaborative efforts of knowledge communities, the networked nature of interactive media allows masses of people to gather on a regular basis at their convenience around a shared idea or goal. Just this act of gathering alone can bring heightened attention to a community, as interactive media platforms are frequently programmed to highlight the most active or popular groups. This pattern extends to the broader context of the media convergence ecosystem as well, as both social and corporate media systems can help bring awareness of a group's activities to new audiences and groups, further expanding the reach of their efforts or message.

For example, LaBeouf's celebrity status and media coverage of his art project added visibility to the 4chan community effort. As word of these efforts spread to other social media platforms and networks that crossed over with /pol/, it brought yet more attention and collaborators to help out. In addition, these professional and digital media systems inadvertently gave the group leads, as users utilized both professional media reporting and social media posts to find LaBeouf's whereabouts. Although perhaps not the most uplifting example of empowerment, the bottom-up knowledge community of 4chan did, in fact, irreverently undermine the aims of the top-down media system in this instance (i.e., the well-known, well-funded, and high-status professionals), even while using it to inform their own efforts. Across a variety of sectors and in a thousand different ways, the potential of such empowerment within knowledge communities gives them the strength to challenge, undermine, or even change power structures in society.[92]

## Conclusion

A common theme seen with interactive media is that a certain "sensibility" derived from its uses leaks out into the broader culture, for better or for worse. The demand protocols we adopt from using these tools begin to modify our expectations in the real world. In other words, over time, the norms of the Internet begin making their way into everyday life.[93] In the case of large online groups, we have borne witness over the past several decades to the rise of a *knowledge culture*, a new cultural understanding of how knowledge is produced and validated, deriving, at least in part, from the diverse, collaborative, and empowering outcomes of collective intelligence.[94] For instance, in today's information environment, there are no prescribed rules for where knowledge comes from; everyone can contribute to it.[95] This means that what is presented as truth, especially if it is a dominant or "mainstream" narrative, is publicly challenged more frequently. Disciplinary experts are not trusted the way they used to be, and every idea, every fact is questioned and entered into an ongoing conversation that seems to have no resolution in sight.[96] Everyone can contribute to these debates, and no one is in charge of refereeing them or making final judgments.[97]

At the same time, this has led to some broader consequences for our society as a whole. There has been a rise in conspiracy theories, allegations of fake news from every direction, and we now have fact-checkers for the fact-checkers. People have lost trust in experts and democratic systems, and we struggle to find an objective source for understanding reality. Established institutions are collapsing, and bottom-up is clashing with top-down globally and across sectors. More and more, the idea of "question everything" is becoming "fight everything," and various groups from all sides of what has been termed the "culture war" have begun to exert their networked power in an effort to silence ideas that are alternative to their own (such as taking out art installations). How, when, and if this will all level out is yet to be seen, but it is evident that we are still in the midst of a significant societal shift, and we will need to develop new skills in order to be able to critically navigate this media environment so that we can utilize it in ways that are helpful rather than harmful.

Writing in 1997, Lévy argued that we were going to need to undergo a period of "apprenticeship" in which we adapted our "mental models and patterns of action" to better suit the benefits that collective intelligence could bring, but that it would take us some time to do so.[98] Nearly twenty-five years later, it would seem that we are still learning. Like adolescents, we have realized our newfound freedom and strength and are currently wielding it in ways that have negative consequences for ourselves and those around us. As Lévy projected, the technology has evolved faster than we could.[99] But the hope is that, like a student or youth learning from their mistakes, we will mature and begin to direct our energies toward more positive and beneficial outcomes, adopting new models and behaviors that respect, incorporate, and build upon one another's knowledge in order to advance humanity forward.

## NOTES

1. Luke Turner, Nastja Rönkkö, and Shia LaBeouf, "Info," accessed December 21, 2020, http://labeoufronkkoturner.com/info/.

2. Lamoureux, "How 4Chan's Worst."

3. Museum of the Moving Image, "Installation: HeWillNotDivide.us." accessed January 31, 2021, https://web.archive.org/web/20170126123442if_/; http://www.movingimage.us/exhibitions/2017/01/20/detail/hewillnotdivide-us/.

4. *BBC*, "Shia LaBeouf's Anti-Trump."

5. *BBC*.

6. Buffenstein, "Shia LaBeouf's."

7. Internet Historian, "Capture the Flag | He Will Not Divide Us," March 15, 2017, Video, 5:00, https://youtu.be/vw9zyxm860Q.

8. "/pol/ - Politically Incorrect," 4chan, updated August 21, 2020, https://boards.4chan.org/pol/.

9. Internet Historian, "Capture the Flag | He Will Not Divide Us," March 15, 2017, Video, 5:00, https://youtu.be/vw9zyxm860Q.

10. Alfonso, "After 4chan Manhunt."

11. Klarreich, "Anonymous 4chan Post."

12. Zoltany, "Shia LaBeouf Flag Capture."

13. Mohney, "Girl Diagnosed."

14. Heaton, "Myrtle Beach Police."

15. Pierpoint, "Reddit Sleuth."

16. Reddit, "For the Identification of Mysterious Objects," September 5, 2010, https://www.reddit.com/r/whatisthisthing/.

17. Reddit, "RBI: Reddit Bureau of Investigation," January 3, 2012, https://www.reddit.com/r/RBI/.

18. *BBC*, "Reddit Apologises."

19. Shirky, *Here Comes Everybody*, 27.

20. Shirky, 27.

21. Shirky, 28.

22. Anderson, "More Is Different," 393.

23. Couldry and Hepp, *The Mediated Construction*, 71; Shirky, *Here Comes Everybody*, 28.

24. Shirky, 92.

25. Shirky, 48.

26. Shirky, 48.

27. CHEEZburger, "I Can Has," accessed December 21, 2020, https://icanhas. cheezburger.com.

28. Reddit, "Cancer: Discussion & Support," June 17, 2008, https://www.reddit. com/r/cancer/.

29. Facebook, "Korean Cooking," updated May 20, 2020, https://www.facebook. com/groups/375989249440033/.

30. Bennett and Segerberg, "Logic of Connective Action," 753.

31. Shirky, *Here Comes Everybody*, 206.

32. Shirky, 181–82.

33. Benkler, *The Wealth of Networks*, 4.

34. Shirky, *Here Comes Everybody*, 19.

35. Shirky, 53–54.

36. Shirky, 236.

37. Gladwell, *The Tipping Point*, 24–25.

38. Jemielniak and Przegalinska, *Collaborative Society*, 4–5; Shirky, *Here Comes Everybody*, 20–21.

39. Shirky, 29.

40. Shirky, 30–31.

41. Shirky, 29.

42. Jemielniak and Przegalinska, *Collaborative Society*, 46; Western, "Autonomist Leadership," 681.

43. Lai, "Can Our Group Survive," 843.

44. Averian, "Digital Ecosystems Software," 40.

45. Castells, *Networks of Outrage and Hope*, 180.

46. Benkler and Nissenbaum, "Common-Based Peer Production," 396; Jemielniak and Przegalinska, *Collaborative Society*, 46.

47. Raymond, "Cathedral and the Bazaar," 24.

48. Castells, *Networks of Outrage and Hope*, 224–25.

49. Shirky, *Here Comes Everybody*, 272.

50. Jenkins, *Convergence Culture*, 54.

51. Braman and Roberts, "Advantage ISP," 442–43; McLaughlin and Vitak, "Norm Evolution and Violation," 301.

52. Shirky, 272.

53. Jenkins, *Convergence Culture*, 54; Lévy, *Collective Intelligence*, 17; McLaughlin and Vitak, 301.

54. Shirky, *Here Comes Everybody*, 29.

55. Shirky, 53.

56. Shirky, 53.

57. Wellman and Gulia, "Virtual Communities as Communities," 185.

58. Wellman and Gulia, 172.

59. Shirky, *Here Comes Everybody*, 50.

60. Shirky, 267.

61. Jemielniak and Przegalinska, *Collaborative Society*, 50.

62. Jemielniak and Przegalinska, 51–52; Shirky, *Here Comes Everybody*, 139.

63. Jones, *Cybersociety 2.0*, 15.

64. Couldry and Hepp, *The Mediated Construction,* 172; Jones, 28.

65. Rheingold, *The Virtual Community* 2nd ed., *xxviii.*

66. Jemielniak and Przegalinska, *Collaborative Society,* 48; Muniz and O'Guinn, "Brand Community," 426.

67. Rainie and Wellman, *Networked,* 124.

68. Couldry and Hepp, *The Mediated Construction,* 171; Porter, "Virtual Communities and Social Networks," 161–63.

69. Shirky, *Here Comes Everbody,* 205.

70. Porter, "Virtual Communities," 162–63; Wellman and Gulia, "Virtual Communities as Communities," 185.

71. Wellman and Gulia, 186.

72. Jones, *Cybersociety 2.0,* 18.

73. Couldry and Hepp, *The Mediated Construction,* 168–70.

74. Couldry and Hepp, 172; Schwier, "Shaping the Metaphor," 68.

75. Jenkins, *Convergence Culture,* 27.

76. Lin et al., "Web-Based Knowledge Communities," 39–40.

77. Lévy, *Collective Intelligence,* 13.

78. Lévy, xxvii.

79. Barrett et al., "Learning in Knowledge Communities," 3.

80. Wellman and Gulia, "Virtual Communities as Communities," 185–86.

81. Lévy, *Collective Intelligence,* 13–14.

82. Surowiecki, *The Wisdom of Crowds,* 29–31.

83. Johnson, *Good Ideas,* 165–67.

84. Barrett et al., "Learning in Knowledge Communities," 1.

85. Duarte et al., "Political Diversity Will Improve," 7.

86. Surowecki, *The Wisdom of Crowds,* 161–62.

87. Lévy, *Collective Intelligence,* 17.

88. Jenkins, *Convergence Culture,* 262.

89. Tapscott and Williams, *Wikinomics,* 236–37.

90. Lévy, *Collective Intelligence,* 15; Tapscott and Williams, 236.

91. Shirky, *Here Comes Everbody,* 107.

92. Lévy, *Collective Intelligence,* 82–88.

93. Castells, *Networks of Outrage and Hope,* 228–29; Jenkins, *Convergence Culture,* 27.

94. Jemielniak and Przegalinska, *Collaborative Society,* 106; Jenkins, 27.

95. Jemielniak and Przegalinska, 112; Jenkins, 52–53.

96. Jemielniak and Przegalinska, 50; Shirky, *Here Comes Everybody,* 119.

97. Jenkins, 53–54.

98. Lévy, *Collective Intelligence,* 77.

99. Lévy, 76.

# Chapter 4

# Networks

## INTRODUCTION: ORACLE OF BACON

Visiting the website www.oracleofbacon.org[1] is like taking a time machine back to the 1990s. Not only do its graphics and design still reflect the amateurish websites of the era, but its purpose—to demonstrate the actor Kevin Bacon's links to any other actor in Hollywood—is a relic of its time. For those of us old enough to remember, the "Six Degrees of Kevin Bacon" was a cultural phenomenon that emerged circa 1994, shortly after the actor was featured in *Premiere* magazine and made the claim that he had probably either worked with, or at least worked with someone who had worked with, every person in Hollywood.[2] In an online "newsgroup" (the closest thing we had to social media at the time), users began to test this claim through a game, in which a member would name a celebrity as a challenge, and the others would attempt to link them up with Bacon through the films they had appeared in. "Try it with anyone, it works!" poster Alexander Wyeth Raven claimed on April 7, 1994.[3] Another user offered up a seemingly difficult task, "Someone do Toshiro Mifune." "Too easy," a third replied, "Toshiro Mifune was in *1941* with John Belushi who was in *ANIMAL HOUSE* with Kevin Bacon."[4]

A group of Albright college students began taking on the challenge as a party trick, finding connections from Bacon to the most obscure and antedated of actors, and gave the trivia game its "Six Degrees" name, in reference to the 1993 film *The Six Degrees of Separation*.[5] They soon publicized their newly found Bacon-linking superpowers, performing them for Jon Stewart on television and Howard Stern on the radio (where Bacon himself even called in and played along).[6] From there, it became a book, a board game, and an oft-cited American cultural reference. Brett Tjaden, a University of Virginia doctoral student at the time, created the original Oracle of Bacon website in 1996,[7] and Google later utilized the concept for a time, allowing users to search the "Bacon number" of any celebrity and returning a result that provided the number of links between them and the actor.[8]

One of the most interesting questions about the phenomenon is this: why Kevin Bacon? Perhaps it's just the fact that he has a funny name, but it's also notable that Bacon has had a long career and been in a lot of productions (he has ninety-four credits to his name according to IMDB[9]). He's also very diverse in his acting roles. Not one to be typecast, Bacon has played everything from everyday heroes to supervillains; he has appeared in dramas, horror films, action movies, supernatural thrillers, and comedies of the "chick flick" and "bro" variety. In addition, he spans media. He's acted on TV and Broadway and worked with independent producers, major studios, and everything in between.[10] This means that he crosses boundaries, transcends divides, connects divergences, and achieves a wide reach. Lastly, he has worked with many other veteran actors, like Tom Hanks, Cuba Gooding Jr., and Julia Roberts, who connect him to a variety of other films. Put together, all of this means that, in the world of film, Kevin Bacon is well-known and well-networked, and this makes the game fun and playable by the average pop culture buff.

However, the "Six Degrees of Kevin Bacon" phenomenon was perhaps less about Bacon himself and more about the impressive power of social networks on display, at a time when a growing awareness of them was just emerging within our collective cultural and scientific consciousness. In fact, once the game became "databased" via oracleofbacon.org (which first utilized imdb.org[11] for its data and now uses Wikipedia[12]), users have discovered that they can put in nearly any two people from its network of 379,000 actors from throughout film history and across the world,[13] and they will typically find three or fewer links between them. Identifying such connections between people is not only fun but fascinating, and Kevin Bacon's prolific film career was simply the mechanism of entry into a 1990s-era "oracle" previewing for the masses a concept we would all soon come to know well: the social network.[14]

## SOCIAL NETWORK ANALYSIS

Facebook CEO Mark Zuckerberg was not the first person to conceive of *social networks*, and he certainly did not create them. Human beings have always existed within, and to some degree been aware of, social networks through our informal social connections with one another.[15] Scholars have been theorizing about them since long before the Internet existed, and began formally studying them as early as the 1930s.[16] Operating under the rubric of different terms, such as "sociometry," "interpersonal networks," "human relations," and "the structural perspective," researchers in a variety of fields coalesced in the establishment of an approach known as "social network analysis" by the 1970s.[17] Social network analysts work to explain and predict social influences on behavior in various contexts by creating interlinking maps representing people as "nodes" and their "ties" or "links" as lines crossing from node to node.[18] Since the 1970s, a growing body of research analyzing social networks has emerged, experiencing a massive surge after the rise of interactive media, and much has been learned about their structures.[19]

During approximately this same stretch of time beginning in the first half of the twentieth century, emerging forms of mass media, and an increased interest in both propaganda and advertising sparked a research agenda focused on better understanding influences over public opinion and how ideas caught on and were diffused throughout society.[20] It was understood that there was a kind of social "contagion" effect wherein people shared ideas with one another, and a lot of power in "word of mouth."[21] We knew that the people we know, and the people they know, played an important role in spreading ideas.[22] Some of us who are older may remember the Fabergé Shampoo commercial from the 1980s (or the parody of this commercial in the 1990s movie *Wayne's World*) in which a woman states, "I told two friends, and they told two friends," repeating the second clause again and again while her image is multiplied several times over on the screen, which captures this idea visually.

While word of mouth is a part of the equation, social network analysts have demonstrated that the way ideas spread across a population is actually more complex than that, and involves the different kinds of connections that we have with one another. It was Michael Gurevitch in 1961 who first began mapping "who-knows-whom" contact links between individuals in a particular sphere of influence in his dissertation titled, "The Social Structure of Acquaintanceship Networks."[23] In 1967, social psychologist Stanley Milgram built on this work, finding that the average number of links between people who do not personally know each other in the United States was relatively low, and estimated an average of about five acquaintance intermediaries, or "degrees," between any two Americans.[24] It was, in fact, playwright John Guare who extended the number of degrees to six, likely because of the nicer-sounding alliteration, when he coined the phrase, "The Six Degrees of Separation" as the title of his 1990 Broadway play on which the 1993 film was based. In it, a character ponders about this scientific theory, "I read somewhere that everybody on this planet is separated by only six other people. Six degrees of separation. The president of the United States. A gondolier in Venice. Fill in the names . . . I am bound to everyone on this planet by a trail of six people. It's a profound thought."[25] While no one has yet been able to test this idea for the entire population of 7.8 billion people on this planet, Facebook's research team did run such an analysis on its sample of 1.6 billion worldwide users in 2016, and found that, in fact, like the Oracle of Bacon demonstrated for Hollywood, there is an average of about 3.57 degrees of separation between any two people in its network.[26] Again and again, when we test the theory, we discover that there are indeed very few connections from one person to another in extremely large populations. How can this be possible? The answer lies in the structure of our informal ties.

## SMALL WORLD NETWORKS

In the last chapter, it was demonstrated how, as groups of people grow in numbers, the complexity of communication increases, and the ability of each person to connect directly with all of the others is increasingly limited. As noted, because of this, in order to achieve some degree of progress, we typically adopt other methods of coming to consensus or making decisions in large groups, by implementing hierarchical structures that ensure at least the representation of smaller subgroups. Even without these formal mechanisms, however, people quite naturally end up communicating in subgroupings.[27] A glance around at any party or other large social gathering will show evidence of people congregating in clusters, typically groups of no more than seven,[28] with certain individuals flitting between them like butterflies.

In informal communication, our social patterns tend to look less like hierarchical pyramids or branching trees, and more like a field of wildflowers or an interconnected web.[29] Even within hierarchically organized institutions, such informally organized links and networks tend to form, such as when Deborah from engineering has lunch with Janelle from accounting, and Janelle, whose husband is the VP of marketing, frequently joins the administrative staff at TGIFriday's for happy hour. In fact, many of the earliest social network analyses involved the mapping of these informal ties within hierarchical organizations, demonstrating their influence outside the more formal, rigidly controlled, and top-down communication structures in place.[30]

This more organically formed structure of informal social ties creates what is called a *small world network*, so named for the "small world" phenomenon that occurs when we first meet someone and find out that we share a common acquaintance of unlikely origin.[31] Duncan Watts and Steve Strogatz discovered this pattern using social network analysis in 1998, and it is represented in figure 4.1 below.

As can be seen, the small world network is made up of smaller, tightly knit clusters that represent the groups of people communicating with one another the most often. These are our families, closest groups of friends, and co-workers—groups where everyone knows everyone, and members all communicate directly with one another on a regular basis. But it doesn't end

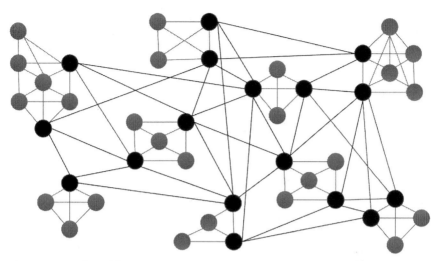

**Figure 4.1 Small world network pattern.** *Figure created by author.*

there. The pattern repeats itself at the larger scale.[32] Although there is not as much overlap between "nodes," the more condensed clusters have links to one another as well (seen in the black lines). Looking at these sparser connections for a moment, one might notice something peculiar about them. Most people do not communicate regularly with anyone outside of their cluster, but there are a few, highly connected people called *Connectors*[33] (the black dots), who typically have not just one, but many, links beyond their smaller clusters to others.[34]

A kind of encoding of the small world network can be clearly seen when we use social media. On Facebook, for example, most of us probably have a relatively small network of very close friends and family with whom we communicate the most often—this is our tightly knit cluster. The Connectors within each cluster, however, can be identified as those with a higher-than-average number of friends (whom they actually seem to know in real life) and likely have a variety of disparate interests on their page. Connectors have also been conceived of in the research as "opinion leaders," "opinion brokers," "network entrepreneurs,"[35] or "influencers"[36] (another term in social media parlance borrowed from the work of social network analysts). Most people are not Connectors, but these few, very highly connected people are the glue that holds the whole small world network structure together.[37] In fact, in those "small world" encounters with a stranger, it is very likely that either one of the people in the duo, or the person they know in common, is a Connector.

Connectors are a special type of person. Typically extroverted "social butterflies," they not only communicate with more people on average than the rest of us, but they also tend to communicate with a lot of different types of people, from a variety of backgrounds and with a diverse set of experiences.[38] We all know someone like this, who seems to run into people they know everywhere they go. Kevin Bacon is a Connector in film because he's been in so many recognized films of different types, and worked within different networks of actors and directors. It's very good to be a Connector, because, as discussed in chapter 3, when a person has access to a wide array of people with a diversity of knowledge and from many walks of life,[39] they are more likely to find answers and come up with better solutions. People who are Connectors tend to be regarded more positively, and are more likely to be viewed as creative thinkers and good problem-solvers.[40]

The small world network structure has provided a great deal of explanatory power as to how there can be so few links between people, as well as to how ideas and messages get spread through society.[41] With so many communication pathways throughout them, small world networks are extremely effective on a variety of levels, especially when compared to the more rigid hierarchical structures of formal institutions. Through Connectors, we are linked to a lot more people than we realize, providing a consistently *efficient* way of getting information around and distributing ideas.[42] In addition, since even the most reclusive among us communicate with at least a couple of people on a regular basis, the structure is *robust* enough to be inclusive of just about everyone.[43] Finally, the small world network is much better at suffering loss, making it more *persistent* than a hierarchy.[44] In a hierarchy, entire systems are dependent on a single link (i.e., the chair of a department, a project manager, or the political representative of a district).[45] If that person should leave the group, he or she has to be replaced or an entire subgroup will be left out of the loop and unable to function properly (see figure 4.2). In a small world network, however, there is a lot of built-in redundancy. If one person leaves a tightly knit cluster, the members are still all connecting directly with each other, and nothing is lost. Even if a Connector should leave a group, there are typically backup Connectors who can bring messages to them from the larger network. The communication still spreads efficiently, and no one needs to be replaced in order for it to function (see figure 4.3). As seen in the Figures below, despite the fact that just two people or "nodes" were removed from each group (the white dots), the hierarchy suffers a great deal more communicative loss.

Based on what we previously learned about the operation of large online communities in chapter 3, which aligns more closely with many of the more informal gathering principles of social organization, it might seem that online communities would be better conceived of as networks. Although there are some who do argue that they are, essentially, the same thing,[46] I do not agree. As noted, small world networks are found everywhere, both online and off, and at scales both large and small.[47] They encompass everyone globally,

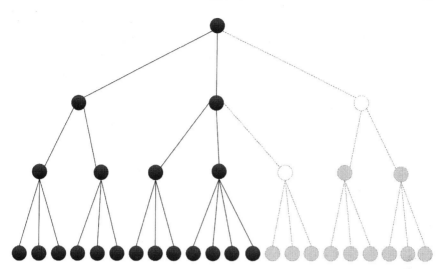

**Figure 4.2 (a) Persistence of small world network versus hierarchy.** *Figure created by author.*

but they also exist in smaller degrees across all of society. The pattern is fractal-like. As when zooming into a map from the planetary view, entering into a cluster that appears tightly knit from a distance will reveal yet more clusters within. To some degree, it depends on how micro or macro that maps are. Seen from the perspective of the entire Internet, for example, an online crafting community might be viewed as a tightly knit cluster. But looking at that community more closely, one would find more frequently communicating

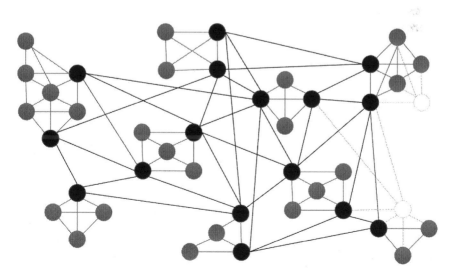

**Figure 4.3 (b) Persistence of small world network versus hierarchy.** *Figure created by*

subgroups within, and even smaller close-knit groups within those. This continues until you get down to the smallest group of just a few communicating individuals. In fact, it has been shown that the tendency of people to aggregate into smaller groups may extend to online conversation patterns as well.[48] So, although a small world network is not the same thing as the large online communities that were discussed in the previous chapter, those communities are made up of, and also found within, small world networks.[49]

In general, the networked and databased design of interactive media readily lends itself to people to organizing themselves in these more organic and informal ways,[50] which are perhaps more in line with our natural social instincts. It is perhaps no coincidence, then, that it was the decade of the 1990s in which *The Six Degrees of Separation* was written, the "Oracle of Bacon" was culturally relevant, and the small world network structure was discovered by Watts and Strogatz. Although social media had not yet come on the scene and would not do so until the early to mid-2000s, something about the type of communication we were beginning to engage in online suddenly got us thinking in new ways about how we are connected to one another. So, although social media did not create social networks, they do help us to perceive them. By both codifying and amplifying the patterns of the small world network, they make them easier to access, more visible, and more public.[51] They also allow us to cultivate our networks by highlighting for us those "latent" links of which we were unaware, encouraging us to activate them through their recommendation features ("you might also like," "who to follow," "you may also know," etc.).[52] Interactive media is increasing the ease with which we can form and maintain our small world networks, and it makes it possible for all of us, if we so choose, to act more like Connectors within them.

## SOCIAL CAPITAL

Whether online or offline, what allows communities and informal networks to function is something called *social capital*, which is the extent to which we perceive and enjoy benefits from existing within them.[53] When someone is a member of the same group or community as us, we tend toward a mode of reciprocity or cooperation with them, even if we don't actually know them. For example, we let strangers go ahead of us in line at the grocery store, offer to jump-start their cars, or lend them a pen if they need one. This is because of something called *the shadow of the future*.[54] We imagine that we might be in that same situation one day, and, depending on the amount of social capital we perceive our shared community to have, we expect that they would have done the same for us. So even though we don't expect a returned favor from that person specifically, there is an expected benefit, a "norm of reciprocity" that permeates the community or group as a whole.[55] These norms of collective support, trust, and cooperation that exist within communities make up the social capital that holds social structures together, which is what allows us to accomplish things as a group.[56] Sociologist Robert Putnam offers a useful breakdown of social capital into two specific types: *bonding capital* and *bridging capital*.[57]

## Bonding Capital

Bonding capital occurs within groups that are more homogenous, or made up of very similar or like-minded people.[58] Members of groups with a lot of bonding capital feel a kinship with one another because they feel understood by people who share the same beliefs, values, ideas, and perspectives. In the small world network pattern, bonding capital is found mostly within the smaller, tightly knit clusters.[59] Bonding capital is important because it builds up group trust and identification, and it is best aligned with the "community" conceptualization of large online groups, in which people gather in an online space, typically oriented around similar interests or passions. Although there is a lot of good to be said about bonding capital, groups that have too much of it can produce an *echo chamber* effect whereby the ideas that are presented are only useful for that group.[60] Although this might not be terrible for a community centered around dog ownership or sports cars, it could lead to problems when the groups' aims are more nefarious.

As discussed previously, groups can more easily form around anything on the Internet, including things that would otherwise meet with social disapproval in the real word, such as unhealthy behaviors,[61] extremist ideologies, or even criminal activity.[62] In such communities, bad ideas are normalized and continually reinforce one another.[63] Communities like these can close themselves off from the rest of the network by ousting those who would act as Connectors for bringing in alternative ideas that challenge the internal status quo.[64] We know when we've stumbled onto a community that is suffering from the problem of the echo chamber when people are viciously attacked for relatively innocuous comments or simply asking questions. Unfortunately, groups like these can still collaborate when they share ideas and knowledge, and they are still empowered by their large numbers when they find each other via interactive media. Despite the fact that they are lacking the diversity outcome of knowledge communities, they can become quite dangerous, to themselves and/or to others.

## Bridging Capital

On the other hand, bridging capital occurs within groups that are more het-erogenous, or made up of diverse individuals.[65] The connections between members are looser and there is not as much trust, but they are able to gain access to alternative perspectives and viewpoints, different from their own.[66] Bridging capital is more inclusive as opposed to exclusive,[67] and the variation in viewpoints, expertise, knowledge, and skills that it brings is the driving force behind collective intelligence.[68] In the small world network pattern, bridging capital can be seen in the looser connections between the tightly knit clusters.[69] Individuals who are Connectors tend to have a lot of bridging capital in their personal social networks because they communi-cate with so many different types of people and groups.[70] Bridging capital is important because it helps people keep an open mind, share perspectives, and gain insights into each other's experiences. This type of social capital is best aligned with the "network" conceptualization of interactive media, and reflected in places where people tend to gather more generally, such as on popular and public social media platforms. For example, there is much diver-sity to be found across all users of Twitter, because their only real reason for "gathering" in this space is the popularity of the platform. This is also why we frequently see references to subgroups such as "black twitter," "academic twitter," or "Catholic twitter" to help users identify the smaller, bonding sub-groups within.

As with bonding capital, groups with an imbalance toward too much bridg-ing capital can also have problems. Because they have mostly loose connec-tions, they lack the trust and kinship that build up in the smaller, tightly knit groups. Such groups are characterized by a tendency toward competition, debate, and conflict,[71] and communicative behaviors like disingenuity, inci-vility, and political posturing are more common. The lack of bonding capital in the broader network of the knowledge culture is also probably in part the impetus behind the endless scrutiny of all positions, and it helps to explain the fighting and debates that are so frequently seen on social media, full of participants seemingly uninterested in finding common ground.

## Conclusion

The most healthy, effective networks have a distributed small world network structure, and strike a good balance between bonding and bridging capital.[72] As we have learned, both types of capital have their merits, but too much of one or the other can produce many of the problems we see on the Internet today. Using interactive media to more intentionally gain both, however, will lead not only to more productive communities and beneficial networks, but also to reaching more people with messages and ideas, which can help to strengthen and improve upon them. In a study of how ideas are related to group structure, Ronald Burt found that the people who had bridging capital as well as bonding capital in their networks came up with the best ideas.[73] He stated that,

> creativity is a diffusion process of repeated discovery in which a good idea is carried across structural holes to be discovered in one cluster of people, rediscovered in another, then rediscovered in still others—and each discovery is no less an experience of creativity for people encountering the good idea. Thus, value accumulates as an idea moves through the social structure; each transmission from one group to another has the potential to add value.[74]

In small world networks with a healthy mix of bonding and bridging, ideas are free to move from one cluster to another, sparking creativity as people make new linkages to other ideas.

The features of interactive media that best support bonding capital are those that offer what Porter calls a *communication capability*, based on conversation and the sharing of visual media, while those that support bridging capital offer a *connection capability*, based on invitations to link together and join new networks.[75] If the goal is to reach people via interactive media, we must use these tools to engage meaningfully not only with those who agree with us but also those who have different viewpoints, ideas, backgrounds, and experiences. Like Kevin Bacon, our oracle of the networked age, we have to be willing and able to work successfully with different types of people for different reasons and in a variety of contexts in order to be recognized, effective, and successful.

## NOTES

1. "The Oracle of Bacon," accessed January 21, 2021, https://www.oracleofbacon.org.

2. Teotonio, "Google Adds Six Degrees."

3. Alexander Wyeth Ruthven, "Kevin Bacon Is the Center of the Universe," *Google Groups,* April 7, 1994, https://groups.google.com/forum/#!topic/rec.arts.movies/-qNue6RwTn8%5B1-25%5D.

4. Alexander Wyeth Ruthven.

5. Internet Movie Database, "Six Degrees of Separation," accessed December 21, 2020, https://www.imdb.com/title/tt0108149/.

6. Fass, *Six Degrees.*

7. Brett Tjaden, "Professor of Computer Science," accessed December 21, 2020, https://users.cs.jmu.edu/tjadenbc/Web/?_ga=2.214424855.1236359426.1590595276 -1153336905.1587317382.

8. Fowler, "Google Introduces 'Bacon Number.'"

9. Internet Movie Database, "Kevin Bacon," accessed December 21, 2020, https:// www.imdb.com/title/tt0108149/.

10. "Kevin Bacon."

11. University of Virginia, "Acknowledgements," Department of Computer Science, Accessed December 21, 2020, https://web.archive.org/web/20000914173848/ http://oracleofbacon.org/ack.html.

12. The Oracle of Bacon, "Acknowledgements," accessed January 21, 2021, https: //oracleofbacon.org/ack.php.

13. Lewis, "Centre of the Movie Universe," 9.

14. Steele, "Bacon Shows the Way."

15. McNeil and McNeil, *The Human Web.*

16. Borgatti et al., "Network Analysis," 892.

17. Freeman, *Social Network Analysis.*

18. Freeman et al., *Research Methods*; Aydin, "Literature Review."

19. Borgatti et al., "Network Analysis"; Couldry and Hepp, *The Mediated Construction*, 60.

20. Eadie and Goret, "Theories and Models," 18–19.

21. Freeman, *Social Network Analysis*, 15.

22. Freeman, 94.

23. Gurevich, "Acquaintanceship Networks."

24. Milgram, "The Small World Problem," 67.

25. Guare, *Six Degrees of Separation.*

26. Bhagat et al., "Three and a Half Degrees."

27. Bakeman and Beck, "The Size of Informal Groups in Public," 381.

28. James, "A Preliminary Study," 477.

29. Lima, *Visual Complexity.*

30. Freeman, *Social Network Analysis.*

31. Shirky, *Here Comes Everybody*, 212.

32. Shirky, 216.

33. Gladwell, *The Tipping Point*, 38.

34. Shirky, *Here Comes Everbody*, 217.

35. Burt, "Social Capital of Opinion Leaders."

36. Erickson, "Some Problem of Inference," 276.

37. Gladwell, *The Tipping Point*, 38.

38. Burt, "Structural Holes," 356.

39. Jenkins, *Convergence Culture*, 54.

40. Burt, "Structural Holes."

41. Shirky, *Here Comes Everybody*, 214.

42. Shirky, 216.

43. Shirky, 216.

44. Shirky, 228.

45. Shirky, 216.

46. Rheingold, *The Virtual Community*, 2nd ed., 359; Bender, *Community and Social Change*, 10–11.

47. Shirky, *Here Comes Everybody*, 218.

48. Dalelio, "Development of a Structural Approach," 93, 122.

49. Rainie and Wellman, *Networked*, 40–41.

50. Watts and Strogatz, "Collective Dynamics," 441; Yang, "Fractals in Small -World Networks," 215.

51. Shirky, *Here Comes Everybody*, 17, 218.

52. Shirky, 220.

53. Coleman, "Social Capital," S101.

54. Axelrod, *The Evolution of Cooperation*, 129.

55. Axelrod, 5.

56. Putnam, *Bowling Alone*, 23.

57. Putnam, 22.

58. Shirky, *Here Comes Everybody*, 222.

59. Shirky, 224.

60. Shirky, 231.

61. Shirky, 206–07.

62. O'Hara and Stevens, "Echo Chambers," 402; Shirky, 210.

63. Benkler et al., *Network Propaganda*, 10.

64. Benkler et al., 10.

65. Shirky, *Here Comes Everybody*, 222.

66. Shirky, 224.

67. Putnam, *Bowling Alone*, 22.

68. Jenkins, *Convergence Culture*, 52.

69. Shirky, *Here Comes Everybody*, 224.

70. Shirky, 228.

71. Gelderblom, "The Limits to Bridging," 1322.

72. Shirky, 215.

73. Burt, "Structural Holes."

74. Burt, 389.

75. Porter, "Virtual Communities and Social Networks," 166.

# Chapter 5

# Amateur Media

## INTRODUCTION: GAME OVER?

The final season of HBO's *Game of Thrones* was an epic disappointment for fans. After the airing of its final episode, there was an outright revolt online, with almost two million people signing a petition to HBO asking them to remake the season,[1] and many threatening to cancel their HBO Now subscriptions.[2] Without getting into any spoilers about the plotline, the general consensus among fans was that, under pressure to wrap up the series according to the predetermined production schedule, the plotting was rushed, the narrative logic lost, and characters were made to behave in ways that were inconsistent with their development.[3] Entertainment journalists and fans who lamented the series' ultimate demise were so upset that they were still complaining about it a year later.[4]

The television series, which lasted eight seasons, was unique in that it was based on an ongoing book series by author George R. R. Martin, which itself (as of this writing) has yet to be completed. Like the *Harry Potter* franchise, which also released a series of films that partially overlapped with J. K. Rowling's writing of the books (though in that case none of the books outpaced their on-screen counterparts), the series has a cult-like following that takes its fandom seriously. It seems that this sense of incompleteness at inception, along with the fact that fans can choose the depth and breadth with which they will engage with the narrative across media, cultivates a kind of empowered participation among fans, characterized by an increased sense of ownership and an expectation of feedback receptivity from series creators. Communities dedicated to *fan fiction* and *fan art* (in which fans produce and share their own creations and extensions of characters and plotlines) abound, and series creators do indeed feed their fandom's frenzy by openly engaging with them about their processes, sharing details about their production prog-ress, and responding to fan feedback.

So, it should have come as no surprise when, three days after the unsatis-factory series' finale aired, Daniel Whidden, a fan and budding screenwriter himself, created a sixteen-and-a-half-minute video essay entitled, "How *Game of Thrones* Should Have Ended" and posted it to his "Think Story" channel on YouTube.[5] With nearly eight million views, Whidden's video has not had quite as many viewers as the actual final episode, which hit a record-setting 19.3 million in ratings;[6] however, it has gotten a better reception. The video currently has approximately 265,000 "likes" and only 18,000 "dislikes." There are over 41,000 mostly positive comments responding to the video, such as "We can always hope George R. R. Martin takes note of the reactions to GoT and writes a more satisfactory ending," "I'd love to see this done like this, I'd even be happy with it being in youtube quality," and "i'm just gonna brainwash myself to think this is actually how it ended."[7] In the process of complimenting Whidden's rewrite, the commenters are also implicitly (sometimes explicitly) critiquing the show runners and writers David Benioff and D. B. Weiss, often referred to as D & D, or more angrily, "Dumb & Dumber," by fans. Since no one is without their detractors in the knowledge culture of the Internet, there is also a smaller subset of comments that are critical of Whidden's rewrite itself, pointing out its own plot holes, and these are typically followed up on with explanations or suggested fixes from others.

The YouTube video presents a narrated commentary splicing together dozens of short clips from the series, interviews with cast and crew, behind-the-scenes footage, and other sources, as well as some stills and visual aids. Most of these are played soundlessly while spoken over by Whidden's explanations and some are visually edited, but others are simply short clips, reproduced exactly from the original, re-cut together. Whidden's video is like many that can be found on YouTube, which comment on products of popular culture while using them within their own productions. In such videos, there is enough editing and transformation of the original content that YouTube's automated copyright checks don't catch them, and, though it would take a court of law to determine this for sure, the video may actually be considered a "fair use," which means it would not require the copyright owners' permis-sion to use these works. While that is left up to a lot of legal technicality (more on this in chapter 10), it probably does not feel "fair" to Benioff and Weiss that their ability to control their own narrative has been undermined by Whidden's reproduction, or that a large chunk of their fan base has praised this version while simultaneously slamming the series that made it possible.

## A THRIVING CULTURE

In graduate school, I took a class called "Media and Culture" with Dr. Jack Bratich. On the first day, he pointed out that these two terms, "media" and "culture," are also used in the field of biology.[8] When a biologist wants to study a bacterial or viral "culture," they place a small amount of it onto what they call growth "media," usually a gelatinous substance like agar, and the culture grows as it spreads through the media. The relationship between media and culture, Dr. Bratich explained, has parallels to our understanding of them in communication, as we can observe how culture, both the good and the bad of it, spreads through media.

The term *culture*, which can be defined as the "distribution of information (ideas, beliefs, concepts, symbols, technical knowledge, etc.) across [a] population,"[9] is also often understood in terms of the works of art, music, and other creative outputs in a society.[10] While the term *media* paints with a relatively broad brush in the popular lexicon today, throughout the twentieth century, it typically referred to one thing: *the* media, meaning the industries of cultural production and their output. This *culture industry*, as scholars have called it,[11] refers to a collection of businesses with particular ways of producing and distributing media, namely through film, radio, print publishing, and television, for the primary purpose of generating revenue. It is represented in the small, pre-1990s box in the media convergence ecosystem represented in chapter 2. Over the last few decades, the use of the term *media* has been vastly expanded to mean anything we use to communicate within this ecosystem, which includes a variety of media production and distribution tools, such as software, devices, applications, websites, channels, networks, outlets, and platforms, as well as any creative output that is shared, by anyone, in some form. When media is produced in today's environment, it is done for a variety of reasons, many of which have nothing to do with making money. Thus, the need for quality media production has diminished, and our cultural output today yields a lot more, frankly, "bad" creations. Paradoxically, that is not necessarily a bad thing.[12] We no longer have to choose between quantity and quality media, because the tools of interactive media allow us to have both.

The Internet is an experimental space, where we can tinker, test, and try things out. As previously noted, users can simply throw things out there, and see what sticks. Because there is less investment in success and fewer potential consequences for failure, our tolerance for "failure" increases.[13] Not only does this give us the opportunity to find those diamonds in the rough, but also those pieces of coal that could be worked into diamonds.[14] According to Henry Jenkins, when we give people who are not professionals, experts, or skilled artists—in other words, *amateurs*—room to create, they "get feedback, and get better," which helps our culture to thrive.[15] In other words, it could be argued, because the "gelatinous substance" of interactive media is so porous, flexible, and accepting, it is well-suited to accomodate faster, freer, and more fruitful cultural growth.

## A HISTORY OF CREATIVITY AND CULTURE

Even though it is modern technology that has made this more participatory environment possible, what we are witnessing with respect to our cultural output today is reminiscent, in some ways, of an earlier cultural era. One lens with which we can view the history of American creative production is the ways in which it has emerged from two sides of a cultural coin: the grass-roots side and the commercial side.[16] The *grassroots culture* comes from the "bottom-up," originating with everyday people—the "roots" of society—and spreads organically through informal social networks.[17] The *commercial culture*, on the other hand, is the "top-down" side, created by people paid to produce it, and is primarily spread through the sales and marketing efforts of a commercial enterprise.[18] Henry Jenkins has outlined a useful history of America from the perspective of creativity and culture, distinguishing three major eras with respect to the relationship between grassroots culture and commercial culture in American history, which I summarize and expand upon below.

### Folk Culture

Jenkins begins in nineteenth-century America, describing the *folk culture* that existed then.[19] At this time, most of culture originated from the grassroots side, as people shared with one another stories, songs, skills, and traditions that were passed down from their ancestors. No one was particularly concerned with who owned or created these works or ideas; they simply shared them as a way of expressing their own cultural identities. The only commercial side of culture that existed was in the form of traveling shows, which emerged as a business model for sharing culture and could appeal to audiences across geographical locations.[20] In this era, the two sides of culture would freely borrow from one another.[21] On the commercial side, the songs, stories, forms, styles, and sometimes even people, were borrowed from the grassroots side as they were produced into stage performances.[22] These performances would then move on to other towns, where new audiences would be inspired by the unfamiliar cultural expressions and incorporate them into their own grassroots expressions.[23] At this time, no one was considered particularly "professional," though sometimes people were paid to perform their cultural acts.[24]

## Mass Culture

During the twentieth century, American cultural output was transformed into an industry.[25] With the introduction of radio, film, and television (all one-way broadcast media largely built on the advertising model), the commercial side took over.[26] Americans became a "mass audience," and the culture industry was born.[27] Major big-budget production companies and labels dominated American culture, gaining influence and power,[28] and even employing the legal system to support their status by getting endless copyright extensions approved by Congress to continue profiting from their productions for as long as possible.[29] Media production became increasingly complex, specialized, professionalized, and expensive.[30] Corporations built up an infrastructure to the point that a mass audience was required in order for this industry to continue to exist, and everything became very standardized, homogenized, and consumer focused.[31]

In this era of *mass culture*, the technical quality of cultural productions went way up, but the grassroots side of culture nearly disappeared.[32] Mostly, the people were turned into passive consumers of culture, "eyeballs" whose role it was to admire and not contribute.[33] Now that there existed a group of people known as the "professionals" of cultural production, regular people were relegated to being "amateurs," those who did not have the budgets or skills to compete.[34] Any grassroots expressions of culture that did exist during this time were limited to local community productions, driven underground, or otherwise out of mainstream awareness.[35] Although subcultures did emerge, they were typically fringe elements, "starving artists" largely marginalized from broader cultural participation.[36] Emerging countercultural movements found within these subcultures, such as the beatniks, hippies, punks, and the hip-hop culture, were each marked by their efforts to challenge the culturally dominant forces of the era.[37] For instance, Andy Warhol's famous "Campbell's soup can" motif raised questions about the idea of art as mass-produced,[38] and punk rockers' in-your-face "do it yourself" (DIY) aesthetic rejected the polished standards of the music industry.[39]

By the late twentieth century, the imbalance between the commercial and grassroots sides of culture had grown to such an extent that most people engaged with the commercial side alone, and any "borrowing" they did was in the form of pop culture fandom. People incorporated industry products into their own expressions of identity through their posters, backpacks, and T-shirts,[40] and by playing party games like the Six Degrees of Kevin Bacon. The audience's main influence over content was relegated to a quantification of their overall consumption in the form of sales and ratings,[41] and the only time the commercial side of culture actively "borrowed" from the grass-roots side was to incorporate any emergent movements that became popular enough to warrant attention.[42] When "incorporated" by the commercial side, however, grassroots movements were sure to be stripped of any underlying critical messages about the dominance of the industry, and relegated to super-ficial forms, styles, and fashion trends[43] (which explains why I had a punk rock Barbie doll as a kid in the 1980s).

## Convergence Culture

With the rise of interactive media, people are again participating in the broader culture in the twenty-first century.[44] As noted, in many ways, the culture that exists today has a lot in common with the folk culture of the nineteenth century.[45] The grassroots side of culture has reemerged in the mainstream, as everyday people are once again producing their own culture as an expression of self, identity, and belonging. As they create and share their creations via interactive media, people are reclaiming cultural ownership with little regard for, or even awareness of, authorship or attribution.[46] Audiences have moved from passive to active, consumers have become producers, and "fandom" has found a voice with which they can speak back to prominent cultural producers.

However, the environment today is also markedly different from folk cul-ture in many ways. The professional media industry still exists, as do mass audiences (though they are more segmented), and the commercial side of culture still dominates in terms of influence and power.[47] That is why Jenkins terms this current age *convergence culture*.[48] Within the media convergence ecosystem, cultural productions from both sides traverse the same media spaces, where they exist alongside each other. In some respects, the media industry benefits from the cultural output of the grassroots side. Fan produc-tions inspired by and incorporating their products can serve as free market-ing,[49] and fan feedback can serve as free market research.[50] But there are also many challenges for the commercial side in this environment.

While the media industry continues to provide high-quality and profes-sionally produced content with technical perfection, the more grassroots participation there is in the culture, the less control the industry has over their own products. Media companies are struggling to maintain their ownership of content, trademarks, and brands in the face of new tools that allow their copyrighted content to be accessed, copied, used, and shared in a variety of unapproved ways.[51] Many grassroots productions also serve as counter-cultural critique, and their direct access to the same audiences means their messages can now be heard without being stripped of their critical edge. In addition, amateur and independent media productions compete with professionally produced ones, and have been known to outperform them, even when they are comparatively "bad."[52] The media industry's continued reliance on consumer models has also become more difficult. Even when simply consuming mass media products, audiences in a convergence culture find ways to be more active and involved, using interactive media to further engage with professionally produced content.[53] Media franchises have found they need to put more effort into marketing, selling, and advertising as they adapt to these active audience behaviors in order to keep them engaged, including needing to work harder to maintain their dominance and credibility in response to public critique and scrutiny online.[54]

## GRASSROOTS CREATIVITY

We now have a cultural system where there is a rebalancing of the grassroots and commercial sides, but it's a balance of tension, not harmony.[55] As the two sides borrow from one another, they are also frequently battling one another.[56] Now that everyday people (i.e., nonprofessionals) are once again participating in the cultural production and output in society, the *grassroots creativity* of the convergence culture has some unique attributes that catch these tensions,[57] three of which are media appropriation, the amateur aesthetic, and convergence apprenticeship.

### Media Appropriation

Much of what is created on the grassroots side of culture remains largely influenced and inspired by the still very dominant commercial side of culture.[58] When creating, it is only natural that grassroots producers would want to incorporate aspects of their shared popular culture into their own work, and, as discussed in chapter 1, the design of interactive media makes it very easy to find, access, copy, and edit commercially produced content. Such "borrowing" from another's media product—form, content, expression, or style—and incorporating it into one's own is called *media appropriation.*[59] When amateur creators borrow the work of professionals, media appropriation can take the form of fan appreciation, fan reporting, parody, narrative deconstruction, or critique, among others. Examples of this abound online. The *Game of Thrones* rewrite on "Think Story," for example, was both a critique and a deconstruction of the official narrative put forth by the show's writers. Another popular YouTube channel, "Honest Trailers," known for its parody trailers of re-cut scenes from movies and TV shows to reveal their tropes, plot devices, marketing tactics, and narrative inconsistencies, refers to their own deconstructions as "the hilarious trailers the producers don't want you to see."[60] In a more positive example, a dedicated *Supernatural* fan with the YouTube username "Wayward Winchester" produces and shares a variety of videos including "season/episode reactions and reviews, top 10 lists, fun parodies, scene breakdowns, ending explained, news, theories, creatively edited juxtapositions," and more,[61] showing an appreciation for the series while also including varying degrees of its appropriated content. Whether critical or celebratory, by creating content of their own that reflects on or re -creates popular industry-produced content, amateurs and fans have found a way to again participate, and have a voice, in their own culture.

From the perspective of copyright law, however, media appropriation is not mere creative expression or cultural participation; it is the unauthorized use of someone else's intellectual property. Legally speaking, all of these videos and other content found online that use clips, soundbites, samples, images, and other elements taken from copyrighted content *should* have first obtained permission from the owners in order to do so; merely giving a credit attribution does not suffice. When it comes to anything that is professionally produced by a media company, however, permission is not guaranteed or even likely, and just the process of asking for it is quite time-consuming.[62] Although I do not know if the examples I've described here have gone to the lengths to obtain the proper permissions to utilize these works, it goes without saying that many such amateur producers have not.

In one particularly elucidating example of media appropriation, a YouTube user named "lim" created a cultural commentary on the seemingly paradoxical instinct of copyright infringement within fandom in her video entitled "Us | Multifandom," which displays a variety of clips from industry-produced products, beautifully transformed and thoughtfully re-combined with digital editing tools to make an artistic statement on the state of copyright in the convergence culture.[63] This meta-analytic production was yet further edited and included in a separate YouTube video posted by anthropologist Michael Wesch titled "An Anthropological Introduction to YouTube," featuring a talk he gave to the Library of Congress in 2008. Wesch points out that "lim" chose to use Regina Spektor's "Us" as her soundtrack, a song that includes the repeated phrase "we're living in a den of thieves, and it's contagious."[64]

The fact that copyright infringement is so frequently committed via interactive media makes copyright rules very difficult to enforce. And the great irony of copyright law today is that, although they do sometimes get caught, on the whole amateur producers actually have more freedom in using others' works than those in the media industry. Professionals working for media companies are at much higher risk of getting sued and destroying their careers if they use the work of their colleagues without going through the proper legal channels. In addition, a professional in the industry creating videos like those described above would not only need to get permission for using others' content, but is also likely to be required to pay royalties or licensing fees in order to be allowed to do so.

## Amateur Aesthetic

While appropriating popular media is common, a lot of grassroots creativity is also quite original and unique. In fact, a kind of *amateur aesthetic* has emerged from the grassroots side, in which new styles, techniques, and genres have developed out of the limitations of producing media in a non professional environment.[65] Amateur productions lack the polish, gloss, and glamour of professionally produced media,[66] as they have limited to no budgets to support their work, and the amateurs producing them have not "earned their stripes" by making their way up the industry ladder, gaining the needed training and know-how as they go.[67] Like punk rock, "doing it yourself" has certain constraints, which in turn create unique sounds, sights, and feels.[68] But unlike the 1970s, today we have so many amateurs in the mediascape that there are countless examples of how amateur and independent producers have influenced the "DIY" aesthetics of both screen and sound.

Although much attention is given to the ways that the grassroots side of culture appropriates from the commercial side, when it comes to the amateur aesthetic, the commercial side has been known to borrow from the grassroots side as well.[69] This is another characteristic that convergence culture shares with early American folk culture, in which the commercial side appropriates the forms, styles, and sometimes even the performers, of grassroots creativity.[70] Although admittedly, when the commercial side takes a cue from this amateur aesthetic, it usually does it better.

One example can be seen in a film movement known as "mumblecore," which emerged around 2010. It was called mumblecore because it was sometimes hard to hear what was being said on screen due to the more realistic, fumbling dialogue and less than technically perfect sound quality.[71] The young filmmakers spearheading this movement shot on digital video and recruited their "nonprofessional" friends and acquaintances to serve as the actors and crew. They had access to cheap cameras and production software, but not big film budgets. As a result, mumblecore films tended to be filled with scenes involving a lot of dialogue and long takes, with subject matter focused on everyday experiences. There is no makeup, spanning cinematography, action sequences, or special effects in these films. The settings are simple, everyday places, and the actors look like everyday people. Despite their amateur nature, the relative success of these films among a niche audience suggested that they had an appeal, perhaps because of their simple relatability, in what Sickels terms a *twenty-first-century sensibility.*[72]

Although mumblecore was a bit of a fad, this mumblecore-inspired sensibility made its way into a variety of Hollywood-produced television shows and films. One example is the HBO series *Girls*, which aired for six seasons between 2012 and 2017.[73] Starring and directed by Lena Dunham, who got her own start on YouTube,[74] the show followed the exploits of four female friends in their twenties trying to make a life for themselves in New York City. Though the show has frequently been compared to *Sex and the City*, which also had six seasons on HBO from 1998–2004,[75] the narrative of *Girls* focuses much more on the struggle and banality, rather than the glitz and the glamour, of New York City living. A *New York Times* article about *Girls* written in 2012 was titled "There's Sex, There's the City, but no Manolos" (Manolos being a reference to the high-end shoes designed by Manolo Blahnik and the focus on designer fashion in *Sex and the City*), and *Girls* has been dubbed "a *Sex and the City* for the 21st century."[76] Like *Sex and the City*, *Girls* provided a self-deprecating and comedic take on womanhood, but like mumblecore, it was much more relatable to the average twenty-something than a cosmopolitan fantasy of the New York high life.[77]

Mumblecore is just one example of an amateur-inspired genre appropriated by the media industry.[78] Other film and TV genres that have been created or significantly advanced by the amateur aesthetic include "found footage" and "shakycam" directorial styles, vlog-inspired "camera confessionals," extreme stunt/prank content,[79] and stop-motion toy animation.[80] In music, amateur production has invented the VIP mix/mashup,[81] as well as strongly influenced the genres of lo-fi,[82] glitchcore,[83] and mumble/Soundcloud rap.[84] Podcasters like Joe Rogan have popularized "extra" long-form audio, with programs lasting upward of three hours.[85] In visual media, we have seen the incorporation of media styles reflecting the aesthetics of "glitch art,"[86] image macros,[87] and animated GIFs.[88] Across the board, "mistake" techniques like overmodulation,[89] pixilation, and digital distortion[90] have also become more widely utilized in professionally produced media. And of course, we all know of stories of actual artists and performers being picked up by media corporations, such as now mega-stars Justin Bieber[91] and Ed Sheeran,[92] who began their careers by self-releasing their songs and performances on interactive media platforms. Some amateur media creators have even made their way into the industry while innovating their own version of *Internet ugly* style, or that which is bad on purpose.[93] Some examples include Perez Hilton, a media personality whose blog became famous for its freehand mouse doodles scrawled on paparazzi photos and saucy commentary;[94] Brad Neely, a television writer and comic book artist who got his start with an intentionally misinformed and "unauthorized" retelling of the *Harry Potter* book series;[95] and Colleen Ballinger, whose entire career (including a Netflix series) is based on her character Miranda Sings, a parody of arrogant and talentless YouTubers.[96]

This influence of grassroots creativity demonstrates that, even as the industry still dominates in the convergence culture, there is more of an exchange between both sides than is typically acknowledged or seen.

## Convergence Apprenticeship

Although amateur media producers often have little to no formal training or industry experience, in a way they do undergo a *convergence apprenticeship* through the communities and media products they are able to engage with through interactive media.[97] Traditional apprentices are mentored by a working professional in order to practice and learn a trade under their guidance. Similarly, there are a variety of online "mentorship" communities, often fan communities, that are specifically dedicated to advancing the work of amateur creators of different varieties, inviting them to share their works, get and receive feedback, exchange production tips and technical advice, and work together to improve and collaborate on productions.[98] In addition to mentorship, traditional apprentices benefit from learning under established artisans because they are free to learn the trade without also having the pressure to innovate their own projects.[99] Working with media industry products can provide this kind of support for amateurs, giving them inspiration and a starting point for their own creativity, so they are able to practice their craft without having to come up with completely original ideas.[100] This idea is captured in the documentary *We Are Wizards* about Harry Potter fandom, when Bradley Mehlenbacher of the "wizard rock" band Draco and the Malfoys explains,

> I've tried to write songs ever since I've been able to play guitar and I could never do it. And I think it was because I could never . . . be confident enough that I actually had something to say about the world that people would care about. And then, when I started writing songs from a fictional character's perspective, it just . . . shattered that, and it just came flooding out. And I think that freed a lot of people up, too.[101]

Finally, traditional apprentices gain access to their mentors' network of customers and collaborators as they learn, which can help to propel their own careers. Albeit unauthorized, utilizing the products of popular culture similarly serves amateur creators in this way, as they tap in to an already existing fan base that is predisposed to appreciate it, which can also help bring attention to and spread their own creations. For someone just starting out, all of these factors combined mimic the benefits of a more conventional career path, as someone moves from novice to expert. For example, *Game of Thrones* rewriter Daniel Whidden, while not exactly an amateur, has posted a lot more videos on his own "Think Story" channel (all focused on various products of pop culture) than he has professional credits to his name. As he advances in his career looking for industry gigs, he is in the meantime getting tons of experience, exposure, and feedback through this independent, unpaid, and unsolicited corpus of work. So, if we can bracket for a moment the legalities of and conflicts between the systems of convergence culture, we can see that maybe these amateur producers are "earning their stripes" after all, just not in ways we have traditionally thought of.

## CONCLUSION

Certainly, interactive media has given a lot of creators a level of access to the cultural sphere that they would not have otherwise had, and can help their creativity to thrive, even when their creations are relatively "bad." But is our culture thriving in this age of convergence, rife with tension as it is? Right now, we are still in the midst of figuring out how all of this should work. Both amateurs and professionals work hard on the media they produce, and both deserve both credit and appreciation for their efforts. However, we have not yet found the best path forward. The battles, legalities, and operations of exchange surrounding cultural contribution and participation have yet to be resolved. We will further explore these concerns and the resulting confrontations with the media industry in chapter 10, and in chapter 11 begin to look at some promising new models that may provide a way through to a culture that is truly thriving. But whether we will accept and adopt those models remains to be seen. There are evolutionary shifts that would need to occur in how we think about and understand creativity and culture, and much of that would need to be worked out, institutionally, before we can again strike a harmonious balance between the grassroots and commercial sides of culture. For now, media producers of all stripes—fans, amateurs, independents, and industry professionals alike—will have to just keep carving out their own paths through the ecosystem, experimenting, innovating where they need to, capitalizing on what they can, and seeing what "sticks."

## NOTES

1. Dylan D, "Remake Game of Thrones Season 8 With Competent Writers," Change.org, accessed December 21, 2020, https://www.change.org/p/hbo-remake -game-of-thrones-season-8-with-competent-writers?recruiter=963393975&recruited _by_id=eee46090-7ba7-11e9-ba90-436ed594c4d9.

2. Lam, "Decrease in HBO Subscribers."

3. Hough, "The End They Want."

4. Britt, "Game of Thrones Ending"; Hayes, "Even Worse"; Ostergren, "One Year Later."

5. Think Story, "How Game of Thrones Should Have Ended," May 22, 2019, Video, 16:33, https://youtu.be/G0mncEl4nVU.

6. Pallotta, "New Viewership Record."

7. Think Story, "How Game of Thrones Should Have Ended," May 22, 2019, Video, 16:33, https://youtu.be/G0mncEl4nVU.

8. Personal communication.

9. Carly, "Theory of Group Stability," 333.

10. Mironenko and Sorokin, "Seeking for the Definition."

11. Kellner and Durham, "Adventures in Media," *xvii*.

12. Shirky, *Here Comes Everybody*, 232; Jenkins, *Convergence Culture*, 140.

13. Shirky, *232*.

14. Jenkins, *Convergence Culture,* 140.

15. Jenkins, 140.

16. Jenkins, 139.

17. Jenkins, 139–40, 175.

18. Jenkins, 139, 175.

19. Jenkins, 139.

20. Lewis, *From Traveling Show*, 1.

21. Jenkins, *Convergence Culture,* 139.

22. Jenkins, 139.

23. Ashby, *With Amusement for All*, 123; Quintero Rivera, "Migration, Ethnicity, and Interactions," 85.

24. Jenkins, *Convergence Culture,* 139.

25. Jenkins, 139.

26. Benkler, *The Wealth of Networks*, 29.

27. Horkheimer and Adorno, "The Culture Industry."

28. Jenkins, *Convergence Culture*, 39.

29. Lessig, *Free Culture*, 134.

30. Jenkins, *Convergence Culture*, 139.

31. Benkler, *The Wealth of Networks*, 30; de Sola Pool, *Technologies without Boundaries*, 15.

32. Jenkins, *Convergence Culture*, 139–40.

33. Jenkins, 66.

34. de Sola Pool, *Technologies without Boundaries*, 83.

35. Jenkins, *Convergence Culture*, 139.

36. Piell Wexler, *Who Paid for Modernism*, 1–2.

37. Kellner and Durham, "Adventures in Media," *xxiv–xxv*.

38. Weekes, "Warhol's Pop Politics."

39. Brown, "Is 'Mumble Rap' the New Punk?"

40. Jenkins, *Convergence Culture*, 142.

41. Jenkins, 66.

42. Hebdige, "Subculture," 155; Jenkins, *Convergence Culture*, 148.

43. Hebdige, 155.

44. Jenkins, *Convergence Culture*, 140.

45. Jenkins, 141.

46. Jenkins, 141.

47. Jenkins, 141–42.

48. Jenkins, 136–37.

49. De Kosnick, "Fandom as Free Labor," 99.

50. Rowley et al., "Customer Community and Co-Creation."

51. Jenkins, *Convergence Culture*, 138, 159.

52. Jemielniak and Przegalinska, *Collaborative Society*, 68–69.

53. Jenkins, 136–38.

54. Jenkins, 138.

55. Jemielniak and Przegalinska, *Collaborative Society*, 64; Jenkins, 175.

56. Jenkins, 142.

57. Jenkins, 132.

58. Jenkins, 141.

59. Jenkins, 167.

60. Screen Junkies, "Honest Trailers—Tuesdays at 10am PST," Video Playlist, accessed December 21, 2020, https://www.youtube.com/playlist?list=PL86F4D497FD3CACCE.

61. Wayward Winchester, "Description," YouTube Channel, March 23, 2016, https://www.youtube.com/channel/UCuuz2D3nqAv6bOBrdStn7Uw/about.

62. Corzine, "Permission to Use."

63. lim, "Us | Multifandom," June 2, 2007, Video, 3:55, https://youtu.be/_yxHKgQyGx0.

64. Michael Wesch, "An Anthropological Introduction to YouTube," July 26, 2008, Video, 55:33, https://youtu.be/TPAO-lZ4_hU.

65. Galloway, *Protocol*, 219; Jenkins, *Convergence Culture*, 136, 153.

66. de Sola Pool, *Technologies without Boundaries*, 83.

67. Jemielniak and Przegalinska, *Collaborative Society*, 61.

68. Galloway, *Protocol*, 219.

69. Jenkins, 136.

70. Jenkins, 139.

71. Sickles, "The Future, Mr. Gittes."

72. Sickles.

73. Yoshida, "Shows About Nothing."

74. Short Takes, "YouTube Beginnings."

75. HBO, "Sex and the City," accessed January 16, 2021, https://www.hbo.com/sex-and-the-city.

76. Lawson et al., "Arts Preview 2014."

77. Pelling, "Why Do Today's Feminists."

78. Jenkins, *Convergence Culture*, 153.

79. Groening, "Aesthetics of Online Videos."

80. Brownlee, "Stop-Motion on YouTube"; Jenkins, "Quentin Tarantino's *Star Wars*," 218–19.

81. THEEDMIST, "The EDM Dictionary: VIP Mix (n.)," The EDMist, March 18, 2016, https://theedmist.co/2016/03/18/the-edm-dictionary-vip-mix-n/.

82. Greenfield, "The Lo-Fi Aesthetic"; Harper, "Lo-Fi Aesthetics."

83. Williams, "Hyperactive Subgenre Glitchcore."

84. Brown, "Is 'Mumble Rap' the New Punk?"

85. Greenwald, "Growth of Podcasts"; *BBC*, "Joe Rogan's Exclusive."

86. Jackson, "The Glitch Aesthetic"; Pomerleau, "Glitch Art Design."

87. Jemielniak and Przegalinska, *Collaborative Society*, 74.

88. Dynel, "'I Has Seen.'"

89. Harper, "Lo-Fi Aesthetics," 20.

90. Jackson, "The Glitch Aesthetic."

91. Mitchell, "Usher Introduces Teen Singer."

92. CBS News, "Ed Sheeran: Reinventing Pop."

93. Douglas, "The Internet Ugly Aesthetic."

94. Gray, "Pop Goes Perez."

95. Dry, "Brad Neely's Adult Swim."

96. Seabaugh, "The Woman Behind Miranda."

97. Jenkins, *Convergence Culture*, 190.

98. Jenkins, 145; Jensen Schau et al., "How Brand Community Practices," 37; Shirky, *Here Comes Everybody*, 99–100; Zittrain, *The Future of the Internet*, 135.

99. Jenkins, 191.

100. Jenkins, 190–91.

101. *We Are Wizards*, directed by Josh Koury, 2008; Argot Pictures, 1:17:37.

# Chapter 6

# Citizen News

## INTRODUCTION: HOST IN THE MACHINE

Cenk Uygur (pronounced "Jenk You-grrr"[1]) is the creator and host of *The Young Turks* (TYT), a popular progressive news program that livestreams daily on YouTube.[2] Although TYT claims "an audience of over 80 million unique viewers"[3] and today operates and looks a lot like a traditional news outlet, it has a noticeably different flavor from that of *legacy media,* or those whose forms predate the Internet. First, TYT embraces audience participation, turning to their "TYT army" (as their followers are called) for story ideas, tips, corrections, fund-raising, and even employees.[4] Uygur and his cohosts also hold a certain irreverence toward the establishment, criticizing politicians on both sides of the political aisle and holding their feet to the fire, even when they come on to be interviewed.[5] Uygur, known for his straight -talking mix of anger and humor,[6] is also very critical of the "mainstream media," especially cable TV news outlets. Yet, many who are familiar with him may know that he also once had a brief stint on MSNBC back in 2011. This short-lived embrace between the so-called mainstream media and the more independent, citizen-oriented, "alternative" variety did not exactly end well. But before we get to that, a bit of background.

In the year 2000, Uygur (who is of Turkish descent and was, actually, young at the time) wrote on his blog that his dream was to be on television. He had a problem, however. Uygur explained:

> Nobody is going to put a young kid who doesn't have any experience, on TV. . . . What are you going to do against such resistance? I'll tell you what I did. . . . I figured, if they don't want to put me on TV, then I'll put myself on TV. . . . That's what The Young Turk is . . . an independently produced television

show from a young guy who wanted to tell everybody what he thought. It is a talk show that specializes in raw honesty.[7]

In the pre–social media, pre-YouTube era, the only way for Uygur to independently share his talk show with others was to air it on local public access television. Within two years he gained, according to him, "3,500 loyal viewers . . . in a town with only 59,000 cable subscribers."[8] After that, he created his blog, launched his show on Sirius Satellite Radio, and then expanded onto the YouTube platform once it became available in 2005.[9] By February 2010, the TYT YouTube channel had over 200 million views, and Cenk had a staff of nine people working for him.[10] In a 2010 video summarizing the history of TYT up until that point, Cenk said "We're the next generation of talk shows. . . . And you know what, old media? We're coming for you."[11] Around this same time, the TYT army began a campaign to get Uygur on MSNBC by pummeling them with letters and emails, and the network began bringing him on to fill in for Dylan Ratigan on a semi-regular basis.[12] Noting that he brought a new audience, the producers eventually granted him a nightly hosting gig for the show *MSNBC Live* in the 6 p.m. slot, which began in January 2011.[13] By July, he was out.[14]

So, what happened? After leaving MSNBC, Uygur took to his own TYT channel on YouTube to tell the story. He explained that, despite the fact that he had good ratings, he was repeatedly instructed to appeal not only to the viewers, but also to "management," and vaguely referenced "people in Washington," who were concerned about his aggressive, somewhat wild, and indiscriminately critical approach.[15] He said that "the head of MSNBC" (Phil Griffin), gave him a talking-to, in which he told Uygur, "we're insiders; we are the establishment."[16] After that, a defiant Cenk decided to ramp up the adversarial nature of his style and tone, and his shows became increasingly unscripted.[17] Though his ratings went up, the network soon brought him in to tell him that he was not going to work out for the 6 p.m. slot, and offered him more money for a reduced role as an MSNBC contributor.[18] As he was giving his audience all of these details and more, Uygur reflected, "it's the perks . . . that's how they suck you in." But he explained that he "didn't want to work at a place that . . . didn't want to challenge power." He ultimately declined the network's offer, explaining to his TYT audience that "the deciding factor for me was that I had to tell you this story." He concluded with this message for the establishment, "more than ever, I'm coming." Since then, Cenk has only grown his empire, and his time "inside the machine," as he's called it, has given him a kind of reverse "street cred," a reference point of firsthand knowledge that serves as a window into the powerful political influences dominating the establishment, "mainstream" media.[19]

## MASS AMATEURIZATION

Because the tools of interactive media have become so mobile, cheap, and easy to use, "publishing" is practically our default mode of communication today.[20] Every day, people of the world cover what is going on by not only capturing, recording, and streaming, but also by editing, commenting on, and speaking out publicly about real-life events and issues. When they do so, such *digital citizens*, or those who use "digital media as civic tools,"[21] often engage in what some refer to as "citizen journalism," though in many cases, it is a stretch to call this mode of news "journalism."[22] Clay Shirky perhaps more accurately calls it "the *mass amateurization* of publishing."[23] Although there is plenty of variation in what, specifically, it looks like when non-professionals participate in news production, there is a certain style that tends to characterize such coverage, which is very distinct from the traditional standards of journalism. These unique features of "citizen news" are detailed in the sections below.

### Personal

It was certainly an anomaly when we watched the TV news reporters fighting back tears as they reported live from downtown Manhattan on September 11, 2001. The fact that they, the consummate professionals, were struggling to maintain their composure was a signifier that what we were witness to was an immeasurable tragedy, and we felt a rare sense of kinship with them. When ordinary people report on the news, however, such "extraordinary" displays are the norm rather than the exception. They cry, they shout, they scream, they curse, they cheer. They get knocked over or start to run, and the scene itself loses composure.[24] In the May 2020 video of George Floyd's murder, for example, as we hear the citizens from behind the camera pleading, "Get off of him!" and "Check his pulse!"[25] we share in their sense of helplessness, outrage, and fear. This is a much more powerful experience than watching a detached news reporter standing on the street corner speaking into a micro-phone as they recount "what happened here."

As a whole, everyday citizens who produce news *are* the communities they are covering, so their reports are much more *personal*.[26] Whether willingly or not, they are frequently "on the ground," in the streets, neighborhoods, malls, schools, parks, or other everyday settings, amidst events as they occur.[27] Even in commentary-based reporting, citizens often record, vlog-style, from more intimate spaces like their home or their car. Unlike professional journalists, everyday people do not feel a need to be objective. They tend to express themselves the way they would in everyday conversation, offering their own subjective opinions and showing bias, sometimes advocating for a cause or encouraging activism. They are more likely to be openly passionate about the issues and events of which they speak or write, and they express their passions through emotions such as anger, fear, sadness, and panic, whether in the moment or upon reflection later on.[28]

It is not only negative emotions that are found in citizen news, however; laughter plays a big role, too. The knowledge culture of the Internet has a characteristically sarcastic and irreverent undercurrent, and a lot of this mass amateurization involves the use of satire or parody to make political points or highlight the absurdities of political systems. Many online news shows, like *The Young Turks* or that of another popular daily YouTube commentator Philip DeFranco, incorporate humor into their news-reporting style as they present their honest and frank analyses of what they see. Some of these works also involve media appropriation, as they borrow from pop culture iconography as an entry point for political critique.[29] Consider, for example, all of the *image macros*, more commonly referred to as memes, that circulate making political points today. They frequently incorporate characters, scenes, and phrases taken from television, music, and film. They might even use the official brand, logo, or slogan of a political campaign as a critique against the candidate whose campaign they were "borrowed" from. The early 2000s advocacy group "True Majority" called this use of pop culture and entertainment while engaging in civic issues *serious fun*.[30]

The ability to deconstruct appropriated media has proven particularly useful for breaking down political rhetoric.[31] Re-cuts of debates, speeches, media clips, or interviews can be used to reveal the messaging strategies of politicians and other public figures.[32] One notable example from the 2012 US presidential election is a video called "The Patriot Game," which creatively broke down the rhetorical strategies of the two nominees for president at the time, Barack Obama and Mitt Romney.[33] The piece, which was created by "The Gregory Brothers" (who first became known for their autotuned remixes of media clips, most famously "Double Rainbow" and "Bed Intruder"[34]), presents a song that re-cuts the two primary nominee acceptance speeches alongside one another, in an epic 1980's video game style battle. What the clip actually reveals, however, is how similar the speeches from the two opposing sides were, even at times overlaying their use of same exact phrases onto one another. Both candidates, for example, stressed having a "choice" for the future, encouraged the "risk-takers" and "dreamers" (both invoking Steve Jobs), focused on overcoming divisiveness and moving forward "together," and cited American exceptionalism in their plans for growth.[35] Even their wives' speeches were compared, in which each emphasized their husbands' humble beginnings, recollecting their early days in small apartments without proper furniture.[36] Because of the similarities, the two candidates' "scores" in the "Patriot Game" were very close, but Romney ultimately won because of extra "Spaceman" points earned for mentioning Neil Armstrong.[37]

Whether funny and entertaining or passionate and opinionated, the more personal side of mass amateurized news has the effect of "bringing the realm of political discourse closer to the everyday experience" of citizens.[38] The "in your face" quality of citizen news is more emotional and relatable, getting the audience more involved. As people engage with these more personal forms of news in spaces both political and non-political, they gain a better sense of their own place and role in the media ecosystem as well.[39] Interactive media offers an invitation to participate in the news environment as we consume these more personal forms of reporting and commentary, even if we never actually take up the offer.[40]

## Record-less

In the professional news environment, journalists adhere to a set of standards in which they will not share information that is identified or agreed-upon as "off the record."[41] They of course do, however, still possess knowledge of this off-the-record information and often share it privately amongst themselves in the process of putting together stories and reports.[42] In a way, this does make them "insiders," and if MSNBC CEO Phil Griffin did say that to Cenk Uygur as alleged, we can't really blame him for stating a fact. But "outsiders" have no such standards; they are not required to,[43] which is why Cenk Uygur had no problem revealing these statements of Griffin's to his audience of millions, despite the fact they were made within a private conversation between the two.

When everyone, everywhere, has the ability to publish, more things go public.[44] The reality is that one can never really be certain that they are in an "off the record" situation anymore.[45] Aspects of closed-door meetings, private briefings, confidential memos, exclusive clubs, invitation-only events, Zoom sessions, and more can be shared with the world if someone not beholden to accepted standards of journalism captures or records something that the public finds worthy of attention.[46] Photos and emails get leaked, off-color comments get shared, hidden relationships get revealed, and dirty secrets get exposed. It is the "age of the whistleblower,"[47] due, in part, to "outsider" organizations like Wikileaks, who release classified documents,[48] and Project Veritas, known for their hidden-camera sting operations aimed at their political enemies.[49] There is even a subgenre of citizen news that has emerged as a form of YouTube "gotcha" journalism, where a public figure is shadowed and sometimes directly confronted, in the hopes of catching them saying or doing something that would reveal something negative about their motives or character.[50] This *record-less* characteristic of citizen news can be both good and bad—good when shining a light on information that the public has a right to know, revealing issues that might otherwise have been ignored, and speaking back to power; bad when information released could bring real harm to individuals or is taken out of context to the point of inaccuracy.

So, who decides where that line is drawn? Whether or not that decision is best left up to professional journalists (as it has mostly been in the past), today there is really no one in charge of setting the boundaries, which is in keeping with the "leaderless" sensibility of networked interactive media. In addition, once something is published via interactive media, we cannot "strike it" from the record. A Pandora's box has been opened that cannot be undone or retracted. It gets replicated and spreads throughout the networks of the media convergence ecosystem, nearly instantaneously. Thus, when Department of Defense spokesman Geoff Morrell demanded in 2010 "that Wikileaks return immediately to the US government all versions of documents obtained directly or indirectly from the Department of Defense databases or records,"[51] it was absurd to think that this was even possible. And while that may be seen as a victory for freedom and truth in the uncontrollable information environment, when Facebook and other platforms struggled to remove millions of videos showing the livestreamed Christchurch shooting in New Zealand in 2019, it revealed the darker side of having no one in charge.[52] The freedom to use interactive media to bypass information control efforts now extends to all digital citizens, for better or worse.

## Networked

While professional journalism is produced within media companies that have a more traditionally hierarchical structure, citizen news occurs within the horizontal, informal communities of the interactive media environment. The *networked* nature of mass amateurization brings in both a grassroots "expertise" that emerges as large groups of people work together to track down information,[53] and a small world network level of efficiency and persistance that makes it more difficult to censor.[54] Thus, citizens get more involved in the process of the news and become less like an "audience" and more like an "army," as noted with *The Young Turks*.

These "armies" of citizens can provide input and feedback on stories, use their collective power to help sift through documents and data, and even engage in a kind of community investigative journalism that seeks to uncover truth.[55] Of course, like the Reddit community that misidentified the Boston Marathon bomber from pictures of the crowd,[56] communities of citizens can be, and often are, wrong. They are collaboratively constructing narratives from bits of available information,[57] and the smallest of details can be uncovered and then amplified to support a working theory, drawing connections that may or may not really be there. This explains a lot of the conspiracy theorizing that tends to occur within mass amateurization as well.[58] Yet it is this same freewheeling environment that has also served to uncover actual conspiracies, such as when the Pentagon's cover-up of key information about civilian casualties in Afghanistan and Iraq was revealed through a whistleblower served by Julian Assange's Wikileaks,[59] when the hashtag #MeToo revealed the undercurrent of rape culture that permeated Hollywood for decades and finally came to bear on predators like Harvey Weinstein, or when a friend of the rich and famous Jeffrey Epstein was arrested for sex trafficking minors in part due to the legal filings of blogger, lawyer, and so-called far right conspiracy theorist Mike Cernovich.[60] In a democratic society that sometimes struggles with transparency, the collective elements of the citizen news environment can serve to both free up, and make up, information, and, as stories are emerging, it can be hard to tell which is which.

## Anti-Professional

The institutional nature of professional journalism can lead to a kind of "professional bias" as outlets determine how they will direct their efforts and what they will cover.[61] For instance, when big news and breaking news override small news and old news,[62] when issues get simplified down to two "sides,"[63] or when the most outrageous political candidate gets the most attention,[64] professional journalists are working within the limitations of their own formats and outlets. This fact can be frustrating for the journalists themselves, as seen in the (leaked) video of ABC News anchor Amy Robach during a break angrily asserting that she had the Epstein story three years before it broke and her network "would not put it on the air" because they assumed there was a lack of public interest and feared blowback from whom it would implicate.[65]

Citizen news, on the other hand, is decidedly unprofessional. It tends to have features of the amateur aesthetic discussed in the last chapter, but there is also an *amateur process* that applies to citizen newsgathering. As discussed, everyday citizens who take it upon themselves to act "journalistic" do not adhere to the same standards and practices of professional journalism,[66] but they are also free from the constraints of a large news organization, corporate pressures, or an editorial review.[67] They don't have insider access[68] or "news leader" status in the first place, so they don't worry about losing it. In other words, citizens operate outside of the "template of news."[69] As a result, they gather and freely share information from varied and sometimes conflicting sources in their personal social and information networks, focus more on publishing what they find than evaluating it, and report it speculatively and without concern for the threats that it might pose to individuals or to the status quo.[70]

More than unprofessional, some independent and citizen news outlets might even be considered *anti-professional* in their approach to journalism, wearing their outsider status as a badge of honor. Many purposefully refer to themselves as "alternative" media in order to place themselves in opposition to corporate media, not financially beholden to anyone or interested in insider access.[71] Influential blogger Matt Drudge, for example, described himself as "free from any corporate concerns."[72] Newsbud boasts, "We do not receive a single penny from corporate advertisers, foundations, NGOs or partisan-affiliated entities."[73] Cenk Uygur has said that his show doesn't "play ball" with the political establishment, who "is used to manipulating the press and getting away with it" because, unlike the mainstream media, they have no interest in getting "access to their weaselly politicians."[74] These alternative outlets sometimes even eschew the term "journalism" entirely when describing themselves, instead using terms like "community,"[75] "everyday citizens,"[76] "misfits,"[77] or "something like a journalist" but more.[78] Such outlets represent themselves as being driven more by a set of values than ratings or views and willing to cover the things that the professionals won't talk about,[79] often in ways that are more openly partisan[80] (yet distrustful of political parties and other "establishment" institutions[81]) or even activist in nature.[82]

## FAKE NEWS

In the less professional nature of the citizen news environment, the problem of *fake news*, or "news" that misrepresents facts or even includes outright falsehoods in order to garner clicks or support an agenda, has been exacerbated.[83] In the open and unchecked environment of the media convergence ecosystem, plenty of examples of the purposeful and coordinated spread of *disinformation*, as well as the unintentional sharing of *misinformation*, abound.[84] In fact, in a small amount of cases, the "people" sharing news may not be real people at all, but misleading and fake proxy accounts (hundreds of which could be run by one person),[85] or sometimes even automated *bots* (programmed algorithms liking, sharing, and commenting on stories to help spread them around).[86] But the term "fake news" has also been applied to describe that which is manipulative or serves as propaganda for a particular political agenda. This muddies the usage of the term, as all news reports, from the grittiest of "on-the-ground" citizen accounts to the most polished of professionally produced segments, are social constructions, created by people with their own opinions and points of view.[87] A subjective and biased perspective, even when unintended, lies at the heart of any story told. In addition, as everything digital can be deconstructed into bits, all content is subject to altering and manipulation. Quotes can be taken out of context, actions misrepresented, scenes cropped, and details left out, in confirmation of a storyteller's aims and/or worldview. While the problem of fake news is nothing particularly new,[88] in the "question everything" knowledge culture, the accusation of "fake news" is thrown at anyone and everyone, and even fact-checking efforts are sucked into the vortex of distortion and distrust.[89]

So, what is a citizen to do with news in an environment like this? Although the old adage, "don't believe everything you read" might seem to apply, our relationship with media, especially interactive media, is more complex than that. It is more akin to, "you are what you eat."[90] Just as a diet of only donuts or apples would not serve our body well in the long run, it is also advised that digital citizens ensure that there is a good deal of variety in their news diet in order to avoid falling into the traps of disinformation and ideological echo chambers.[91] Both professional and citizen news have their advantages, but each presents a perspective that is limited and can be informed by the other.[92] It can be advantageous for individuals to have exposure to many different types and sources of media—professional, independent, activist, alternative, international, local, and investigative, as well as engaging with editorial perspectives from across the political spectrum. Despite the typically adversarial nature of these different sources, together they can actually coalesce to provide a more nuanced, developed, and well-rounded perspective. Something can be learned from all of them, and they can be compared in order to enhance one's understanding of issues and events. While this may sound a bit overwhelming, the databased design principle of interactive media actually makes it relatively easy to curate and follow a variety of perspectives in the feeds of social media and news aggregator sites.[93] However, people need to learn to consciously cultivate a sense of appreciation for dialogue, at least in their own consumption habits of news, even if the media outlets don't engage in it themselves.

At the same time, it is important to be aware of the manipulation and disinformation tactics that can exploit media systems, neither accepting claims at face value nor dismissing them out of hand. We can apply the underlying principles outlined in chapter 1 to critically read each form of media according to their particular weaknesses for spreading falsehoods, even as they evolve. For instance, on social media, engaging with news stories beyond their headlines and evaluating and weighing the perspectives presented against others both supportive and critical can help to mitigate false claims and generate more nuanced understandings. When reading news articles, we can also attend more to the primary sources that are cited (such as public data, court records, and peer-reviewed research) than to the ways in which they are interpreted. We can likewise seek out the raw, unedited versions of visual or audio content, especially that which is shared in real or near–real time, in order to gain more angles and details informing our understanding of something that took place. In fact, if an individual or outlet never or rarely links to such primary or unedited sources in their reporting, that is a good indicator they are more focused on manipulation than facts. Additional indicators of the credibility and authenticity of sources can be found by looking into the backgrounds of those producing them. Whether professional, independent, or everyday citizen, looking through their media archives, posting history, and networks, not for the purposes of "calling them out," but for our own personal evaluative purposes, can offer insight into their ethics, motives, goals, and biases. Finally, when we ourselves share media with others, we can include qualifiers to let people know if we have identified the source as problematic in terms of bias or credibility, or have not yet fully assessed the story or audiovisual representation in these ways.


## THE PUBLIC SPHERE

As more digital citizens engage in and activate around "news" via interactive media, it has also created a resurgence of participation in the *public sphere*, an aspect of society in which private citizens come together in public spaces to debate and discuss the important issues of the day, with the intent of influencing the direction of the society's governance.[94] In the early days of America, citizens would discuss politics and civic issues in public spaces like "a public square, on the courthouse steps—or in the pages of a newspaper or pamphlet."[95] The role of pamphlets and newspapers, the "media" of the day, was to reflect and circulate the perspectives represented in these public spaces so that others could learn about them.[96] As newspapers became more widely available throughout the nineteenth century, "the press" initially served to expand the public sphere "beyond the bounds of the bourgeoisie," bringing working-class and populist perspectives into the public arena.[97]

When "mass" media emerged in America, however, the press took over the public sphere nearly entirely.[98] Paralleling the processes by which amateurs were removed from participating in creative and cultural production over the course of the twentieth century (discussed in chapter 5), civic and political activity was increasingly professionalized, specialized, and commercialized into the domains of journalism and public relations.[99] Citizens' main role in the public sphere was thus largely reduced to that of its consumer audience,[100] and by the time news media had moved to television, politics had become a mere spectacle, "a game only for the players, not even for the fans."[101] As mass media became more dominant throughout the twentieth century, they also became more entrenched with the structures of power in society (i.e., the wealthy, the two major political parties, the corporations, and the government), and the viewpoints they portrayed again began to more closely reflect the perspectives of the powerful.[102] Although any given individual journalist would likely still have seen themselves as adhering to the principle value of serving the interests of the people in their own work,[103] over time, "the press," broadly conceived, moved from informing the public about debates that were happening among the citizenry, to constructing those debates themselves.[104]

Meanwhile, if citizens wanted to reach the public with their own information or perspectives, they had to either find a way to access and be chosen by a media gatekeeper (in which their story would be subject to the whims of said gatekeeper's framing),[105] or, like the counterculture movements described in the last chapter, run their own smaller, community, and underground outlets (often for the purpose of resisting this corporate domination).[106] As this version of the public sphere driven by one-way broadcast and print media effectively censored citizens' participation in it,[107] most eventually lost interest in even trying.[108] By the 1990s, the average American citizen felt so removed from and disgusted with the political process that voter turnout reached an all-time low.[109] Seen through the lens of the public sphere, then, we might more accurately conceive of citizens in the twentieth century as "the audience formerly known as 'the people'" rather than accept the more popular conceptualization that citizens in the twenty-first century are "the people formerly known as the audience."

## The Digital Public Sphere

With the rise of interactive media in the twenty-first century, citizens once again began participating in what might be called a *digital public sphere*, which is actually larger, more directly accessible, and more global than anything that existed in the early days of America. The long-suppressed desire of people to engage civically and have their stories told publicly was unleashed through the Internet, and the earliest adopters of interactive media for political purposes were those who had a higher tendency to be distrustful of mass media.[110] Citizens from all over the world now use these spaces to propose topics and identify the issues of importance, as well as represent their own perspectives, directly, in discussions and debates, in ways that are more naturally integrated with their everyday social and non-political lives.[111] Digital citizens can bring attention to significant happenings and events and, depending on their closeness to a situation, they can even clarify misunderstandings or provide information or knowledge that sheds new light.[112] Through this online discourse, people have begun to highlight other ways of seeing the issues outside of the way the media frames them.[113] They have also begun picking up on, pointing out, and critiquing news media strategies, which then serve as further points of discussion.[114]

In addition, the networked interactive media platforms through which people gather to have these conversations are not merely a representation of the public places where people gather to deliberate and debate the issues of the day, they are themselves the spaces where it happens. People's contributions, exactly as they posted them, can be preserved and available for all to see, and may be brought back up, added to, refuted, or supported at any future point. The databased nature of interactive media also allows for the identification of trends, keywords, and visualizations, providing snapshots of the public's interests, opinions, and sentiments.[115] Thus, this data in a way provides a literal "encoding" of the public sphere. The digital public sphere, thus, is again reflecting rather than constructing the public conversation, and in a way that is more direct than any pamphlet, newspaper, or television network could have ever done.

While the digital public sphere has given some power back to the people, there are, of course, problems. For one, these tools are not accessible to all people. As Papacharissi explains, "access to online technology is as binding to digital citizenship as national geography is to national citizenship."[116] The gap between the citizens of the world who are connected to and able to use the tools of interactive media and those who are not is known as the *digital divide*,[117] and there are many today who have limited or no access because of economic obstacles, poor infrastructure, or a lack of technological knowledge or ability.[118] This inequality must be considered in any serious discussion of the public sphere today, as certain perspectives continue to be left out of the public conversation, which can serve to reinforce social stratifications in society.[119] Meanwhile, among those who do have access, civic discussions are rife with conflict, bullying, shaming, and harassment, which can also result in the silencing of certain voices.[120]

As noted, over the course of the twentieth century, citizens were more or less completely removed from, and thus unpracticed in, civic engagement, and for generations, the primary model we had to turn to for what a public sphere should look like were commercialized forms of media.[121] Then, suddenly and seemingly out of nowhere, we were given our own platforms. Many have simply continued to adopt the commercial models,[122] talking without listening and focused on reaching as many people as possible. Those who do attempt to engage with one another, largely untrained in the art of debate and deliberation, make a lot of rookie mistakes,[123] and public discussions frequently devolve into toxic spaces full of unproductive, divisive, and personal *ad hominem* attacks (i.e., name-calling).[124] Lastly, as news consumers, we often use these tools to decrease, rather than increase, the diversity of viewpoints we are exposed to by joining communities and self-selecting news that only serve to reinforce our worldviews. Rather than a public sphere, then, we fragment ourselves into what Gitlin calls "separate public sphericles."[125]

This is a far cry from the idealized public sphere required for a truly partici-patory democracy.[126]

Meanwhile, the public sphere of the Internet has again grown into a largely corporatized space.[127] The competing agendas of media gatekeepers and political elites still dominate the public conversation,[128] and a trend of media consolidation that began in the 1990s continues as the increasingly influen-tial "Big Tech" companies merge into fewer and fewer mega-corporations.[129] Interactive media sites like Facebook, Twitter, and YouTube are not, actually, public squares where we all have a right to free speech, but private compa-nies themselves[130] with their own rights to filter, block, or otherwise suppress citizens' messages on their platforms, which they have been under increasing pressure to do.[131] In addition, the data that they collect and host can also be used against citizens by a variety of actors wishing to track or target them in manipulative ways, which can have further chilling effects on free speech (see chapters 12 and 13 for more details).

## Digital Citizenship

Despite all of the problems of the digital public sphere, for many today it is the space where we engage in and enact much of our citizenship, so it is of the upmost importance to address these issues, and there are things that we can do to improve it.[132] After all, citizenship comes with "both rights and responsi-bilities."[133] If the goal of digital citizenship is to bring about an understanding of a multitude of perspectives in an "idealized form of public reasoning,"[134] we can start by adding more bridging capital and branching out from our own "sphericles" into others. As explained in previous chapters, the more diversity we have in our networks, the more effective and useful our ideas and solutions will be.[135] As responsible digital citizens, it is also important to broaden our understanding of the world to incorporate others' viewpoints and ideas.[136] While social media tends to exacerbate a simplistic "us" versus "them" mentality that paints a caricatured position of the "opposition," such negativity and cynicism only serves divisiveness and shapes our collective in extremely unhealthy directions.[137] The goal of freedom of speech, after all, is not to achieve a unified consensus, but rather to give room for the dialectic voices of the citizenry, so that: a) none may be oppressed (thus invoking the feelings of desperation that lead to violence),[138] and b) we can identify points of commonality from which to drive human progress.[139] When we trust that all may have something worth saying, something that is "belief-worthy," we start with a position of mutual respect for one another's humanity.[140]

Rather than promoting the censorship, blocking, or "cancelling" of those with whom we disagree (effectively sticking our heads in the sand in denial of their existence), then, we can learn to communicate across divides, engendering respectfulness, listening, and dialogue in our efforts.[141] We needn't be afraid of the conflict that characterizes this ecosystem today, but find ways to lead by example, engaging with it gracefully, with care for one another.[142] It is important to be cognizant of the "public" nature of the debates that we have online, and consider the perspectives and feelings of all who might in some way be witness to them.[143] As one of the benefits of online speech is the removal of immediacy, we can take our time to think through our responses to someone, reflect, and come up with a way to say what it is we want to say with openness and respect. Before responding, for example, we can ask ourselves: Is this helpful? Is it necessary? Is it true? Is it kind?

Simply being aware of the negative human tendencies that online talk feeds into can help to negate them, as can consciously engaging others with a dose of humility.[144] Attending to those times when we ourselves are being disingenuous just to win an argument and subsequently course correcting can help to ensure that we are engaging in as authentic and sincere a manner as possible.[145] We can also guard against dysfunctional communication tendencies such as hearing things that weren't said or making assumptions about another's line of thought by instead asking those with whom we disagree questions focused on uncovering what it is that has convinced them of their position.[146]

If possible, another powerful way to engage with another's perspective is through a "*steel man*" approach, in which we seek to represent and respond to the strongest parts of the opposing arguments (the opposite of a "straw man" approach).[147] From there, we can work toward improving our knowledge through mutual understanding[148] and identify the coalescent starting points for a productive, even mind-changing discussion or relationship.[149] If one is starting with the intent to persuade another, however, they are starting at the wrong place. True and beneficial dialogue requires a degree of openness to adjusting and reconfiguring our own perspectives as we engage with others.[150] Thus, the first step to a productive dialogue is to listen, as it is only when we have a full understanding of all standpoints and perspectives that we can make any headway toward more wise and just solutions.[151] Lastly, we need not shy away from expressions of emotion in these discussions, but rather find ways to express those passions while maintaining respect for the other and combine that with a reasoned approach that helps to strengthen our case.[152] In 2008, Paul Graham developed a "hierarchy of disagreement," with which we would all do well to familiarize ourselves if we are going to engage in debates online (see figure 6.1). Aiming to keep our arguments within the top three levels of this hierarchy will help us to be more reasoned and "less mean."[153]

At the same time, it is also important to know when to disengage. There do exist those who just want to provoke us, spread hatefulness, or merely shout without making any efforts to listen, and we only bring more attention

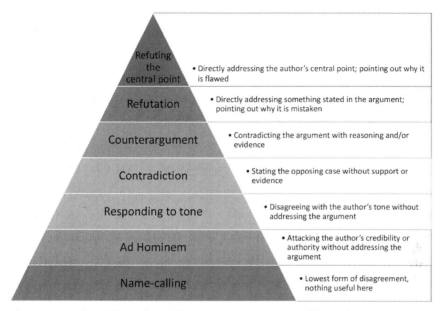

**Figure 6.1 Graham's hierarchy of disagreement.** *Figure created by author.*

to their message by arguing with them online. Once we come to the realization that this is whom we are debating with, the healthiest response—both for us and for the public sphere in general—is simply to ignore them. We can also heighten our awareness to when we ourselves might be getting caught up in such a mentality by noting our own emotional state—strong feelings of self-righteousness or rage directed at another person or group are a good indicator that this is happening. It is important to know when we are not in the right state of mind to be self-aware in our approach, which takes a lot of mental strength and energy to accomplish. Sometimes we just need to step away from the screen and enjoy the real world instead. In general, too much time online has been shown to be linked with depression and anxiety, and a healthy balance is needed in our lives regardless.[154]

## CONCLUSION

If we want to be engaged digital citizens, we will, of course, need to use interactive media to consume news and participate in the digital public sphere, but we can resolve to do so thoughtfully. Not everyone needs to start their own news outlet, but we could each join an "army" or two, speaking back to influence news coverage and offering our own knowledge. An added benefit of demanding of ourselves more conscientious civic engagement as we interact online is that it can encourage us to expect the same from the news outlets that we follow. It can better prepare us to recognize when they are not living up to that same standard (which they will inevitably fail to do at least some of the time). Engaged with properly, the added value of the increased diversity in the current media convergence ecosystem is that it can create a system of mutually beneficial reciprocal information exchange for both news producers and consumers.[155] Above all, we need to remember that all of us, together, are shaping the direction of interactive media as we use these tools every day.[156] We are never going to achieve perfection or all be of one mind (nor would we want to), but the more of us who model open-mindedness, responsible information assessment, and fair argumentation tactics, the more we can contribute to a healthier public sphere, both online and off.

## NOTES

1. Waywire, "How To Pronounce 'Cenk Uygur,'" May 13, 2013, Video, 0:58, https://youtu.be/7A3JBT34EXQ.

2. The Young Turks, "About," YouTube Channel, December 21, 2005, https://www.youtube.com/c/TheYoungTurks/about.

3. The Young Turks, "Why Hillary Campaign Tried to Silence Mika Brzezinski," December 13, 2016, Video, 11:46, https://youtu.be/jZ3ToluZBRY.

4. The Young Turks, "A Brief History of The Young Turks," April 19, 2010, Video, 4:58, https://youtu.be/cdgPFgWAwqo.

5. Madlena, "Cenk Uygur on the Success."

6. Bee, "I Like Cenk Uygur"; Amusa, "Bold New Media Mogul."

7. Cenk Uygur, "The Turk." The Young Turk, December 6, 2002, https://web.archive.org/web/20000619155751/http://youngturk.com/theyoung.htm.

8. Cenk Uygur.

9. The Young Turks, "A Brief History of The Young Turks," April 19, 2010, Video, 4:58, https://youtu.be/cdgPFgWAwqo.

10. Madlena, "Cenk Uygur on the Success."

11. The Young Turks, "A Brief History of The Young Turks," April 19, 2010, Video, 4:58, https://youtu.be/cdgPFgWAwqo.

12. Rainey, "On the Media."

13. Johnson, "Keith Olbermann Exits MSNBC."

14. Democracynow.org, "Rejecting Lucrative Offer."

15. The Young Turks, "Why Cenk Uygur Left MSNBC - Part 1," July 20, 2011, Video, 11:54 (3:41), https://youtu.be/HrKKkGl3TnY.

16. "Why Cenk Uygur Left."

17. "Why Cenk Uygur Left."

18. "Why Cenk Uygur Left."

19. The Young Turks, "Why Hillary Campaign Tried."

20. Shirky, *Here Comes Everybody*, 89.

21. Papacharissi, *A Private Sphere*, 104.

22. Tewskbury and Rittenberg, *News on the Internet*, 51.

23. Shirky, 60; italics added.

24. Stork, "Online Videos of Police."

25. Hill et al., "How George Floyd."

26. Bruns, *Gatewatching and News Curation*, 23; Kenix, *Alternative and Mainstream Media*, 22.

27. McNair, "Trust, Truth and Objectivity," 81.

28. Blaagaard, "Situated, Embodied, and Political," 44.

29. Jemielniak and Przegalinska, *Collaborative Society*, 75; Jenkins, *Convergence Culture*, 233.

30. Jenkins, 218.

31. da Silva and Garcia, "YouTubers as Satirists," 109.

32. da Silva and Garcia, 90.

33. *New York Times*, "Patriot Game: Obama vs. Romney | Op-Docs | The New York Times," September 17, 2012, Video, 2:30, https://youtu.be/ekQSpbwKkdg.

34. The Gregory Brothers, "About," accessed December 26, 2020, https://www.thegregorybrothers.com/about.

35. *New York Times*, "Patriot Game: Obama vs. Romney | Op-Docs | The New York Times," September 17, 2012, Video, 2:30, https://youtu.be/ekQSpbwKkdg.

36. "Patriot Game."

37. "Patriot Game."

38. Jenkins, *Convergence Culture*, 219.

39. Papacharissi, *Affective Publics*, 114.

40. Jenkins, *Convergence Culture*, 290; Jenkins, *Spreadable Media*, 159.

41. Lakshmanan, "Why Off-the-Record."

42. Lakshmanan.

43. Jemielniak and Przegalinska, *Collaborative Society*, 65.

44. Shirky, *Here Comes Everybody*, 11.

45. San Miguel, "Taking Back the Tweet."

46. Jenkins, *Convergence Culture*, 280; Shirky, *Here Comes Everybody*, 64–65.

47. Mandelbaum, "The Age of the Whistleblower."

48. Wikileaks, "What Is Wikileaks," November 3, 2015, https://wikileaks.org/What-is-WikiLeaks.html.

49. Project Veritas, "Overview," accessed December 26, 2020, https://www.projectveritas.com/about/.

50. Castells, "Communication, Power," 255.

51. Poulsen, "Pentagon Demands Wikileaks."

52. Liptak, "Facebook Says."

53. Bruns, *Gatewatching*, 30; Jenkins, *Convergence Culture*, 27; Leavitt and Robinson, "Upvote My News," 12.

54. Shirky, *Here Comes Everybody*, 216–17.

55. Jenkins, *Convergence Culture*, 226–27.

56. Shontell, "When Reddit Wrongly Accuses."

57. Gulbrandsen and Just, "Collaboratively Constructed Contradictory Accounts," 579.

58. Robertson, *UFOs, Conspiracy Theories*, 16.

59. *New York Times*, "The War Logs: An Archive of Classified Military Documents Offers Views of the Wars in Iraq and Afghanistan," October 23, 2010, https://archive.nytimes.com/www.nytimes.com/interactive/world/war-logs.html.

60. Briquelet, "Jeffrey Epstein"; Cernovich, "Jeff Epstein Arrested"; Gerstein, "Weird Court Case"; Murdock, "Arizona Senate Candidate."

61. Shirky, *Here Comes Everybody*, 65.

62. Hooton, "Justin Bieber Arrested."

63. Wihbey and Ward, "Communicating about Climate Change."

64. Silver, "How Trump Hacked."

65. Project Veritas, "VIDEO: Leaked ABC News Insider Recording EXPOSES #EpsteinCoverup 'We Had Clinton, We Had Everything'," November 5, 2019, Video, 7:36, https://youtu.be/3lfwkTsJGYA.

66. Atton and Hamilton, *Alternative Journalism*, 83.

67. Atton and Hamilton, 89; Dalhgren, "Professionalism and Citizen Journalism," 249.

68. Atton and Hamilton, 91.

69. Shirky, *Here Comes Everybody*, 61–62.

70. Atton and Hamilton, *Alternative Journalism*, 111–12; Bruns, *Gatewatching*, 27.

71. Jenkins, *Convergence Culture*, 227–28; Kenix, *Alternative and Mainstream Media*, 20.

72. Matt Drudge, "DrudgeReport Passes 1 Billion Hits in Past Year," Drudge Report Archives, November 12, 2002, http://www.drudgereportarchives.com/data/2002/11/12/20021112_180331.htm.

73. NewsBud, "About NewsBud," accessed December 26, 2020, https://www.newsbud.com/about-us/.

74. The Young Turks, "Why Hillary Campaign Tried to Silence Mika Brzezinski," December 13, 2016, Video, 11:46, https://youtu.be/jZ3ToluZBRY.

75. Global Voices, "What Is Global Voices?" accessed December 26, 2020, https://globalvoices.org/about/.

76. Common Dreams, "About Common Dreams," accessed December 26, 2020, https://www.commondreams.org/about-us.

77. The Conservative Treehouse, "Rag Tag Bunch of Conservative Misfits," accessed December 26, 2020, https://theconservativetreehouse.com.

78. Wikileaks, "Wikileaks: Writer's Kit," accessed December 26, 2020, https://wikileaks.org/wiki/Writer's_Kit.

79. McLintock, "The Destruction of Media," 575.

80. Atton and Hamilton, *Alternative Journalism*, 82; Broersma and Peters, "Introduction," 7; Jenkins, *Convergence Culture*, 231.

81. Atton and Hamilton, 19.

82. Atton and Hamilton, 112; Kenix, *Alternative and Mainstream Media*, 8.

83. Tandoc et al., "Defining 'Fake News,'" 2.

84. Tandoc et al., 4.

85. Nansen et al., "Proxy Users," 297.

86. Bruns, *Gatewatching and News Curation*, 165; Woolley, "We're Fighting Fake News."

87. Tandoc et al., "Defining 'Fake News,'" 4.

88. Tandoc et al., 2; Holiday, "Fake News Problem."

89. Leetaru, "The Daily Mail"; Pareene, "How Political Fact-Checkers."

90. Dill, *How Fantasy Becomes Reality*, 232.

91. Dubois and Blank, "The Echo Chamber," 740; Dvir-Gvirsman, "One-Track Minds," 490.

92. Leavitt and Robinson, "Upvote My News," 1; Rohlinger, "American Media and Deliberative," 123.

93. Bruns, *Gatewatching*, 156.

94. Habermas, "The Public Sphere," 73; Schudson, *The Good Citizen*, 12.

95. Schudson, 12.

96. Carey, "The Press, Public Opinion," 235; Schudson, 37–38.

97. Habermas, "The Public Sphere," 77.

98. Savigny, "Public Opinion, Political Communication," 6.

99. Atton and Hamilton, *Alternative Journalism*, 24; Nevue, "Four Generations," 83, 86.

100. Carey, "The Press, Public Opinion," 229.

101. Carey, 239.

102. Atton and Hamilton, *Alternative Journalism*, 23, 26–27; Carey, 248; Kenix, *Alternative and Mainstream Media*, 143–44, 151; Savigny, "Public Opinion, Political Communication," 6.

103. Ryfe and Mensing, "Citizen Journalism," 34.

104. Bourdieu, "On Television," 332; Carey, 248.

105. Carey, "The Press, Public Opinion," 241.

106. Atton and Hamilton, *Alternative Journalism*, 24.

107. Bourdieu, "On Television," 329–30.

108. Bimber, *Information and American Democracy*, 204; Carey, "The Press, Public Opinion," 239; Kenix, *Alternative and Mainstream Media*, 140.

109. Bimber, 198–200; Carey, 230; McNair, "Journalism and Democracy," 409.

110. Bimber, 219.

111. Wright, "From 'Third Place,'" 13.

112. Dalelio and Weinhold, "'I Know from Personal,'" 16; Leavitt and Robinson, "Upvote My News," 12–13; McNair, "Trust, Truth and Objectivity," 81.

113. Dalelio and Weinhold, 16.

114. Batsell, *Engaged Journalism*, 25.

115. Volkmer and Firdaus, "Between Networks and 'Hierachies,'" 105.

116. Papacharissi, *A Private Sphere*, 104.

117. Hargittai, "Second-Level Digital Divide."

118. Papacharissi, *A Private Sphere*, 104–05.

119. Papacharissi, 104.

120. Keats Citron and Penney, "When Law Frees Us," 2319.

121. Booth, *Modern Dogma*, 201–02.

122. Kenix, *Alternative and Mainstream Media*, 81.

123. Weger and Aakhus, "Arguing in Internet Chat," 31.

124. Habernal et al., "Before Name-Calling," 386.

125. Gitlin, "Public Sphere," 173.

126. Dahlberg, "The Habermasian Public Sphere," 7–10.

127. Kenix, *Alternative and Mainstream Media*, 150.

128. Kenix, 20, 26, 111.

129. McLintock, "The Destruction of Media," 582–83.

130. Cope and Greene, "Ninth Circuit."

131. Asarch, "Steven Crowder Incites"; Conger et al., "Violence on Capitol Hill"; Edelman, "Stop Saying Facebook"; Mangan, "'Don't Touch Me'"; Marantz, "Free Speech Is Killing Us"; Maratnz, "Reddit and the Struggle."

132. Mahailidis, *Civic Media Literacies*, 19–20.

133. Hanitzch, "Journalism, Participative Media," 204.

134. Dahlberg, "The Habermasian Public Sphere," 7.

135. Landemore and Page, "Deliberation and Disagreement," 234–35.

136. Dahlberg, "The Habermasian Public Sphere," 7–8.

137. Bickford, "Emotion Talk," 1035.

138. Baker et al., "The Art of Being," 28–29.

139. Booth, *Modern Dogma*, 111.

140. Baker et al., "The Art of Being," 29.

141. Dahlberg, "Taking Difference Seriously," 127.

142. Mihailidis and Viotty, "Spreadable Spectacle," 11.

143. Dahlberg, "The Habermasian Public Sphere," 7.

144. Dahlberg, 8.

145. Dahlberg, 7–8.

146. Dahlberg, 9.

147. Mattes, "Techniques for Communicating," 15.

148. Lankes, "Trusting the Internet," 112.

149. Young, "Communication and the Other," 125.

150. Baker, "The Art of Being," 18; Turkle, *Reclaiming Conversation*, 298.

151. Young, "Communication and the Other," 128.

152. Bickford, "Emotion Talk," 1036; Dahlberg, "Taking Difference Seriously," 115–16.

153. Graham, "How to Disagree."

154. Shensa et al., "Social Media Use," 10.

155. Kenix, *Alternative and Mainstream Media*, 170; Tewksbury and Rittenberg, *News on the Internet*, 49.

156. Webster, *The Marketplace of Attention*, 150.

*Chapter 7*

# Collaboration

## INTRODUCTION: BIRDSONG

After the COVID-19 pandemic spurred on a social distancing shutdown across North America in March 2020, "stephieb," a self-employed massage therapist from Ottawa, Canada, wrote a poem to express her feelings about potentially being out of work and having to cancel a long-awaited trip:[1]

> It's not the end of the world
> It's just a glitch
> And although your plans have gone to shit
> While the world holds its breath
> The days continue to get longer
> And the planet continues to spin
> So listen to the birdsong and stand with your face in the sun
> And pay attention to the opportunities that you would have missed
> Had your path not been blocked[2]

"Bokoblinvertigo," who had just lost his own job at a restaurant in Texas, recorded some of these lines on his phone. "Analaura," from Torreón, Mexico, did the same. Meanwhile, "Epocadofim," a filmmaker and writer in New York,[3] took some video footage of the eerily empty streets in the city. A year earlier, "create_self," a data scientist,[4] had recorded her own video in Taiwan, of she and her grandfather joyfully dancing on a rain-soaked outdoor promenade.[5] And back in 2016, "Kerrnie," a woodwind instrumentalist and composer from New Jersey,[6] had made a recording of some long, low tones that she played on a clarinet. Parts of these creations, along with the contributions of nineteen other people from all over the world, were beautifully pieced together in May 2020 to create a digital short film called "Change of Plans." The film was featured in the premiere episode of a six-part YouTube

Originals series called *Create Together #WithMe*,[7] which was the brainchild of actor Joseph Gordon-Levitt. He announced the series in a YouTube video on May 11, saying, "So, we're all gonna make a show together, starting now!" Episodes were released every Monday for six weeks, each one soliciting continued participation from the audience, and the final miniseries utilized the works of more than five hundred contributors.[8] And here's the kicker: They all got paid for it.

How did Gordon-Levitt do it? It wasn't the YouTube platform that made this possible, but in fact his own pet project, a platform called HitRecord. Artists, professionals, and everyday people have been using his site for over ten years to collaborate on creative works by purposefully and openly using each other's work. Whenever someone on the site shares a creation, it's called a "record," and whether it's a piece of writing, a drawing, a painting, photography, animation, acting, voice-over work, music samples, or anything at all—it is made downloadable. Any time someone uses another community member's record in their own contribution, the new record is linked to the original as a "remix" of it, and any records that are used in a remix are likewise linked out from it as "resources." Here, media appropriation isn't something to watch out for, but rather, that's the point. According to community members, "getting remixed" is the exciting part; that's when the magic happens.[9] Unlike a lot of creative sharing platforms out there, which tend to be about promoting oneself and one's own work, HitRecord has an ethos of collaboration.[10]

Almost as an aside, HitRecord is also a production company. Gordon-Levitt has taken works that he's chosen and directed from the community to the market, including films, albums, video game graphics, books, commercials, and an Emmy award–winning TV show,[11] and all contributors to these works get paid for their contributions. Over the years, the company has paid out a sum total of over three million dollars to its contributors.[12] But, according to Gordon-Levitt, "I certainly wouldn't include money in the third or fifth or even 10th sentence of why people come to HitRecord."[13] In fact, in the beginning, money wasn't even a factor. It started out as a simple message board that he and his brother created so that he could keep up with his fans.[14] He explains, "what we noticed was . . . more than just checking out the stuff that I was making, that the people on this message board wanted to make things together. . . . It wasn't even our idea, it was just something that the community was doing organically, and we started leaning into it."[15] Today, there are over one million members on the site,[16] and nearly three million "records" posted.[17] As Gordon-Levitt has said, "being creative alone can be hard, but doing it together, we have found over the years of doing this, it can unlock something."[18] Indeed, looking through the site, it is like a beautiful cacophonous birdsong of its own, an aggregate collection of unleashed creativity.

## TIERS OF COLLABORATIVE EFFORT

There is nothing particularly new in the idea of collaborative groups; they have always existed, especially in the realm of media production (just sit through the credits of a movie some time). But traditional collaboration tends to be limited to the professional realm, as networks of people working within companies or institutions join together on assigned or approved-of projects.[19] However, with the use of interactive media, collaborative groups today can be larger, more widely dispersed, and more open to participation.[20] People everywhere are using interactive media to jump into collaborative efforts to varying degrees, without the need for special access or an invitation from above.[21] According to Clay Shirky, such efforts can be observed across four tiers of increasing involvement and complexity: sharing, cooperation, collaborative production, and collective action.[22]

### Sharing

*Sharing* is the first and simplest tier of collaborative effort.[23] It involves large groups of people providing content, whether textual, visual, or aural, for others to access. For example, Twitter is primarily the sharing of words, Instagram the sharing of photos, and YouTube the sharing of videos. Sharing does not ask much more of people than to simply post something and leave it there, but on the whole it creates what is known as a *commons resource* that anyone can contribute to and anyone can use, for free.[24] The term "commons" might be more conventionally understood as something like a community garden, where people can both contribute to and take from what is there. Digital commons resources, however, are somewhat different. They do not suffer from what is known as *"the tragedy of the commons,"* which is what happens when too many freeloaders take from the resource without contributing, leading to its ultimate depletion.[25] That is because digital resources are not taken; they are copied.[26] When we look at something on the Internet, we are actually looking at a copy of it.[27] When we download something from the Internet, we are making an exact replication of it to keep for ourselves, but the original resource remains.[28] So, while nothing gets taken away when people use a digital resource, value is still added when they contribute to it.[29] Thus, in the sphere of interactive media, content flows more like ideas through a society: openly shared, freely spread, and belonging to anyone.[30]

## Cooperation

*Cooperation* is a degree more difficult than simply group sharing, because it has to do with not just content but also behavior.[31] When members of large groups cooperate, they synchronize their behavior as a way of organizing and making sense of shared content.[32] This is seen, for example, when a hashtag emerges and people begin using it to join in on the conversation, or when people @ each other to get them to participate in the latest social media "challenge." Such coordinated efforts are in part driven by the features and functions available on a specific platform, but the platforms also develop in concert with evolving group norms around how they are used,[33] such as when Twitter (and then later Facebook, Instagram, and others) added the hashtag capability after seeing users employ it in other systems,[34] or when Reddit added the "Live Thread" format after their communities demonstrated extremely useful collective information-gathering behaviors during breaking news events.[35]

Sharing and cooperation serve to create a whole new kind of non-market production model, where no money exchanges hands and yet highly valuable resources are created.[36] For instance, I could look on CNN's website today and find a gallery of the thirty-four "press" photographs that they chose to represent the George Floyd protests that have been recently going on around the world,[37] or I could go on Flickr.com and find an instant photo essay of over 32,000 high-quality images created by thousands of individuals who not only shared them but also cooperated by tagging them with similar relevant keywords.[38] While CNN is paying for the photographs, as well as employing someone who chose and captioned each of them, no money exchanged hands to create the much larger gallery on Flickr. In addition, the photographers on Flickr provided their own captions, dates, and other information surrounding the photographs, and other users viewed, "faved," and commented on them. Thus, while it is the social platforms that make such commons resources possible, it is the cooperating community of users that collaboratively creates them.[39]

## Collaborative Production

Collaborative production, also known as mass collaboration[40] or peer production,[41] is a form of large-scale collaboration that involves users participating in projects with shared outcomes or products for which no single individual can take credit.[42] Collaborative production is more involved than simply sharing or cooperation, because participants' contributions tend to take the form of an iterative work process, a back-and-forth exchange, leading to some "thing."[43] HitRecord is great example of collaborative production, where people are working together to create collaborative art. Another, more well-known example is Wikipedia, where people are working to write, edit, translate, and check articles in order to create something that is "encyclopedia-like."[44] The shared vision or goal underlying collaborative production suggests that group members' level of investment is greater than what might be found in cooperation or simple group sharing.[45]

## Collective Action

Collective action is the most difficult kind of collaborative effort.[46] It is "action that is undertaken in the name of members meant to change something out in the world."[47] Members commit themselves to a particular cause together and generally remain dedicated even if they don't necessarily support the decisions that are collectively made.[48] For this, not only do group members perceive a strong sense of group identity, but their individual identity must also be tied into the effort.[49] Dedicated members of collective actions offer their skill sets and work together on iterative tasks, and also express themselves frequently in terms of their cause. They share in not only the goals and group vision, but also a sense of responsibility for what the group achieves.[50] Because of the level of involvement required, in most cases interactive media alone does not suffice for collective action, and the most effective movements are undergirded by the efforts of real-world actions, networks, and organizations.[51] Interactive media can serve to strengthen such efforts, however, and increasingly act as a site through which grassroots movements emerge.[52] The role of interactive media in collective action will be explored in more detail in the next chapter on activism.

## THE OPEN-SOURCE MODEL

Whatever the level of involvement, when large groups of people use interactive media to collaborate, it tends to reflect a more *open-source model* of group effort.[53] The term "open-source" derives from the programming community, as it was first used to describe the opening up of the "source code" of a computer program to a community, so that anyone could write and share new code to modify its functionality, and programmers would work together, collectively, to improve the software over time.[54] But the term "open-source" has since been applied to refer to anything where people are given free access to the "source," or origination, of something in order to make and share their own modifications.[55] Wikis open up the "source" of documents, as anyone can click an "edit" button to change them, and Wikipedia is an open-source encyclopedia where people can add, write, or alter article entries.[56] HitRecord is an open-source creative hub where anyone can access original artistic pieces and works to build on in order to create their own.[57] While some things are more technically "open-source" than others, the open-source model to a degree permeates everything we do via interactive media, and it is beginning to make its way into science, architecture, design, education, and more.[58] Thus, the characteristics and processes of the open-source model, as detailed in the sections below, may be found, to varying degrees, all over the place.

## Self-Organizing

Collaboration in the open-source model is the result of many contributions added with no formal workflow, each serving the effort in different ways.[59] It is a spontaneous, self-organizing division of labor, in which people choose when and how often they want to contribute, and in what ways.[60] Because of the small world network structure that underlies these groups, they are able to operate without hierarchy, assigned roles, oversight, or requirements. Yet, due to the large numbers of people participating, major undertakings can still be accomplished.[61] In a continuing theme of natural processes serving as apt metaphors for social processes via interactive media, through the open-source model we tend to operate more like a self-organizing species, such as a giant flock of birds or a colony of ants, getting more done "on-the-fly" and with less planning.[62]

As the boundaries between producers and consumers dissolve, the entire audience of something also has the potential to contribute to it. Any of the millions of daily readers of Wikipedia,[63] for example, can become proof-readers, editors, fact-checkers, or reference-finders at any point and as they please.[64] Browsers of Flickr can become commenters, curators, or photographers themselves. People who read news on Twitter can become distributors and editorialists when they share and respond to stories. Shoppers on Amazon can become product reviewers or recommenders. We saw in chapter 5 how fans of media productions can become content creators, and in chapter 6 how citizens can become journalists and media outlets themselves. This self-organizing feature influences the creative processes users experience as well, as they try out new roles and tasks inspired by their fellow users. As HitRecord member "LatteSundae" from the UK explains, "at the core, I am a writer, and that's the whole reason why I joined HitRecord. But, you can't just stay in your lane, because you get tempted with all these different possibilities and people remixing you into something that you never would have dreamed to be a part of."[65] As is typical of artists on the site, she has contributed beyond her "core" motivation for participating, and has begun singing, performing, and composing music with her fellow collaborators.[66]

## Unequal

Even though equal participation is theoretically possible with open-source collaborations, not everyone participates equally.[67] In fact, the way that they participate is almost always decidedly *unequal*, with a lot of contributions from a small number of "super" participants, plus a large number of participants who contribute very little.[68] It tends to look like this:

This pattern is called a *power law distribution*, and it represents the typical output of informal, voluntary, networked communities (figure 7.1).[69] This means that, unlike the traditional world of work, where everyone is expected to put in 100 percent or face consequences, people can contribute as much or as little as they want and still work together in relative harmony.[70] Even though they are collaboratively producing something, no one is resentful toward others for their level of effort or lack thereof, since everyone is participating informally and voluntarily.[71] Even on a site like HitRecord, where users might end up getting paid, the business model is not based on evenly distributed labor or assigned tasks, but rather members are paid based on the percentage of their contribution that ends up in the final product.[72]

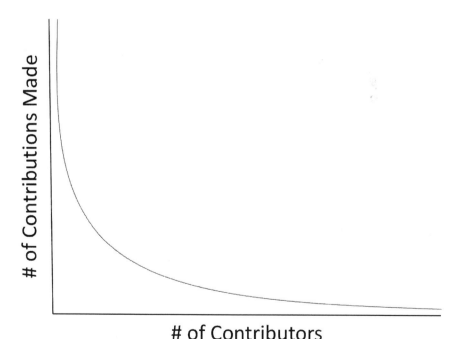

**Figure 7.1 Power law distribution.** *Figure created by author.*

## Self-Healing

When everyone has the ability to make changes to or alter something, there may also be those who do so badly. They may make a mistake or misjudgment, or even actively engage in sabotage.[73] But open-source collaboration also has a tendency to be *self-healing*.[74] This means that such errors or problems, "bugs" in tech-speak, are fixed with relative expediency and frequency.[75] For instance, despite the open-source nature of Wikipedia, it has been found that the average number of errors per article (at a given point in time) was on par with the number found in the Encyclopedia Britannica.[76] Considering the fact anyone can edit a Wikipedia article at any given point and put in false or erroneous information, and that Encyclopedia Britannica is pored over and approved of by paid experts, how can this be so? Because in the open-source model, the larger the community, the more eyes will be looking at something at any given moment.[77] Since the overwhelming majority of users tend to be more interested in good content rather than bad, there is an inherent positive "net value,"[78] and such "errors" can be caught very quickly and buried or eliminated.

In addition, errors are just as easy, if not easier, to "undo" than they are to make.[79] Because of the digital and databased nature of interactive media, previous messages, efforts, and output are typically archived and can be brought up again, reintroduced to the effort. On Wikipedia, for example, people can go into the history and reinstate an earlier version.[80] Similarly on HitRecord, everyone has the ability to go back to the original resources if they want to change or "fix" the way something is remixed, and redo it in their own style.

Some sites, like Reddit and YouTube, even take ratings into account, allowing users to collectively highlight and filter items with their "up" votes, bringing them to the surface, or "down" votes, burying them at the bottom. Amazon likewise lets users rate the raters by marking reviews as "helpful," which moves them up the list.[81] Whether or not the "bad" content remains somewhere in a site's archives, the "good" can always be highlighted and brought back up to be continued.

## Open-Ended

Although things can get done more easily via large groups collaborating via interactive media, they are also never really done.[82] Such efforts are usually left *open-ended*, meaning they may always be built upon or added to at any point.[83] The goal of these communities is not to achieve some final complete outcome.[84] Even when there is a "product" being developed in collaborative production, such as an encyclopedia entry, a photo gallery, or a digital short film, it is always only a "snapshot," a moment in time amidst an ongoing effort. This makes sources like Reddit, Wikipedia, Twitter, and Youtube good places to go for the latest information and breaking news, as they never close out a "final report."[85] New information, opinions, and images can always be posted, in real time. In creative processes, every production, every scene, every line is opened up to limitless reinterpretation and carries the potential of new contextual uses (a photograph of Michael Jordan crying, a screenshot of Kermit the Frog sipping tea, or the line "one does not simply walk into Mordor" from *The Lord of the Rings*, for example). As "LatteSundae" said, in describing a HitRecord musical project she worked on, "even though in my mind, it was finished . . . there's no limit to where [the community] can take it."[86] Even the conversations we have via interactive media tend to have this open-ended nature, as they go on without resolution, with no goal of coming to an agreement or collectively agreed-upon solution, rarely a final "goodbye" even uttered, but rather just left in ellipses, an implied "until next time" in perpetuity.

## DIGITAL LABOR

Although it is clear that the motivation behind collaborative efforts in the open-source model is not primarily money, people are still doing work. Why? Some argue that it is a labor of love, driven by passion, altruism, a sense of belonging, or even a kind of egotism, desiring to leave one's mark on the world.[87] In a way, nearly everyone contributing, voluntarily and for free, via interactive media is (in their mind at least) doing it "for the good," sharing with others something they think others might want or should have.[88] This is a communal model, as opposed to a commercial model, of labor, and it has made us all aware that we are capable of great things, even without being market-driven.[89] Kevin Kelly has even called it a kind of "digital socialism," that is voluntary, "leaderless," and outside of state rule.[90] Without anyone forcing us to, and with little to no concern for property, we have created a "workforce composed entirely of free agents" neither market-driven nor tax-funded, providing a new model for how we understand work.[91] While there is perhaps a lot of promise and hope in this view, we must also recognize that this is largely uncompensated labor, and thus there is a point at which taking advantage of people's generosity and willingness to perform their labor of love may become exploitative.[92] It was Linus Tovalds, after all, inventor of the open-source model with his Linux programmer community, who said of his motivation, "I'm basically a very lazy person who likes to get credit for things other people actually do."[93] People engaging in collaborative efforts through interactive media are engaging in *digital labor*, expending resources, time, and energy, that others are benefitting from. So, it is important to take a long, hard look at a collaborative effort of any tier to critically assess who is benefiting, how much, and to what end.

There must be a fair balance on both sides of the digital labor coin. For example, if Joseph Gordon-Levitt was selling products made by the community and not paying contributors but rather keeping all profits for himself and his company, it would not be ethical, despite the fact that contributors are not creating for the purpose of compensation. In fact, even though he has found a very fair and transparent process for paying contributors from sold products, Gordon-Levitt has been accused of cutting corners by using HitRecord for "spec work," which is "when professionals work for free in hopes of getting paid later" as they compete for contract bids.[94] Wikipedia's approach, on the other hand, is to remain not-for-profit, so although it does have employees,[95] most of its contributors are not paid at all, and in fact it is against their policy for users to be paid to contribute to their site.[96] Meanwhile, social media platforms like Twitter, Facebook, and Instagram make money off of all of their user-contributed data through advertising and influence models (more on this in chapter 12), and sites like YouTube allow only the most popular of contributors to get paid through their advertising programs. While some of these arrangements may seem more fair than others, in all cases no one is being forced, or even asked, to contribute to these sites, and there are benefits for those who do. So, what trade-offs should we be willing to accept for the benefits we receive from producing digital labor? It is not an easy question to answer, especially as we experiment with commercially viable ways to support participation in society, culture, and the public sphere (more on this in chapter 11). But in this age of transition, with new models popping up all the time, it is at the very least a question we should continually be asking ourselves.

## CONCLUSION

Interactive media has brought about the possibility of large-scale collaboration, and the processes of the open-source model quite clearly reflect their comparatively looser, freer, and more open structures. No one exactly asked for all of this sharing, cooperation, collaborative production, and collective action to take place; it just happened. But we now know that people have a clear drive to work together, regardless of whether or not they need to do so for the purposes of their livelihood. The interesting thing moving forward will be to see how this affects the structures and institutions we used to think we needed to get things done.

As newer generations enter the workforce, interactive media tools like Slack, Confluence, and BitBucket are becoming more commonly used to manage projects, share knowledge, and organize workflows according to these newer, more open, and less formalized rules for collaboration.[97] In a 2018 *TechCrunch* article entitled, "Why *Minecraft* predicts the Future of Collaborative Work," Jim Fowler, executive in the tech industry, wrote the following after watching his kids play the open, iterative, collaborative, brick-building video game *Minecraft*:

> We're already seeing this kind of spontaneous, highly effective collaboration at work in the corporate world. As CIO, I've watched people get more comfortable exploring and finding their own best way to use data. Earlier in my career, I tried to dictate how people used technology. Now, I just keep the maximum amount of data flowing to whomever wants it. I set up sensible guard rails, but, otherwise, I let people explore and experiment. Sometimes I feel like I'm playing referee for an open-ended, open-source, high-stakes game played with resources and data.[98]

As the collaborative tools, processes, and mindsets of interactive media increasingly dominate the workforce, many questions arise about what effects this will have and what the future of work will look like. For instance, will employees more freely cross boundaries in their duties and knowledge application, or be free to voluntarily work on projects as much or as little they wish? Will entire sectors open up their ideas, research, and working processes to one another, or even to nonprofessionals, in order to generate new ideas? If so, how can we protect ideas, ownership, and attribution in such an open environment? How can we ensure quality and avoid exploiting people's goodwill? How much, really, of the open-source model can apply, when livelihoods *are* at stake? There is much that needs to be figured out in determining what is fair and workable in a for-pay environment, but there is one thing that we can say for sure about the future of work: It will be collaborative.

## NOTES

1. HITRECORD, "Scream with Me Because It Works," May 18, 2020, Video, 13:32, https://youtu.be/yhKUCZI4s1c.

2. stephieb, "Glitch," HitRecord, March 13, 2020, https://hitrecord.org/records/4249907.

3. Eric Tortora Pato, "About + Sobre," accessed December 26, 2020, http://etortorapato.com/sobre.

4. Vivian Peng, "About," accessed December 26, 2020, https://www.vivianpeng.com/about.

5. create_self, "Dancing with Grandpa 3," HitRecord, April 29, 2019, https://hitrecord.org/records/3797413.

6. Marybeth Kern, "Biography," accessed December 26, 2020, http://marybethkern.com.

7. HITRECORD, "Scream with Me Because It Works," May 18, 2020, Video, 13:32, https://youtu.be/yhKUCZI4s1c.

8. HITRECORD, "Create Together #WithMe," YouTube Playlist, last updated July 10, 2020. https://www.youtube.com/playlist?list=PLB0rl-bjxkI6gwIOA6paIZlOjp0f42zOq.

9. Joseph Gordon-Levitt, "Live from Sundance—it's HITRECORD Live Labs!!" Facebook Video, 1:09, January 24, 2020, https://www.facebook.com/JoeGordonLevitt/videos/465281754143323/.

10. HITRECORD, "YouTube, meet HITRECORD," March 14, 2019, Video, 1:22, https://youtu.be/CLbvYEH9Ncg.

11. Protalinski, "'GitHub for Creativity.'"

12. HitRecord, "Be Creative. Together," accessed December 26, 2020, Video, 2:25, https://hitrecord.org/how_it_works.

13. Clark, "Joseph Gordon-Levitt's."

14. Joseph Gordon-Levitt, "Live from Sundance—it's HITRECORD Live Labs!!" Facebook Video, 21:58, January 24, 2020, https://www.facebook.com/JoeGordonLevitt/videos/465281754143323/.

15. "Live from Sundance," 22:08.

16. HitRecord, "People," accessed December 26, 2020, https://hitrecord.org/explore/users.

17. HitRecord, "Records," accessed December 26, 2020, https://hitrecord.org/explore/records.

18. Joseph Gordon-Levitt, "Live from Sundance—it's HITRECORD Live Labs!!" Facebook Video, 24:27, January 24, 2020, https://www.facebook.com/JoeGordonLevitt/videos/465281754143323/.

19. Tapscott and Williams, *Wikinomics*, 10.

20. Shirky, *Here Comes Everybody*, 48.

21. Jemielniak and Przegalinska, *Collaborative Society*, 46–48.

22. Shirky, *Here Comes Everybody*, 48–51.

23. Shirky, 49.

24. Lessig, *The Future of Ideas*, 19–20.

25. Lessig, 22.

26. Lessig, 96.

27. Kelly, *The Inevitable*, 61; Lessig, "Remix: How Creativity," 161.

28. Lessig, *The Future of Ideas*, 58, 94.

29. Lessig, 21.

30. Lessig, 116.

31. Shirky, *Here Comes Everybody*, 49.

32. Shirky, 49–50.

33. Raymond, "Cathedral and the Bazaar," 27; Orlikowski, "Using Technology and Constituting," 407; Zittrain, *The Future of the Internet*, 223–25.

34. Salazar, "Hashtags 2.0."

35. Leavitt and Robinson, "Upvote My News," 15.

36. Benkler, *The Wealth of Networks*, 59; Jemielniak and Przegalinska, *Collaborative Society*, 43.

37. CNN, "Protests Across the Globe."

38. Flickr, "Photos," accessed December 26, 2020, https://www.flickr.com/search/?text=george%20floyd%20protests.

39. Shirky, *Here Comes Everybody*, 136.

40. Jemielniak and Przegalinska, *Collaborative Society*, 41; Tapscott and Williams, *Wikinomics*.

41. Benkler and Nissenbaum, "Commons-Based Peer Production," Jemielniak and Przegalinska, 41.

42. Jemielniak and Przegalinska, 41; Shirky, *Here Comes Everybody*, 50.

43. Jemielniak and Przegalinska, 41; Shirky, 50.

44. Shirky, 114–15.

45. Jemielniak and Przegalinska, *Collaborative Society*, 43; Shirky, 50.

46. Shirky, 51.

47. Shirky, 51.

48. Shirky, 53.

49. Shirky, 51; Turner-Zwinkles and van Zomeren, "Identity Expression Through Collective," 2.

50. Shirky, *Here Comes Everybody*, 51.

51. Bennett and Segerberg, "The Logic of Connective," 754.

52. Bennett and Segerberg, 754.

53. Jemielniak and Przegalinska, *Collaborative Society*, 4–5; Shirky, *Here Comes Everybody*, 254.

54. Jemielniak and Przegalinska, 18; Shirky, 240.

55. Jemielniak and Przegalinska, 18; Shirky, 254.

56. Tredennick, "Wikipedia."

57. Protalinski, "'GitHub for Creativity.'"

58. Levine and Prietula, "Open Collaboration for Innovation."

59. Shirky, *Here Comes Everybody*, 122.

60. Benkler and Nissenbaum, "Common-Based Peer Production," 402; Crowston et al., "Self-Organization of Teams"; Shirky, 118.

61. Shirky, 104.

62. Averian, "Digital Ecosystems," 38–39; Rheingold, *Smart Mobs*, 176, Shirky, 122.

63. Anderson et al., "Wikipedia at 15."

64. Shirky, *Here Comes Everybody*, 119–22.

65. Joseph Gordon-Levitt, "Live from Sundance—it's HITRECORD Live Labs!!" Facebook Video, "Live from Sundance," 1:15, January 24, 2020, https://www.facebook.com/JoeGordonLevitt/videos/465281754143323/.

66. "Live from Sundance."

67. Shirky, *Here Comes Everybody*, 123.

68. Graham and Wright, "Impact of 'Superparticipants'"; Shirky, 120.

69. Shirky, 123–24.

70. Shirky, 121.

71. Jemielniak and Przegalinska, *Collaborative Society*, 48; Raymond, "Cathedral and the Bazaar," 43; Shirky, 121.

72. Gordon-Levitt, "Community Collaboration."

73. Shirky, *Here Comes Everybody*, 136–37.

74. Rosenzweig, "Can History Be," 136; Shirky, 116.

75. Raymond, "Cathedral and the Bazaar," 29.

76. Giles, "Internet Encyclopedias."

77. Rosenzweig, "Can History Be," 133.

78. Shirky, *Here Comes Everybody*, 296.

79. Rosenzweig, "Can History Be," 133; Shirky, 272; Zittrain, *The Future of the Internet*, 154.

80. Benkler and Nissenbaum, "Common-Based Peer Production," 398; Shirky, *Here Comes Everybody*, 136.

81. Hanna, "Amazon on a Positive Note."

82. Shirky, *Here Comes Everybody*, 119.

83. Jemielniak and Przegalinska, *Collaborative Society*, 59; Shirky, 122.

84. Shirky, 139.

85. Bruns, *Gatewatching and News Curation*, 30; Shirky, 116.

86. Gordon-Levitt, "Live from Sundance," 1:14.

87. Benkler and Nissenbaum, "Common-Based Peer Production," 405–9; Shirky, *Here Comes Everybody*, 131–33.

88. Benkler and Nissenbaum, "Common-Based Peer Production," 409; Gauntlett, *Making Is Connecting*, 169.

89. Shirky, *Here Comes Everybody*, 258.

90. Kelly, "The New Socialism."

91. Kelly.

92. Shirky, *Here Comes Everybody*, 134–35.

93. Raymond, "Cathedral and the Bazaar," 27.

94. Gordon-Levitt, "Community Collaboration."

95. Wikipedia, "Wikimedia Foundation," accessed February 27, 2021, https://en.wikipedia.org/wiki/Wikipedia:Wikimedia_Foundation.

96. Pinsker, "The Covert World."

97. York and Johnson-Eilola, "Enduring Designs, Transient Designers."

98. Fowler, "Why Minecraft Predicts."

# Chapter 8

# Activism

## INTRODUCTION: "QUIET" RIOT

On Saturday, January 21, 2017, a beautifully performed a cappella song was heard rising up from the crowd of over 470,000 people in a sea of pink hats during the first Women's March on Washington, DC.[1] In perfect, soulful harmony, a diverse group of twenty-six women sang together, "If I don't say something, if I just lie still, . . . If I let them hear what I have to say, I can't keep quiet, no-oh-oh-oh-oh . . . A one woman riot, oh-oh-oh-oh."[2] Alma Har'el, an Israeli filmmaker and director, was wandering through the crowd looking for a friend when she came across the women singing and quickly pulled out her phone to record them.[3] She soon posted the video, which captured the moving performance mid-song, to her YouTube channel, as well as her Twitter and Facebook feeds.[4] By the next morning, the video had already been viewed three million times.[5]

The song, titled "Quiet," was cowritten one year earlier by little-known Los Angeles musician Connie Lim, aka "MILCK," and producer Adrianne "AG" Gonzalez.[6] In the months leading up to the Women's March, Lim envisaged bringing the song to D.C. that day as a guerilla-style *flash mob*, which is when a group of people coordinate via interactive media to show up at a specified time and place to perform a unifying action,[7] in support of the march's message.[8] She found several choirs in the DC area and began emailing them, ultimately recruiting two to join her: a professional group called *Capital Blend* and another called the *GW Sirens* from George Washington University. From there, all details about when and where the women would meet, as well as the sharing of the score and verses of the song, were arranged via email and Skype.[9] On the morning of the march, which itself was organized on Facebook,[10] the singers met together for the first time to practice their song. They did not know what to expect when they went out to the crowd to sing, but they soon found that their performances resonated. *GW Sirens* member Tessa O'Rourke recounts, "Every time we sang we saw people watching, and there would be people looking right at us, crying. And then we would look at each other and start crying. It was all just so emotionally charged."[11]

The resonance of the performance did not end there. The video was shared all over social media, including by actresses Emma Watson, Amy Poehler,[12] and Debra Messing, and the hashtag #icantkeepquiet began trending. Lim and her fellow singers were invited to perform the song on *Full Frontal with Samantha Bee* five days later,[13] and it was soon dubbed the "anthem" of women's rights.[14] Then others started performing and sharing their own versions of the song all around the world, in places like Ghana,[15] Sweden,[16] and Austria,[17] where groups of women sang together, flash-mob style in public places,[18] at concerts,[19] and in large groups.[20] It clearly struck a chord with people, especially women, many of whom were sexual assault survivors and reached out to Lim expressing gratitude for the song's empowering message.[21] By summer of that year, Lim began a website, www.icantkeepquiet.org, encouraging such women to tell their stories to the world so they would no longer have to keep quiet, and calling her fans "Gentle Rebels."[22]

When the #MeToo movement emerged along these same lines a couple of months later, Lim, who had by then signed with Atlantic Records, got permission from her label to release the official studio recording of "Quiet" earlier than planned via her YouTube channel. In the description, she called it her "musical #METOO," explaining that it was originally written as her own source of healing after having been sexually assaulted herself.[23] She later added, "it is critical for our individual and collective voices to be heard. With this song, I'm saying I am NOT the woman who is going to stay quiet where there are figures who promote oppression. I want to encourage others to give a voice to whatever they may have silenced, political or personal."[24]

No longer just a "one-woman" riot, the journey of this activist-musician and her song across 2017 underscored what *Wired* magazine called "the year women reclaimed the web."[25] Citing movements like the Women's March and #MeToo, writer Issie Lapowsky explains, "in 2017, women . . . reminded us all of the upside of connecting online. Joining together around the world, . . . they were able to find and support one another, despite geography and circumstance, and to subvert the power structures that have silenced them for so long."[26] The voice given to Lim and so many others since in sharing their stories has demonstrated the value of interactive media in those times when people, individually and together, wish to be silenced no more.

## SHARED AWARENESS

Activism and protest movements gain traction in a society as more and more people come to share in an awareness around some problem or issue. Such *shared awareness* is not just limited to social injustice, but plays a role in the identification of any problem that large groups of people collectively become aware of.[27] According to Clay Shirky, it happens across "three levels: when everybody knows something, when everybody knows that everybody knows, and when everybody knows that everybody knows that everybody knows."[28]

For example, imagine watching a Superbowl in which there are repeated flags called against one team only. Some of these calls seem a bit unfair, while the other team seems to be getting away with similar penalties that aren't getting called. At first, everyone watching the game begins to realize that something is not right with these calls, but no one has said it out loud yet. This is the first level of shared awareness: when "everybody" knows, on their own, that the game is unfair.[29]

Next, people might begin to wonder if they are alone in this realization, and decide to test the notion. "Does anyone else think that ref is being a little one-sided?" they might begin to ask their fellow spectators. Others express their agreement. They then begin to discuss the ways in which the referee identified penalties against one team but let the other team get away with them, and even those who are fans of the benefiting team are forced to admit that they noticed it. All across the nation, people are having similar discussions about this game. This is the second level of shared awareness: when "everybody" becomes aware that they agree that the game is unfair.[30]

Then people begin to look online to see what others are saying. They find that, indeed, many people are talking about it on social media, and they continue to talk about it, even after the game ends. A petition is started, calling for the referee's firing and a rematch, and fans are posting replays online in slow motion to prove how the calls were biased. Fans begin claiming there was collusion, and hashtags like #riggedbowl start trending. Now it is even reaching people who aren't football fans and didn't watch the game, and within twenty-four hours, the critiques are so prevalent that it seems no one, including the commissioners of the NFL, could be ignorant of it. This is the third level of shared awareness: when it is so obvious that "everybody" is aware that the game was unfair, that no one, including those in charge, can pretend not to know.[31]

This third level of shared awareness is key, and it is the goal of most collective action.[32] That is because it is the point at which something must be done, as the "authorities," whomever they may be, are forced to respond in some way.[33] In this case, it is the commissioners of the NFL, but in more serious cases, it might be the leaders of a government who cannot pretend that they are not aware of its people's oppression, or a local representative who cannot pretend that he doesn't know that his constituents are accusing him of corruption. When the third level is reached, something has to give. The NFL would have to put out a statement, fire the ref, or maybe even host another game to appease their fans; government leaders would be forced to take action to fix the system or respond to support a community; politicians would be forced to publicly apologize, explain themselves, or resign. The tools of interactive media make achieving the third level of shared awareness easier, because, once the online voice is loud enough and public enough, a tipping point is reached where the benefits of responding to a particular message outweigh the risks, and that is when the larger systems of media, business, or government will do so.[34]

## DIGITAL ACTIVISM

In *digital activism*, citizens apply interactive media to collective action by bringing visibility to their concerns, organizing themselves into a movement, raising awareness, building momentum, and sharing information in real time.[35] This creates a perfect storm of characteristics that shifts the balance of power more in the activists' favor.[36] It is not just the larger numbers of people in communities and networks online that empowers them, but also their ability to harness the tools they use to communicate toward a cause, in varying ways.[37] These are detailed in the following sections, along with some of the benefits and limitations of each.

### Microactivism

Recall from the open-source model in chapter 7 that large-scale collaboration done via interactive media tends to result from the combination of a small, core group of people contributing a lot, and a large number of people contributing just a little.[38] Applied to activism, this means that movements benefit from a kind of *microactivism*, in which the sum total of a large number of people participating in small ways can be extremely effective.[39] The majority of people do not have the level of motivation or passion needed to actively work for a cause on a daily basis, yet if they care about it, interactive media allows them to help in small but potentially powerful ways.[40] For example, consider the level of effort, energy, and resources a person expends to share a link to an online petition or fund-raising site on their Facebook page (with, let's just say, three hundred friends) versus standing on a street corner for three hours, trying to get people's attention and explaining over and over again what the cause is and why they should care. The likelihood of someone actually volunteering three hours of their time is much lower than that of them agreeing to share a link.[41] Because interactive media lowers the cost of participating, a lot more less-motivated people can be recruited to do simple and easy tasks that help.[42]

In addition to the ability to recruit more people to help, there are other benefits of interactive media for microactivism. For one, it adds an *exponential* value to the message's reach as it extends through the small world networks encoded by social media.[43] On social media for instance, each individual who is motivated to act (sign, donate, etc.) is given a secondary and equally simple task: to share the link with their own three hundred or so friends, expanding the potential for attention. In addition, the bonding capital within our networks provides a kind of automatic targeting for message campaigns.[44] It is much more likely that, if one person cares about a particular cause, their friends will also care about it.[45] Rather than just reaching strangers who happen to be walking by on a public street at a particular time on a particular day, people sharing activist messages on Facebook reach people they know, within communities likely to share similar concerns.[46] It also creates a space for follow-up discussion and debate with anyone who doesn't share the movement's concerns (see chapter 6 for how to do so productively), which at the very least raises awareness through an ongoing conversation.

On the other hand, the use of interactive media for activism can be a double-edged sword, as it also has the potential to encourage *slacktivism*, which is when people are given the feeling that they are doing something without actively engaging with the causes and actions that they are supporting.[47] Messages on social media tend to be very ego-driven, and people might attach their name to a cause as a form of *virtue signaling*, a mere performance with little dedication to, understanding of, or even concern for, the actual movement they claim to represent.[48] They might identify with a cause in the same way they would with a brand, to jump on a bandwagon, or act as a fan rather than a follower.[49] This can ultimately be problematic for the cause, because when those challenging conversations do come up with those who disagree, slacktivists may misrepresent and even do harm to the movement's intended message. In addition, people engaging in microactivism do not always do their due diligence to seek out the authenticity of movements, are not skilled in activist strategies, and may be inadvertently backing efforts that actually undermine the causes they seek to support.

## Virtual Organizing

Digital activists can also use the tools of interactive media to plan, coordinate, and recruit for their efforts in a relatively short time frame and without ever having to meet in person.[50] Such virtual organizing was exemplified in this chapter's opening story and the flash mob phenomenon in general. The level of effort required and advanced planning needed is significantly decreased when we can organize virtually,[51] and because of this, activist campaigns and efforts can be coordinated by anyone, whether "officially" an activist or not. It was retired lawyer and grandmother Teresa Shook, for example, who created the event on Facebook that started the Women's March on Washington.[52]

Again more in line with the open-source model, anyone and everyone can work to start, bring attention to, coordinate, and lead an effort within a networked movement, and these roles are fluid and interchangeable.[53] The decentralized nature of such movements can serve them well, as they benefit from the flexibility, persistence, and efficiency of small world networks. For instance, the ability for anyone to come up with an idea, propose a strategy, and lead an effort at any time means that these groups' tactics are harder to predict and plan for.[54] When not even the movement's members know what's coming next, it can be difficult for the authorities to quash their actions.[55]

When it comes to on-the-ground events, those that are organized virtually can be especially difficult to predict and plan for.[56] Although group actions may be proposed in public view via social media, the number of people who come, which people will come, and what will happen if and when they do come, remains an unknown until the day of.[57] This can make preparation impossible and participation risky.[58] Because of interactive media, on-the-ground activist efforts today frequently take place simultaneously in multiple locations around the world,[59] and no one wants to be the only one in their town to actually show up. On the other hand, an event that ends up being unexpectedly large or having opposition groups show up in a given location have an increased potential for violence.[60] In the days leading up to an event, the potential activists, the local authorities, opposition groups, and the media are all attempting to extract information indicating what might happen on the day of an event, and usually from the same online sources.[61]

But the horizontal, "leaderless" nature of these virtually organized efforts can also leave a lot of room for infighting, infiltrations, and the muddling of a movement's message.[62] Occupy Wall Street, for example, a movement that took place across 2011 and 2012 and coined the phrase "We are the 99%," was famously panned for its lack of clear goals or outcomes.[63] The Women's March on Washington fell apart after intersectional disagreements emerged about what kinds of women the movement represented.[64] A Black Lives Matter Facebook page organizing a march in Baltimore in 2016 was discovered to be a fake account linked to the Russian government in an effort to divide the American electorate.[65] Hashtags and social media accounts associated with any movement can be used to represent a sentiment, a community, or a series of established activist organizations, and there may be disagreements about when and how they should be used.[66] In addition, violence and hateful conduct can be done in the name of a movement that does not condone it, messaging can go off the rails, and, with no one in charge to tell a movement's members to stop or redirect their efforts, things can get out of control.[67]

## Real-Time Information Sharing

The widespread availability of mobile devices also makes it possible to coordinate large groups of people "on-the-fly."[68] This is as true for us making plans with our friends tonight as it is for hundreds, even thousands, of activists engaging in an on-the-ground campaign. Just as we can send a group text to let everyone know where we are planning to be at any given moment, activists can employ posts, hashtags, and livestreams to coordinate with each other.[69] Such real-time information sharing allows protestors to work together to avoid dangerous areas, form blockades, and circumvent attempts at suppression.[70] Like a flock of birds, they use the mobility of interactive media to call out to one another, project their next moves, and "swarm" in a kind of choreographed formation.[71]

Protestors can also use real-time information sharing to give their own "reports" about what is happening and counter any mischaracterizations of their efforts as portrayed by news organizations or opposition groups.[72] In chapter 6, we saw how citizen-driven news outlets frequently merge with activism; here, we see how activism can also begin to shade into a form of citizen journalism, as they share relevant news, produce "calls to action," and provide live "on-the-ground" coverage of street events.[73] Camera drones have even been employed by protestors to provide bird's-eye views of marches and document activities across wide expanses.[74] Meanwhile, activists' livestreams and hashtags are closely monitored by a movement-oriented "audience" who follows along online.[75] These "watchers" help to share, distribute, and highlight any injustices or significant events taking place as they happen.[76] As this information spreads in real time through the decentralized networks of social media, it becomes very difficult to censor or suppress documentation of overly aggressive tactics of the state,[77] which, when shared, further bolsters the fight against injustice.

In an effort to tip the scales back in their favor, the response of some governments and local authorities around the world has been to simply shut down access to the Internet altogether in regions where there is unrest. In the year 2019 alone, thirty-three countries imposed 213 Internet shutdowns on their citizens, the majority of which were aimed at suppressing protests and dissent.[78] While Internet and cellular shutdowns may be effective in stifling protests (or not[79]), they also hurt the global economy,[80] violate free speech rights,[81] and provide a threat to public safety as people lose the ability to communicate in emergency situations.[82] Yet it is a tactic that has even been used in the United States. In August 2011, a protest that was planned in the Bay Area Rapid Transit (BART) subway system in San Francisco after a homeless man was fatally shot by police was thwarted after underground cell phone service was shut down.[83] It was the local BART system that disabled its own network in the name of public safety,[84] but the move was widely regarded by organizations like the Electronic Frontier Foundation (EFF) and the American Civil Liberties Union (ACLU) as unlawful[85] and a violation of human rights.[86] While it is good news that BART's blatant attempt to restrict speech was not seen as acceptable in the United States, the Internet is a global community, and efforts to restrict access around the world are increasing.[87] In addition, there are subtler ways that Internet access can be thwarted, filtered, or otherwise interfered with, and we need to be vigilant about all such efforts to do so. These issues will be explored in more detail in chapter 12.

An interesting illustrative example of both the positive and negative sides of digital activism can be seen in the user-generated technique known as the social media "blackout." This method was first used on January 18, 2012, in response to the "Stop Online Piracy Act" (SOPA) and "PROTECT IP Act" (PIPA) bills that were being proposed in Congress. Online activists, including many major technology companies, opposed these bills for their over-reach, essentially allowing for the shutdown of any site that a user could potentially employ to engage in piracy. Because this includes nearly every site that allows for user-generated content, an awareness campaign called "Internet Blackout Day" was headed up by Reddit, which major tech sites like Wikipedia, Google, Amazon, and many others joined, showing black homepages with messages about the how the bills would allow for wide-spread online censorship.[88] Similarly, many users of social media supported the effort by replacing their profile pictures with blacked-out images,[89] and got hashtags like #blackoutSOPA trending.[90] This campaign has been widely acknowledged as effective, as the bills were ultimately voted down,[91] and the method has since been used in other efforts looking to demonstrate shared awareness around a cause.[92]

When this same blackout method was applied in support of the George Floyd protests against police violence in 2020, however, it ended up having adverse effects. In response to an effort emerging out of the music indus-try with artists calling for #BlackoutTuesday on June 2nd to acknowledge racism,[93] millions of users again began posting blacked-out squares on sites like Twitter and Instagram, and people were finding their entire feeds dominated by a sea of them.[94] While this was no doubt well-intentioned, designed to demonstrate shared awareness and widespread support for the cause, it was not what was needed at the time. Delivered one week into an on-the-ground campaign that had already successfully achieved visibility and was still underway in multiple cities around the world,[95] protestors found that their efforts were actually undermined by the blackout, as it overtook their hashtags and silenced their own voices on social media, making it more difficult for them to coordinate their campaigns and get their messages out.[96] It was as if their own supporters, not the state, had shut down their access to the network. The key takeaway here is to understand that, although methods of digital activism can be effective, it is not always appropriate to apply them in a one-size-fits-all approach, and users of social media looking to help causes can best help by identifying, following, and taking their cues from those who are most genuinely and closely involved with a cause or movement.[97]

## HACKTIVISM

Another kind of activism that is specific to interactive media is *hacktivism*, which is when people skilled in the application (and hacking) of information technologies and distributed networks utilize those skills for political purposes.[98] Unlike the term "hackers," which could be applied to anyone breaking into a secured database for unlawful reasons, "hacktivists" are working for a cause.[99] They are not averse to breaking the law, but their actions must align with their guiding ethics, which Steven Levy outlined in 1984.[100] Peter Ludlow sums these up as: (1) "information should be free," and (2) "mistrust authority and promote decentralization."[101]

Hacktivists have been around since the very earliest days of computers and the Internet in the 1980s, and these principles are aligned with the characteristics and models of interactive media, which they identified very early on. The idea of "freeing" information reflects the accessible, un-censorable, and empowering nature of networked media, and the distrust of authority and promotion of decentralization goes hand in hand with the horizontal small world network structures that these tools support. Hacktivists view any hierarchical or condensed form of power as illegitimate. Adopting the flattened, open-source ethos of the Internet, they prefer end-to-end networks of communication over authoritative control structures.[102] According to Ludlow, their politics "can't be characterized in terms of left versus right so much as individual versus institution."[103] They also embrace the strength of information networks as reflected in their own activism, refusing to tie their message and efforts in with any one person or leader to be targeted or taken out to destroy their momentum, but rather keeping it distributed throughout the network. As a hacker going by the name "The Mentor" wrote shortly after his arrest in 1986, "you may stop this individual, but you can't stop us all." Two well-known names within hacktivism today, Wikileaks and Anonymous, embrace these ideals while also providing interesting extensions of the more traditional notions of both activism and journalism.

Since it began in 2006, Wikileaks has been responsible for publishing more classified data than has been leaked in all of US history.[104] Two of its biggest leaks in the United States include an unprecedented account of the wars in Afghanistan and Iraq that provided previously unknown details about civilian casualties in 2010,[105] and a database of emails from the Democratic National Committee (DNC) that included those of presidential candidate Hillary Clinton in the months leading up to the 2016 election.[106] Reflecting the first principle of hacktivism to "free" information, Wikileaks' founder, Julian Assange, justified his motives in a 2010 documentary by saying that, "the public has a right to know . . . and the historical record has a right to have, materials of diplomatic, political, ethical, and historical significance. If something is interfering with that process, we will undo it."[107]

While leakers and whistleblowers have traditionally turned to journalists to share their secrets, Wikileaks, which utilizes encryption technology to protect sources so that even Assange cannot decipher their identities,[108] has been the dominant source in recent decades. After a Wikileaks release, which tends to include thousands of records and files, journalists are left to comb through the data looking for information along with the rest of the Wikileaks community, relying on its collective intelligence to highlight and identify the pieces and patterns that reveal something worth reporting on. Perhaps in an attempt to reclaim journalistic authority in this domain, legacy newspaper the *Wall Street Journal* attempted to take a cue from Wikileaks in 2011 and launched a site called *WSJ Safehouse*, their own secure portal that whistleblowers could use to share information with the outlet.[109] But it was quickly noted that, unlike Wikileaks, the site didn't adopt all of the encryption protocols required for maximum security, and even included in the "Terms of Use" that they "reserve the right to disclose any information about you to law enforcement authorities or to a requesting third party, without notice, in order to comply with any applicable laws and/or requests under legal process."[110] For a whistleblower risking their life and livelihood to release information to the public, Wikileaks would appear to be the safer bet. The irony is that it is only the professional journalists and outlets that have shield law protections giving them an exemption from being legally compelled to reveal their sources.[111] Hacktivists have no such protection but little regard for the law, and Assange himself was arrested in April 2019 after spending seven years as a political asylee holed up in an Ecuadorian embassy in London.[112]

While Julian Assange put himself out there as the public face of his organization's hacktivist efforts, the hacktivist collective known as "Anonymous" attempts to evade law enforcement by hiding themselves within a distributed community identity. Like news reporters out of an apocalyptic sci-fi movie, media communications from within the group are uniform in their adoption of a somewhat creepy aesthetic steeped in anonymity, as members wear Guy Fawkes masks to cover their faces[113] and use computerized voiceovers to speak their words.[114] These communications often activate their followers, by calling for campaigns involving collective actions like *"directed denial-of-service" (DDoS) attacks*, the takedown of companies' or institutions' websites and communications systems by overwhelming their servers with automated traffic.[115] Anonymous' reliance on faceless and leaderless efforts reflects the second principle of hacktivism: decentralization. It has, however, also left them vulnerable to infiltration and infighting, creating confusion of its own in their messaging.[116]

Although this infighting ultimately deactivated the network for a time in 2016,[117] it was brought back to life in 2020 by the efforts of an unlikely source: Korean pop (K-pop) music fans. Realizing their potential in numbers as they supported and effectuated causes promoted by their favorite teen idols,[118] K-pop fans actualized in an effort to help George Floyd protestors on the ground. They began utilizing a method that closely resembles Anonymous' directed cyberattacks called *culture jamming*, in which groups direct their efforts at interrupting the communication ability of a company or institution they want to thwart by flooding their media systems with critical, alternative, or unwanted messages.[119] After police precincts around the country began putting out requests for reports of riots, looting, and violence via their police watch apps and social media accounts, the K-pop community began overwhelming the police systems with memes and "fancams" featuring their favorite performers in order to obscure any reported activity of BLM protestors, ultimately shutting down many of the police's reporting systems.[120] When Anonymous saw the K-pop fans' passion and collective power for a cause they also supported, the two groups began coordinating on a series of campaigns targeted at hijacking the opposition's hashtags and engaging in other directed efforts utilizing their large peer-to-peer networks.[121]

There is, of course, a lot of potential for problems within hacktivism. While their efforts may be laudable and their intentions good, they are making themselves the arbiters of what should and should not be allowed in public communication. Information released by Wikileaks reaches not only citizens who have a right to know, but also terrorists and other enemies that can use classified information against troops on the ground. Similarly, taking down emergency communication systems can put citizens in danger, and silencing the opposition can result in forcing everyone to live in a mob-ruled echo chamber. The same decentralized environment that empowers groups and networks to speak out can promote a kind of remarginalization of those voices existing outside of the new majority, and feed the dangerous groupthink frenzies that have resulted in *cancel culture*, where people are called out for perceived (and sometimes long-ago) bad behavior and then viciously attacked and shamed by large groups via social media in an effort to remove them from public prominence.[122] Some bad actors have even been involved in the targeting of opponents by finding and then publishing their names and addresses, in some cases causing private citizens to lose their jobs and putting them in real physical danger[123] (more on this in chapter 13). So, although hacktivist campaigns mostly involve efforts that are delivered and arranged entirely through virtual means, what happens online does not always stay online, and intended and unintended consequences can have serious impacts on the lives of real people.

## CONCLUSION

In sum, activism today is different. It has a truly unique character and flavor that largely derives from the application of interactive media to collective action. In fact, the "open-source" version of collective action is so different in nature that Bennett and Segerberg have proposed that it instead be called *connective action*.[124] The more organic, grassroots, and networked nature of digital activism means that, as in other arenas we have looked at, it is more spontaneous, ad hoc, unpredictable, and uncontrollable than traditional activist movements.[125] When applied to collaborative efforts that are as political and significant as collective action, the positive and negative implications of these models are serious. Interactive media can allow movements to be more effective, persistent, and empowered, but it also opens them up to the dangers of groupthink, misrepresentation, and infiltration. Mob rule has the potential to win the day over public safety, protected and private information can be released, and microactivist campaigns can effectively silence authentic voices, even those they support, and drown out dialogue. As the balance of power tips in the favor of activist networks, we must be wary of using that empowerment to impose a new authority or cause unnecessary harm.

The good news is that re-balancing corrections can also be found within the typical patterns of small world networks, the ever-questioning knowledge culture, and the self-healing open-source model. Authentic movements can thrive if their authenticity is preserved among their networks. Heated as it may sometimes get, in the limitless spaces of interactive media, activists can find ways to be empowered while also allowing others to have a voice, work to point out and document injustices while also minding people's safety, and embrace the diverse polyvocality of the interconnected masses to come up with better solutions. A heightened awareness of these challenges and pitfalls will help to ensure that, as we use these tools to engage in collective action and digital activism, we are helping more than we are hurting, empowering more than marginalizing, and giving a voice to more than silencing others, as we highlight, document, and fight against the injustices of the world.

## NOTES

1. Blair, "A Song Called 'Quiet.'"
2. Almaharel, "#IcantKeepQuiet #Anthem."
3. Blair, "A Song Called 'Quiet.'"
4. Almaharel, "#IcantKeepQuiet #Anthem in the Women's March on Washington," January 22, 2017, Video, 2:50, https://youtu.be/zLvIw8J8sWE; Hilton, "A Flash Mob Choir."
5. Almaharel (video description).
6. Chandler, "MILCK."
7. Couldry and Hepp, *The Mediated Construction*, 172; Shirky, *Here Comes Everybody*, 165.
8. Chiarito, "This Woman's Unplanned Anthem."
9. Blair, "A Song Called 'Quiet.'"
10. Davis, "Maui Woman."
11. Blair, "A Song Called 'Quiet.'"
12. Chiarito, "This Woman's Unplanned Anthem."
13. Blair, "A Song Called 'Quiet.'"
14. Chiarito, "This Woman's Unplanned Anthem."
15. Global Platform Ghana, "I can't keep quiet with Dagbanli," Facebook Video, March 7, 2017, https://www.facebook.com/globalplatformghana/videos/763478933818299/.
16. Church of Stonewall, "Church of Stonewall 'Quiet' Flashmob Stockholm Central Station 8 March 2017," March 9, 2017, Video, 6:47, https://youtu.be/yyx4Lpz_vjg.
17. eva-maria danko-bodenstein, "#icantkeepquiet Vienna," March 28, 2017, Video, 4:30, https://youtu.be/C_tEVj8MpDY.
18. Eric Faw, "Flash Mob Protest—MILCK's (I can't be) Quiet, Richmond, VA #ICANTKEEPQUIET," April 8, 2017, Video, 5:39, https://youtu.be/bi6aUbgqExM.
19. Aurora Chorus, "Aurora Chorus of Portland, OR performs 'Quiet,'" May 11, 2018, Video, 3:16, https://youtu.be/iba6rHYJVv0.
20. Choir! Choir! Choir! "MILCK + Choir! Of 1300 Can't Keep Quiet!" February 17, 2017, Video, 6:15, https://youtu.be/1cc_neVdjb4.
21. Fleshman, "Got MILCK?"
22. Icantkeepquiet.org, "#ICan'tKeepQuietFund," accessed December 27, 2020, https://icantkeepquiet.org/fund.
23. MILCK, "MILCK—Quiet (Official Video)," November 3, 2017, Video, 3:34, https://youtu.be/Tl_Qfj8780M.
24. Hilton, "A Flash Mob Choir."
25. Lapowski, "The Year Women Reclaimed."
26. Lapowski.

27. Canan and Sousa-Poza, "Pragmatic Idealism."

28. Shirky, *Here Comes Everybody*, 163.

29. Shirky, 163.

30. Shirky, 163.

31. Shirky, 163–64.

32. Keyes, *The Hundredth Monkey*, 17–18.

33. Innes and Gruber, "Planning Styles in Conflict," 182.

34. Shirky, *Here Comes Everybody*, 168–69.

35. Baruh and Watson, "Social Media Use During," 208.

36. Jemielniak and Przegalinska, *Collaborative Society*, 157–58; Shirky, *Here Comes Everybody*, 164.

37. Castells, *Networks of Outrage and Hope*.

38. Shirky, *Here Comes Everybody*, 181.

39. Barberá, "The Critical Periphery"; Shirky, 181–82.

40. Shirky, 181–82.

41. Vitak et al., "It's Complicated," 112.

42. Bennet and Segerberg, "The Logic of Connective," 748; Shirky, *Here Comes Everybody*, 182.

43. Kaplan and Haenlein, "Two Hearts," 255.

44. Bennet and Segerberg, "The Logic of Connective," 751.

45. Shirky, *Here Comes Everybody*, 221.

46. Crossley and Diani, "Networks and Fields," 152–53.

47. Jemielniak and Przegalinska, *Collaborative Society*, 98; Morozov, *The Net Delusion*, 191.

48. Orlitzky, Marc, "Virtue Signaling," 178.

49. Morozov, *The Net Delusion*, 202.

50. Shirky, *Here Comes Everybody*, 171.

51. Karpf, "Online Political Mobilization," 15.

52. Kearny, "Hawaii Grandma's Plea."

53. Carty, *Social Movements*, 183; Western, "Autonomist Leadership."

54. Keating, "The George Floyd Protests."

55. Castells, *Networks of Outrage and Hope*, 222; Lohmann, "The Dynamics of," 69; The Mentor, "The Conscience of a Hacker."

56. Shirky, *Here Comes Everybody*, 169.

57. Shirky, 169.

58. Lohmann, "The Dynamics of"; Shirky, *Here Comes Everybody*, 169.

59. Almeida and Lichbach, "To the Internet," 252; Castells, *Networks of Outrage and Hope*, 223.

60. Lohmann, "The Dynamics of."

61. Thorburn, "Social Media, Subjectivity," 58.

62. Ganz and McKenna, "Bringing Leadership Back In," 189; Gerbaudo, "Digital Vanguards," 194; Western, "Autonomist Leadership," 679.

63. Rushkoff, "Think Occupy Wall St."

64. Kelly, "Founder of the Women's March."

65. O'Sullivan and Byers, "Fake Black Activist Accounts."

66. Keating, "The George Floyd Protests."

67. Keating.

68. Rainie & Wellman, *Networked*, 99.

69. Rheingold, *Smart Mobs*, 157–58, Shirky, *Here Comes Everybody*, 174.

70. Neumayer and Stald, "The Mobile Phone," 123.

71. Rheingold, *Smart Mobs*, 162.

72. Thorburn, "Social Media, Subjectivity," 56; Shirky, *Here Comes Everybody*, 186–87.

73. Baruh and Watson, "Social Media Use During," 205–06; "Neumayer, "Nationalist and Anti-Fascist," 305.

74. Choi-Fitzpatrick, "Drones for Good," 24–25.

75. Thorburn, "Social Media, Subjectivity," 56–57.

76. Baruh and Watson, "Social Media Use During," 208; Castells, *Networks of Outrage and Hope*, 223.

77. Thorburn, "Social Media, Subjectivity," 57; Shirky, *Here Comes Everybody*, 169, 171.

78. #KeepItOn, "Targeted, Cut Off, and Left in the Dark: The #KeepItOn Report on Internet Shutdowns in 2019," AccessNow, accessed December 27, 2020, https://www.accessnow.org/keepiton/.

79. Gerbaudo, "The 'Kill Switch.'"

80. Griffiths, "Internet Shutdowns Cost."

81. Higgins, "BART's Cell Phone Shutdown."

82. Galperin, "Want Public Safety?"

83. Wolchover, "How Did BART Kill."

84. Wolchover.

85. Higgins, "BART's Cell Phone Shutdown."

86. Arulanantham, "Free Speech and BART."

87. #KeepItOn, "Targeted, Cut Off."

88. Wortham, "Political Coming of Age."

89. Finn, "#BlackoutSOPA."

90. Chansanchai, "2.4 Million SOPA Tweets."

91. Engleman, "Google Protest."

92. Kleinman, "'The Day We Fight Back'"; Watercutter, "Instagram Users."

93. Seemayer, "Music Industry Calls."

94. Ho, "Social Media 'Blackout.'"

95. Taylor, "George Floyd Protests."

96. Ho, "Social Media 'Blackout.'"

97. Bakare and Davies, "Blackout Tuesday"; Ho, "Social Media 'Blackout.'"

98. Ludlow, "Wikileaks and Hacktivist Culture," 25.

99. Jemielniak and Przegalinska, *Collaborative Society*, 100.

100. Levy, *Hackers*.

101. Ludlow, "Wikileaks and Hacktivist Culture," 25.

102. Coleman, *Coding Freedom*, 136.

103. Ludlow, "Wikileaks and Hacktivist Culture," 26.

104. Greenberg, "Wikileaks Reveals."

105. *New York Times*, "The War Logs."

106. BBC, "18 Revelations from Wikileaks."

107. *WikiRebels*, directed by Jesper Huor and Bosse Lindquist, released 2010, Svergies Television, 57:25.

108. Burns and Somaiya, "Confidential Swedish Police Report."

109. Kessler, "*Wall Street Journal* Launches."

110. Greenberg, "Full of Holes."

111. Hodgson Russ Media Law, "Assange Indictment."

112. BBC, "Julian Assange."

113. Waites, "V for Vendetta Masks."

114. KCRA News, "Anonymous video threatens cyber-attack on Sacramento," January 7, 2016, Video, 1:53, https://youtu.be/m_3axJSK-fM.

115. Mansfield Devine, "Hacktivism."

116. Gilbert, "Anonymous Declared War."

117. Glibert.

118. Ohlheiser, "How K-Pop Fans."

119. Couldry and Hepp, *The Mediated Construction*, 88; Wells and Li, "How Tik-Tok Users."

120. Tiffany, "Why K-Pop Fans."

121. Kim, "K-Pop Fans, Maestros."

122. Bouvier, "Racist Call-Outs."

123. Douglas, "Doxing."

124. Berger and Segerberg, "Logic of Connective Action."

125. Castells, *Networks of Outrage*, 26.

# Chapter 9

# Convergence Consumerism

## INTRODUCTION: SIGNATURE SNACK

When thinking of high fashion, which brands come to mind? Givenchy? Prada? Dolce & Gabbana? How about . . . Cheetos? Likely not. And yet, during New York's Fashion Week in 2019, as Vice reporter Bettina Makalintal put it, "Cheetos. Fashion. Show. Those words, in that order, as inexplicable as it may seem."[1] Hosting an event called "The House of Flamin' Haute," the brand sent nearly two dozen Cheetos-inspired looks down the runway, many of which were designed by popular fashion *social media influencers*,[2] or people who have a significant enough online following to guide product trends and consumer purchases.[3] Cheetos' runway show was followed by a stage performance of rapper Saweetie, donned in her own "Flamin' Hot" look, and a "style bar" where people could get beauty treatments like Cheetle-dusted "caught snacking" nails, Cheetah tail braids, and applications of bright orange eyeshadow and lipstick.[4] They also served hors d'oeuvres and drinks incorporating Cheetos ingredients.[5] "Many, many Instagram videos were being filmed,"[6] and the dazzling spectacle was "a made-for-the-internet activation par excellence."[7] How did this come to be, one might ask, and . . . why? Over the past several years, the Cheetos brand has taken a winding trip through the media convergence ecosystem, copiloted by the active audience and their own marketing department, leading them to this place.

Although they have been around for over seven decades,[8] Cheetos, especially the "Flamin' Hot" variety, has gained attention in recent years as a cult favorite.[9] A form of junk food that is deliciously addictive yet has virtually no nutritional value, it fits well into the self-deprecating and guilty-pleasure confessional style of humor that is so often displayed on social media,[10] an easy target for its somewhat comic universality and meme-able relatability.[11] For instance, a social media challenge involving taking a bath in Hot Cheetos that emerged in 2013 persists to this day.[12] A Cheeto shaped like Harambe, the gorilla whose killing was the subject of much Internet outrage in 2016, sold for $100,000 on eBay.[13] Popular YouTuber "Marlin," who calls himself "The King of Hot Cheeto DIYs,"[14] has made a Hot Cheetos Turkey,[15] Hot Cheeto Bacon Corn Dogs,[16] and Hot Cheeto Waffles.[17] Another YouTuber, "grav3yardgirl," posted a video using Cheetos to curl her hair, to surprisingly amazing results.[18] Instagrammer "skelotim" posted a makeup look "inspired by a hot Cheetos bag,"[19] as have many others in response to the "lookin' like a snack" makeup challenge.[20] And that's just the tip of the orange-colored iceberg. As Cait Munro of *Urban Daddy* wrote in 2018, "we are truly living in the age of the Flamin' Hot Cheeto."[21]

Of course, professionals across a variety of industries have incorporated Cheetos' popularity into their own products as well, bringing them yet more attention. Burger King offered Mac n' Cheese–filled Cheetos for a limited time,[22] and Kentucky Fried Chicken (KFC) came out with a "Cheetos sandwich."[23] Hot Cheetos were referenced in the first episode of the FX series *Atlanta,*[24] and a film featuring the story of Richard Montañez, the man who created the "Flamin' Hot" flavor, is reportedly in the works.[25] Chromat clothing designer Becca McCharen-Tran sent Cheetos-eating models down the runway in 2018,[26] and hairstylist Helena Palacio created a Hot Cheetos inspired colormelt that same year.[27] All of this follows an ongoing trend of popular reality competition shows like *Project Runway* and *America's Next Top Model* partnering with brands to sponsor contestant challenges using their product as a way of selling advertising.[28]

Although the Cheetos brand may not approve of all of the ways that their product has been used in the media convergence ecosystem, this level of uninitiated (and largely unpaid for) advertising is a marketer's dream. Given these trends, the "House of Flamin' Haute" runway show begins to look less inexplicable and more inevitable. With all of this attention, why wouldn't Cheetos get in on the fun? Director of marketing Brandi Ray said of this fashion venture beyond their salty-snack milieu, "we are so excited to continue to celebrate our fans and their creativity."[29] And this was not the first time they have done so. In 2017, they partnered with the crowdfunded fashion retailer Betabrand (think "open-source" clothing design) to create a spring line of products that made Cheetos-eating easier.[30] After the Harambe Cheeto, they teamed up with *Ripley's Believe It or Not* to install a "Cheetos Museum," collecting the most recognizably shaped Cheetos through a hashtag contest with fans.[31] And no doubt they were involved in at least some of the professional industry incorporations noted above. So, how much of Cheetos' success can be credited to their marketing department and how much to their grassroots Internet stardom? While this is not fully quantifiable, there is one thing that can be said for sure: As the top-selling snack for the last three years running,[32] this brand has found a way to ride the interactive media rainbow all the way to the pot of Flamin' Hot gold.

## THE TWENTY-FIRST-CENTURY CONSUMER

All of the features of interactive media that have given more visibility and influence to amateurs, citizens, and activists have done so for consumers as well. The twenty-first-century consumer no longer just shops; they traverse the landscape of the media convergence ecosystem to be actively involved with brands, franchises, and companies.[33] The prosuming audience simultaneously produces while consuming, sharing their consumerism via interactive media, deriving inspiration from brands, providing them with feedback, and making them their own.[34] As each product and service is entered into a public conversation, customers and potential customers also actively seek out and access user-generated reviews, criticisms, suggestions, promotions, and ratings.[35] People are thus more informed about products and services, engaging with them on their own terms.[36] Finally, consumers have become more demanding, as they now expect to have more control over their products, tailoring them to their preferences, speaking back to companies, and getting "what they want when they want it."[37]

Meanwhile, the commercial audience for products has grown increasingly *segmented* while at the same time becoming more globalized. Long gone are the days of "mass markets," where brands could reach huge swaths of the nation's population in a matter of moments by purchasing a single "one-to-many" advertisement on one of three broadcast networks.[38] Instead, consumers today access an endless array of niche channels and outlets in ways that are "on-demand" and less predictable,[39] and spend more of their mediated time amidst the networked depths of many-to-many communication. Meanwhile, any marketing done online has the potential to reach consumers across cultures, countries, and time zones, making it more challenging to market products in ways that will be appropriate, appealing, and relevant to all who may see it.[40]

In other words, the twenty-first-century consumer has markedly different needs, demands, behaviors, and access points, and is a moving and constantly evolving target.[41] This creates new challenges for advertisers, marketers, and public relations professionals, as they have found the promotion of their brands to be an exceedingly complex and demanding enterprise.[42] Less top-down and more bottom-up, less straightforward and more collaborative, less by-the-book and more fluid, less "mass" and more networked, navigating the waters of convergence consumerism can be a wild, erratic, and frequently risky ride for anyone trying to sell a product or service.

## CONVERGENCE MARKETING STRATEGIES

Rather than attempt to retrofit the old marketing models, many companies have begun to adopt new strategies that aim to capitalize on the interactive media landscape and all that it offers. These are largely focused on harnessing and appeasing a group of consumers known as the *loyals*, or those who have a clear dedication to, and passion for, a particular product or brand.[43] Often, the most hard-core, committed, and outspoken loyals, called *inspirational consumers*, can be key to spreading brand awareness as they extol a product's virtues, "inspiring" others in their network to love and enjoy it as much as they do.[44] This consumer dedication has proven to be especially valuable in the media convergence ecosystem, where the endorsement of communities, collectives, and networks is on par with that of celebrities and experts.[45] Loyals are more attentive to brand-related messages and information, more likely to buy and display brand-related products, and more effective than blanket advertising at bringing in new customers.[46] Like the microactivists sharing a message they believe in with their friends on social media, loyals who believe in their brands are more likely to have an effect on their reputations within their own personal networks.

### Brand Community Engagement

Because of their passion around a brand, loyals tend to use interactive media to gather in *brand communities* online. These communities are made up of people who bond over their love of a particular brand or product, and they provide a useful and accessible entry point into a franchise's consumer base.[47] Brand communities can form around nearly any product we can think of, and they are easy to collectively create and find, as the brand's unique trademarked name serves as an automatic hashtag and keyword to utilize and search on social media, forums, wikis, or other sites employing user-generated content and groups. As with any community that forms online, members of brand communities can develop a high degree of group identification, even developing their own communicative norms, lingo, activities, and events surrounding their beloved brands, which further reinforces their brand loyalty.[48]

As the Cheetos example opening this chapter demonstrates, an active brand community is the holy grail of marketing today, and can benefit brands in multiple ways. The collective intelligence of these communities serves as free market research, a source of creative inspiration, and a way to collect feedback about how to improve on both products and advertising campaigns.[49] Companies can also release sneak peeks to these communities and their influencers, who serve as "connectors" within their networks, as a way of generating grassroots buzz and preempting potential issues.[50] Some brands make a point of actively, openly, and transparently attending and responding to their brand community and inspirational consumers, embracing their feedback as a form of creative labor in *"participatory branding."*[51] This allows them to cocreate value for their brand with their consumers[52] and build up social capital, allowing them to more easily "ride out" any missteps or public relations crises that may arise.[53]

If a company does not see active communities organically forming around a particular product, their instinct may be to try to cultivate one themselves. While it certainly makes sense for brands to provide spaces and ways for people to gather in brand communities via their official social media accounts and websites, this alone does not guarantee that one will form.[54] In fact, a lack of active consumer engagement online may be an indication that the brand is missing a core base of loyals to begin with, an important piece of the puzzle in today's commercial enterprise.[55] This likely has more to do with the quality and reputation of the brand than it does any particular tools or content that they happen to make available, and trying to artificially impose a brand community without first addressing these core issues can easily backfire.[56]

## Emotional Advertising

Researchers have found that loyals' willingness to be so attentive to their favorite products is largely driven by emotion.[57] Thus what Jenkins terms *affective economics*, which focuses on fostering emotional connections in order to mold consumer desires and spark passions around a brand, has been the focus of marketers in recent decades.[58] This means more than just creating commercials that make us laugh or pull on our heartstrings; it is about *brand relatability*, making the brand something that people can identify with, as people.[59] Marketers focus on giving the brand a personality, aligning it with positive human characteristics like "funny," "creative," or "exciting," to elicit feelings that mimic those we might experience when desiring to get to know someone better.[60] Many have even begun using official brand social media accounts to express a more personal voice, with posts sounding more like they came from a friend than a company, and generating thousands of likes and shares.[61]

In 2006, Kevin Roberts of the advertising firm Saatchi & Saatchi coined the term *lovemark* to describe those companies that are seen as "more than" a brand, both highly loved and highly respected by their customers.[62] Apple (especially in the Steve Jobs era) is widely cited as the epitome of a lovemark, seen as innovative, cool, young, and fresh, and garnering a following of consumers so loyal that they would camp outside stores overnight just to be first to get the latest product releases.[63] A lovemark is something that goes "beyond" a brand (respected, but not loved), a fad (well-loved, but not respected), or a product (neither well-loved nor respected).[64] See the lovemarks matrix in figure 9.1 below.

Loyals find meaning in their lovemarks, relate to them, and see them as a part of who they are.[65] They proudly display logos, mascots, and slogans on social media profiles, clothing, and other personal items[66]; some even permanently "brand" their own bodies with tattoos of corporate trademarks.[67]

As noted previously, twenty-first-century consumers want to be more actively involved in the products they consume, and giving consumers an opportunity to personalize a brand's campaigns, products, and offerings allows advertisers to feed in to those desires while also supporting their own marketing goals.[68] In an effort to tap in to consumer "love," brands will often ask consumers to share their own stories, memories, testimonials, or creative uses of their product, make their own creations and share them with others, or customize the product to their own preferences.[69] When Cheetos held their #CheetosMuseum contest, for instance, they were getting consumers to personally participate in the product while also sharing their love for Cheetos with others on social media. When they spray-painted cheetah spots on people's hair or gave them Chester "pawlish" nail treatments at their fashion show style bar,[70] people were literally wearing the product for anyone to see, both in person and in amplified ways when sharing the images online. In

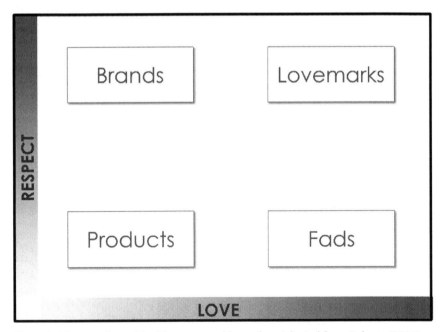

**Figure 9.1 Lovemarks matrix.** *Figure created by author. Adapted from Roberts (2004).*

addition to making the brand personal, such efforts make Cheetos look like a "fun" brand, one that's in on the joke and takes it good-naturedly, as opposed to one that simply uses social media to put out information "about weekly promotions and new products and services in an innocuous tone."[71]

Many of these convergence marketing strategies extend beyond just messages, and are incorporated into the products themselves, especially in the realm of media and technology.[72] For example, interactive assistants like Siri, Google Echo, and Amazon Alexa give their consumers an actual personalized voice to relate to and interact with. Smartphones, computers, televisions, and other devices, along with websites like Netflix, Amazon, and most social media, let users customize their own preferences and/or make tailored recommendations based on their usage data. *Interactive television* emerged when reality shows like *The Voice* and *America's Got Talent* let viewers vote for their favorite contestants to keep them on the show.[73] Now companies have begun creating interactive series like *Black Mirror: Bandersnatch* and *Minecraft: Story Mode* that allow viewers to choose plot points and change the direction of the narrative according to their preferences.[74] Video games and massively multiplayer online (MMO) games give people the ability to create and style their own avatars, and sometimes build houses, cities, and even entire worlds of their own making. These design features have been shown not only to be effective at keeping people coming back to these products again and again, but in fact, they feed right into the addictive tendencies of human psychology.[75]

While the personalization methods of brands help to address the "love" side of lovemarks, emotional advertising is also used to earn respect through social messaging.[76] A brand that stands for something is a brand we can believe in. Thus, another strategy that has emerged in recent years, known as *brand activism*, involves brands focusing on popular social justice issues.[77] A famous example was Nike's ad campaign featuring Colin Kaepernick, the NFL quarterback who was fired after leading a player protest of kneeling during the national anthem in support of the Black Lives Matter movement.[78] Kaepernick himself tweeted the ad, which showed a black-and-white close-up of his face and read, "Believe in something, even if it means sacrificing everything. #JustDoIt."[79] While stepping into the realm of activism can be controversial and risky for brands, it can also pay off, as it did for Nike, who, despite some boycotting backlash, boasted a 31 percent increase in sales after the campaign.[80] However, corporate executives capitalizing on messages of social justice for the purpose of selling products is bound to make a lot of people uneasy, and, like microactivism, if uninformed can be problematic for those within an authentic movement.[81]

### Experiential Marketing

Another way to acquire loyals and tap in to emotion is to give consumers an experience that leaves them with a lasting impression.[82] As Steve Olenski put it in *Forbes* magazine, "most people go out of their way to avoid commercials, yet most will also go out of their way for a new experience."[83] *Experiential marketing* is when brands market to their consumers in ways that are interactive, memorable, and participatory, engaging people through their senses, cognitions, and/or other abilities and typically employing multiple modalities.[84] It could include everything from giving fans an interactive participatory billboard in New York's Times Square[85] to creating a months-long *alternate reality game*, requiring the collective intelligence of large communities to work together to uncover, decode, or unlock a series of brand-related *easter eggs* ("extra features" hidden within media)[86] that traverse interactive, virtual, and real-world spaces and objects.[87] Experiential marketing also includes the hosting or sponsoring of real-world events such as Cheetos' "House of Flamin' Haute."[88]

A type of experiential marketing involving *immersive entertainment* utilizes the construction of permanent or temporary theme park–like attractions and real-world installations that people are invited to enter into, in order to participate in highly visual, sensory, interactive, and sometimes virtual or augmented reality experiences[89] (Universal's *Wizarding World of Harry Potter* is one famous example). Perhaps unsurprisingly, entertainment products like films, television shows, and video games were among the first to utilize this method of marketing, inspired by their fans' near-obsessive level of engagement with their products.[90] Loyals of such franchises desire to enter into the worlds that have so captivated them on the screen, and immersive entertainment is one way to give that to them.[91] It is within this environment that San Diego's annual Comic Convention (Comic-Con) went from a fringe event attended by a few hundred social outcasts to a major industry marketing venue drawing hundreds of thousands of people.[92] Like Comic-Con, other annual entertainment industry events, such as the Sundance and Tribeca Film Festivals,[93] the South by Southwest (SXSW) Conference & Festivals,[94] and the Coachella Valley Music and Arts Festival,[95] have begun offering a variety of sponsored immersive entertainment experiences that cater to the fans and generate a lot of buzz online.[96]

While most of these sponsored experiences and immersive installations tend to look more like attractions than ads, those within the video game industry have begun to look more like sports. The category of *e-Sports*, in which video game players compete at live events for cash prizes, has begun to be recognized as a legitimate sport[97] and is reportedly going to be included in the 2024 Summer Olympics.[98] In fact, with the level of attention and profits e-Sports has generated through both the live events and their online stream-ing audience, it is beginning to be recognized as an industry in and of itself.[99]

## Transmedia Franchises

With so many ways to reach the twenty-first-century consumer, compa-nies have begun to morph into what Henry Jenkins calls *transmedia fran-chises*.[100] This means ensuring that a product's marketing spans across media, with the main goal of being as "everywhere" as possible.[101] This includes pro-viding multiple entry points into a brand throughout the media convergence ecosystem by tailoring campaigns to various interactive platforms,[102] such as official social media accounts, apps, texts, and others, and providing content that is dynamic (updated and added to on a regular basis); on-demand (free, customizable, downloadable); and participatory (openly seeking consumers' insights and feedback). It can also be aided with *brand extension* through the sponsoring of and partnership with other media outlets and brands.[103] These other outlets and brands do not even need to be relevant to the product itself,[104] such as when Cheetos partnered with Saweetie to have her perform at their fashion show; it is simply a way of associating the brand with good feelings, accessing other brands' loyals, and keeping the name on people's minds.[105] *Product placement*, a form of brand extension in which advertisers pay for products to be featured within the content of another media product like a film, TV show, or video game, has also been increasingly used as a way of getting around consumers' interactive ability to skip over ad and commercials.[106]

*Transmedia storytelling*, in which a narrative plot is designed to be revealed across media forms and formats,[107] is another strategy commonly employed by a transmedia franchise. It can be seen in any advertising campaign that involves a cross-platform narrative component (where a televised ad invites us to visit a brand website to see "what happens next," for example).[108] While transmedia storytelling relies on and influences consumers' ability to access and seek out content across a variety of formats and devices, it also extends to influence the way that the stories are told. For example, recent decades have seen television series with increasingly serialized narrative arcs span-ning seasons rather than episodes, relying on cliffhangers, and creating a more immersive and binge-watchable experience.[109] Plots have become more mysterious, disjointed, and puzzle-like, "designed to be discussed, dissected, debated, predicted, and critiqued" by brand communities in the time between episodes or seasons.[110] At the same time, this trend can be seen in the broader movie "universes" spanning several films with interchanging characters, such as in the *Marvel Comics* and *Star Wars* franchises, which have become increasingly popular in recent years.[111] Narrative media of all stripes today offer plenty of supplementary content beyond the main product that expands their story universes, providing "extra" plotlines and details for the more hard-core fans to find, discuss, and curate via interactive media, as in the experiential marketing strategies discussed earlier.[112]

## CHALLENGES AND PITFALLS

While all of these marketing techniques (and no doubt yet more to emerge) can be very effective at getting the already actively involved audience of one's product to become even more engaged, intentionally opening up one's franchise or brand to the more participatory and public nature of convergence consumerism is not without its challenges. Fostering brand participation gives loyals, inspirational consumers, and brand communities a sense of ownership over their lovemarks,[113] and this can be a double-edged sword for marketers. Sanctioning consumer participation can leave brands vulnerable to losing control of their messaging,[114] yet companies that attempt to exert too much control will also be criticized for a lack of receptiveness.[115] Meanwhile, encouraging too much consumer involvement can be perceived as taking advantage of loyals and will likewise be received negatively.[116] The biggest challenge of convergence marketing is to stay within the middle lane of consumer engagement, without veering off into either consumer estrangement or consumer enragement.

The heightened scrutiny that brands experience today includes that which emerges from their core consumer base. Loyals are so invested that they begin to feel a sense of personal responsibility for maintaining a product's expected quality, and inspirational consumers will be just as outspoken about any perceived failure of the brand as they are about its virtues.[117] Similarly, products that have achieved lovemark status have higher expectations to live up to.[118] Remember, lovemarks are loved, but they also need to be respected in order to maintain their high status.[119] If they do something wrong or out of step with expectations, they risk losing that respect.[120] Since brand communities already have the group organization tools and structures available to them via interactive media, they can easily turn on a company in collective action.[121] Recall the *Game of Thrones* fans in the introduction to chapter 5, who were so upset about the final season that they started a petition calling on HBO for a do-over, and then worked to rewrite the season themselves.[122] Transparency, authenticity, and listening to consumers' concerns and feedback, in addition to admitting when mistakes were made, can go a long way toward earning consumers' trust.[123]

In addition, loyals are so tuned in to the brand that even its advertising and marketing campaigns become subjects up for discussion.[124] Consumers' identification with their lovemarks means that it's not business, it's personal, and overly commodifying their relationship with the brand can send the message that brands don't care. So, it is important that convergence marketing strategies guard against going too far and exploiting their brand community, as this will be recognized and brought to public attention as well.[125] For instance, industry incorporations have been accused of ripping off fans' ideas,[126] brands have been criticized for attempting to exploit hashtag trends[127] and memes,[128] and both companies and influencers have been skewered for having undisclosed partnerships with one another.[129] Transmedia franchising can go sour, too, when the attempt to "be everywhere" is perceived as overkill by consumers.[130] Targeted advertising on social media, for instance, can be viewed as "creepy,"[131] and product placements that are too obvious, don't make sense, or occur too often will receive consumer backlash when they are pointed out online.[132]

In the knowledge culture that questions everything, any company engaging in brand activism is also bound to be met with cynicism and critique.[133] For instance, the parent company Unilever was harshly criticized online for the hypocrisy of encouraging body-positive messaging in its Dove "real beauty" campaign but objectifying women in its commercials for Axe Body Spray.[134] Similarly, after Gillette's advertisement critiquing the culture of "toxic masculinity" aired, people began circulating images of the "Gillette girls" dressed in skintight blue bodysuits with the company's name emblazoned on their behinds.[135] A company embarking on social messaging can guard against these types of errors, but in order to do so, the social messaging effort needs to be authentic.[136] Three ways to ensure that this is the case are to: (1) take care that the campaign's social message is aligned with the brand's values, history, and consumer base; (2) if it isn't, openly address that publicly first, acknowledging any mistakes that were made, and meaningfully righting any wrongs that need to be corrected; and (3) allow the campaign to be directed by, and in partnership with, individuals who are genuinely involved with the movement or cause it supports.[137] If a brand is going to talk the talk of social messaging, they had better also be willing and able to walk the walk.

Finally, any time a brand actively allows or encourages consumer participation via interactive media, there is a chance it could be used against them in a purposeful sabotage effort. One infamous example is when McDonald's employed the hashtag #McDstories and it took off as people shared their worst experiences with the franchise's food.[138] Brands can avoid this to a degree by being aware of and addressing core product-quality issues before they open themselves up to participatory campaigns.[139] But even just the mere fact of having official accounts on social media can leave brands open to this kind of brand attack, as Cheerios learned when its Facebook page was culture-jammed by food activists criticizing the company for using genetically modified organisms (GMOs) in its ingredients.[140] Commendably, Cheerios' parent company, General Mills, did respond by subsequently removing GMOs from all of their cereals, and, though they did not acknowledge these activists as the reason for doing so,[141] being open and receptive to criticism, rather than going on the defensive or completely ignoring the issue, is the more effective and responsible strategy.

## CONCLUSION

In sum, marketing has become a much more collaborative, "co-creative" process between brand and consumer, with both good and bad outcomes for both. It is good to see consumers having more of a voice and more access to one another to be better informed about products. It is also good to see brands being more responsive to consumers' concerns, suggestions, and feedback. But as marketing invades more and more of our everyday spaces in an effort to reach us, the omnipresence of commercialism is continuously increasing in a culture that was already well dominated by it. The more time we spend with our devices, the more influence they have over us, which leaves us, as human beings, more subject to manipulation. While it is good that knowledge-culture-fueled consumers will recognize and criticize marketing that goes too far, unfortunately there are also many invisible methods that we don't see, as interactive media sites work with companies to exploit our usage data (more on this in chapters 12 and 13). For brands, they face more risk in the media convergence ecosystem than they did in the pre-1990s era, but for the most part they are adapting in ways that are creative and advantageous for their brand promotion and marketing goals. Together, consumers and brands get to have fun with, and be inspired by, one another, and the relationship is usually pretty harmonious. But even when it's not, the heightened degree of volatility, criticism, and vulnerability that companies have to deal with in this environment will keep them from going too far and force them to be tuned in to their consumers' needs. In the end, that's a good thing, so a good bit of advice, both for consumers and for brands, would be to keep vigilant, keep watching, and keep 'em on their toes.

## NOTES

1. Makalintal, "Inside the Dazzling."
2. Frito-Lay, "Orange-Dusted Fingerprints."
3. De Vierman et al., "Marketing through Instagram Influencers," 798.
4. The Marketing Arm, "House of Flamin' Haute."

5. Makalintal, "Inside the Dazzling."

6. Makalintal.

7. Hore-Thorburn, "Cheetos Brings."

8. Timeline Maker, "The History of Cheetos Timeline," May 7, 2014, https://www.timelinemaker.com/blog/featured-timeline/history-of-cheetos-timeline/.

9. Nunez, "12 Flamin' Hot Cheetos."

10. Munro, "Why Are Flamin' Hot."

11. Nunez, "12 Flamin' Hot Cheetos."

12. Sam Gold, "Stop Bathing In Flaming Hot Cheetos," September 15, 2018, Video, 11:07, https://youtu.be/FmJ7Y4GIBMA.

13. Griffin, "Cheeto That Looks Like."

14. Marlin, "Trying Hot Cheeto Diys!!!" November 9, 2019, Video, 14:34, https://youtu.be/uCsSVLg1oZI.

15. Marlin, "How to make: HOT CHEETOS TURKEY!!!" November 23, 2017, Video, 12:38, https://youtu.be/XJ0dGEsl_9I.

16. Marlin, "DIY HOT CHEETO BACON CORN DOGS!!!" December 28, 2016, Video, 5:15, https://youtu.be/6-cXj13buPA.

17. Marlin, "DIY HOT CHEETO WAFFLE!!!" September 18, 2016, Video, 4:17, https://youtu.be/k7ZCW9b8N2Y.

18. Wu, "YouTuber Curls Her Hair."

19. skelotim (@skelotim), "Tbt to when my fatass got inspired by a hot Cheetos bag lol! One of my favorite looks!" Instagram photo, July 26, 2015, https://www.instagram.com/p/5OA7zNtlX-/.

20. Morphe, "Looking Like a Snack Makeup Challenge w/ Louie Castro & Daisy Marquez," September 27, 2019, Video, 7:48, https://youtu.be/towMfbXkm1M.

21. Munro, "Why Are Flamin' Hot."

22. Gladwell, "Burger King."

23. Campbell, "KFC's Cheetos Sandwich."

24. Smalls, "Run Willy Run."

25. N'Duka, "Eva Longoria."

26. Wang, "Chromat Had Cheetos."

27. Norris, "Hot Cheetos Hair."

28. Havrilesky, "'Top Chef' Just Improves."

29. Frito-Lay, "Cheetos Puts Its Orange-Dusted Fingerprints All Over Fashion and Beauty World With 'House Of Flamin' Haute,'" Cision PR Newswire, August 29, 2019, https://www.prnewswire.com/news-releases/cheetos-puts-its-orange-dusted-fingerprints-all-over-fashion-and-beauty-world-with-house-of-flamin-haute-300908872.html.

30. Weiss, "Cheetos Designed A Line."

31. Scott, "Cheetos And Ripley's."

32. Hiebert, "America's Favorite Snack."

33. Jenkins, *Convergence Culture*, 122–23.

34. Bruns, *Blogs, Wikipedia, SecondLife*, 11–12.

35. Brennan and Schafer, *Branded!*, x.

36. Brennan and Schafer, 50.

37. Jenkins, *Convergence Culture*, 253–55.

38. Jenkins, 66.

39. Jenkins, 67; Kimmel, *Marketing Communication*, 3.

40. de Mooij, *Global Marketing and Advertising*, 5.

41. Gobé, *Emotional Branding, xviii.*

42. Gobé, 243.

43. Jenkins, *Convergence Culture*, 74–76.

44. Roberts, *Lovemarks*, 192.

45. Brennan and Schafer, *Branded!*, 6, 102.

46. Jenkins, *Convergence Culture*, 63, 76.

47.Couldry and Hepp, *The Mediated Construction*, 183; Jenkins, 79.

48. Jensen Schau et al., "How Brand Community Practices," 35–38; Muñiz and O'Guinn, "Brand Community."

49. Muñiz and O'Guinn, 427.

50. Muñiz and O'Guinn, "Marketing Communications," 74–75.

51. Meisner and Ledbetter, "Participatory Branding," 3.

52. Gong, "Customer Brand Engagement Behavior," 294.

53. Brennan and Schafer, *Branded!*, 128.

54. Amine and Sitz, "How Does a Virtual," 4; Solis, *Engage!*, 107.

55. Solis, 7.

56. Fournier and Avery, "The Uninvited Brand," 197.

57. Khamitov et al., "How Well Do Consumer."

58. Jenkins, *Convergence Culture*, 61–62.

59. Beltzer, "Why Brand Relatability Matters."

60. Solis, *Engage!*, 137.

61. Zeger, "How Corporations."

62. Roberts, *Lovemarks.*

63. Blunt, "Apple Fans."

64. Roberts, *Lovemarks.*

65. Eslinger, *Mobile Magic*, 127.

66. Jenkins, *Convergence Culture*, 142.

67. Orend and Gagné, "Corporate Logo Tattoos."

68. Bleier et al., "Customer Engagement."

69. Jenkins, *Convergence Culture*, 70.

70. Makalintal, "Inside the Dazzling."

71. Zeger, "How Corporations."

72. Bleier et al., "Customer Engagement," 78.

73. Jenkins, *Convergence Culture*, 59.

74. Netflix, "Interactive TV Shows and Movies on Netflix," Help Center, accessed December 29, 2020, https://help.netflix.com/en/node/62526.

75. Lanier, "Ten Arguments," 11, 16.

76. Vrendenburg et al., "Brands Taking a Stand," 445.

77. Vrendenburg et al., 444.

78. Vrendenburg et al., 444.

79. Colin Kaepernick (@Kaepernick7), "Believe in something, even if it means sacrificing everything. #JustDoIt," Twitter image, September 3, 2018, https://twitter.com/Kaepernick7/status/1036695513251434498.

80. Beer, "One Year Later."

81. Ortegon, "The Danger of Branding."

82. Calder et al., "Creating Stronger Brands," 223.

83. Olenski, "3 Reasons Why."

84. Calder et al., "Creating Stronger Brands," 226.

85. Workman, "Coke Launches."

86. Montfort and Bogost, *Racing the Beam*, 59.

87. Gaming Street Staff, "How Baskin-Robbins."

88. Calder et al., "Creating Stronger Brands," 227.

89. Scholz and Smith, "Augmented Reality," 150.

90. McGonigal, "'This Is Not a Game."

91. Jenkins, *Convergence Culture*, 62.

92. Chafin, "San Diego Comic-Con."

93. Porges, "4 Trends That Could."

94. Hultgren, "Big Bets in Experiential."

95. Event Marketer, "Coachella Roundup."

96. Bishop, "How HBO's *Westworld*."

97. Rosell Llorens, "eSport Gaming."

98. Schaffhauser, "Esports Joining Olympics."

99. BBC, "Esports 'Set for £1bn.'"

100. Jenkins, *Convergence Culture*, 98.

101. Jenkins, 66.

102. Jenkins, 122.

103. Jenkins, 68–69.

104. Jenkins, 69.

105. Jenkins, 69.

106. Balasubramian et al., "Audience Response," 116.

107. Jenkins, *Convergence Culture*, 97.

108. Draughton, "The 3-Act 'Cliffhanger.'"

109. Jenkins, *Convergence Culture*, 133.

110. Jenkins, 25, 122.

111. Murawski, "Marvel Makes Films."

112. Lawardorn, "Is the Mainstream Ready."

113. Gong, "Customer Brand Engagement Behavior," 288.

114. Jenkins, *Convergence Culture*, 200.

115. Jenkins, 197.

116. Couldry and Hepp, *The Mediated Construction*, 185; Jenkins, 62–63.

117. Muñiz and O'Guinn, "Brand Community," 427; Roberts, 170.

118. Pansari and Kumar, "Customer Engagement Marketing," 11.

119. Jenkins, *Convergence Culture*, 70.

120. Jenkins, 89.

121. Shirky, *Here Comes Everybody,* 178–80.

122. Dylan D., "Remake *Game of Thrones*"; Think Story, "How *Game of Thrones*."

123. Eslinger, *Mobile Magic*, 146; Khadim et al., "Revisiting Antecedents"; Quinton, "The Community Brand Paradigm."

124. Jenkins, *Convergence Culture*, 88.

125. Couldry and Hepp, *The Mediated Construction*, 185; Jenkins, 88.

126. Duribe, "Kim Kardashian Urged."

127. Petri, "#WhyIStayed, Digiorno."

128. Chen, "Hold My Meme."

129. McCormick, "PewDiePie and Other YouTubers."

130. Jenkins, *Convergence Culture*, 90.

131. Björn, "Why Targeted Advertising."

132. Immersely, "The Good, the Bad."

133. Vrendenburg et al., "Brands Taking a Stand," 445.

134. Kurtzleben, "Do Dove and Axe."

135. Cicalese, "Toxic Persuasion"; Olson, "After Man Hating."

136. Vrendenburg et al., "Brands Taking a Stand," 445.

137. Vrendenburg et al., 455.

138. Glikerson and Tusinski Berg, "Social Media, Hashtag Hijacking," 141–42; Lubin, "McDonald's Twitter Campaign."

139. Glikerson and Tusinski Berg, 152.

140. *Huffington Post*, "Cheerios' Facebook Hijacked."

141. Shemkus, "Why Are Food Activists?"

# Chapter 10

# Media Industry Concerns & Confrontations

## INTRODUCTION: FAKE OFF

Southern California–based blogger and lawyer Mike Cernovich, who rose to prominence in 2016,[1] is frequently characterized as a misogynistic,[2] racist,[3] far-right[4] *troll* (one who intentionally provokes others with controversial statements).[5] So, it may surprise some to find Bernie Sanders supporters, academics, and Black Lives Matter leaders among those featured in his 2019 documentary *Hoaxed*.[6] Rather than politics or identity, what all of these interviewees had in common was a keen awareness of the media industry's collective power to alter reality (in many cases, having personally experienced media mischaracterization firsthand).[7] Citing himself as one of the film's many subjects of unfair media treatment, Cernovich fills the more than two-hour documentary with evidenced examples of "fake news" hoaxes and misinformation originating not from the likes of him, but from the most prominent and trusted of news outlets.[8]

The documentary also highlights the advantages that interactive media has given to independent and amateur journalists over corporate media professionals. In one scene, independent journalist Tim Pool explains,

> I think the new media is finding faster, better, and more efficient ways to cover the story than the old media ever can. When I . . . report, I have a GoPro [camera] . . . and my phone. And I can strap the phone to my chest, which does a high-definition, live broadcast. . . . And then I look over to my side and I see a big satellite truck that costs ten times, a hundred times as much as my cell phone plan. . . . I'm [doing] the jobs of four people in one person, and they still can't get the speed and content that I can.[9]

Reflecting on Pool's account, it is hard not to feel for professionals working in the media industry today. They have, in fact, suffered significant economic losses in the wake of interactive media, and are in competition with a growing number of smaller outlets for the same audiences that sustained their industry for decades.[10] And while *Hoaxed* does a lot to point out the real and significant problems with the news media's often superficial and distorted coverage that frequently fails to accurately represent the more nuanced reality,[11] the documentary is also guilty of oversimplification itself. It presents the media industry as full of evil propagandists with an agenda intentionally designed to deceive. However, like the interview subjects of *Hoaxed*, the reality of media professionals working today is much more complex than that. Many are just attempting to stay afloat amidst a sea of intersecting historical, economic, political, and technological realities,[12] and despite all of this, many of them are still managing to do very good work.[13]

Cernovich's first line in the film states that "all media is narrative,"[14] and this is true of his own documentary as well. But his last line is a question: "How do you know what's true or what's not true?"[15] This question is one that many people are asking themselves today, as the very idea of truth seems to be growing ever more elusive in a world of competing narratives, suspicion toward authoritative sources, and mistrust of dominant institutions. Some argue that it is personalities like Cernovich who created this crisis in the first place by undermining media narratives with disinformation, and that he is just projecting his own "fake news" methods onto the professionals.[16] Whether or not that is true, often those who make such arguments also happen to be those who perceive these amateur and independent producers as a threat to their own goals and livelihoods.[17]

The adversarial nature of Cernovich's approach reflects the ways in which media professionals working in the industry are regularly challenged by those responding directly, loudly, and sometimes even dishonestly or unlawfully, to the content they produce today. As media producers from news to music to movies struggle to maintain control of their content, these tensions have played out in varying ways, through "information wars,"[18] copyright battles,[19] and fact-checking and content-flagging "combat."[20] While some of these fights are framed as protecting property and others as protecting democracy, the ways in which they play out—elite groups utilizing their dominant status to stamp out broadening participation in media—are remarkably similar. And indeed, *Hoaxed* was removed without explanation from Amazon Prime,[21] a platform whose owner, Jeff Bezos, also happens to own the *Washington Post*.[22] Still, despite the industry's continued efforts to weed out such unwelcome invaders into their media landscape, these new media uses and behaviors seem to be here to stay. And until and unless we can find a way to achieve more of a harmonious equilibrium between the many interacting parts of the media convergence ecosystem, these confrontations, and the confusion, distrust, and division that marks our age, will continue to persist.

## THE INSTITUTIONAL DILEMMA

Institutions, by their very nature, have limitations on their resources (i.e., people, time, equipment, and money), so they must pick and choose a limited number of efforts on which to spend them.[23] Thus, as institutions working to inform or entertain the public, media companies face an *institutional dilemma* in which they must decisively select what they will focus on from all of the available possibilities that exist.[24] This is as true for movie studios, television networks, and record labels as it is for book publishers and news organizations. Although there are countless possibilities for scripts that could be produced, series that could be piloted, artists that could be signed, authors that could be contracted, and issues or events that could be covered, *gatekeepers* at media organizations must make decisions about whom or what they are going to put their resources into, and then assign people and budgets to them.[25]

Gatekeeping applies not only to what content gets selected in the media industry, but also to decisions about how that content is produced.[26] In a film or TV show, for instance, a story is told through the limited range of perspectives and representations belonging to those who were chosen to work on the series. The music released on a label is chosen, recorded, and styled in concert with the select preferences and ideas of the producers assigned to each artist or album. And even the most objectively oriented journalists must choose certain details, quotes, visuals, and perspectives to feature in their reporting, which inevitably introduces a certain narrative *framing*, or prioritizing of an interpretation.[27] All of these producers also have the added challenge of needing to make money in order to support themselves, which means that they must take ratings, advertisers, and marketing into account in their decision-making.[28] These factors, combined with the fact that almost all media companies today are consolidated under six major umbrella corporations,[29] mean that media productions are subject to a range of influencing factors, and professionals are actually quite restricted in terms of what they can and cannot produce.[30] When they were all working within these same parameters in a pre-Internet era, however, this was not much of a problem for professionals.[31] In the freewheeling and unpredictable landscape of the media convergence ecosystem, however, it raises a variety of significant issues and concerns for those who are working in the industry.

## INDUSTRY CONCERNS

As discussed in earlier chapters, a large proportion of the media created today is produced by people existing outside of institutions, who thus face no institutional dilemma. With interactive media, we can access stories, ideas, perspectives, and content from everyone, everywhere (at least in theory), published directly, without gatekeepers, and often with little to no concern for financial viability.[32] So, media producers working within the confines of the institutional dilemma are exceedingly challenged to keep up with those who are not,[33] the overall impact on the industry has been significant,[34] and professionals have a variety of resulting concerns.

### Competition

Today, we simply have a lot MORE—more words, more ideas, more artists, more creators, more content—and media professionals struggle to attract and sustain the needed audience in this overloaded media landscape.[35] Finding themselves in competition with the people "formerly known as the audience" as they have been called,[36] media companies are floundering.[37] Amateur and independent producers have more freedom to do things that the constraints of the industry simply do not allow.[38] They can attract audiences in ways that professionals cannot, by experimenting with new and untested forms, being outrageous, openly speaking their minds, and appealing to niche inter- ests.[39] They can form entire communities around a single individual, issue, or idea.[40] With the older business models, large media outlets cannot afford to have such a narrow focus, as their costs demand that they have enough variety and generalizability to appeal to larger "mass" publics.[41] Independent outlets can also interact more directly with their smaller audiences,[42] which, as we learned in the last chapter, offers a level of active involvement and participation that is more captivating and loyalty-inducing.[43] In addition, the collective intelligence of hyperfocused online communities and networks has been known to collaboratively create or uncover stories in ways that a small group of professionals simply cannot do working within the confines of their own organizations.[44] Meanwhile, professionals also endure the heightened scrutiny of the "active audience," as observers and commentators like Mike Cernovich publicly criticize most of what they do, often using their own con- tent against them in these critiques.[45] The combined result of these activities generates yet further losses to media companies' bottom lines.[46]

## Scarcity

In the world of media, a piece of information, a story, a TV program, a song—all of these things are more valuable the harder they are to come by.[47] In fact, such scarcity is what media outlets rely on to function.[48] Because they own the rights, have the exclusive, or get the scoop, if we want it, we have to go to them to get it. This need for scarcity is what causes media companies to cling to copyright, as it allows them to maintain control of and access to their content, charging audiences, advertisers, or other creators in order to use it.[49]

As much as corporate media want or need to maintain scarcity, however, their ability to do so has been significantly diminished in the media convergence ecosystem. Content is shared freely (even if illegally), anyone can scoop a story if they are at the right place at the right time, and people are getting exclusives and breaking news straight from the subjects of stories on social media. Stars, celebrities, athletes, musicians, and public figures are sidestepping industry middlemen to reach audiences directly,[50] and citizens are reporting live from the ground.[51] So, if Odell Beckham Jr. is negotiating a trade or there's a tornado in Tennessee, the news outlets are often monitoring social media to find out what's going on right along with the rest of us. In addition, when things are digital, unauthorized copies of industry content spread through peer-to-peer small world networks at exponential rates, and neither the media companies nor the government can possibly keep track of it all.[52] Copyright, which was meant to protect such unauthorized use, has done little to give corporate owners control in this environment[53] (more on this in "Legal Issues" below). In the twenty-first century, the "products" of the media industry are no longer scarce, and media professionals are experiencing a loss of ownership, not only over their own productions but also over the culture "industry" that they had built up in the decades prior.[54]

## Status

As non-professionals find their own audiences and realize that they no longer need to turn to industry gatekeepers in the hopes of being chosen, professionals have also begun to lose their status and authority in society.[55] The respect and reverence once given to media professionals has been eroded as users have opened up, deconstructed, and brought into question the formerly enshrined and untouchable products and processes of the media industries. *Game of Thrones* fans deride the showrunners by referring to them as "Dumb and Dumber,"[56] for instance, or Cenk Uygur reveals that MSNBC executives unethically defer to "people in Washington."[57] In many ways, this culture of irreverence acts as a check on power,[58] which can be a good thing even for professionals working in the industry. After all, it was in this same environment that the #MeToo platform was used by many in the industry to reveal publicly that gatekeepers like Harvey Weinstein abused their high positions to sexually harass and assault women for decades.[59] But at the same time, a loss of status also reflects a loss in value, and an industry losing its value is an industry under threat.

## Survival

Professional media production and journalism are things we can hardly imagine ceasing to exist today, but it wouldn't be the first time an entire profession disappeared after the introduction of a new media technology.[60] As Clay Shirky has pointed out, once movable type was invented in the 1400s, the profession of "scribe" was no longer needed.[61] Scribes, who handwrote copies of important texts so that they could be handed down from generation to generation, had a critical role in society, and were highly regarded as the keepers of all knowledge.[62] While it may seem clear to us today that scribes would no longer be needed once the printing press came out in 1450, the revolutionary effect of this technology's introduction was not immediately recognized in society at the time.[63] We now know that the subsequent spread of literacy and knowledge, a form of mass amateurization, would change history, but this did not happen right away.[64] Scribes struggled to maintain their revered status for some time, and stuck around past their usefulness in society for several decades.[65]

Like scribes, many of the functions that media professionals served in the past no longer need them in order to be accomplished,[66] and it has already had a major effect on the industry. For instance, cable and satellite television companies lost 3.2 million subscribers in 2018, and 5.5 million in 2019.[67] Over 2,000 American newspapers have shut down since 2004,[68] and newspaper employment has gone down 23 percent since 2008.[69] Piracy has been estimated to cost billions to the film, TV, video game, and music industries,[70] and an estimated 7,800 jobs in media were lost in 2019,[71] even as job numbers were surging across other sectors.[72] In light of these statistics, it is clear that media professionals have not just been impacted by the rise of interactive media, but are in an ongoing financial crisis.[73] Some of these trends reflect shifts in the industry that are more about form than content, however, as the analog versions of media—newspapers, magazines, television, radio—are increasingly replaced by digital. In addition, unlike scribes, media professionals are actually creating, not merely copying, content. So, while it is unlikely that we will witness the disappearance of all professional media, those who can find a way to focus on serving the purposes that they, and only they, can serve, will significantly increase their chances of survival.[74]

## Quality

Professionalism produces quality, as highly skilled people with training adhere to standards, principles, and practices that have been well-developed over time.[75] If the media professions were to lose too much revenue or disappear entirely, they would no longer be able to produce all of the high-quality media content that currently acts as a source of inspiration, provides legitimate content to share, reference, and comment upon,[76] and offers a standard to adopt.[77] Yet increasingly, as Andrew Keen has put it, "the monkeys are running the show."[78] Thus, the industry concern about losing quality is perhaps a nobler one, compared to the more self-serving concerns in this list so far.

In fact, quality as a virtue has the potential to act as a salve for many of these other industry concerns,[79] as it is the primary value that is added by professionals, and could be the primary means by which leaders in the industry maintain their role in the ecosystem.[80] By capitalizing on their professionalism, the industry can lead in terms of balancing out, rather than exacerbating, the tensions within the media convergence ecosystem. Quality and quantity are no longer mutually exclusive categories in this saturated environment; they can both exist, and even thrive, by building upon one another. When media professionals dominated in the twentieth century, we basically had quality only. To prevent devolving into quantity only in the twenty-first century, however, professionals can take the lead in preserving the virtues of professionalism. Seen from this perspective, the quality-oriented institutional constraints on professionals are a strength, not a weakness, and actually give them their best competitive advantage.[81]

For instance, taking the time to put together technically superior and high-quality productions can support rather than hinder scarcity. Focusing on the use of methods that are out of the reach of independents and amateurs, such as the use of interactive data visualizations, 360-degree cameras, 3D filming, computer-generated imagery (CGI) animation, immersive media, state-of-the-art live experiences, and the ability to travel the world, will keep industry professionals on the leading edge.[82] Although some of these quality-ensuring methods might seem slow compared to the instant access of social media, consumers have proven that they are willing to wait for a product, even in today's fast-paced and demanding environment, if they expect that it will be of high quality.[83]

In addition, properly serving a broader audience rather than increasingly appealing to niche interests can help to unify people, act as a bridge across differences, offer experiences to bond over, and provide points of contact and coalition, serving as a refreshing oasis in the echo-chambered desert of interactive media. In the same way that Connectors act as the glue that holds our small world networks together (see chapter 4), professionally produced media can serve as the glue that holds our society together by meeting the information and entertainment needs of a wide variety of people. But the social capital that is needed for such a role also requires trust, and trust in media has reached an all-time low.[84] Leaning into their ethical standards and educational training can help media producers earn back trust, as they are better equipped than amateurs to guard against irresponsible messaging that can have negative consequences for an individual, organization, or group of people in society.[85]

Professionals who leave the reckless characterizations, sensationalizing, misinformation, partisanship, and tit-for-tat bickering to the non-professionals will rise above the fray. In journalism, for instance, those who invest their time and resources in investigative reporting aimed at uncovering wrongdoing in the public interest rather than engaging in "feeding-frenzy journalism"[86] will benefit from a reputation of credibility and respect.[87] Thus, instead of trying to mimic their less-professional counterparts in an effort to compete,[88] media organizations can recognize the fact that amateur, independent, and alternative media producers are still by and large responding to, and even helping to distribute, their industry-produced content.[89] In this way, industry outsiders might be seen not as competitors, but rather as *opinion brokers*, or those "who carry information across the social boundaries between groups,"[90] bringing industry content to new audiences and communities who might not otherwise have been exposed to it.

This should not by any means be understood to suggest that the industry should revert to or remain stuck in the past, nor that they should see themselves as better than their alternative counterparts. On the contrary, media companies should observe, engage with, be informed by, and learn from independents, amateurs, and citizens, while adapting their new models in ways that support rather than interfere with professional quality.[91] In other words, learn from what's good; avoid what's bad. As we discussed in the last chapter, embracing the tools of interactive media to listen to one's audience is another key to earning trust. So, for example, media entertainment companies might treat their audiences not as "eyeballs" but rather as *co-creators*," or consumer communities who bring value to and influence a brand's identity and products in varying ways.[92] Similarly, journalists might evolve into what I call "journalisteners," hosting online communities created for the express purpose of listening to the passionate perspectives of their audiences, and then summarizing, representing, and responding to those perspectives in a product delivered in the way that a professional is trained to do.[93] (More specific ways in which these new models might be more effectively incorporated into the production of media, both creatively and financially, are explored in more depth in the next chapter.)

## LEGAL ISSUES

The blurring of lines between categories of media access, consumption, and production are creating challenges not only for the industry, but also for the law. This has perhaps been most prominently evidenced in terms of the intellectual property issues surrounding copyright law, but it is also reflected in the evolving legal definitions of the increasingly muddled words we use to describe media industry professions and practices.[94] As media companies and legislators spent the better part of the twentieth century working out the legal requirements for the industry based on the one-to-many "mass" communication model, any proposed or potential changes made to media or communications related laws will be inextricably linked to the above-noted concerns of professionals. Some implications of interactive media uses as related to law, as well the current state of perspectives on and propositions for addressing these issues, are detailed in the following sections.

### Copyright Law

Many of the industry concerns noted above have been made manifest in the battle over copyright. More than two decades into this fight, the major incongruency between what is legally allowed to be done with copyrighted content and what is commonly done with it via interactive media has yet to be resolved. Without getting too much into the weeds of copyright law, a brief history is in order. Copyright protection was enshrined in Article 1, Section 8 of the US Constitution, which authorizes Congress "to promote the progress of science and the useful arts, by securing for limited times to authors and inventors the exclusive right to their respective writings and discoveries."[95] It was initially created to support innovation by giving creators sole ownership over their expression of ideas for a defined period of time.[96] In 1790, the first US copyright act was passed, giving exclusive rights to one's own works for a fourteen-year term, and allowing the author to apply for one fourteen-year extension.[97] So, a creator could retain copyright for up to twenty-eight years, and then the works would go into *public domain*, meaning anyone could use and access them, for any reason and without needing permission.[98]

Since that initial law, copyright has been revised countless times, particularly in the second half of the twentieth century.[99] These revisions focused on extending the copyright terms and were often the result of legislation efforts put forth by major media lobbying organizations like the Motion Picture Association of America (MPAA) and the Recording Industry Association of America (RIAA).[100] As of the most recent extension in 1998, the Digital Millennium Copyright Act (DMCA), the current copyright term has been extended to be the life of the author, plus seventy years.[101] This is why works from as early as the 1920s are still owned by companies like Disney,[102] and why we still don't have public domain access to important historical content like Martin Luther King Jr.'s "I Have a Dream" speech from 1963.[103] Copyright was initially created to support innovation by encouraging creators to create more due to the benefits of ownership. Yet, it would seem that we have meandered far past the law's original intent when we are still "incentivizing" a creator for seventy years beyond the end of his or her life.[104]

Still, even the original intent of copyright law to maintain scarcity and control over content for a period of time has become increasingly difficult to protect. Although not technically legal, anyone can access, and download, nearly any works that they want to in full, even the most recently released and proprietary of productions.[105] Thus, media companies have pursued efforts to take down copyrighted content from sites like YouTube, sued users for illegally downloading content, and encouraged the government to go after file-sharing sites like The Pirate Bay.[106] However, companies actively pursuing copyright infringers risk angering their consumers by prohibiting their engagement with the product.[107] In addition, taking down copyright infringers is often a fruitless effort, sort of like whack-a-mole, where something that gets removed in one place simply just pops up somewhere else.[108] Several of the copyright-infringing activities take place outside of the borders of the United States, where media companies, lobby organizations, and the US government do not have legal authority to act.[109] Each time copyright infringers get caught, new platforms are invented, new workarounds are devised, servers are moved offshore, and people continue on infringing until the industry catches on again.[110] It is an endless game of cat and mouse, and in the endless small world networks of interactive media, there are simply too many mice to catch them all.[111]

Several bills have been proposed in Congress that would give copyright enforcers even more power to punish infringers and potential infringers (such as SOPA, PIPA, and COICA), but to date, these have all been shot down because of activism and public outcries against them as violations of free speech and hindrances on public participation.[112] Many opponents of these laws feel that copyright law is already too restrictive as it is.[113] As legal scholar Lawrence Lessig has pointed out, the lingering restrictions on copyright in the age of interactive media constrain innovation and creativity, and corrupt society by turning all citizens into law-breakers simply for engaging as they are able to in their own culture.[114] Activists in the free culture movement (sometimes called *pirates*) subscribe to the idea that culture, like information, "wants to be free," and their aim is to free it so that all can participate.[115] In fact, they argue, piracy should not be considered stealing, because when copying digital files, no "thing" is taken.[116]

When this was written in 2021, no clear legal path for resolving these copyright dilemmas has been laid out.[117] There are two areas within existing laws that could provide promising future avenues; however, barring a major perceptual shift in the industry, it does not seem likely that a critical mass of professionals will embrace either of them anytime soon. The first is *fair use*, a protection built into copyright law to allow for certain uses of copyrighted content—such as for the purposes of review, critique, reporting, or parody—without needing to obtain owners' permission.[118] Although the works of many amateur and independent creators might fit under fair use, this has been a historically fuzzy legal concept to nail down, largely handled in the courts, and is thus difficult to build into automated identification systems.[119] Instead, copyright filters simply use content-matching scanners to identify any uses of existing industry content at all, without taking fair-use exceptions into account.[120] This means that on sites like YouTube, fair use–protected works are frequently taken down without question, and their creators need to then appeal to the platforms to have them reinstated.[121] Because content moderation systems work in concert with the industry, they are essentially preferencing the industry's right to ownership within copyright law over the public's right to employ an exception built into the law for fair use.[122] Introducing laws against the use of automated systems that do not account for fair use could help to deal with some of these issues in a way that is more equitable and reflective of the reality.[123]

The second area of promise is the use of *creative commons licensing*, developed by Lessig and others, which is a revised copyright license that owners can apply to intentionally give up certain rights over their works in order to allow and even encourage others to use them without permission.[124] These creative commons (CC) licenses can be used as filters when searching on sites like Google, YouTube, Flickr, and Soundcloud, allowing people to find and access works that can be legally used in certain ways, such as for non-commercial purposes or with modifications.[125] Although the currently 1.6 billion works[126] using CC licenses mostly belong to amateur and independent creators, forward-thinking leaders within the industry could put them on promotional items, perhaps, or on less popular and "retired" productions that are not generating revenue.[127] For news organizations, CC licenses could actually improve their reach and impact (*ProPublica* already does this), even helping to support sustainability for smaller outlets.[128] If media professionals were to take the lead in considering ways to begin adopting and even benefiting from these alternative copyright models, we might begin to see a more balanced approach to copyright emerge.

## Legal Definitions

With respect to the enshrined legal definitions relating to what have traditionally been treated as media industry roles, legislators are continuing to debate the directions the law should take to address these challenges. For instance, who or what counts as a "journalist," "sponsor," or "publisher" today? This is important because all of these terms have legal implications. For instance, professional journalists are given *journalistic privilege*, such as legal protections from having to reveal the names of sources,[129] but these cannot be given to everyone with a smartphone and a Twitter account. Often these protections are only given to people who are employed or paid by a news organization,[130] but as discussed in chapter 6, bloggers, independent journalists, and everyday citizens can contribute to news in important ways as well. Similarly, the lines between sponsored and unsponsored content are not nearly as clear for social media influencers and product reviewers as they are for professional media publishers, who are required by law to disclose their advertisements.[131] When it comes to publishing, we are also losing clarity on who should be considered liable for the spread of false and defamatory information. As it stands right now, the one-to-many "broadcast" media publishers can be sued or fined for allowing lies about a person or event to be shared via their platforms, yet social media sites (wherein a large portion of misinformation originates) are shielded from such penalties.[132]

The question over who should be treated as a media publisher has been brought into particularly high relief in recent years as politicians have been engaging in increasingly public debates over Section 230 of the 1996 Communications Decency Act (CDA). Section 230 states that interactive media companies are allowed, but not required, to block content posted by users that they deem to be potentially harmful, such as harassment, hate speech, obscenity, disinformation, or the promotion of violence.[133] This actually gives them quite a bit of freedom in terms of how they can choose to manage content (or not) on their sites, as compared to more traditionally defined media publishers. Thus, many public figures and politicians on the left want to change Section 230 to give it more teeth, obligating, rather than simply allowing, these companies to block such harmful content, holding them responsible in the same way that media publishers are held responsible for what is published on their platforms.[134] However, like fair use, the boundaries that define hate speech, obscenity, or harmful content are not easily identified, and thus difficult to moderate with automated systems. Legally requiring platform owners to seek out and take down all such content on their platforms would not magically make them able to do so. Meanwhile, many on the political right take a free speech stance on the issue, arguing that platform owners can use the allowance to moderate content without limits as a shield to cover the censorship of ideas or perspectives they don't like, and that it should be taken away from them if abused.[135] But again, the vagaries surrounding the definitions of protected speech make it exceedingly difficult to prove in court that content moderation decisions are being made in bad faith to silence certain perspectives.[136]

It may be tempting for those in the industry to want interactive media sites to be subject to the same restrictions as they are, able to be sued for copyright violations, false advertising, or anything that could be viewed as slanderous, libelous, harmful, or potentially dangerous on their sites. Factually speaking, however, interactive media companies are not publishers reviewing every piece of content before it goes out; rather, they are the hosts of the public platforms that we, the users, stand on in order to be heard. In addition, as has occurred with copyright takedowns, interactive media platform owners' efforts to moderate content are both imperfect and inevitably result in restricting the participation, creativity, and freedom that those outside of the industry have to engage with the public in online spaces. Public space is important, because, as Castells explains, it "is the space of societal, meaningful interaction where ideas and values are formed, conveyed, supported, and resisted."[137] But unlike the platforms that people might stand on in the public space of the offline world in order to gain a voice, these digital platforms have the capacity to reach up and muzzle us if and when they choose to.[138] This makes them the *de facto* "builders and caretakers"[139] of our public space, giving them more power than we may realize over the direction our society takes (more on this in chapter 12). Thus, it is exceedingly important to address their responsibilities to the public good, however we must also take care to avoid doing so in ways that can set us back to the more easily controlled and thus increasingly homogenized "mass" distribution models that the industry would likely prefer.

## CONCLUSION

In light of the seismic shifts that have taken place in media over the past few decades, it is understandable that professionals in the industry would have a variety of concerns related to the ways that interactive media have "enabled broader public participation in society, culture, and commerce" (definition from chapter 1). Major changes have happened, are happening, and will continue to happen. But rather than go down fighting, it will take an equally seismic shift in the industry's perspective in order to properly address all of these changes. From an outside perspective, it is clear to see that the old institutions of media are failing and the old models are fading away, but, squinting at the future, we also struggle to see what will fill in the voids they leave behind.

For industry insiders, it's scary, like a silent freight train coming through the fog, and the industry response has thus been largely resistant,[140] making only incremental changes when they have to.[141] By doing so, however, they are continuing to stand in the same place on the tracks.

Yet, from other angles within the media convergence ecosystem, standing outside of the "corporate, professional" box has elicited a variety of innovative models for both content production and financial viability. Thus, a change of positioning toward these new participatory practices could similarly help industry media companies avoid the impact. Such an embrace, done with professionalism and without compromise, could serve them well, even allowing them to use their dominant status to proactively envision and lead us into the future. Therefore, perhaps the most beneficial question every media industry professional could be asking themselves is, am I simply standing in the same place fighting, or am I changing my perspective to find ways to benefit from these new opportunities and models? Such potentials for these new opportunities will be discussed in the next chapter.

## NOTES

1. Darcy, "Right-Wing Troll."
2. Goldhill, "Wondering What Trolls."
3. López et al., "Mike Cernovich's Far-Right."
4. Stack, "Who Is Mike Cernovich?"
5. Binns, "DON'T FEED THE TROLLS!," 547.
6. *Hoaxed: Everything They Told You Is a Lie*, directed by Scooter Downey and Jon Du Toit, released 2019, El Ride Productions, 2:08:11.
7. Toto, "Cernovich's 'Hoaxed' Torches Media."
8. *Hoaxed: Everything They Told You Is a Lie*, directed by Scooter Downey and Jon Du Toit, released 2019, El Ride Productions, 54:45.
9. *Hoaxed.*
10. Jurkowitz, "The Losses in Legacy."
11. Butovsky, "Phony Populism," 92; Franklin, "Social Policy, the Media," 4; Hass, "False Equivalency," 96; Herman and Chomsky, *Manufacturing Consent*; Klein and Naccarato, "Broadcast News Portrayals," 1614–15; Yousman, "Challenging the Media/Incarceration," 143.
12. Borchardt et al., *Are Journalists Today's*, 15; McClure Haughey et al., "On the Misinformation Beat," 3.
13. Carey, "The Press, Public Opinion," 232; Cernovich, "Jeff Epstein Arrested"; Kenix, *Alternative and Mainstream Media*, 21.
14. *Hoaxed: Everything They Told You Is a Lie*, directed by Scooter Downey and Jon Du Toit, released 2019, El Ride Productions, 2:18.
15. *Hoaxed*, 1:59:22.

16. Darcy, "Right-Wing Troll"; Stack, "Who Is Mike Cernovich?"

17. Bogaerts and Carpentier, "The Postmodern Challenge," 67–68; Bruns, *Gatewatching*, 46.

18. Stengel, *Information Wars*.

19. Netanel, *Copyright*, 62.

20. Anderson and Søe, "Communicative Actions," 127; Taylor et al., "Industry Responses"; Solomon, "Fair Users or Content," 238.

21. Aubert, "Mike Cernovich's Documentary"; Toto, "'Hoaxed' Doc Cancelled."

22. Denning, "Why Jeff Bezos."

23. Shirky, *Here Comes Everybody*, 19–20.

24. Bruns, *Gatewatching and News Curation*, 26; Shirky, 64–65; Shoemaker and Vos, *Gatekeeping Theory*, 63.

25. Shoemaker and Vos, 1, 28.

26. Shoemaker and Vos, 49.

27. Entman, "Framing," 52.

28. Shoemaker and Vos, *Gatekeeping Theory*, 80–81.

29. McLintock, "The Destruction of Media," 582–83.

30. Baker, "Media Concentration," 908; Horkheimer and Adorno, "The Culture Industry," 42.

31. Benkler, *The Wealth of Networks*, 55; McLintock, "The Destruction of Media," 583.

32. Bennett, "New Media Power," 34.

33. Bennett, 34.

34. Jurkowitz, "The Losses in Legacy."

35. Tewksbury and Rittenberg, *News on the Internet*, 18; Webster, *The Marketplace of Attention*, 50–51.

36. Rosen, "The People Formerly Known."

37. Kenix, *Alternative and Mainstream Media*, 25–26.

38. Kenix, 106.

39. Tewksbury and Rittenberg, *News on the Internet*, 78–79.

40. Benkler, *The Wealth of Networks*, 55; Tewksbury and Rittenberg, 18.

41. Benkler, 55; Tewksbury and Rittenberg, 35.

42. Bruns, *Gatewatching*, 29.

43. Quinton, "The Community Brand Paradigm," 922.

44. Kenix, *Alternative and Mainstream Media*, 22; Tewksbury and Rittenberg, *News on the Internet*, 57.

45. Kenix, 109.

46. Tewksbury and Rittenberg, *News on the Internet*, 40.

47. Lessig, *The Future of Ideas*, 75; Shirky, *Here Comes Everybody*, 79.

48. Hutchins and Rowe, "From Broadcast Scarcity," 355; Jemielniak and Przegalinska, *Collaborative Society*, 38; Langenderfer and Cook, "Copyright Policies and Issues," 280.

49. Lessig, *The Future of Ideas*, 238.

50. Hutchins, "The Acceleration of Media," 237.

51. Bruno, "Tweet First, Verify Later," 7.

52. Kelly, *The Inevitable*, 61–62.

53. Lessig, "Remix: How Creativity," 161.

54. Jenkins and Deuze, "Editorial: Convergence Culture," 6, 9.

55. Couldry, "Beyond the Hall," 50; Kenix, *Alternative and Mainstream Media*, 21; Tewksbury and Rittenberg, *News on the Internet*, 2012.

56. Heim, "'Game of Thrones' Producers."

57. The Young Turks, "Why Cenk Uygur Left," 3:41.

58. Grady, "Some Say."

59. Williams, "Women in Hollywood."

60. Shirky, *Here Comes Everybody*, 66.

61. Shirky, 67.

62. Meyrowitz, *No Sense of Place,* 160; Shirky, 67.

63. Shirky, 67–68.

64. Shirky, 66.

65. Shirky, 68.

66. Shirky, 79.

67. Rizzo and Fitzgerald, "Cord-Cutting Accelerated."

68. McIntyre, "Over 2000 American Newspapers."

69. Greico, "U.S. Newspapers."

70. Quintais and Poort, "The Decline of Online," 809.

71. Goggin, "7,800 People Lost."

72. U.S. Bureau of Labor Statistics, "Job Market Remains."

73. Shirky, *Here Comes Everybody*, 75.

74. Shirky, 79.

75. Tandoc et al., "Defining 'Fake News,'" 4.

76. Tandoc et al., 4.

77. Leavitt and Robinson, "Upvote My News," 3.

78. Keen, *The Cult of the Amateur*, 9.

79. Batson, *Engaged Journalism*, 49.

80. McNair, "Trust, Truth, and Objectivity," 80–81.

81. Tewksbury and Rittenberg, *News on the Internet*, 175.

82. Barnhurst, "'Trust Me,'" 220.

83. Giebelhausen et al., "Worth Waiting For," 901; Stock and Balachander, "The Making of," 1182.

84. Salmon, "Media Trust."

85. Donovan and boyd, "Stop the Presses?" 344–45.

86. Carey, "The Press, Public Opinion," 231.

87. Price, "How to Feed," 1329–30.

88. Donovan and boyd, "Stop the Presses?," 344.

89. Atton, "Separate, Supplementary, or Seamless?," 134; Jenkins, *Convergence Culture*, 141; Kenix, *Alternative and Mainstream Media*, 20, 26, 111.

90. Burt, "The Social Capital of," 37.

91. Kenix, *Alternative and Mainstream Media*, 170.

92. Smith, *Brand Fans*, 15

93. Graham, "Talking Back," 126.

94. Shirky, *Here Comes Everybody*, 70.

95. U.S. Const. art. I, §8, cl. 8.

96. Lessig, *The Future of Ideas*, 106.

97. Copyright Act of 1790, §1; Lessig, 107.

98. Langvardt, "Historic Copyrighted Works," 942.

99. Lessig, *The Future of Ideas*, 107.

100. Lee, "Why Mickey Mouse's."

101. Lessig, *The Future of Ideas*, 107.

102. Lee, "Why Mickey Mouse's."

103. Langvardt, "Historic Copyrighted Works," 942–43.

104. Kelly, *The Inevitable*, 209.

105. Aguiar et al., "Catch Me If You Can," 1.

106. Aguiar et al., 1; Lessig, *Free Culture*, 185, 190; Lindgren and Linde, "The Subpolitics of," 148.

107. Jenkins, *Convergence Culture*, 138, 195.

108. Aguiar et al., "Catch Me If You Can," 2.

109. Denniston, "International Copyright Protection."

110. Aguiar et al., "Catch Me If You Can," 2.

111. Kelly, *The Inevitable*, 61–62.

112. Benkler et al., "Social Mobilization"; Postigo et al., *The Digital Rights Movement*, 4.

113. Lessig, *Free Culture*, 292–93; Postigo et al., 175–79.

114. Lessig, 207.

115. Lhooq, "How Did the Pirate"; Postigo et al., *The Digital Rights Movement*, 6.

116. Raustiala and Sprigman, "Copying Is Not Theft."

117. Kelley, "The CASE Act."

118. Copyright.gov, "More Information on Fair Use," U.S. Copyright Office Fair Use Index, last updated October 2020, https://www.copyright.gov/fair-use/more-info.html.

119. Langvardt, "Historic Copyrighted Works," 967.

120. Lessig, 256; Trendacosta, "Unfiltered."

121. Trendacosta.

122. Trendacosta.

123. Lessig, *The Future of Ideas*, 257.

124. Lessig, *Free Culture*, 282.

125. Creative Commons, "Frequently Asked Questions," last updated August 28, 2020, https://creativecommons.org/faq/.

126. Creative Commons, "The Growing Commons," accessed January 7, 2021, https://creativecommons.org/about/.

127. Kramer, "It's Time for News."

128. Kramer.

129. Gleason, "If We Are All," 376; Shirky, *Here Comes Everybody*, 70.

130. Gleason, 381–82; Peters, "Shield Laws"; Shirky, 71–72; Weinhold, "Watching the Watchdogs," 1.

131. Luong, "All That Glitters," 574.

132. Balkin, "Free Speech," 1178.
133. Communications Decency Act of 1996, 47 USC §230.
134. Bambauer, "Day After Section 230."
135. Bambauer.
136. Robertson, "Social Media Bias Lawsuits."
137. Castells, *Communication Power*, 371.
138. Castells, 371.
139. Castells, 371.
140. Witschge, "Transforming Journalistic Practice," 164.
141. Kenix, *Alternative and Mainstream Media*, 31.

# Chapter 11

# New Models for Converging Media

## INTRODUCTION: IMPOSSIBLE MATH

Christian filmmaker Dallas Jenkins, who focuses on making faith-based entertainment, saw his burgeoning Hollywood career implode before his eyes in early 2017. After the disastrous box office numbers from the opening weekend of his first big film, *The Resurrection of Gavin Stone*, the promising opportunities Jenkins had been considering, including a dream plan drafted with movie studios to finance multiple faith-based projects over a ten-year period, vanished in an instant.[1] As he prayed with his wife, Amanda, over this "extreme low-point" in his career, she told him that the message "I do impossible math" came to her, as if from God.[2] They thought that maybe this meant that the box office numbers would magically turn around that weekend. They didn't.[3]

Jenkins was ready to give up and walk away from filmmaking all together, but a few months later, he agreed to make a short film for his church's Christmas Eve service.[4] The 23-minute production, entitled *The Shepherd*, was shared with Jeffrey and Neal Harmon, cofounders of a company called VidAngel.[5] At the time, VidAngel was more of a tech platform than a media production company, providing a family-friendly filtering service that can be used with streaming sites like Netflix and Amazon to skip over unwanted content, such as profanity, nudity, or graphic violence.[6] But they were looking to get into original content production themselves, and *The Shepherd* inspired them to take this next step.[7] They told Jenkins that they wanted to work with him to produce his idea for a multiseason series about the life of Jesus, but that they would have to finance it through *crowdfunding*,[8] a backing model based on smaller donations solicited from a large community of followers.[9]

(At the time VidAngel was facing a financial crisis itself, having just been sued for $62 million by Hollywood movie companies for its original service, which streamed digitally edited films rather than layering a filter onto existing streaming platforms.[10])

Jenkins was, of course, excited about the idea of producing the series. But when he heard that it would need to be crowdfunded, he said,

> Then I got really depressed. Because crowdfunding rarely works, it's usually for very small projects, and the all-time crowdfunding record was $5.7 million for a project that was famous. All the projects in the top 5 crowdfunds of all time for media projects are famous shows or movies that had a big fanbase. We had nothing, and I was coming off of a big bomb.[11]

They estimated that they would need a budget of $10 million to produce the first season of the series. He told the Harmons he would be surprised if they raised $800, but with nothing to lose, he agreed to try.[12] So, VidAngel released *The Shepherd* via social media, pitching it as the pilot episode of an original series called *The Chosen*,[13] "not your grandma's Jesus show."[14] The video received over fifteen million views,[15] and they kicked off a donation campaign, employing a unique model called *equity crowdfunding*, in which backers can become investors serving as part owners and share in any profit returns that may result.[16] By January 2019, the team of producers not only met but exceeded their unprecedented and seemingly impossible goal, raising nearly $10.3 million from over 15,000 donors.[17] The moment Jenkins and his wife watched the ticker hit its target and become the top crowdfunded media project in history,[18] Amanda suddenly remembered the message she had received nearly two years earlier, and said to him with tears in her eyes, "I do impossible math."[19]

The full first season of *The Chosen* was made available in November 2019, and, as I write these words, funding has been completed for the second season as well, with production underway.[20] Jenkins, who was astonished by the success of the campaign, sees this model as a hopeful step toward restoring the public's trust in entertainment.[21] He said of *The Chosen*'s audience, who access the show for free via a downloaded app and are welcome but not required to donate to support its future, "they don't need a subscription. They don't need approval. They don't need a gatekeeper. And that has allowed us to get into people's hands, even with the coronavirus, even with economic strife. And even with the distrust of institutions that many people have."[22] So, what does this story tell us, that it takes a miracle to successfully implement a legitimate alternative model to the traditional economics of professional quality media production? On the contrary, it supports the idea that we've seen again and again throughout this book, that the openness and freedom of the interactive media environment can create enough room to allow for even the most unlikely, unexpected, and seemingly impossible of accomplishments. But in order to tap in to that potential, there needs to be a willingness to take a risk. One might even say that it requires a leap of faith.

## REVERSED PUBLISHING PROCESS

In a pre-Internet era, anything or anyone that was not chosen by media industry gatekeepers was by and large unknown to the public.[23] Because of the institutional dilemma, the "material" of the world was filtered "in advance" of reaching the public.[24] This older publishing model is what Clay Shirky has called the *filter-then-publish* model.[25] Because it was so narrowly defined, this situation was destined to produce a mediated view of the world that was hardly adequate to capture the breadth and depth of true lived experience, with all of its cultural, social, and artistic intricacies.[26]

With interactive media, however, a new publishing model has reversed that process.[27] Collectively, online, we adopt a process of *publish-then-filter* (see figure 11.1).[28] The "material" of the world is there for all to see, and we can, at least in theory, capture a more authentic view of it.[29] Instead of gatekeepers, community filtering tools serve to highlight the most interesting, important, or popular items from the massive amounts of content that are published from anyone, anywhere, all over the world.[30] Some of these filtering tools are based on ratings or votes, some are based on shares or reposts, some are just based on views. Save for the interference of the hosting platforms used (which will be further explored in the next chapter), it is by and large the preferences and

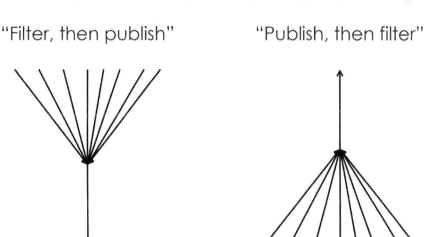

"Filter, then publish"     "Publish, then filter"

Figure 11.1 Filter-then-publish versus publish-then-filter. *Figure created by*

behaviors of the crowd that filters the content and pushes it to the top of the attention-getting stack.[31] So now, not only are users generating media content, but in *user-generated filtering*, they are serving the editorial function of media organizations as well.[32]

Certainly, we wouldn't want the publish-then-filter model to be the only way we access content, as it would leave us entirely to our own, untrained, low-quality, and mob-ruled devices. As discussed in previous chapters, there are advantages to both forms of publishing continuing to exist. So, how can media producers benefit from this reversed version, without losing the value of quality that filter-then-publish can bring? In fact, there are several new trends in professional media production that are tapping in to the publish-then-filter model.

## NEW TRENDS IN MEDIA

While it is sometimes applied only superficially, as mere window dressing on more typical "business as usual" corporate media productions, there have also been some very good examples of professional media organizations thoughtfully and authentically engaging with the reversed publishing model in ways that actually benefit and enhance their own products. These trends have gone by many names and appeared in different media sectors, but those that we have seen thus far have tended to fall under a few separate but interrelated themes, detailed in the following sections.

### Crowdsourcing

*Crowdsourcing*, in which a community, network, or audience is solicited to contribute content or ideas to a production,[33] is a concept closely related to the publish-then-filter model. But whether or not it is used in a true, authentic, publish-then-filter process depends on whether or not the filtering of choices is also user-driven. For instance, nearly every election cycle, we see candidate debates in which a set of questions are submitted "from the audience" via interactive media. This seems more democratic, as these represent questions from everyday people, rather than media professionals.[34] But who decides which questions are chosen out of the thousands submitted? If there is still a media professional, company, or outlet that is making those decisions, it is really just the filter-then-publish model, dressed up in user-generated packaging.[35]

To truly understand how publish-then-filter could be embraced in a way that is authentic and beneficial for both the professionals and their audience, it is helpful, for a moment, to go back in Internet history, to the year 2009.

At that time, a site called Digg, a news aggregator that has taken a variety of forms over the years, used to use crowdsourcing to put together something called "Digg Dialoggs."[36] A public figure, such as Ozzy Osbourne,[37] Nancy Pelosi, or Al Gore,[38] would agree to be interviewed, and then the community would submit and vote on questions to ask them. The "most-Dugg questions,"[39] meaning the top 10 most voted on by the community, would be used to conduct the interview. This is true, bottom-up, user-generated filtering, as the users, collectively, both wrote *and* chose the questions. As might be expected, some of the questions that ended up being asked were a bit ludicrous, such as when Al Gore was queried about his strategy for spreading "ManBearPig" awareness (a reference to a *South Park* episode making fun of the former vice president). But other questions were also quite hard-hitting, such as when then Federal Communications Commission (FCC) chairman Julius Genachowski was asked, "Who do you think you are to enforce what my children can or cannot see [on television]?" And yet others were very critical, such as when Arnold Schwarzenegger was asked, "What makes you a Republican?" These were not typical news interviews, yet, as they gained popularity, Digg began partnering with professional journalists to conduct them.

The Digg Dialogg in which *Wall Street Journal* editor Alan Murray interviewed Timothy Geithner, treasury secretary at the time, gives some insight into how such a crowdsourced interview could be advantageous to professional journalists. Murray started the interview by explaining, "I'm merely a prop in this exercise. My job is to ask the questions that have been offered up by the Digg online community. . . . I'm going to ask you the top 10."[40] This setup was helpful later on, when Murray was able to press a bit further and follow up on some of the questions critiquing the Federal Reserve for its lack of transparency with the public.[41] This interview demonstrates how the journalists, knowledgeable about the subjects they were interviewing, could use these "top-dugg" questions as jumping-off points for a more in-depth discussion. And yet, they didn't have to be the ones doing the asking. It took the onus off of the journalist from being perceived as too critical or aggressive, but still allowed them to ask the tough questions, which could now genuinely be framed as something "the people want to know."

In addition, because the entire process of generating and filtering the questions was open, transparent, and available for all to see, neither the interviewee nor the audience could accuse the interviewer of pursuing his or her own agenda, misrepresenting public sentiment, or editing out questions (which is exactly what happened when Google *didn't* ask one of their topvoted-on questions in their similarly crowdsourced "hangout" with President Obama in 2012[42]). As a bonus, if a public figure were to back out of an interview because they didn't want to answer a certain top-voted-on question, everyone could easily see the reason why, and it would reflect poorly on him or her to do so. So, a journalist could secure the interview, ask the hard-hitting questions that people wanted to know, and get a good interview that earned them the respect of the audience, without being personally responsible for any offense that the interviewee might take. That seems like a pretty good trade-off for having to ask the occasional silly question about ManBearPigs.

Unfortunately, it seems like professional media producers' embrace of this kind crowdsourcing went away for the most part, and today we generally only get the top-down variety. While it is true that there is some risk of saboteurs and culture jammers gaming the system to gain a platform, if this were to become a regularly employed process in news reporting, as common as featuring selected social media posts is today, such adversarial efforts would likely lose their punch and diminish. In addition, organizations who are concerned about such sabotage could mitigate the possibility by keeping their crowdsourcing limited to a membership audience.[43] And maybe it isn't for everyone. But, done with commitment, openness, and transparency, the bottom-up crowdsourcing model could be a potential key for media outlets looking to be innovative and earn the respect of their audience, while also giving them more freedom to engage with stories, ideas, or perspectives that might be seen as extending beyond the boundaries of their usual "template." For instance, the regular featuring of such an audience-driven interview on a news network; a debate or two each election cycle using truly crowdsourced (and voted-on) questions; an occasional "follow-up" article reproducing the highest-rated comments and discussions stemming from a previously published one; or entire publications or programs dedicated to covering the top-voted-on user-suggested stories, could do a lot to earn trust through reciprocity with the audience.[44] On the entertainment side, things could go further, too, with *crowdsourced storytelling*, in which companies could have the audience generate and vote on ideas for where a storyline could go next, which characters should be the focus of a plot, or which series or films they want to see produced. We have already seen inroads into such ideas through innovative video games like Fortnite and interactive media productions created by companies like Netflix.[45]

## Transparency

Because transparency has become so key to building audience trust, many media producers are taking it upon themselves to "open up" their production and storytelling processes for their audiences. Rather than limit their output to a final product, they "show their work," sharing more of the behind-the-scenes workings in the process of creating it. This serves many purposes that can be valuable to both the products and the processes of media production. First, it gives the fans a way to be more involved by engaging with this "extra" content, generating a community of loyals (see chapter 9). Second, it can serve to educate those prosumers within the audience, who are pursuing their own careers in media and can create and share content that will bring free marketing and new audiences to the product. Third, it can support producers' ability to anticipate what their audience wants, ultimately creating a product that is more well-received.

Because *The Chosen* deals with topics and subjects that are quite literally sacred to most of their viewing audience, the producers have embraced this idea of transparency as a way of earning their fans' trust. They are constantly posting updates about what they are doing and have provided copious amounts of behind-the-scenes footage—including table sessions consulting with Bible scholars, tutorials on industry lingo, insights into production struggles and decision-making challenges, and responses to fan questions and criticisms—along the way.[46] Jenkins has even created a video called, "Can you trust *The Chosen?*" to explain in-depth their approach to writing and producing a show that is based on the sacred text of the Bible.[47] Transparency is a value that the team frequently communicates with their public, not only in their rhetoric, but also in their actions.[48]

In news, embracing this "show-your-work" ethic[49] is often referred to as *open journalism*, as reporters share with and involve their audiences in their news-making processes, including providing information about values, bias, and funding sources, producing source material such as the complete datasets or raw unedited video that they are working with, and providing a running log of all updates, changes, or corrections made to an article.[50] As Gabriel Kahn noted in 2017, "authority and trust will only return if reporters share some of the messy sausage-making process with the audience."[51] Some have argued that the resulting transparency in journalism may be even more important than the more traditional value of objectivity, which we now recognize as an genuine impossibility with any narrative or visual representation.[52]

One of the most successful and popular journalistic investigations in recent years, Sarah Koenig's *Serial* podcast, has been frequently cited as an effective example of open journalism. Called by *Slate Magazine* "a master class in investigative journalism,"[53] the podcast presented a series of episodes revealing Koenig's discoveries over the course of her months-long investigations into cold case files related to murders and disappearances.[54] The clues she uncovered, interviews she conducted, and leads she followed didn't always provide fruitful answers, but her opening up of the process found an audience of sixty million listeners[55] and educated people on how investigative journalism is done.[56] It is also credited with helping to bring podcasting to the masses.[57]

Combined with crowdsourcing, open journalism might also be seen as a kind of *participatory journalism,* in which reporters can benefit from following the leads, perspectives, and tips provided by their audience.[58] Journalist Eugenia Chien, who created such a participatory project by utilizing a website encouraging citizens to report issues experienced with the notoriously problematic public transit system in San Francisco, said, "rather than turning citizens into unpaid journalists, you can get the best out of your readers by creating a space where conversations lead to ideas and stories."[59] Crowdsourced participation can also serve to make journalism spaces those where civic participation thrives, as journalists work with citizens to gather and input needed public information[60] in the same way that scientists and researchers have done for the last decade with citizen science projects.[61] News organizations employing another newer trend called *data journalism,*[62] which is the use of data in journalistic reporting,[63] can then visualize this citizen data in useful and interactive ways that best serve the identified needs of various publics.

*The Guardian* in the United Kingdom has been a leader in implementing many of these new journalistic trends for the past decade, and has demonstrably shown how a thoughtful, quality, transparent, and data-driven approach to professional journalism is possible, even for a broad-reaching journalistic organization that serves a wide-ranging audience. Incidentally, in 2017, the publication also reached the point where it is now funded more by its readers than it is by advertising,[64] a fact that they share frequently to show how they are kept independent and accountable to their audience. Across their site, they display the slogan "available for everyone, funded by readers," and solicit both contributions and subscriptions to support their reporting, without requiring either of anyone.[65]

In order to preserve the quality of journalism, however, it is important that reporters are clear about what it is they are sharing when they embrace such open trends.[66] Even as they have purposefully collaborated with their audience in their reporting, *The Guardian*'s primary value and motto has been that "facts are sacred."[67] Being too quick to share some piece of information gathered on social media without taking the time to verify it can get professional journalists into a lot of hot water, as a higher quality is expected from them.[68] But a simple disclaimer that this was something that was shared by a viewer, reader, or listener and that, without proper context, "we are working to gather more information" can help to guard against this sort of error and present it as a part of the "sausage-making" reveal, provided that all such claims are indeed followed up on with either confirmation or denial.[69] Facts can be clearly presented as verified information, and speculation as possibility.[70] Such transparency can work to guard against the accusations of manipulation, obfuscation, and propagandizing that will inevitably arise in the broader knowledge culture and serve to undermine trust, respect, and credibility.

## Engagement

In media, *engagement* with the audience sometimes means crowdsourcing, sometimes means transparency, but above all it means finding ways to listen to the audience, in advance of production investments, in order to best serve their needs. A legendary cautionary tale of the Internet is that of the never-produced television series *Global Frequency*.[71] After Warner Brothers rejected the series in 2005,[72] the pilot episode leaked on the Internet, and fans loved it. They shared and spread it via illegal download sites, and began a campaign to implore the network to reconsider making the show.[73] But the company's executives, more focused on the fans' piracy than their passion, responded, "copyright infringement is not a productive way to try to influence a corporate decision."[74] That's precisely *not* listening to the audience, and, as a result, they left money on the table. Afterward, the show's would-be head writer and producer, John Rogers, said that next time, "I would put my pilot out on the Internet in a heartbeat. Want five more? Come buy the boxed set."[75] Fourteen years later, this is essentially what Dallas Jenkins and the creators of *The Chosen* did. They released a pilot episode and made a pitch to see if people liked the idea, and, when they saw that they did, they asked for their followers' help in getting it made, releasing four episodes at a time and sharing with them the process along the way. That's listening to the audience, and as a result, they have earned millions of dollars in funding support.

This idea fits closely with a new trend that Philip Smith calls "pull journalism" (as opposed to the old model of "push journalism"),[76] which, though focused on journalism, could be applied to any industry media product.[77] The *push* variety of media, Smith says, is when an organization invests a lot of time, resources, and energy into a putting together a production, based on a hunch about what will resonate with the audience, and then pushes hard to get it "in front of as many people as possible in the hope that it will reach the people who need that information the most," or, in terms of entertainment, those most likely to want or enjoy it.[78] The alternative he proposes, *pull* media, is when media producers talk with their audience about their hunches before they ever produce the product.[79] This is not strictly crowdsourcing, but rather presenting ideas while being open to being proven wrong, discovering some other project, or going in a different direction than originally thought, as a result of engaging with the audience.[80] It could also involve discussing with the audience what format this production should take, and how it could best be distributed, as the idea develops further.[81] The most active group of participants in each of these project conversations then acts as a kind of beta-testing group, regularly tapped for input as they preview various iterations of the project throughout the different stages of its production.[82] Keeping this smaller group of interested participants involved throughout the process gives them a level of investment and excitement that they inevitably share with their own social networks, supplying a tailored audience likely to have similar media needs and desires, and reducing the need to invest so many resources into pushing out the final product.[83]

Journalists may find themselves especially skeptical of such an engagement approach, concerned that such conversations would end up looking a lot like their comments sections (for those organizations that still even allow them), overrun with conflict, racist and offensive remarks, and unhelpful, uncivil criticisms.[84] But Jennifer Brandel, CEO of a consumer engagement company called *Hearken* (which means "to listen),[85] has experimented with this approach, which she calls "*public-powered journalism*," and found that seeking questions from the audience before reporting is done is infinitely more productive than seeking their comments after the fact.[86] Unlike comments on an article, she says, questions posed by the audience beforehand are "curiosity-based," "inherently flexible," "open-minded" and "positively contagious."[87] In addition, anticipating the objection that all the audience would want to know about is celebrity gossip, Brandel explains that "the feedback loop that results in a never-ending naked Kardashian clickhole is *not* created because journalists are starting stories with audience questions. (That happens because journalists are chasing metrics.)"[88] In fact, she says, the questions drummed up by the audiences of the real news organizations that she has worked with have resulted in more original, relevant, and popular stories than those generated by a team of editors sitting around a conference table in an enclosed newsroom.[89]

## NEW AND EVOLVING BUSINESS MODELS

There may be some who are reading this thinking, sure, all of these ideals about involving the audience are great, but what about the money? The traditional advertising and sales models supporting the media business are failing to sustain it as they used to, and something more is needed.[90] But new business models have emerged as well, and they are in fact most effectively employed alongside the above cited new trends in media production. While there are no doubt others to come, to date the new and evolving business models that have seen some success in, and thus hold the most potential for, supporting professional-level media productions are summarized here, along with the advantages and challenges of each.

## Crowdfunding

The first is *crowdfunding*. As in the example of *The Chosen*, media producers can tap in to the power of the crowd by asking their audiences for donations to support ideas, products, or services. Current popular platforms that anyone can utilize to employ this model for the purpose of funding media projects include Kickstarter and Indiegogo. Some organizations, such as Wikipedia and *The Guardian*, also solicit and collect user donations through their own websites as a way of fund-raising support for their services. Crowdfunding capitalizes on all that is right about involving one's audience in the process of production. Because followers literally invest in a project, they are more passionate about seeing its success and will be more likely to promote it within their own networks. It adds a grassroots, organic component to the traditionally more one-way process of media production, generates a buzz, and brings both fans and funds to the effort.

As noted by Dallas Jenkins in the opening example, however, crowdfunding has generally been more successful for smaller side projects, or for those franchises that already have a strong fanbase, such as the $5.7 million campaign that brought the television show *Veronica Mars* back to life.[91] In addition, soliciting donations is viewed in a negative light by some, seen as "cyber-pan handling,"[92] or passing the buck of responsibility for an organization's success or failure onto the audience.[93] Finally, it is never guaranteed that enough funds will be raised to support a project or service, so it cannot be relied on the way other funding sources can when planning for the future.[94] For these reasons, it is perhaps best employed by large media organizations with a degree of balance, not too excessively or fervently, and in conjunction with other funding sources. Not to be feared, however, crowdfunding could be viewed as a potential opportunity to listen to one's audience in a way that can also serve to financially support certain aspects of production.[95]

## Networked Labor

Another new business model employs the use of *networked labor*, or finding ways to get things done through networked communities, running along a spectrum of paid and contracted work to that which is free and volunteered. For instance, although contract jobs have long been a part of the media industry's mode of operation, freelancer communities like Upwork, Fiverr, and Contra offer more consistency to this model by providing a large database of companies, jobs, pitches, and talents that can be tapped in to on an as-needed basis.[96] Some smaller media organizations adopt this model by appealing directly to their audience as a community of freelancers, asking them to submit ideas and content that they will pay them for if featured, as on humor site Cracked[97] or culture hub Buzzfeed.[98] And of course, there is the unpaid labor that is provided for free through crowdsourcing and engagement with the audience. The financial benefits of such a model for the media companies are clear: They do not need to have as many full-time employees on staff and can rely at least part on their community to serve as resources.

But, as discussed in chapter 7, when it comes to digital labor, companies would be well-served to avoid exploiting those from whom they benefit. While freelancer communities allow people to find contract work more consistently, giving them independence and freedom from a nine-to-five job, freelancers can also be taken advantage of when contracts unfairly address issues like copyright, content control, and profits.[99] Likewise, sites seeking freelance submissions from their audiences should be extremely clear about the process, giving them information about the percentage of submissions that gets selected, the payment structures utilized, and the proposed handling of acknowledgments or attributions. When soliciting free, volunteered contributions from an audience or community, producers should always take care not to ask for too much. Balance and transparency are key in all of these methods. In general, if the benefits to a media producer or company far outweigh the benefits to those they are working with in networked labor, they risk being exposed for taking advantage of their position and having their reputation soiled as a result.

## Subscriptions and Memberships

Finally, subscription models, such as *paywalls*, where one must be a paying customer in order to access any content,[100] and *freemium content,* where some aspects of content or services are given for free but one can pay to access more, better, or ad-free aspects,[101] have evolved with the rise of interactive media. Like advertising, the subscription model is a carryover from an earlier era, but it has been a bit of a double-edged sword in the interactive media environment. On the one hand, it has been shown that streaming sites employing these models, such as Netflix and Spotify, have reduced file-sharing and piracy more effectively than copyright battles.[102] Print media outlets, the companies that have perhaps been most negatively affected by the new media environment, have used *metered paywalls,* a type of freemium content in which free access is given to a limited number of articles per month but a paid subscription is required in order to access more,[103] as an effective way to support themselves through digital revenue.[104] Meanwhile, independent and entrepreneurial media producers who have found their own audiences through social media sites have begun using subscription-based platforms like Patreon, Locals, and Substack to offer more exclusive content and enjoy interacting in a more intimate, often friendlier, space with their core audience.[105]

But there are also drawbacks to these models. For one, people tire of paying for several subscriptions at once,[106] and having too many for too high of a price in the marketplace has already begun to weaken their collective sustainability.[107] In addition, subscriptions limit the reach that an outlet can have in the media convergence ecosystem, and the blocks put up by metered paywalls create a negative user experience, generating annoyance and frustration, the exact opposite emotions to those necessary to convince a consumer to pay for one's product.[108] Finally, in the case of journalism especially, it reduces the important role that media can play in the lives of everyday citizens, and results in further disadvantaging already disadvantaged people who don't have the expendable incomes to subscribe.[109] The best antidote to these issues thus far has been to create a *membership* model, as *The Guardian* has done, where people are required to sign up for a free account once they hit a certain content limit. These account-holding members are then encouraged, but still not required, to donate to support this service that they so clearly enjoy and help expand its reach to others.[110] Combining this model with some of the new trends involving crowdsourcing, transparency, and audience engagement, such members could also be offered more of a say in the media that is ultimately produced, increasing both their degree of loyalty and likelihood of future financial support. In a similar way, *The Chosen* encourages those who viewed the series for free via their app to "pay it forward," donating to help others likewise watch the series for free, and encourages them to send "thank you" messages to those who made their own viewing possible. Such models take dedication, but they serve to address three major keys to survival in the media convergence ecosystem: (1) generating goodwill toward the media franchise for providing their content for free, (2) giving those who have the means within the core audience a way to express their passion for the product, and (3) offering a metric that media producers can use to ensure that they are continuing to maintain the quality, trust, and respect that their fans have come to expect.

## CONCLUSION

While the constant flux of new, evolving, and emerging trends and models for media will no doubt continue, this chapter offers a basic understanding of the core principles that can help media producers become more adaptable in the ever-present face of change, and demonstrates ways in which those principles have been successfully implemented thus far. There is no singular way to do media production anymore, there is no singular type of content distribution or delivery, and there is no singular business model supporting any of these. In the media convergence ecosystem, we can have filter-then-publish, publish-then-filter, and everything in between. Learning to see these new trends and models as opportunities rather than roadblocks can elucidate the ways that they can be used wisely to improve upon media offerings.

Regardless of the kind of media produced, level of audience involvement engaged with, or combination of funding sources utilized, there are three main principles to which all media producers would be advantaged to adhere: (1) focus on providing and maintaining a high-quality product, (2) earn trust and respect by being authentic and transparent with the audience, and (3) ensure fairness and balance in terms of who contributes to the product and how they benefit from those contributions. These principles might sound a bit idealistic in an age of extreme cynicism, where mere attention is viewed as value. But attention only lasts for a moment and consistent negative attention leads to a loss in value over time. As discussed in chapter 9, consumer loyalty and respect are what produces lasting value today. When so much of what we do is based on carelessly publishing first and filtering later, it is just these attributes of integrity—quality, authenticity, openness, and fairness—that can earn media producers the loyalty needed to rise, and stay, above the noise.[111]

# NOTES

1. *The Chosen*, "What God told me," 2:45.

2. *The Chosen*, 3:01, 3:59.

3. *The Chosen*, 5:38.

4. *The Chosen*, "'I'm in a tough spot," 2020 Chosen update," July 5, 2020, Video, 8:27, https://youtu.be/Px-FPr--nRQ.

5. *The Chosen*, "The Story Behind," 1:56.

6. VidAngel Studios, "You Have the Power to Skip the Unacceptable in Movies and TV," accessed December 31, 2020, https://www.vidangel.com.

7. *The Chosen*, "The Story Behind The Chosen," September 15, 2018, Video, 8:58 (2:09), https://youtu.be/3-fxe-4fvlc/.

8. *The Chosen*, "What God told me about my failure that led to The Chosen | Dallas Jenkins," October 15, 2019, Video, 11:03 (8:40), https://youtu.be/evqanx-4XpI.

9. Mollick, "The Dynamics of Crowdfunding," 1.

10. Maddaus, "VidAngel Hit."

11. *The Chosen*, "What God told me about my failure that led to The Chosen | Dallas Jenkins," October 15, 2019, Video, 11:03 (8:53), https://youtu.be/evqanx-4XpI.

12. *The Chosen*, "The Story Behind The Chosen," September 15, 2018, Video, 8:58 (3:48), https://youtu.be/3-fxe-4fvlc/.

13. VidAngel Studios, "About The Chosen," Campaign, Accessed December 31, 2020, https://studios.vidangel.com/the-chosen-reg-cf.

14. *The Chosen*, "Not your grandma's Jesus show," April 8, 2020, Video, 6:07, https://youtu.be/mGWnwIvZopc.

15. Parke, "Story About Life."

16. Bond, "Largest-Ever Crowdfunding Campaign"; VidAngel Studios, "About The Chosen."

17. Parke, "Story About Life."

18. Parke.

19. *The Chosen*, "What God told me about my failure that led to The Chosen | Dallas Jenkins," October 15, 2019, Video, 11:03 (9:53), https://youtu.be/evqanx-4XpI.

20. TheChosen (@thechosentv), "TheChosen," Twitter profile, accessed January 1, 2021. https://twitter.com/thechosentv.

21. Moore, "Elgin Filmmaker."

22. Bond, "Largest-Ever Crowdfunding Campaign."

23. Shoemaker and Vos, *Gatekeeping Theory*, 4.

24. Shirky, *Here Comes Everybody*, 97.

25. Shirky, 98.

26. Benkler, *The Wealth of Networks*, 209.

27. Shirky, *Here Comes Everybody*, 98.

28. Shirky, 98.

29. Mandiberg, "Introduction," 2–3.

30. Shoemaker and Vos, *Gatekeeping Theory*, 123.

31. Brabham, *Crowdsourcing*, 49–50; Surowiecki, *The Wisdom of Crowds*, 234.

32. Jenkins, *Convergence Culture*, 275; Leavitt and Robinson, "Upvote My News," 6; Nadler, "For Every Citizen Journalist"; Tewksbury and Rittenberg, *News on the Internet*, 94.

33. Brabham, *Crowdsourcing*, xv.

34. Bruns, *Gatewatching*, 156; Jenkins, *Convergence Culture*, 271.

35. Jemielniak and Przegalinska, *Collaborative Society*, 73–74; Jenkins, 278.

36. Digg, "Digg Dialogg." Digg TV, archived November 14, 2009, https://web.archive.org/web/20091117120239/https:/tv.digg.com/diggdialogg/.

37. Diggnation, "Ozzy Osbourne TELLS ALL—What is Iron Man REALLY About ? – Digg Dialogg," June 17, 2010, Video, 34:19, https://youtu.be/4isrVLnyZ5w.

38. Nadler, "For Every Citizen Journalist."

39. CNN, "'Digg Dialogg.'"

40. *Wall Street Journal*, "Digg Dialogg with Timothy Geithner," August 25, 2009, Video, 19:47, https://www.wsj.com/video/digg-dialogg-with-timothy-geithner/A0A13568-043B-468A-A8A9-0D5426057FEF.html.

41. "Digg Dialogg with Timothy Geithner."

42. Shaw, "President Obama Misses."

43. Kilgler-Vilenchik and Tenenboim, "Sustained Journalist-Audience Reciprocity," 269.

44. Kilgler-Vilenchik and Tenenboim, 279.

45. Morgan, "Welcome to the New."

46. *The Chosen*, "TheChosenSeries," YouTube Channel, accessed January 1, 2021, https://www.youtube.com/c/TheChosenSeries/.

47. *The Chosen*, "Can you trust The Chosen?" December 27, 2019, Video, 10:47, https://youtu.be/S1E-gFGKVWw.

48. Sahms, "The Chosen's Dallas Jenkins."

49. Thompson, "6 Reasons Journalists Should"; Rosen, "Show Your Work."

50. Rosen, "Show Your Work"; Sill, "How to Begin Practicing"; Silverman, "Show the Reporting."

51. Kahn, "Transparency Is the New."

52. Empson, "Jeff Jarvis: When It."

53. Levin, "*Serial* Wasn't."

54. Kahn, "Transparency Is the New."

55. Landes, "Koenig's 'Serial' Wins Peabody."

56. Levin, "*Serial* Wasn't."

57. Bishop, "How 'Serial' Is Making."

58. Sill, "How to Begin Practicing."

59. Chien, "4 Ways Muni Diaries."

60. Schmidt, "It's Not 'Citizen Journalism."

61. Zooniverse, "Publications," Accessed January 1, 2021. https://www.zooniverse.org/about/publications.

62. Hickman, "How We Used Facebook."

63. Loosen, Reimer, and De Silva-Schmidt, "Data-Driven Reporting," 1249.

64. Viner, "A Mission for Journalism."

65. Arroyo Nieto and Valor, "How *The Guardian* Capitalized."

66. Rosen, "Show Your Work."

67. Viner, "A Mission for Journalism."

68. Broersma, 30.

69. Rosen, "Show Your Work."

70. Rosen.

71. Grebb, "Rejected TV Pilot Thrives."

72. Grebb.

73. Grebb.

74. Grebb.

75. Grebb.

76. Smith, "Push Journalism vs. Pull."

77. Smith.

78. Smith.

79. Smith.

80. Smith.

81. Smith.

82. Smith.

83. Smith.

84. Dalelio and Weinhold, "'I Know from Personal.'"

85. Hearken, "About Hearken," accessed January 1, 2021, https://wearehearken.com/about-us/.

86. Brandel, "Questions Are the New."

87. Brandel.

88. Brandel.

89. Brandel.

90. Tewksbury and Rittenberg, *News on the Internet*, 34–35.

91. Catapooolt, "Top 10 Highest Crowdfunded."

92. Pela, "I Hate Crowdfunding."

93. Moritz, "Newspapers: Don't Lecture."

94. Gen, "Read This Before You."

95. Moritz, "Newspapers: Don't Lecture."

96. Younger, "Contra and Other Platforms."

97. Hill, "Write for Cracked."

98. Sanders, "How to Pitch Essays."

99. Salamon, "E-lancer Resistance."

100. Tewksbury and Rittenberg, *News on the Internet*, 177.

101. Gu et al., "Selling the Premium," 10; Tewksbury and Rittenberg, 178.

102. Herbert and Lotz, "Approaching Media Industries," 358; Quintais and Poort, "The Decline of Online Piracy."

103. Tewksbury and Rittenberg, *News on the Internet*, 178.

104. Arroyo Nieto and Valor, "The NYT Proves."

105. Fischer, "Ad Models Break."

106. Moritz, "Newspapers: Don't Lecture."

107. Barrett, "You're About to Drown"; Bode, "The Rise of Netflix"; Stokel-Walker, "To Compete with Netflix."

108. Howard, "Three Reasons Why."

109. Howard.

110. Arroyo Nieto and Valor, "How *The Guardian* Capitalized."

111. Howard, "Three Reasons Why."

*Chapter 12*

# The New Gatekeepers

## INTRODUCTION: THE CATCH

Mark S. Luckie was the strategic partner manager for global influencers at Facebook for over a year.[1] Before he left the company, he circulated a 2,500-word memo to his colleagues that thoughtfully engaged with what he called Facebook's "black people problem."[2] In addition to detailing some of the company's internal issues with racial discrimination, the memo outlined a variety of processes on the platform itself that have particularly adverse effects for its African American users, most notably removing content and accounts inaccurately flagged for "hate speech."[3] Receiving no formal response from the company, Luckie decided to make the memo available to the public by posting it to, of all places, Facebook.[4] The post itself was soon deleted for violating "community standards."[5] Perhaps Luckie shouldn't have been surprised, but he couldn't help but laugh. "I've been on so many phone calls and email threads with people having this issue," he said. "In an ironic twist, I am dealing with this."[6]

The practice of removing content that is not explicitly unlawful or illicit is antithetical to the many benefits that interactive media have had for people, especially those whose perspectives have long been underrepresented. Yet this practice is also perfectly legal and within the host companies' rights to do so, and it has been occurring at an increasing rate. In response to criticisms that they are not doing enough to protect their users from bullying, harassment, toxicity, and exposure to misinformation,[7] the major interactive media companies have begun to expand their *content moderation* protocols, employing more aggressive filters and "nets" designed to catch, subdue, restrict, or otherwise divert away unwanted elements through a combination of automated, human, and artificial intelligence (AI) processes. Although this has perhaps successfully limited the reach of the bad actors these platforms have inadvertently empowered, it has also effectively closed the same doors on those who had benefited most from their formerly more open accessibility.

As noted by Luckie, "black people are finding that their attempts to create 'safe spaces' on Facebook for conversation among themselves are being derailed by the platform itself."[8] Activists, educators, and advocates regularly see their content deleted and accounts suspended for discussing racism, even though they are fighting against these issues and working to bring them to light.[9] Although these decisions can be appealed and reversed[10] (this was ultimately the fate of Luckie's post[11]), such takedowns create significant roadblocks to discussion, especially when they occur pervasively within a particular community.[12] In addition, it often requires the attention of professional media coverage to bring about such a decision reversal,[13] thus reintroducing elite gatekeeping over citizens' access to the public sphere, and disadvantaging those who have not yet achieved a significant enough following to warrant such media attention. The process of being content-moderated out of existence on interactive media platforms has become so common among activists that they have begun to use codes to talk around keywords and employ buddy systems to alert followers when a partner has "been sent to Facebook jail."[14] But these hardly seem like equitable or sustainable solutions, and the changes have left many users stuck in a catch-22. As the platforms that they first flocked to because of their freedom and connectivity now increasingly silence their voices, they can neither leave nor stay without it having a negative impact on their efforts.[15]

These upticks in moderation have proven to be a catch-22 for social media companies as well, as their attempts to address criticism from one corner of the knowledge culture are only met with criticism from another. The suppression of individuals and outlets from across the political spectrum has frequently resulted in negative backlash as it is used against them as evidence of bias.[16] And the reality is, these decisions are biased. As in storytelling, any judgments made to filter out content will be unavoidably subjective; even automated judgments follow rules created by humans influenced by things like culture, opinion, experience, and background.[17] Additionally, when such rules are applied to the vast sea of content that is posted freely, dynamically, and constantly by millions of people from all over the world, it is impossible to enforce them in a way that is entirely clear, comprehensive, consistent, and without error.[18] So, what is a social media company to do? Luckie's recommendation is to use more humans—albeit humans trained in cultural competency—to make these decisions.[19] While this would certainly be a positive step, like many of the solutions proposed today, it does not address the core problem, which is the real and pervasive enormity of these platforms overall. Because the biggest catch-22 of all is that, by using these companies' services for so many of our communications, we have simply given them too much power, and now neither we, nor they, know exactly what to do about it.

## Three Categories of New Gatekeepers

Throughout this book, we have largely focused on all that has been made possible by interactive media, and the democratizing, empowering, and diversifying successes of its end-to-end, networked design. As the Internet has grown into an increasingly commercialized, corporatized space, however, we have unwittingly put our lives into the hands of a small number of powerful corporations. In addition, because these private companies keep the mechanisms of their products' workings behind the black box of trade secrets, we do not know exactly how they interact with, or make decisions about, the information they both collect and provide in various ways.[20] So, although the design principles of interactive media have allowed us to largely circumvent the gatekeeping of the traditional media industry, these technology companies now dominating the interactive media landscape have emerged as *new gatekeepers*. They not only filter, but collect, amplify, and control a majority of the information we access today, and have the power to do so in ways that can interfere with our access and agency in mediated public spaces.[21] As Manuel Castells explains, "different forms of control and manipulation . . . in the public space are at the heart of power-making."[22] When it comes to such "power-making" in the twenty-first century, there are three categories of new gatekeepers—access providers, manufacturers, and social/information services—who not only have the ability to control and manipulate, but also to exploit, our communication and information. These are detailed in the following sections.

## The Access Providers

The *access providers* are the companies that give us access to the Internet through our computers or mobile devices. They include wireless companies, like Verizon and AT&T, and Internet Service Providers (ISPs) such as Xfinity and Frontier. Their services hook us up to the underground cables, satellites, and cellular towers that bring us to the Internet, and manage the amount of data that can be accessed by an individual user at a given time. Technically, they have the ability to exert control over whether or not someone is able to access online information at all.

Because they provide the means of connection required for many of the basic communication functions needed in today's world, the access providers have the most potential to infringe upon our freedoms. It is for this reason that these companies in particular have been in the past regulated by the Federal

Communications Commission (FCC) to follow rules of *Net Neutrality*, meaning that they are not allowed to block, slow down, or limit in any way the Internet access of their paying customers.[23] These rules ensure that, in the same way that water and electric companies cannot discriminate in the level of service they provide, access providers give everyone the same degree of access to the Internet, no matter the use or the user.[24] However, these legal requirements have vacillated in their existence, application, and enforcement over the years.[25] In fact, the rules were not formally applied at the federal level in the United States until the year 2015, and were then subsequently eliminated by the FCC in 2017.[26]

The wireless companies in particular are in a unique position to control access, as they not only connect us to the Internet, but also directly to each other via phone calls, voice mails, and text messages. Similar to home utilities services, companies that help connect people so that they may communicate with one another, such as traditional phone line companies, are classified as "common carriers," and they are expected to "serve the public indiscriminately."[27] However, "the laws that forbid common carriers from interfering with voice transmissions on ordinary phone lines do not apply to text messages."[28] In fact, texting might better fit into the category of social and information services discussed below, which have far fewer restrictions.

It seems odd that phone companies would be seen as common carriers with respect to phone calls but not text message communication. From a consumer's perspective, we see little difference between the two, and would reason that the same rules for phone calls should apply to texting, or for that matter any of the telephone-like "calls" that we make through our phones on video applications like FaceTime and Zoom. But, they do not.[29] While phone lines are considered "telecommunications services" offering merely the means for the *transmission* of information,[30] text messages, video calls, and (as of 2017) ISP connections to the Internet,[31] are considered "information services" offering various *capabilities* to express information via this transmission.[32] This distinction is subtle, but the reason it matters is that the government has much less authority to make it illegal for companies in the latter category to interfere with our communications in a nondiscriminatory manner.[33] Both common carriers and public utilities have traditionally been ruled as neither "authorized [nor] required to investigate or regulate the public or private conduct of those who seek service at their hands."[34] Those deemed information services, however, are allowed to both investigate and regulate what we do via their services, and yet they are still not legally required to do so. As noted in chapter 10, however, the difficulty we now have distinguishing between the legal categories for media and communications related companies, services, and activities is making the application of the current laws increasingly confounding.

## The Manufacturers

The *manufacturers* are the companies that create the devices—the hardware—through which we use interactive media. They include the companies that create computers, tablets, mobile phones, and smart devices (i.e., smart watches, smart TVs, smart speakers, etc.), such as Apple, Samsung, LG, and Dell. We know that many of these devices are created with built-in global positioning systems (GPS) that continually track their location, microphones that pick up sound (and, in many cases, are always listening for system "wake-up" cues), and cameras that can capture images and video. This means they have the potential to collect information about their users that could invade their privacy and essentially put them under constant surveillance. There are, of course, privacy regulations in place that do not allow them to do this without the customer's knowledge and consent, or to use it against people for the purposes of exploitation or control, but there are a lot of gray areas within the application of the law that are still being worked out (more on this in chapter 13).

In addition, these companies make the final determinations about what systems will be preloaded on their devices—the software—which controls how they will work, whom they will work with, and when they will be updated, even forcing these updates regardless of the user's wishes long after they have purchased and "own" the product.[35] For instance, Apple's iPhone currently requires that all application ("app") icons appear on the home screen(s), while Android smartphones allow the user to decide which ones will be accessed via the home screen(s). These are mostly little things, but consider what might happen if all of these companies decided at once to limit users' ability to control privacy settings such as turning off location tracking or microphone listening. Or imagine if a smartphone were built to implement controls on users' ability to use their own recording features, such as turning them off based on location or time of day. Indeed, Apple has filed patents revealing plans to stop iPhone users from being allowed to film at live concerts—working with the venue to install a system that will turn off the cameras upon entry—to help curb copyright violations from people filming in the audience.[36] While that may be a well-intentioned use, it is not hard to imagine other more nefarious uses that would interfere with citizens' ability to capture and share documentation revealing injustices or corruption in certain locations.

The manufacturers also have the capacity to build into their machines blocks to *interoperability*, or the adaptability of tools to work across hardware and software systems, and they frequently engage in this practice today.[37] By being incompatible with other companies' products, our use of these devices "locks us in" to an ongoing relationship with the brand, and acts as a means to force us to continue to buy products from their company and only their company.[38] This "*lock-in*," as Pariser defines it, "is the point at which users are so invested in their technology that even if competitors might offer better services, it's not worth making the switch."[39] From a business perspective, of course this makes sense; why give competitors an edge? However, from a consumer rights perspective, this has reduced our freedom of choice, as our ability to discontinue use of a service, should they cross a line of control or exploitation that we are uncomfortable with, is complicated by the fact that we cannot even take our own digital or physical "stuff" with us when we leave.

## The Social/Information Services

The *social/information services* are the companies that offer us digital interface tools—software, apps, and websites—that can be used for a variety of communicative, connective, or informational purposes. They include social media companies like Instagram, Snapchat, Facebook, and Twitter, but also search engines like Google and Bing, and email services like Gmail and iCloud. As noted earlier, these companies, which are legally referred to as "information services"[40] also include text messaging and video calls, as these are understood as services that go beyond simply "transmission," or making a connection from point A to point B. The problems discussed in the opening introduction to this chapter were solely derived from the use of these social and informational services, and these new gatekeepers are probably the most complicated when it comes to the control and power that they can exert over information. Because they host such a large portion of our communications today, they have a tremendous potential to control the conversation. The complexities and consequences of the myriad ways in which these services do so is explored in further detail in the next section.

As all three categories of new gatekeepers become more and more embedded in our daily existence, we are also bearing witness to their increasing consolidation, helping them to grow in market dominance.[41] Some companies, such as Microsoft, Google, Apple, and Amazon, are big players as both manufacturers and social/information services, developing hardware and software. In addition, they are continually buying one another up. Facebook, for instance, owns both Instagram and WhatsApp,[42] Google owns YouTube,[43] and Amazon owns Twitch.[44] The access providers, too, have crossed categorical lines, such as when Verizon bought Yahoo! and AOL.[45] And sometimes the new gatekeepers join forces with the old gatekeepers of legacy media (already concentrated into what we call the "big six" media corporations), such as when Comcast acquired NBCUniversal, or when AT&T merged with Time Warner.[46] As one might imagine, these mergers put yet more power and control into the hands of fewer and fewer mega-corporations, which only intensifies their capacity to dominate and manipulate our daily and increasingly mediated existence in varying ways.

## CONTINUUM OF FILTERING

In the past, our tendency to assume that technology is unbiased or neutral has led us to believe that interactive media companies, particularly the social/ information services, provide us with an unadulterated "public square" for the free expression and exchange of ideas and knowledge (indeed, they even promote themselves that way).[47] Thus, we have come to expect such freedom in the global and decentralized spaces of the Internet. The reality, however, is that the First Amendment protecting against the infringement of our freedom of speech only applies to the domains of the US government.[48] Our right to exercise that freedom does not necessarily extend to the spaces we interact in that are owned by private corporations (who are far from neutral),[49] despite the fact that we might feel as if they are "our" public spaces. The social/ information services do not have to give everyone a platform or equal access to reach the world through their services, although in earlier years of their existence, other than illegal activity, they mostly did.[50] In addition, they often filter and promote certain content, not to censor it, but instead for the purposes of providing people with a better user experience or to improve upon their advertising models.[51] Finally, when we consider interactive media as not just subject to US laws and regulation, but rather as the global phenomenon that they are, what we collectively experience in terms of "filtering" content might be best conceived of as a *continuum of filtering*, extending from the most harmless of recommendation practices all the way to the intentional censorship of certain information, perspectives, or ideas.

### Algorithmic Gatekeeping

The social/information services are based on programming code functions, or *algorithms*, that provide instructions on what the system should do in a given situation.[52] These algorithms provide the mechanisms for how the system interacts with the information that it collects and then outputs, such as the algorithm controlling the ordering of search results when we Google something, or the algorithm determining what content is recommended to us on social media sites.[53] Since they are not open-source or available for review, we don't know, exactly, how these algorithms make such determinations, or why certain content gets promoted over others.[54] We do know, however, that these companies have spent the last decade or so using the massive amount of user data they have collected in order to continually refine and adjust their models in ways that maximize our time and attention on their websites.[55] The result is an array of algorithms that have gotten extremely effective at feeding on human weaknesses.[56] As the dominant interactive media platforms engage in this *algorithmic gatekeeping*, they are evolving from transmission services into curation services,[57] and we are once again seeing media that was originally used to reflect and broaden the public conversation move toward directing those communications in ways that benefit them more than us.[58]

In transparent or open filtering that clearly and visibly ranks each piece of content based on user ratings, votes, or likes, we can bear witness to something closer to true, bottom-up crowdsourcing, a reversed publishing model as described in chapter 11. However, black box algorithms insert themselves in the end-to-end process of user input and response, acting as intermediaries interfering with our capacity for control on both an individual and collective level, and thus reducing the interactivity of interactive media (see definition, chapter 1). In addition, many of these filters take into account other aspects of the communication, prioritizing things like the popularity and reputability of the sender, the usage history of the receiver, and other characteristics about both the user and/or the content they are being shown.[59]

These indicators might seem harmless enough, indeed even helpful, but there are also repercussions of each. By prioritizing the popularity of a channel, for instance, YouTube deprioritizes the content creators who are just starting out, making it harder for them to reach an audience than those who have an already established one.[60] By prioritizing source reputability, Google filters out alternative news sites from its news search, highlighting only what professional media outlets are covering, and leaving independent and citizen perspectives and information out entirely.[61] By prioritizing someone's usage history, Facebook prevents its users from seeing articles that they are less likely to "like," even though less enjoyable information might actually help them to gain a more nuanced understanding of the world they inhabit.[62] Over time, the combination of this kind of content filtering with the adaptations that communicators make to their messaging so that it best satisfies what seem to be the algorithms' "preferences," results in a significant homogenizing, narrowing of the range of diversity in the content that we access on these platforms.[63]

## The Filter Bubble

Eli Pariser coined the term *"the filter bubble"* to describe the world of our own making that we exist in when we use interactive media, specifically due to the customization protocols of these sites' algorithms.[64] When customization is consumer-focused, such as when it is used for targeted advertising or recommending products and entertainment content that we might like, this may be relatively innocuous.[65] However, when these same targeting or recommendation principles are applied to everyday conversations, news content, political information, or social messaging, they can have the effect of keeping us unknowingly within an ideological echo chamber.[66] As humans, we already have a tendency to seek out social and political content with which we agree.[67] Conservatives watch Fox News; liberals watch MSNBC. This is not, actually, healthy, and helps no one but the cable news outlets. Interactive media has the potential to expose us to how other people see things, giving us a more diverse and realistic perspective on the world. When they utilize customized filtering, however, the social/information services only exacerbate our tendency for self-selection by further limiting our exposure to other viewpoints.[68] And it is more insidious than the cable news networks, because we don't even realize it's happening.[69] We just look at our feeds full of seemingly regular people who all seem to agree with us and see fewer and fewer of those who disagree, confirming our belief that they are the weirdos. Meanwhile, those "weirdos" are seeing the exact opposite on their screens, and thinking the same thing about us. This may be comforting for us psychologically, but it is very dangerous for us socially.[70] It limits our worldview and eliminates opportunities for bridging capital and dialogue.[71] It is the stuff of division, polarization, hostility, and distrust, all characteristics that have been steadily increasing across American society in recent years.[72]

## Content Moderation

Although the filter bubble is the largely unintentional effect of customized delivery protocols, moving further down the continuum of filtering we find a more intentional kind that takes place via content moderation. As noted in the opening example, the social/information services use content moderation to attempt to "clean up" their platforms for the purposes of limiting hate speech, harassment, misinformation, and other ills. While these are good reasons to moderate content, these categories are not always entirely clear,[73] and such efforts have gotten increasingly aggressive over the last few years.[74] There is also no transparency about these processes. A given site's algorithms are subject to constant updates and tweaks influenced by a variety of factors behind the scenes—estimated of up to thousands of times per year[75]—and users are kept completely unaware of these changes.[76] Exacerbating these complications, automated algorithms tend to identify and take down a lot of "false positives" that are removed without due cause.[77]

In addition to activists fighting racism, others who are more likely to experience this "collateral" deplatforming, restriction, and removal of content or accounts include those who highlight violence in their content (such as those documenting war crimes[78] or police watchdog groups[79]), alternative and citizen news outlets,[80] those who use provocative speech to "disrupt the narrative"[81] or challenge mainstream ideas,[82] and those who advocate for less widely accepted causes (such as anti-abortion[83] or alternative medicine groups[84]). Such moderation provides a solid grounding for which to accuse site owners of political meddling, dialogic interference, and social exclusion.[85] For conspiracy theorists, takedowns only add fuel to the fire, as targets can now provide proof that they are, indeed, being silenced by the "establishment." Perhaps the worst consequence of all is that such moderation practices can result in sending certain groups and communities away from the mainstream platforms and off to other, more closed-off spaces, breaking the ties between the clusters of small world networks and reducing bridging capital in the broader society (see chapter 4). If this continues, the social media landscape will end up looking like a less-enjoyable Baskin-Robbins: "32 flavors of censorship-supported echo chambers. Choose your favorite and never engage in dialogue again!" We will be left with a host of unlinked, tightly knit clusters, each sorely lacking in diversity of thought and access to alternative viewpoints—active breeding grounds for bad and even dangerous ideas.[86]

## Censorship

Finally, the most extreme form of filtering on the continuum is the outright *censorship,* or blocking of content that contains information or ideas that a certain state actor finds undesirable. Working in concert to varying degrees with different nations' governments and laws, interactive media companies agree to block certain terms, sources, or sites, in which they will not allow them to be accessed at all.[87] Although in the United States such automated blocks have largely only been applied to content implicated in unlawful activity, in other countries they are often used to comply with rules that we would consider unjust.[88] For instance, in China, the government will only allow its citizens to access Google if the company agrees to block search results showing images or information about the 1989 Tiananmen Square massacre[89] (which they no longer agree to do[90]). In 2021, Twitter blocked over five hundred user accounts critical of the Indian government under threat of having their local employees in that country arrested if they did not comply.[91] The global nature of the Internet makes the most popular interactive media companies international companies by default, and international companies must comply with the laws of other countries if they want to do international business. But we, the users, do not have these same business concerns. Thus, as we consider this most extreme end of the continuum of filtering, it is important that we recognize the relationship between these gradations of content interference so that we can recognize and identify when the lines threatening human freedom are being crossed.

## PHASES OF ACCESS AND CONTROL

In America, where we value freedom of speech so highly that it is the first amendment listed in our bill of rights, it is difficult to know what to do about these issues, to what degree these companies should be regulated, and in what directions. The current situation raises more questions than it does answers, but it might be helpful to look at a brief history of Internet regulation for context. In 2010, John Palfrey outlined four phases of Internet regulation with respect to access and control[92]; I add one more to the list below.

### Phase 1: The Open Internet (1960s–2000)

Palfrey calls the first phase of the Internet the *open Internet*, lasting from its birth in the 1960s (though it really did not get off the ground until the mid-1990s) to the year 2000.[93] In these early days, the Internet was seen as another world; we called it "cyberspace."[94] It was a beacon of freedom where anyone could say or do practically anything and it had little to no bearing on the real world.[95] So, at that time, there was little to no need for limiting access or regulating control mechanisms. But the Internet's earliest adopters recognized the potential for such interference.[96] They warned against allowing any sort of government or even commercial intrusion into their free online world, as they knew it would lead to putting limits on their activities.[97] While these principles of freedom continue to persist within the culture of the Internet, as it became more and more integrated with our lives and important to our economy and culture, many varied interests began to take notice.

### Phase 2: Access Denied (2000–2005)

The second phase, lasting from the year 2000 to 2005, is called the *access denied* phase.[98] As Palfrey explains, in this phase, "states and others came to think of the activities and expression on the Internet as things that needed to be blocked or managed."[99] Governments around the world began to note the Internet's importance, and lawmakers began to apply regulation from the offline world to the speech and organization taking place in the online world. More authoritarian countries began the outright censorship of information by implementing blocks against certain domains and URLs.[100] Filtering mechanisms began to be applied in more democratic societies in this phase, too. Europe began filtering out child pornography, and the United States began to regulate access from libraries and schools.[101] Although many of these filtering efforts can be circumvented by tech-savvy people anyway,[102] this phase introduced the idea that, across the board, the government does indeed have a say in what can and should be allowed on the Internet.

### Phase 3: Access Controlled (2005–2010)

In the third phase, *access controlled*, lasting from 2005 to 2010, more subtle mechanisms for control and limiting access began to be used as well, which were more subject to waver with changes in the cultural and political climate in a given country.[103] For example, governments began using the Internet for surveillance and monitoring of the population, and technologies of authentication and identity verification became more prevalent.[104] There were even calls to require users to obtain a license to use the Internet.[105] These kinds of identity-based controls can have a chilling effect on free speech and, in more oppressive states, be used to help identify journalists and activists so that they can be arrested or otherwise detained.[106] With the rise of smartphone use in this phase, mobile tracking added an important layer of location data that law enforcement could access in order to track down wanted individuals. It was also in this phase that governments around the world began working with private corporations like Google, Facebook, and YouTube to get them to cooperate with their control mechanisms.[107]

### Phase 4: Access Contested (2010–2015)

Writing in 2010, Palfrey proposed the fourth phase, *access contested*, in light of the public's growing awareness of and backlash against state interference efforts to control and regulate online communication.[108] As we began to see that the Internet was no longer a separate sphere of existence, we realized the necessity of its freedom to our own. Palfrey was correct in his identification of this new phase, as these contestations continued on after he wrote of this in 2010. It was in 2013, for example, that NSA whistleblower Edward Snowden revealed that the US government was accessing citizens' usage data in much more comprehensive ways than was previously realized, and concerns started to be raised about abuses of that power.[109] In response, interactive media companies for the most part joined in the public's outcry against such government interference during this phase, and began to make efforts to be more transparent about the data that is being collected from their users and what is done with it.[110]

## Phase 5: Controls Debated (2015–2020)

Palfrey's pattern of five-year phases has continued, as a new perspective emerging around 2015 and lasting through 2020 reflects what I am calling the *controls debated* phase. In this phase, citizens started to more readily recognize that there were very serious negative consequences of interactive media freedom. It gave everyone a voice, even those who we would rather not have one, and even those who would use these tools for real harm. In addition, we began to notice the ways in which the tools themselves were feeding into negativity and even encouraging bad behavior.[111] Thus, in an odd reversal of phase four, there was a shift in attitudes back toward Internet control rather than away from it.[112] This changing culture was exacerbated by increasing global efforts to crack down on dangerous speech worldwide, particularly due to new regulations put in place by the European Union after terrorist attacks in France and Germany in 2015.[113] Rather than adapt their rules for European users only, however, some platforms changed their blanket "Terms of Use" for everyone, in effect requiring all of their users to adopt the EU's new laws.[114] The efforts of the technology companies to meet these demands has led to a debate in the United States about the degree to which they should have the power to limit or promote access to certain kinds of content, people, or even platforms.[115] During this phase, the CEOs of major companies like Facebook, Twitter, Apple, Google, and Amazon have been brought into congressional hearings to discuss their services' role in things like election interference, the spreading of misinformation, and anti-trust violations.[116]

The ideological whiplash experienced between phases four and five signals that we are still in the midst of a significant transition period.[117] In such an unpredictable time, it is difficult to say what the next phase will look like, however the current debates over things like Net Neutrality and Section 230 (see chapter 10) may give us a clue. It is possible that in the next phase we will see a move toward "controls redistributed" with the introduction of new regulations and products aimed at breaking up corporate dominance in the technology sector and requiring practices more supportive of fairness, transparency, and consumer choice.[118] We may need to reconsider what should be treated as a "public service" and what that means for how these companies should be regulated.[119] The decisions we make, however, depends on a lot of factors, not the least of which is our ability to see beyond short-term problems and interests and consider how we are collectively shaping the future direction of our evolving media convergence ecosystem.[120] Whatever happens next, as we work to achieve a balance between freedom and responsibility in this age, it is important to be aware of this history so that we can understand that the Internet as we know it today is not simply "the way things are" but rather an ongoing and continuing work-in-progress, subject to change for better or for worse based on the choices that we collectively make.[121]

## CONCLUSION

As we witness and take part in the ongoing evolution of technological offerings that we have available to us today and into the future, it is important to fully understand the power these new gatekeepers have to both amplify and suppress our public and private information, and question the ways in which they can affect our society as a whole. To whom shall we turn to solve these problems? Relying on the same corporate, profit-driven entities who created these tools to do so is a very tenuous position to be in. In addition, technology companies will only be able to come up with technological solutions. As we've seen, these technologies extend our capacity to enact the same social processes that both empower the marginalized and embolden the dangerous.[122] But AI-enabled algorithms and filters do not have the capacity to understand if a communicative process is being applied in ways that are good or bad, only that it is being applied, so the technological response is to stop the process, which only results in disempowering everyone.[123] The problems that we want these companies and tools to fix are not, primarily, technology problems; they are humanity problems. The technologies just help to bring them out.

Perhaps, then, we could turn to the government for solutions. As noted, this seems to be the direction we are currently headed, and international and national policies affecting our uses of technology are still very much taking shape at this moment in time.[124] But like algorithms, regulatory policy is based on rules, and rules govern process, not outcomes. In addition, as we've seen, in those legal contexts where the rules are less straightforward and require adjudication on a case-by-case basis, such as those involving fair use and hate speech, the rules are undermined by the interactive media environment, where they are insufficient to operate at scale. When it comes to the interactive media space, whether law, algorithm, or company policy, the code must outline a set of predetermined and universally applied rules, which creates the context for what is possible[125] regardless of whether we, personally, approve of the outcomes. So, the question we need to answer is not in which cases we should apply the rules, but rather: To what extent and in what ways should the rules control our communicative and social processes in these spaces at all?[126] Until we can come to precise agreement on that answer, we will be unable to effectively proceed regarding new legislation and government regulation.[127]

In a free society, the policies, protocols, and rules that both corporations and the government adopt are heavily influenced by cultural norms.[128] So when it comes to shaping the future of the rules that govern interactive media, we should also look to ourselves. If we encourage more interference and control in our uses and demands, then that is the direction the rules will take. If we would rather control ourselves, however, we must learn to do so. The reality is that we all have a public platform now, our own social machine (however big or small our reach), and unless we outlaw interactive media wholesale, that is not going to change. As any public figure will tell you, having a public platform is a huge responsibility; it's time we start seeing it as such. As discussed in chapter 6, we can endeavor to use these services conscientiously ourselves, recognizing and acknowledging that the ways in which what we ourselves say and do, what we encourage and promote in these public spaces, could be problematic.

Importantly, we can also use our collective voice through these platforms to weaken not the power that we have through them, but rather the power that they have over us. This means that we should recognize when these companies are being inconsistent in their application of their mechanisms and/or policies, call it out, and identify the consequences. This also means that we should not be so dependent on a particular site or service that we simply and unquestioningly accept whatever they want to do with our data. Instead, we can encourage a redistribution of controls by choosing to utilize sites and services that are more transparent and have clear, open, and consistent filtering processes. In sum, we need not feel we are powerless to effect change when it comes to solving our technology-enabled social problems. On the contrary, we must recognize that we can take more personal responsibility for participating in their solutions. There are a variety of roles we can play in improving this situation moving into the future, many of which are offered in more detail in chapter 14.

## NOTES

1. Mark Luckie, "About," accessed January 1, 2021, http://www.getluckie.net/.
2. Luckie, "Facebook Is Failing."
3. Luckie.
4. Luckie.
5. Levin, "Facebook Removed Post."
6. Levin.
7. Asarch, "Steven Crowder Incites"; Conger et al., "Violence on Capitol Hill"; Edelman, "Stop Saying Facebook"; Mangan, "'Don't Touch Me'"; Marantz, "Free Speech Is Killing Us"; Marantz, "Reddit and the Struggle."

8. Luckie, "Facebook Is Failing."

9. Guynn, "Facebook While Black"; Silverman, "Black Lives Matter Activists."

10. Guynn, "Facebook's Secret Rules."

11. Levin, "Facebook Removed Post."

12. Guynn, "Facebook While Black."

13. Guynn.

14. Guynn.

15. Silverman, "Black Lives Matter."

16. Cochran, "I Blew the Whistle"; Damon, "Google Intensifies Censorship"; Givetash, "Laura Loomer Banned"; Myers, "Patreon Is a Threat"; Sheffield, "'Fake News' or Free."

17. Gillespie, "The Relevance of Algorithms," 169.

18. York, "Facebook's Latest Proposed Policy."

19. Luckie, "Facebook Is failing."

20. Fuchs, "Propaganda 2.0," 73.

21. McChesney, *Digital Disconnect*, 145; Shirky, *Here Comes Everybody*, 221.

22. Castells, *Communication Power*, 371.

23. Wu, "Network Neutrality, Broadband Discrimination," 167–68.

24. Barratt and Shade, "Net Neutrality," 296.

25. Trendacosta, "The FCC Has Made."

26. Brodkin, "To Kill Net Neutrality."

27. de Sola Pool, *Technologies without Boundaries*, 14; Hall, "Common Carriers," 413.

28. Liptak, "Verizon Block Messages."

29. McSherry, "When Academic Freedom."

30. The Communications Act defines a telecommunications service as "the offering of telecommunications for a fee." It defines *telecommunications* as "the transmission, between or among points specified by the user, of information of the user's choosing, without change in the form or content of the information as sent and received." Communications Act of 1934, 47 U.S.C. § 153.

31. Brodkin, "To Kill Net Neutrality."

32. The Communications Act defines an "information service" as "the offering of a capability for generating, acquiring, storing, transforming, processing, retrieving, utilizing, or making available information via telecommunications, and includes electronic publishing, but does not include any use of any such capability for the management, control, or operation of a telecommunications system or the management of a telecommunications service." Communications Act of 1934, 47 U.S.C. § 153.

33. Trendacosta, "The FCC Has Made."

34. *People v. Brophy*, 49 Cal.App.2d 15 (Cal. Ct. App. 1942).

35. Gillmor, "The Facebook Template."

36. Boyle, "Apple Has Patented iPhone."

37. Doctorow, "Adversarial Interoperability."

38. Pariser, *The Filter Bubble*, 40–41; Venkatesan et al., "Measuring and Managing," 65.

39. Pariser, 40.

40. Communications Act of 1934, 47 U.S.C. §153.

41. Andrejevic, "Work of Being Watched," 244.

42. Shead, "Facebook Owns."

43. Luckerson, "A Decade Ago."

44. Willens, "Once Dominant."

45. Kastrenakes, "Verizon Now Officially Owns."

46. Cook, "AT&T and Time Warner."

47. Dorsey, Jack (@jack), "Twitter cannot rightly serve as a public square if it's constructed around the personal opinions of its makers. We believe a key driver of a thriving public square is the fundamental human right of freedom of opinion and expression." Twitter, September 5, 2018. https://twitter.com/jack/status /1037399105306324993; Gillespie, "The Relevance of Algorithms," 181; York, *Silicon Values*, 14.

48. Braman and Roberts, "Advantage ISP," 422.

49. Couldry and Hepp, *The Mediated Construction*, 33; Ochigame and Holston, "Filtering Dissent," 85; Pedro-Carañana et al., "Introduction," 10.

50. Citron, "Extremist Speech, Compelled Conformity," 1036–37; York, "Reddit banned."

51. Donovan and boyd, "Stop the Presses?" 339–40.

52. Gillespie, "The Relevance of Algorithms," 167; Ochigame and Holston, "Filtering Dissent," 85.

53. Donovan and boyd, "Stop the Presses?" 339–40.

54. Pariser, *The Filter Bubble*, 10.

55. Donovan and boyd, "Stop the Presses?" 339; Hobbs, "Propaganda in an Age," 523.

56. Lanier, *Ten Arguments*, 12; Pariser, *The Filter Bubble*, 14–18.

57. Bruns, *Gatewatching and News Curation*, 159; Donovan and boyd, "Stop the Presses?" 7; Eisenstat, "How to Hold Social Media"; Kumar, "The Algorithmic Dance," 4.

58. Wu, *The Master Switch*, 6.

59. Pariser, *The Filter Bubble*, 38.

60. Granka, "The Politics of Search," 369–70.

61. Damon, "Google Intensifies Censorship."

62. Mott, "Don't Dismiss Debate."

63. Kumar, "The Algorithmic Dance," 15.

64. Pariser, *The Filter Bubble*, 9.

65. Pariser, 18.

66. Pariser, 9–10.

67. Stroud, "Media Use and Political," 358.

68. Pariser, *The Filter Bubble*, 127.

69. Pariser, 10.

70. Spohr, "Fake News and Ideological," 151.

71. Pariser, *The Filter Bubble*, 17.

72. Iyengar and Westwood, "Fear and Loathing," 691.

73. Citron, "Extremist Speech, Compelled Conformity," 1052; York and Greene, "Facebook's Latest."

74. York and Greene, "Facebook's Latest."

75. Grind et al., "How Google Interferes."

76. Gillespie, "The Relevance of Algorithms," 178.

77. York, "Reddit Banned."

78. Asher-Schapiro and Barkawi, "'Lost Memories';" Schulman, "YouTube Wants to Fight."

79. Alcorn, "Left-Wing News Sites."

80. Damon, "Google Intensifies Censorship"; Sheffield, "'Fake News' or Free."

81. Johnstone, "Twitter Shut Down."

82. BBC, "Twitter-Ban Feminist Defends"; Givetash, "Laura Loomer Banned"; Higgins, "The Bizzarre Political"; Myers, "Patreon Is a Threat."

83. Cochran, "I Blew the Whistle."

84. Haynes, "Is Google Suppressing."

85. Kumar, "The Algorithmic Dance," 14–15.

86. Benkler et al., *Network Propaganda*, 73.

87. Gillespie, "The Relevance of Algorithms," 179.

88. Citron, "Extremist Speech, Compelled Conformity," 1037–38; Lessig, *Code*, 80; Zittrain et al., "The Shifting Landscape," 2–3.

89. Mulligan and Griffin, "If Google Goes."

90. Sheehan, "How Google Took On."

91. Singh, "Twitter Blocks Accounts."

92. Palfrey, "Four Phases."

93. Palfrey, 981–84.

94. Gibson, *Neuromancer.*

95. Curran, "Rethinking Internet History," 40.

96. Barlow, "Declaration of Independence."

97. Kelly, "We Are the Web."

98. Palfrey, "Four Phases," 985–89.

99. Palfrey, 985.

100. Palfrey, 985–86.

101. Palfrey, 987.

102. Palfrey, 988.

103. Palfrey, 989.

104. Palfrey, 990; Lessig, *Code*, 48–52.

105. Agence France-Presse, "UN Agency Calls."

106. Palfrey, "Four Phases," 990.

107. Palfrey, 991.

108. Palfrey, 991–93.

109. Reitman, "3 Years Later."

110. Whittaker, "Five Years On."

111. Lanier, *Ten Arguments*, 44–45.

112. Asarch, "Steven Crowder Incites"; Conger et al., "Violence on Capitol Hill"; Edelman, "Stop Saying Facebook"; Mangan, "'Don't Touch Me'"; Marantz, "Free Speech Is Killing Us"; Marantz, "Reddit and the Struggle."

113. Citron, "Extremist Speech, Compelled Conformity," 1037.

114. Citron, 1038.

115. York, McSherry, and O'Brien, "Beyond Platforms."

116. Rosoff, "Congress Grills Tech CEOs"; Tracy and McKinnon, "Tech CEOs Square Off"; Watson, "Mark Zuckerberg's Testimony."

117. Jenkins, *Convergence Culture*, 11.

118. Nadler, Crain, & Donovan, "Weaponizing the Digital Influence," 40–44.

119. Braman and Roberts, "Advantage ISP," 444; Miège, "Theorizing the Cultural Industries," 98.

120. Lanier, *Ten Arguments*, 109–10; Wu, "Network Neutrality, Broadband Discrimination," 143.

121. Lanier, 103; Lessig, *Code*, 32.

122. Shirky, *Here Comes Everybody*, 208.

123. Galloway, *Protocol*, 142.

124. Citron, "Extremist Speech, Compelled Conformity"; Zittrain et al., "The Shifting Landscape."

125. Galloway, *Protocol*, 142; Lessig, *Code*, 77.

126. Lessig, 276.

127. Lessig, 24.

128. Lessig, 124.

# Chapter 13

# Privacy and Surveillance

## INTRODUCTION: HEART-SHAPED DOX

On a flight from New York to Dallas, two strangers struck up a conversation on a plane. They were young, they were attractive, they had a lot in common, and they flirted with each other a bit. Little did they know, they were also about to become the unwitting stars of a reality romcom that would bring a whirlwind of unsought public attention to their lives.[1] Why? The couple sitting in the row behind them, Rosey Blair and Houston Hadaway, decided to entertain themselves by eavesdropping on the pair to find out if their chance encounter would spark a new romance.[2] While this type of people-watching speculation is not altogether uncommon in public and shared spaces, rather than keeping it between her boyfriend and herself, Blair, an actress and photographer,[3] decided that this would make a great story for her Twitter following. She posted a tweet-thread in which she enthusiastically narrated the strangers' entire encounter through captioned photos and short video clips that she had secretly taken of them.[4] "They have been talking nonstop since we took off," she wrote, and "No wedding rings in sight!!!!!!" She drew hearts over their touching elbows viewed between the seats. She gushed over their adorable reactions to the small child who waved at them from a few rows ahead. She interspersed selfies of herself and her boyfriend watching with excitement and interest. The post soon went viral, earning over 900,000 likes,[5] and the hashtag #PlaneBae was born.[6] The story was covered on the *Today Show* and *Good Morning America*.[7] The humor, the drama, the suspense, and the feel-good narrative about a blooming romance simply captivated people.[8] It was, as Blair captioned in one of the photos, "compelling stuff."[9]

There were, however, a few dissenting voices responding to the story that expressed discomfort with the violation of the unaware subjects' privacy. For instance, @Chelsea_Fagan tweeted, "it's unreal how the internet has poisoned our . . . concept of basic privacy so much that u could be 100 tweets deep on something like that & not feel weird about it."[10] But amidst the overwhelming flood of positive and uncritically accepting responses, these detractors also expressed a felt sense of being a lone voice in the wilderness. As @TomandLorenzo noted, "My reaction to that apparently beloved viral plane romance tweetstory makes me think my expectations for privacy are wholly out of line with everyone else's."[11] Others even expressed a hint of shame about their downer responses to the story, tempering their comments with qualifiers like, "I didn't say anything earlier because I feared being a buzzkill,"[12] and "I didn't want to be cynical but . . . "[13]

Although these dissenters might have been in the minority, it turns out they were right. While Blair was cautious enough to scribble out the couple's faces in her photos[14] (though, oddly enough, not that of the waving child), she was not fully aware of the Internet's insatiable and collective ability to de-anonymize people and figure things out. This was not so bad for the man in the duo, who was a former pro soccer player and already used to a bit of public attention. Unfortunately for the woman, a more private person, she did not fare so well. "My personal information has been widely distributed online," she later wrote in a public statement under what shred of anonymity she had left, "I have been doxxed, shamed, insulted and harassed." (*"Doxing"* is when someone's personally identifiable information, such as their name, school, employer, and address, is given out publicly without their permission.[15]) "Voyeurs have come looking for me online and in the real world," she continued. "I did not ask for and do not seek attention."[16] Commentators and journalists then began reframing the story as a cautionary tale about "the dark side" of social media.[17] Blair herself felt awful.[18]

It speaks to a growing surveillance culture[19] in which so many thought it was cute and fun to follow, share, and openly discuss the surreptitiously recorded interactions of two strangers on a plane for entertainment. This was not an isolated incident, but rather one of the more prominent examples in a disturbing trend of privacy boundary[20] encroachment spurred on by the use of interactive media.[21] Whenever we participate in or even passively accept such surveillance of others as simply par for the Internet course, however, we are treating them as objects on a screen rather than the human beings they are: real people with lives, jobs, families, and responsibilities that were never intended for nor set up to handle such invasiveness or public consumption. We are also, by default, demonstrating a growing acceptance of different types of surveillance, from a variety of sources, into all of our lives.[22] Because the simple reality is that all information has become less controllable, including information about ourselves.[23] And until and unless we begin to adopt a more mature and measured set of privacy norms that oppose such intrusions into one another's lives, we should be prepared for a dox on all our houses.

## SITUATIONAL AWARENESS

In a world before interactive media, people generally had a clear understanding of the communication situation they were in. In a living room, for example, we knew that our actions and words were only observed by those present in the room. On a plane or in a restaurant, it was accepted that strangers might see or hear what we were saying, but we knew our communication was still limited to those within sight or earshot. It was only when speaking on a stage or through mass media that one's messages were understood as having "an audience," an ambiguous conglomeration of people in the hundreds, thousands, or even millions, most of whose reactions were not immediately (or ever) perceivable, and a communicator was not able to know exactly who received their message nor how they received it.[24] But even then, there was enough information that could be gleaned from what was known about the delivery format and the targeted audience[25] that we could imagine the type of person that might ultimately access our message and in what situations.[26] This *situational awareness* is an important factor in our messaging and communication behavior.[27] As Joshua Meyrowitz put it, "separation of situations allows for separation of behaviors."[28]

The removal of time and space from online communication, however, has reduced our capacity to be fully aware of the contexts that we are communicating in.[29] The variety of situations in which our behaviors, messages, or performances may be received is limitless and unpredictable, even in the most interpersonal of interactions.[30] Whether intended for the public or not, our communication can be shared, archived, copied, and redistributed with ease, and this inevitably amplifies its social consequences, for the better or for the worse.[31] This *social amplification* means that we have an extended capacity to collaborate, connect, and interact with one another via interactive media, but it also makes it easier to scrutinize, criticize, and mischaracterize each other.[32]

Due to this situational ambiguity and unpredictability, we now communicate not within a definition of the situation, but rather within a range of likely potentialities.[33] There are, essentially, three categories of potentialities that every message or communication behavior now carries with it. The first is the number of people who will receive a message.[34] A communicator may intend a message for just one or two people and end up having it reach millions, or it may be intended for a larger audience and reach only a few. The second category of potentialities is the ways that people may interact with, edit, remix, and re-present our communication, as a given message may find itself included in any number of creative, political, comedic, social, or cultural contexts.[35] The third category is the time frame(s) in which a message may be accessed or resurface, as the archived nature of interactive media gives people the ability to call up messages from months, years, or even decades earlier, to be received in a completely new time and context.[36]

There are times when an individual is more or less aware of all of this potentiality when they are communicating online, such as when someone records a vlog that is to be posted publicly on YouTube with the hopes of attracting attention. This awareness is what digital anthropologist Michael Wesch has termed *context collapse*.[37] As he describes it, this involves the knowledge that we are communicating in "an infinite number of contexts collapsing upon one another in that single moment of recording . . . the little glass lens becomes the gateway to a black hole sucking all of time and space—virtually all possible contexts—in on itself."[38] This phenomenon creates a heightened sense of self,[39] detached from situational awareness in a way that has never been experienced before by humanity. The *"networked audience"* of interactive media, as Marwick and boyd describe it, contains everyone known and unknown, expected and unexpected, and the situation is "both potentially public and personal."[40] As a result, communicators often "acknowledge multiple concurrent audiences" in their messaging and craft their identities in collaboration with their fans.[41]

More often, however, people use interactive media to communicate in very personal, social, or intimate ways without being fully aware of all of these potentialities.[42] In these instances, the extension of one's message or communication behavior to near infinite contexts, spaces, and times is neither intended nor in one's thought process when they are crafting or engaging in it. Without all these potentialities in mind, messages are not so carefully constructed. These communicators are then taken off-guard and feel violated when they find that their information is being used in other contexts that they had not anticipated.[43] This idea that we cannot control what happens with our communication and personal information can be very difficult for humans to accept, as we seem to have an innate sense of our right to privacy.[44] As a result, we live in a sort of ongoing state of denial and continue to be surprised every time we find that something we have communicated moves beyond our control in the interactive media space. Susan Barnes refers to as the *privacy paradox*, and it speaks to the lack of boundaries we actually have around our own information when we communicate (or are captured communicating) via interactive media.[45]

## THE EROSION OF PRIVACY

As the introduction of interactive media has blurred the lines between personal, private, social, and public communication, our ability to keep our own information within our preferred spaces is diminishing. But technology is not the only thing that is creating privacy challenges in the twenty-first century. Concurrent shifts in the law, the data economy, and the culture are also moving in this direction, and together all of these interrelated factors are continually influencing one another in ways that advance the ongoing erosion of privacy.

## The Law

In America, the notion that we have a human right to privacy has been enshrined in the Fourth Amendment to the Constitution. This clause states that citizens have a right "to be secure in their persons, houses, papers, and effects, against unreasonable searches and seizures," which "shall not be violated, and no Warrants shall issue, but upon probable cause, supported by Oath or affirmation, and particularly describing the place to be searched, and the persons or things to be seized."[46] This means that law enforcement entities are required to make a case before a judge that evidence of a crime may be found within a citizen's personal effects in order to be allowed to access them, and then only in limited ways.[47] Much of what would have formerly been stored in the physical manifestations of our "persons, houses, papers, and effects," however, is now stored digitally, which makes it easier to access and harder to contain. Information, whether personal, private, or public, flows relatively freely through the media convergence ecosystem beyond any single entity's control and may be collected and used by anyone, including the government.[48] Meanwhile, the inability of the legal system to keep up with technological developments has created numerous loopholes allowing government agencies to effectively operate as if "the very act of using modern technologies is tantamount to a surrender of your privacy rights."[49]

The truth is that our Fourth Amendment rights were never that well-protected by the courts to begin with.[50] In the past, however, there were physical barriers and obstacles to gathering and/or publicly sharing private citizens' personal information.[51] The process of collating a dossier of someone's unvolunteered background information and personal details, such as how they spend their free time, what their political opinions are, and who they associate with, was difficult, and required the employment of investigators with specialized skillsets, access, and knowledge to obtain.[52] In addition, journalists and editors, the only ones who really had the ability to publish information about a person's name or likeness on a wide scale, were careful about weighing confidentiality against the public's right to know.[53] Thus, in the past, instances of a citizen's private information being involuntarily obtained, let alone published, were few and far between, rare and distinct, and generally needed some strong justification to be supported.[54]

For reference, the big fear that kids in my generation had—and that grown-ups were constantly warning us against—was that we might do something, even just one thing, that was so bad that it "would go down on our permanent record!" Today, however, practically everything we do is logged, with immediacy, to a permanent record of our lives.[55] Sharing personal information and social monitoring is the rule, not the exception we're trying to avoid. Still, the law also recognizes that even those convicted of crimes should have a right to recover from past mistakes by allowing for an expungement of offenses from their records after a sufficient period of time.[56] Yet whatever is logged via interactive media can come back to haunt us at any point in the future, with no legal limits on how long it can be archived.[57] This is why the European Union asserted a legal "right to be forgotten" in 2014, requiring interactive media companies to delink a person from all personal data, including search results, if they should request it.[58] But even those tools that we use that are supposedly private, like email, texts, and direct or private messages, result in the storage of all our communication on interactive media companies' servers for an often undisclosed period of time, and these messages are frequently shared with law enforcement in criminal investigations as well.[59] We also carry with us everywhere we go smartphones, which have within them everything we never wanted anyone to know about us, and these, too, are often scooped up by police from crime scenes or during arrests.[60]

## The Data Economy

Giving over aspects of our private lives to companies and increasingly commodifying our identities might seem like a fair exchange for the opportunity to connect, express ourselves, and participate in public, civic, and social discussions online. But many are not fully aware of the extent to which these companies and organizations benefit from our data, employing super computers that constantly mine all of our information to identify trends and patterns for a variety of reasons and in quite powerful ways. As Eric Schmidt said when he was CEO of Google back in 2010, "if I look at enough of your messaging and your location, and use Artificial Intelligence, we can predict where you are going to go. Show us 14 photos of yourself and we can identify who you are."[61] The massive amounts of data that these companies collect are used to track what people have done and predict and even manipulate what they will do. In the aggregate, they create proprietary datasets and models that can be sold to others at a premium.[62] This kind of social data has eclipsed oil as the most valuable commodity in the world,[63] and it is all supported by our willingness to go along with this "fair" exchange.

The "Terms of Use" contracts that we agree to when using these sites codify this willingness by including our approval to share our user data with "third-party" entities, a vague reference covering a wide variety of groups and organizations that exist outside of the interactive media company itself.[64] But these contracts, notoriously dense and difficult to understand, either require our all-inclusive acceptance for use or are simply obtained through a disclaimer somewhere stating that, by using the site, we agree to its terms by default.[65] Most people do not pay much attention to these agreements or think about what they mean,[66] but rather are focused on the benefits for themselves when they sign up; the exchange is not fully thought through.

It may be that we simply choose to trust these companies and assume that they will not allow our private data to be shared with unwanted entities like criminals or the government. But what happens with the data that they collect is not fully under their control. Identity thieves can easily triangulate data points that we share publicly to find out everything they need to know about us. For instance, it has been shown that with just three data points—birthdate, zip code, and gender—a person can be accurately identified 87 percent of the time.[67] In addition, egregious violations have already happened via these platforms and without their full awareness. In 2013, National Security Agency (NSA) whistleblower Edward Snowden revealed to the public documents showing that the government has back-end methods for accessing these companies' databases.[68] In 2016, a company called Cambridge Analytica allegedly scraped Facebook profile data and used a psychologically oriented "personality test" to send users targeted and predictive behavior-modifying messages to influence their vote.[69] Additionally, any institution that collects and digitally stores people's private data, including government entities like the Internal Revenue Service (IRS), is subject to back-end data breaches and hacks by malicious actors.[70] Lastly, even if a particular company or CEO could somehow assure us that the data they have about us is fully protected today, that data will be archived on their servers for potentially decades to come, continually vulnerable to the shifts in leadership, ethics, principles, and bottom lines that inevitably occur in organizations over time.[71] The fact is that we have put our trust in corporations as the sole remaining barrier to losing one of the most basic rights that our society was founded upon, an illusion that provides us with a false sense of security as we give it all away to anyone and everyone who wants it.

## The Culture

Our willingness to accept this exchange when we use these companies' sites is also related to a cultural shift that first emerged with the popularity of reality TV in the 1990s, in which people are increasingly willing to put themselves—their image, name, ideas, thoughts, and behaviors—out there in a sort of volunteer celebrity-ism.[72] This trend has continued into the twenty-first century with the introduction of webcams and vlogs,[73] and was spurred on by social media. This shift towards "self-surveillance" also contributes to a culture in which corporate and government surveillance is more easily accepted, viewed as acceptable, and increasingly voluntary.[74] Since the Fourth Amendment does not protect us from private companies, ourselves, or each other, but rather solely from the direct intrusion of the state, we have no legal protections against mass scale surveillance of the citizenry through the information that we ourselves have willingly volunteered,[75] nor against private companies collecting and using this information in a variety of ways.[76]

## OPEN-SOURCE SOCIETY

In some ways, this chapter seems antithetical to what has been discussed in those previous, which have presented arguments for the opening up of things as a way of rooting out problems and addressing them. Indeed, early on, some of the pioneers of the Internet argued that using social media would make us more authentic and honest overall, and less likely to act immorally, since our lives would be an open book.[77] But we can see now that that hypothesis was wrong. In fact, in many cases we have witnessed the exact opposite happening over the past few decades; online communication has encouraged the spreading of falsehoods, bullying, harassment, and other bad human behavior.[78] So, if the open-source model is a way of capitalizing on the benefits of interactive media for improving things, why has it not created a better, kinder, more ethical populace? This is because an important part of being human is the freedom to express different dimensions of ourselves in different situations.[79] When we lose situational awareness, when all contexts are collapsed, when our own "sources" are "opened up" in this way, we lose that freedom to adapt and tailor our behavior as needed. Daniel Solove explains this paradox: "We want information to flow openly, for this is essential to a free society, yet we also want to have some control over the information that circulates about us, for this is essential to our freedom as well."[80] The extent to which the release of information can support or hinder human freedom and flourishing has in large part to do with the directionality of the information flow, and the sources toward which the "opening up" is targeted.

### Surveillance

"Surveillance" is a French term, combining the terms "sur" (meaning "on top of" or "above") and "veiller" (meaning "to watch")—thus the term means to "watch from above,"[81] as a mother watching over her children. The instinct behind such watching over on a societal level is not a bad one; the goal is to protect, and maintain a level of safety and security for, the citizens. If we're not doing anything wrong, the argument goes, then surveillance should make us feel safe; it is only those who are behaving badly that would be bothered by it.[82] Of course, however, we know that a surveillance-based society is a hindrance to human freedom because it is fundamentally punitive in orientation, and only serves to become incrementally more so over time,[83] ultimately creating an asymmetry of power in favor of totalitarian control.[84]

But even if we could somehow be assured that surveillance would only ever be used in just and ethical ways in order to protect us, we would still have a natural human instinct toward keeping some things private from others.[85] After all, having a camera in every room of our house with a live feed to the police department would be maximally effective as a preventive safety measure. Yet, no one is comfortable with the idea of being constantly monitored in their most private spaces, no matter what the benefits might be. As Simson Garfinkel has explained, "privacy isn't just about hiding things. It's about self-possession, autonomy and integrity . . . the right of people to control what details about their lives stay inside their own houses and what leaks to the outside."[86] We resist the opening up of our lives because our ability to control what others know about us is necessary for our sense of self, our personal growth, and our human dignity.[87] So, although the introduction of interactive media into our lives has indeed removed some of our social mores about what is acceptable to share publicly, we still largely recoil at the dehumanizing idea of giving up our privacy completely.[88]

## Sousveillance

Instead, many have argued, since increased surveillance seems to be inevitable with the rise of technology,[89] citizens' only recourse today is to "watch the watchers" by taking it upon ourselves to conduct our own surveillance on those in power.[90] This is known as "sous"-veillance, as "sous" is French for "under" or "below."[91] The *sousveillance* conceptualization, also sometimes called "co-veillance,"[92] is based on the idea of empowering the citizenry to likewise "watch from below."[93] In such a society, we would equally keep an eye on the police, the politicians, and the corporations through our own tools of heightened scrutiny to uncover and reveal their wrongdoing as well, including wrongdoing with respect to their excessive surveillance of us. The rise of Wikileaks, the revelations of Edward Snowden, and the increased use of personal cameras for livestreaming injustices committed by law enforcement during traffic stops and at protest events are just a few examples of how citizens have turned the watchful lens around to keep a close eye on the actions of those in power.[94]

The problem with sousveillance, however, is that it is not always and only directed upward. Our monitoring can be similarly turned on each other.[95] And in many cases, when it is directed in this lateral manner from citizen to citizen, interactive media creates a situation in which some individuals or groups can end up unjustly or unethically taking advantage of others' open information vulnerabilities. This can be evidenced in cases such as *revenge porn*, when a hurt ex-lover publicly distributes privately recorded intimate interactions with their former partner as a form of vengeance;[96] when stalkers use social media to track down and locate the object of their obsession;[97] when people's houses are robbed after posting that they are away on vacation;[98] or when people with large social media followings sic their army of fans on an individual who has committed some perceived slight in order to find and harass them.[99] In fact, as stories like #PlaneBae and trends toward cancel culture and increasing censorship show, we seem to be moving in an increasingly unbalanced direction in which we are engaging in efforts to demand more transparency of our fellow citizens, while giving the dominant systems of control (the state, major media platforms, and large corporations), who remain hidden behind their black boxes of "confidential" or "proprietary" secrecy,[100] yet more power over us.

## Dansveillance

Open-source, as a model, is about disintegrating the black boxes and breaking down what Frank Pasquale calls "the logic of secrecy."[101] It does this by opening up the mechanisms of systems to the participation of individuals who operate within them. In order to achieve the benefits of the open-source model for society as a whole, however, the one thing that should precisely *not* be open is the personal information and behavior of those participating individuals, so that they will feel free to continue to participate. Perhaps it is neither surveillance nor sousveillance that we need. Perhaps what we need is a third option, which I am calling *dansveillance*. "Dans" is the French word for "in." Thus, dansveillance is "watching from within." By watching the world we live *in*, highlighting its injustices, and demanding transparency of it, we keep our focus on that which we have a morally justified right to keep a critical eye on.

Integral to this concept is the fact that we do not exist within other people, only alongside them. People are separate and autonomous from one another; therefore, they are beyond the boundaries of what we may ethically monitor.[102] Because we are not a part of them, other human beings are not ours for taking, controlling, experimenting with, participating in, breaking down, altering, remixing, or customizing to our liking.[103] We have no claim or right to peek into the minds of other people, understand their inner workings, hack their patterns and trends to make conclusions about who they are, assume their motivations and goals, or predict or manipulate their behavior. Thus in a dansveillance society, these would be things we would recognize as wrong.[104] The people in such a society would not be driven to violate one another individually, and refuse to engage in behaviors that enable or support superfluous citizen monitoring for the purposes of security, vengeance, curiosity, or voyeurism, out of respect for individual human dignity and the collective protection of all of us.[105]

We do, however, exist within systems. We have a right to understand the inner workings of the technological, governmental, legal, educational, social, corporate, or informational structures and systems that so intimately affect our lived realities in complex ways. Thus, the systems of our world can and should be opened up, carefully watched, and continually deconstructed, and it is properly our place to demand more openness and transparency of them.

In a dansveillance society, then, norms and regulations would be directed toward both our right to keep a watchful eye on the systems and structures within which we must all operate, and our right to protect human persons from being watched in ways they don't actively consent to, from any source. Whistleblowers, journalists, and activists would be supported in their efforts to highlight the moral wrongs and injustices of these systems we live within. At the same time, we would develop behaviors such as asking ourselves if what we are about to share could reveal something personal about someone else, getting others' consent before taking or posting pictures of them or their children, and not participating in or encouraging the doxing and mob-shaming of others, even when they've done something objectively wrong. Succinctly put, we would be driven by an ethic of mutual and reciprocal protection of human personhood,[106] while also demanding transparency and intelligibility of the systems we function within.[107] Such an ethic is becoming increasingly necessary as we fight to protect ourselves from corporate and state surveillance because, if we as equal human individuals are not even willing to protect one another from such intrusions, there is really no justification for the expectation that the structures of power in a society would be.

Is it too idealistic to hope that such a new ethic could be propagated throughout a society such that the majority of people would behave accordingly? Maybe, but as these tools get more and more integrated into our lives, new ethics and new behaviors are being adopted all the time,[108] and so I would argue that a little intentionality and thoughtfulness behind those adoptions could push us more directly in the right, rather than the wrong, directions. In addition, there is another, more pragmatic reason to focus our watchful efforts on systems rather than individuals. As noted in chapter 7, giving people access to the "source code" of a system, or the mechanisms that make it work, allows them to collectively identify the problems within it and work together to fix those problems.[109] This same method could be applied to improve societal systems of communication and institutions at a variety of levels, but only when targeted at the systems themselves. Social problems like discrimination, racism, misogyny, bigotry, oppression, marginalization, delegitimization, and misinformation would not be as potent if they were not encouraged by the larger systems within which they exist.[110] But whenever we take the focus off of the system and turn it onto individuals, we ignore not only the complexities of individual differences, but also the mechanisms supporting these problems.[111] We should keep a watchful eye on systems and not individuals because the individual is inevitably acting in concert with the systems within which he or she exists,[112] and working to fight the flaws of systems is an overall more effective target for correction.[113]

## Public-Powered Systems

An open-source society so properly directed could also go a long way to resolving many of the issues with the new gatekeepers brought up in the last chapter. This is because any technological platforms that are public-powered systems—meaning that they generate their primary value from *social data*, which is both personal and public—on a massive scale, would above all be encouraged toward transparency.[114] This includes, of course, the major social media sites and search engines, but also things like ecommerce platforms (i.e., Etsy and Amazon), voting and elections systems, and public information databases. Instead of accepting the black boxes of these systems and the ways they disempower us, we would seek to use systems that make available the source code to all their mechanisms and structures—not the data itself, but the code directing their processes and algorithms for data collection and output—for public review.[115] Seeing how these systems actually work would not only keep the companies honest in terms of how they traffic, route, and transmit our data,[116] but also allow people to collectively identify where problems are and work with the companies to cooperatively solve them.[117] And while it's true that some users could take advantage of this information to "game the system" and get their content to the top of the pack, this would only be possible to the degree that the sites themselves utilize algorithmic gatekeeping to amplify and manipulate content to improve their advertising models. Thus, opening up the code in this way could instead encourage a return to the simple, chronological, user-curated, and bottom-up crowdsourced designs that dominated content-ranking decisions on most user platforms before the 2010s.[118]

While it may seem like a radical suggestion to require private companies to open up the way their systems work for all to view and basically give up their gold mine, it has become clear that keeping these mechanisms behind the black box of "trade secrets" has created far more problems for the public at large than these companies are equipped to properly handle.[119] This isn't the secret recipe for spaghetti sauce, after all; these are the systems wherein people live out their lives, enact their democracy, and earn their living, with real impacts on our communities and our society.[120] As a general rule, when it comes to technology that is used for public purposes, we need something broader than the capitalist venture lens, and we need to think differently in terms of both scale and solvability.[121] As has been shown throughout this book, these tools were developed and distributed throughout society at a rate faster than any scientific, political, social, economic, or legal framework could anticipate, and the resulting consequences of each decision made are only just now beginning to be fully understood.[122] Just because something *is* a certain way right now, or even has been that way for a while, does not mean that that is the way *it has to be*.[123] Our solutions need to include those that are as potentially radical, disruptive, and impactful as the introduction of the technologies themselves has been.

## CONCLUSION

In sum, while we do not need to stop using interactive media entirely[124] or be afraid to speak our minds publicly, it is important to ensure that when we do use these tools, we have a clear picture of what information we are giving up, potentially to whom, and how it might be used. We do not want to blindly accept technologies just because of convenience or FOMO (fear of missing out), but instead determine for ourselves where the lines should be drawn and attend to those times when we feel they are being crossed. Above all, we should not simply accept that privacy is dead and that there is nothing that can be done.[125] This notion is not a reality, but rather an ideology that lulls us into passively handing over the entirety of our lives to a conglomerate of corporations that have figured out a way (and been legally allowed) to profit off of them.[126] It is we who engage in various types of activities and behaviors via interactive media sites, and we have more power than we realize to determine whether or not these services will be used, and how. Of the major influences over the directions that our society takes—whether they be technological, governmental, market-driven, or cultural—what we, collectively, do (or not) is a primary driver of all of them. Thus, it is our responsibility to act in ways that are aimed at protecting ourselves and one another against unwanted, unwarranted, or unethical intrusions into our lives.[127]

## NOTES

1. Garber, "Two Strangers Met."
2. Garber.
3. Dawson, "The Dark Side."
4. Rosey Blair (@roseyblair), "Last night on a flight home, my boyfriend and I asked a woman to switch seats with me so we could sit together. We made a joke that maybe her new seat partner would be the love of her life and well, now I present you with this thread." Twitter post, July 3, 2018, https://web.archive.org/web/20180703213132if_/https://twitter.com/roseybeeme/status/1014122893805015041.
5. Dawson, "The Dark Side."
6. Garber, "Two Strangers Met."
7. Garber.
8. Garber.
9. Rosey Blair (@roseyblair), Twitter photo, July 3, 2018, https://web.archive.org/web/20180703213132if_/https://twitter.com/roseybeeme/status/1014122893805015041.
10. Chelsea Fagan (@Chelsea_Fagan), "it's unreal how the internet has poisoned our brains & concept of basic privacy so much that u could be 100 tweets deep on something like that & not feel weird about it." Twitter post, July 5, 2018, https://twitter.com/Chelsea_Fagan/status/1014867464646221824.
11. Tom and Lorenzo (@tomandlorenzo), "My reaction to that apparently beloved viral plane romance tweetstory makes me think my expectations for privacy are wholly out of line with everyone else's." Twitter post, July 4, 2018, https://twitter.com/tomandlorenzo/status/1014514891485564928.
12. Katherine Cross (@Quinnae_Moon), "So, I didn't say anything about this earlier because I feared being a buzzkill, and in these times I know people need a reason to smile. But, yeah, that 'couple falling in love on a plane' viral thread going around today? It's a bit skeevy." Twitter post, July 4, 2018, https://twitter.com/Quinnae_Moon/status/1014402748249444352.
13. Mara Davis (@MaraDavis), "I didn't want to be cynical but I felt exactly the same way. Thank you." Twitter post, July 4, 2018, https://twitter.com/MaraDavis/status/1014520816942374914.
14. Abel-Santos, "Plane Bae."
15. Douglas, "Doxing," 199.
16. Lorenz, "Unidentified Plane-Bae."
17. Cross, "The Dark Side"; Dawson, "The Dark Side."
18. Rosey Blair (@roseyblair), Twitter photo, July 10, 2018, https://web.archive.org/web/20180711051321if_/https://twitter.com/roseybeeme/status/1016711281670225927.
19. Lyon, "Surveillance Culture," 824.
20. Petronio and Child, "Conceptualization and Operationalization," 77.
21. Andrejevic, "Work of Being Watched," 233.
22. Lyon, "Surveillance Culture," 829.
23. Solove, *The Future of Reputation*, 30.
24. Meyrowitz, *No Sense of Place*, 43.

25. Ong, "The Writer's Audience," 11.

26. Marwick and boyd, "I Tweet Honestly," 128.

27. Goffman, "The Interaction Order," 3.

28. Meyrowitz, *No Sense of Place,* 41.

29. Couldry and Hepp, *The Mediated Construction*, 146.

30. Castells, "Communication, Power," 247.

31. Barnes, "A Privacy Paradox," 3; Couldry and Hepp, *The Mediated Construction*, 153–54; Solove, *The Future of Reputation*, 29.

32. Shirky, *Here Comes Everybody*, 11–12.

33. Couldry and Hepp, *The Mediated Construction*, 159.

34. Solove, *The Future of Reputation*, 198.

35. Wesch, "YouTube and You," 22–23.

36. Hooks, "Cancel Culture: Posthuman Hauntologies," 3.

37. Wesch, "YouTube and You," 23.

38. Wesch, 22.

39. Wesch, 23.

40. Marwick and boyd, "I Tweet Honestly," 130.

41. Marwick and boyd, 129.

42. Barnes, "A Privacy Paradox"; Solove, *The Future of Reputation*, 199.

43. Barnes.

44. Petronio, "Communication Boundary Management," 320–21.

45. Barnes.

46. U.S. Const. amend. IV.

47. Snowden, *Permanent Record*, 229.

48. Barnes, "A Privacy Paradox."

49. Snowden, *Permanent Record*, 230.

50. Neier, *Dossier*, 188.

51. Kerr, "Applying the Fourth Amendment," 1013–14.

52. Folberg, "Search Warrants and Digital," 331.

53. Solove, *The Future of Reputation*, 194–95.

54. Folberg, "Search Warrants and Digital," 330.

55. Solove, *The Future of Reputation*, 17.

56. Solove, 72–73.

57. Solove, 17.

58. Zuboff, *Surveillance Capitalism*, 59.

59. Rozenshtein, "Surveillance Intermediaries," 114–15.

60. Rozenshtein, 114.

61. James Nixon. "No Anonymity on Future Web Says Google CEO." Thinq, archived August 15, 2010, https://web.archive.org/web/20100815042507/http://www.thinq.co.uk/2010/8/5/no-anonymity-future-web-says-google-ceo/.

62. Zuboff, *Surveillance Capitalism*, 8.

63. *The Economist*, "The World's Most Valuable."

64. Zuboff, *Surveillance Capitalism*, 47–48.

65. Zuboff, 48.

66. Zuboff, 49–50.

67. Sweeney, "Simple Demographics," 1.
68. Greenwald, "Revealed: How US."
69. Zuboff, *Surveillance Capitalism*, 278–79.
70. McCoy, "Cyber Hack Got Access."
71. Ghoshal, "Why We Should Collectively."
72. Andrejevic, "The Kinder, Gentler Gaze," 267–68.
73. Andrejevic, 268.
74. Couch et al., "COVID-19—Extending Surveillance," 812–13.
75. Solove, *The Future of Reputation*, 196–97.
76. Zuboff, *Surveillance Capitalism*, 480–81.
77. Schneier, "Google and Facebook's."
78. Lanier, *Ten Arguments*, 47–48.
79. Solove, *The Future of Reputation*, 69.
80. Solove, 35.
81. *Online Etymology Dictionary*, s.v. "Surveillance," accessed March 27, 2021, https://www.etymonline.com/word/surveillance.
82. Esguerra, "Google CEO Eric Schmidt."
83. Neier, *Dossier*, 192.
84. Havel, "Dear Dr. Husák," 52.
85. Garfinkel, *Database Nation*, 4.
86. Garfinkel, 4.
87. Floridi, "On Human Dignity," 311.
88. Tene and Polonetsky, "Theory of Creepy," 63.
89. Brin, "The Transparent Society"; Hamelink, *The Ethics of Cyberspace*, 131.
90. Brin; Kelly, *The Inevitable*, 260.
91. Mann et al., "Sousveillance," 332.
92. Kelly, *The Inevitable*, 259.
93. Mann et al., "Sousveillance," 332.
94. Kelly, *The Inevitable*, 262–63.
95. Brin, "The Transparent Society"; Couldry and Hepp, *The Mediated Construction*, 138.
96. McGlynn et al., "Beyond 'Revenge Porn,'" 26.
97. Chandler, "Social Media Is Fostering."
98. Liebowitz, "Social Media Status Updates."
99. McCarthy, "Kathy Griffin Calls For."
100. Pasquale, *The Black Box Society*, 3.
101. Pasquale, 2.
102. Floridi, "Four Challenges," 112.
103. Floridi, 111.
104. Floridi, 111.
105. Floridi, "On Human Dignity," 312.
106. Floridi, 311.
107. Pasquale, *The Black Box Society*, 8.
108. Castells, "Communication, Power, and Counter-Power," 250–52.

109. Lévy, *Collective Intelligence*, 61; Raymond, "Cathedral and the Bazaar," 29; Rosenzweig, "Can History Be," 133; Shirky, *Here Comes Everybody*, 116.

110. McCall, "The Complexity of Intersectionality," 1782.

111. McCall, 1782; Zuboff, *Surveillance Capitalism*, 344.

112. Moradi, "(Re)focusing Intersectionality," 120.

113. Moradi, 121.

114. Pasquale, *The Black Box Society*, 89.

115. Gehl, "The Case for Alternative," 6; Pasquale, 145–46.

116. Gronka, "The Politics of Search," 369.

117. Benkler, *The Wealth of Networks*, 323.

118. Helmond, "The Algorithmization of the Hyperlink."

119. Pasquale, *The Black Box Society*, 83.

120. Pasquale, 193.

121. Zuboff, *Surveillance Capitalism*, 343.

122. Lévy, *Collective Intelligence*, 13.

123. Lanier, *Ten Arguments*, 103; Lessig, *Code*, 32; Shafto, "Why Big Tech."

124. Though there are those who recommend it. See Lanier, *Ten Arguments*.

125. Zuboff, *Surveillance Capitalism*, 522.

126. Zuboff, 224.

127. There are advocacy groups like the Electronic Frontier Foundation (eff.org) and Demand Progress (demandprogress.org) that actively work to protect privacy and other human rights against technological interference, and educate and inform about these issues via the resources they provide. There are also tools provided by Solid (solidproject.org) and Tor (torprject.org) that are designed to protect against unwanted data collection and surveillance. These are all great organizations to follow on social media as well, as they can bring attention to new resources and important privacy- and surveillance-related news and updates.

## Chapter 14

# Heading into the Future

## INTRODUCTION: BEATING THE GAME

In an episode of the futuristic 1990s-era sci-fi series *Star Trek: The Next Generation*, the crew of the *Starship Enterprise* got carelessly caught up in a wearable headset holographic video game that rewarded them with increasingly intense serotonin boosts to the pleasure centers of their brains.[1] It was introduced to the ship's top commander, Will Riker, by an alien race in order to interfere with the crew's capacity for higher reasoning so that they would be subject to mind control, and it spread so quickly throughout the ship that all 1000+ passengers on board were hooked on it within days. While the writers of this episode didn't quite get right that the reality of the addictive machine would be much more insidious than a single game with cheesy Atari-style graphics, the scenes in which everyone was sitting around focused only on this gadget and barely capable of even answering a question were eerily similar to those we see when we look around at people attached to their devices today.

Interestingly, it was the teenagers onboard the ship, Wesley Crusher and Robin Lefler (played by then-college-age Wil Wheaton and Ashley Judd), who, more interested in each other than some new gadget, ultimately resisted the game, recognized its harms, and freed everyone else from it. All of the so-called grown-ups—the scientists, doctors, engineers, psychologists, and warriors, even the serious and stoic Captain Picard—couldn't resist its manipulation tactics. In a way, it had to be the kids. In one scene, as the young couple was sitting in the ship's lounge bonding over their shared experiences growing up around the technology of their parents ("My first friend was a tricorder." "Really? My very first friend was a warp coil."), they suddenly looked around to notice the creepiness of what was happening all around them, and began to realize that they had to do something about it.[2]

Their skepticism mirrors that which many of us feel when we snap out of our mediated worlds and recognize the problems technology has introduced or exacerbated in our society today. But it is crucial to know that we are not powerless to solve them. Pendulum swings happen all the time in society; we are never moving only and unstoppably in one direction.[3] And I have witnessed a significant shift reflected in the students I have taught over the past decade. The initial excitement they had about interactive media ten years ago has increasingly turned to concern today, and their hypotheses and questions have moved from a focus on the benefits of these tools to their harms. They worry about how technology is affecting their younger kin. They complain, sounding like curmudgeons at the ripe old age of twenty, "my cousin just got her first phone—she's only eight!" or "all these kids do is play video games all day long. We used to play outside!"

This shift has also been reflected in the scholarship on interactive media, which has gone from an early hopeful optimism about the potential that it had for democratization, empowerment, diversification, and consciousness-raising, to a more skeptical and critical mode of highlighting its real harms and effects.[4] In fact, the trajectory of this book has in some ways taken us through that story, with the earlier chapters focused on all that has been made possible by interactive media and the latter chapters focused on new forms of exploitation and control. But the picture I've tried to paint here is neither one of naïve optimism nor of cynical pessimism. The idealists were not entirely wrong, but the critiques have likewise been well-warranted and helped to bring the early utopic visions back down to earth.

Aboard the *Starship Enterprise*, as Wesley and Robin were hatching their plan to save their superiors from the hold of technological control, they also knew that they would need to employ the help of their friend "Data," a benevolent and artificially intelligent android not subject to the game's physiological interferences. Similarly, today we need to understand that we are not headed straight for a dystopic hellscape but remember that there have indeed been many positive outcomes that technology has brought about, supporting our efforts to help ourselves and each other. As we move into the future, we need to pursue a realistic and reasoned approach based on core principles and underscored by the need for boundaries and balance, rather than getting caught up in the trappings and particulars of the latest shiny object. In order to do so, we will not only need to get a handle on recognizing the ways in which interactive media can be used to both exploit our human weaknesses and support human freedom, and pass this knowledge and understanding on to the next generations. In other words, if we want to stay ahead of the game moving forward, we will need the kids onboard.

## CRITICAL DIGITAL LITERACY

Throughout this book, I have suggested a variety of themes and principles of interactive media that we can use to reflect on and apply to our communicative behavior in a critically engaged way. This is what is known as *critical digital literacy*.[5] Literacy, construed broadly in the digital realm, involves the ability to apply an informed and increasingly complex level of "decoding, comprehension, interpretation, and analysis" to the various forms of "texts" that we encounter through interactive media.[6] Because these tools have become so embedded into our lives, critical digital literacy requires "defamiliarization," a breaking away from the invisible, everyday, mundane, and typical uses of interactive media in order to engage with a more distanced, thoughtful, bigger-picture perspective on what they are, what they make possible, what they complicate, and why any of it matters.[7] This approach encourages "a more systematic understanding of how the media operate, and . . . more reflective use of the media"[8] that can inform our way of "thinking and being in the world."[9]

As noted in chapter 2, what interactive media has introduced into our world has been notoriously unpredictable. But whatever comes next, if we are armed with critical digital literacy, we will be able to think outside of the box and identify the challenges and opportunities that are presented. Moreover, we will have some idea of how to best handle those challenges and take advantage of those opportunities in order to help lead the way toward a better future. What I like about this approach is that it focuses on what we can do, individually and collectively, dispelling that sense of inevitability and helplessness that we sometimes internalize when we talk about the future of technology as "taking over." There are many things that we cannot control about the future, but we are by no means helplessly or passively along for the ride. In fact, due to its open, networked, digital, and databased design, interactive media is especially subject to going down the paths that we, the users, take it.[10] But we have to know that we can.

## DIRECTING THE PATH

As noted throughout this book, a large part of what drives the direction that both technology and the law takes is our cultural norms.[11] Those behaviors that we accept as normal will continue to occur, and those that we view as abnormal are not as likely to catch on.[12] But, like media and technology, norms can be invisible to us, unquestioned because we are so used to them.[13] Sometimes we need to look around at the norms we accept and ask ourselves,

Should this be the way it is? Should this behavior be acceptable? And if the answer is no, what can we do about it? There is no rule book for using interactive media that says we have to use it to engage in rude and uncivil discourse, bully or harass one another, call one another out and violate each other's privacy, or unquestioningly accept what is presented as fact. But these are the norms that we do, in many cases, collectively adopt.[14]

While these tools might lend themselves to feeding into our human weaknesses,[15] there is nothing that says we are forced to use them in these ways.[16] A hammer might "lend itself" to breaking someone's car window when they make us angry, but that doesn't mean that's how we have to use it. Hammers also help us to build and fix things, and that more positive norm is the one that we generally ascribe to their use. How we talk about and conceptualize our tools influences what we expect them to do and what uses we do and do not see as acceptable. Interactive media are also tools. They may be programmed to do things, such as learn, model, promote, filter, and predict, but the driving force behind them is still human.[17] As Melvin Kranzberg explains, "the same technology can have quite different results when introduced into different contexts or under different circumstances."[18] With intention, we could *choose* to view the tools of interactive media differently, and promote those uses that support, rather than undermine, humanity's progress.

Although it cannot be said with specificity what is coming next, there are certain projections that futurists and technologists can make, based on what is already in development and what has been theorized. As computers grow ever more powerful and capable of collecting and processing massive amounts of data, it is assumed that much of what has already begun will continue to be accelerated.[19] It is projected that artificial intelligence (AI) systems will grow ever more sophisticated, able to make better predictions about and anticipate our needs and behaviors on both an individual and a societal scale.[20] It is also expected that sensors, cameras, and monitors will become ever more ubiquitous in real spaces, collecting data and increasing the potential for different kinds of surveillance.[21] The presence of screens and other interactive devices, both throughout our homes and out in the world, is also likely to increase.[22] Our personal technology will become more wearable and even implantable due to advances in nanotechnology.[23] Increasingly immersive gaming and entertainment experiences will be developed through virtual reality, 3D, and holographic projections, and computer-generated graphics will be easier to create and so realistic that they will be indiscernible from actual footage or real experience.[24] Cloud-based systems that give us access to everything by way of services could result in us needing to own fewer and fewer "things" for ourselves.[25] More people and vendors could begin using and accepting *cryptocurrencies*, decentralized digital money systems that are unregulated by any government and unverified by any central bank.[26] Moreover, the *blockchain* technology they are built upon, which establishes trust and accountability through a distributed system whereby transactions are verified and tracked via a chain "log" saved in real time on the machines of all users in a global peer-to-peer network, is likely to be applied in a variety of other sectors and industries.[27]

As we consider these projections, focusing on all of the intersecting roles that we can play in determining where this all leads—and there are many, and they are important—empowers us to impact the direction our society takes in more positive and productive ways. We do not need to simply accept the negative consequences technology might have,[28] but rather we can anticipate and mitigate those consequences while seeking out the ways that we can use these tools to assist. As Kevin Kelly explains, "once [the roots of digital change are] seen, we can work *with* their nature, rather than struggle against it."[29] In an effort to give some insight into the roles that each of us can play in society today, tomorrow, and into the future, in the following sections I speculate about the potential future challenges and opportunities for each, from a perspective of critical digital literacy.

## AS LEADERS

As we move into the future, we can lead by directing our uses in more positive ways and with more balance in our lives. As role models, parents, educators, coaches, mentors, public servants, managers, and business owners, there are many ways in which we can lead others toward adopting better, more ethical, and more responsible behaviors and perspectives. When we model critical digital literacy, the things that we do or don't participate in, the things that we question, and the things that we refuse to passively accept can inspire others to ask themselves: Do things have to be this way? Additionally, we can actively lead in working to not just point out the problems with these systems, but work together to identify and highlight possible solutions.

As new technologies emerge and current ones evolve, one of the biggest challenges we face will be leading the generations that come after us by way of protection. We already know that there was a huge spike in mental health problems for those who were middle school–aged and younger when social media entered the scene.[30] Generation Z, or *iGen* as Jean Twenge has called them,[31] have overwhelmed the mental health services on most campuses as they have entered college.[32] Among other reasons, their formative experiences of being constantly connected to a network of friends, strangers, and frenemies has left them with a permanently heightened sense of anxiety and self-doubt, a feeling of being "always on," and increased loneliness and depression.[33] They are suffering from the consequences of what Nicholas Carr predicted in 2010 when he warned us against "welcoming the digital frenziedness into our souls."[34]

We can help these and future generations by encouraging them to find more balance in their lives, and show them that it is possible by doing it ourselves. Being aware of the mechanisms of attraction and addiction that these tools capitalize on can help us to find ways to prevent ourselves from falling prey to them. This includes things like deleting or silencing apps, turning off notifications, and consciously limiting daily screen time. Just as there are no rules saying that we have to use these tools in negative ways, there is also no rule that says they need to be our sole or even primary way of communicating with one another and informing our understanding of the world. We can resist this by intentionally reading books, attending live performances, interacting face-to-face with others, finding solace in true, uninterrupted solitude, and seeking real, concrete, and hands-on experiences. Meanwhile, even as more and more devices get embedded into public and private spaces, we should always have nature to retreat to. Thus, we should ensure that we preserve and regularly enjoy its unmediated serenity, and invite along our younger counterparts so that they, too, can develop a sense of appreciation for it.

We can leave our devices at home or turn them off when we are doing these things or when we need to focus. We can begin creating more "device-free" spaces, such as camps and programs where kids—and adults—are required to learn about themselves and what they are capable of on their own and together, by solving problems collaboratively and face-to-face. We can take back a portion of our life from the intrusions of media and its devices, as a way of mitigating the hold they can have over us. While this may hinder our ability to be "on call" and respond to messages immediately, the more of us who do this, the less there will be a generalized expectation or a demand protocol of an immediate response. And we can learn for ourselves that there really is little to no "missing out" that results from finding more equilibrium in our relationship to interactive media in our life. In fact, we might just discover how much we really were missing out on because of our constant attention to it. Taking a more reasonable approach to using these tools can also help to ensure that we will have a healthier relationship with them and a sense of perspective that makes us more able to recognize any harmful effects they may be having on our communication.

When we do use interactive media, we can resolve to do so in ways that demonstrate their potential for good, such as learning, creativity, empowerment, and encouragement, and show that there are other, better uses than the merely social or performative. For instance, one of interactive media's greatest potentials as we move into the future is its growing capacity to help us deeply understand other cultures, spaces, and historical eras.[35] Just imagine the amount of detailed documentation we will have about this time in history in the future. Combined with graphical and 3D improvements and immersive, wearable technologies, studying the past could be like traveling back in time! Using interactive media tools to take a lifelike journey through—or even build—another version of society can help to engender an understanding that there are other ways of doing and seeing things. This kind of perspective can free us up to imagine something different, something better. With the strong caveat that it is imperative that we consciously maintain a degree of balance in our perspective and understanding that this is indeed mere simulation, such experiences can embolden us to reflect upon the reality that we exist in, as well as others that might be possible, in ways that can be healthy and productive.

## AS COMMUNITY MEMBERS

As technology becomes more and more enculturated into our daily, "normal" existence, we need to also keep in mind our role as community members who are responsible for caring for one another and for the spaces that we collectively share, whether they be physical or digital, local or global. We must be balanced not only in our positioning toward using interactive media in our own lives, but also in weighing their benefits against their harms for the world at large. Taking responsibility for how our usage of interactive media could negatively affect the lives of others can help us better understand how to use them to raise awareness about these issues, as well as help those who might be left behind in their wake.

As members of communities, our biggest challenge is to ensure that no one is marginalized or exploited by our increased usage of interactive media. Even as these tools are integrated more and more into many of our everyday lives, the digital divide is not going away, and countless others continue to be excluded from the digital sphere. Much of this is for economic reasons. The lack of competition for broadband providers in certain communities means the companies can increasingly raise their prices with little recourse, leaving the most economically disadvantaged among us without the ability to get access at all.[36] In addition, while historically each new medium quickly became more cheaply available as it was introduced into society in order to garner a larger audience,[37] interactive media is beginning to go in the opposite direction as subscription-only and paywalled models replace the older, cheaper-access alternatives.[38] The devices themselves demand a lot from our pockets as well, as the built-in planned obsolescence means that they will not last more than a handful of years before becoming unusable.[39] Again the older models—a single old-school television set or radio tuner, for example—were more accessible, lasting much longer (they can still be found today and will plug in and work) and requiring less financial investment in the long run. Meanwhile, the production and disposal of computer-based technologies is not environmentally friendly or safe,[40] and the manufacturers often keep up with the ever-increasing demand through the exploitation of workers in other countries not subject to US labor laws.[41]

Those of us who do have access to these tools can ensure that we take advantage of the opportunities they create to raise awareness about these issues and demand better options for everyone. Rather than always demanding the "next best thing," we should be using our collective voice to encourage technology companies to slow down and reassess not only their product distribution models but also the ethics of their business practices. New developments should prioritize the ways we can ensure higher-quality, longer-lasting hardware that is compatible with previous generations, and work toward achieving better infrastructure and access throughout the world. Meanwhile, we should support regulatory efforts that are aimed towards emphasizing consumer choice. New innovations should be accompanied by or quickly followed up on with cheaper and more universal alternatives as they are diffused throughout society, not only to be inclusive economically, but also to accommodate and support people across spectra of neurodiversity and ability.

One positive use of both AI systems and robots is that they can be employed toward these ends without requiring such massive demands on human labor.[42] It is essential, however, that we also carefully weigh the human need for connection and community when determining in what contexts and situations the use of such tools is appropriate. For instance, as new technologies are developed that can help assist in the care for people who most need it—such as the elderly and those suffering from illnesses—we should also ensure that such people are given frequent and daily access to live human beings in order to maintain a sense of wholeness and dignity.[43] In the world of today and the future, we should all work together to ensure that everyone has a degree of balance in their lives, and that none are excluded from either technology or community.

## AS CREATORS

Undoubtedly, the thriving creativity that has resulted from the introduction of interactive media into our society has been one of its most wonderful and exciting outcomes. Everyday people actively participating in collaborative cultural production, entertaining and inspiring one another, has been a net positive that should be not only preserved but more actively encouraged as we move into the future. As the increasingly consolidated profit-driven platforms through which we create and share encourage a narrower and more homogenized range of artistic possibilities, however, user creativity is being hindered.[44] The earlier, open, more "generative" spaces of interactive media were more experimental, informal, loose, and disrupt-able, and, as its structures become more closed and rigid, we are losing the freedom to tinker, innovate, and create.[45]

Just as the old gatekeepers did, the new gatekeepers are increasingly building up technical and legal infrastructures that keep them the only game in town,[46] which gives them a greater degree of control over what creators can and cannot do if they want to be able to reach people with their work.[47] Legal blocks to creative participation in culture need to be reconsidered, both in terms of those lingering from the twentieth century (i.e., overly restrictive copyright laws preventing media appropriation[48]) and those that have been introduced for the twenty-first (i.e., legal definitions that enable "digital prior restraint"–style content filtering[49]). In both cases, laws that were initially designed, and used, to protect creative freedom and innovation are being taken too far such that they are now serving to stifle it.[50] Both copyright- and content-moderation protections could be better understood in terms of balance if new ways of thinking around ownership, copying, transformation, and restriction of content that maximize freedom and competition are embraced.[51] Thus, we should also support regulation that prevents companies from monopolizing certain cultural or public spheres through competition laws and other avenues.[52] Encouraging such *competitive compatibility*[53] means that content would not have to be platform or system specific if we don't want it to be, and creators would have the freedom to work seamlessly and easily across platforms, amidst "an absence of walls," as Zittrain puts it.[54]

Provided these challenges can be overcome in a fair manner that leaves the cultural sphere open to all who want to participate in it, the opportunities on the horizon are seemingly limitless for creators across artistic, musical, and cultural spheres. As complex production tasks become increasingly automated and "cognified" by AI processes, creating things like 3D films, virtual worlds, and video games will become easier and more accessible to the average creator.[55] "Audiences," if we can even continue to conceive of them that way, will continue to be paramount, and value access, engagement, and interactivity over ownership.[56] New interactive media spaces that allow for creative collaboration through social networking, different kinds of information visualizations, and various forms of media applications will be able to be developed without the need for computer-programming knowledge.[57] Creating at a high technical quality will become ever easier and cheaper, lowering the boundaries for following through on a creative instinct or idea.[58]

## AS CITIZENS

One of the most important roles we take on as we move into the future is that of citizens, both of our own countries and of the world. Thus we need to seek out and promote the ways in which interactive media and new technologies could be used to enhance rather than hinder our orientations toward those things that most prominently affect our civic life, such as law, activism, news, politics, and systems of control and power. Blocks to civic participation in the digital age include increasing censorship, divisiveness, polarization, misinformation, *deepfakes* (videos that very convincingly digitally alter the face of someone to make them appear as someone else[59]), and the chilling effects of surveillance on self-expression.[60] We can work to improve the quality of the digital public sphere by more thoughtfully evaluating the technology we use and incorporating new tools that can help to encourage open, rational, and civilized debate, tease out facts from opinion, and identify falsehoods from reality.[61]

Perhaps most importantly as citizens, we must keep an eye on surveillance. As improvements in scanning technologies and AI systems increase the accuracy of facial recognition and other biometric indicators to identify people, law enforcement will want to use that (indeed, it already has) to aid their work.[62] But a digital representation of our unique face, linked to other identifying or personal information about us, makes us vulnerable to the control of malicious actors, both within and outside the state.[63] If we want to remain "secure in" our "persons, houses, papers, and effects" as the Fourth Amendment was designed to guarantee, we need to encourage the scaling back of laws that are too permissive in allowing broadscale warrants for information on large swaths of the population,[64] as well as the introduction of legislation that prevents the unwarranted collection of personal and social data by law enforcement.[65] In addition, we need to more specifically build into our legislative processes the continued and regular revisitation of these laws to add new restrictions in light of newly developed technologies moving forward.[66]

In order to be fully enough aware of the issues at hand that we can continue to fight for our digital rights, however, it is of the utmost importance that citizens' access to the public sphere and capacity for agency via interactive media be protected and upheld.[67] When major corporations filter out or promote certain content and hide the ways in which they do so, they are controlling and manipulating our public participation through an exertion of their dominance, further increasing their influence and reducing our own.[68] If these platforms are where the public sphere has finally reemerged after having been nearly snuffed out of existence by the dominating corporate media of the twentieth century, then we should support those laws and models that give us more collective freedom over our participation in that sphere.

While, of course, platform owners should work with law enforcement to mitigate any clear and present violations of the law taking place on their sites, whatever efforts they make to actively control user content beyond that (even content that we disagree with) should be received with an extreme dose of skepticism. The companies who host these platforms are not governmental bodies prevented from violating our First Amendment rights,[69] but rather private entities focused on their bottom lines. However, we could encourage the legal classification of the most prominent platforms as "gatekeepers" (as European Union legislators have recently proposed in the Digital Markets Act), which would obligate them to follow a different set of regulatory rules.[70] We could also support legally redefining these gatekeepers according to their primarily public function, which would put limits on their ability to interfere with the legal speech of their users.[71]

While this may lead to an increase in the problems of misinformation and toxicity created by certain users on these sites, it would also encourage the platforms to focus on other ways of diminishing bad content, such as providing their users with more sensitive measures and preference settings to rate and control what they see, rather than making these filtering decisions for them.[72] They could also be encouraged to open up their systems to interact more readily with outside developers who are innovating more socially responsible filtering solutions.[73] In this way, the major platforms would be not only upholding the rights of speakers on their sites but also those of listeners who do not want to be exposed to certain kinds of speech.[74] We could push developers in these directions by choosing to use systems that more closely align with the principles of open source, transparency, distributed accountability, and consumer choice, and support anti-trust legislation aimed at preventing few companies from dominating the marketplace.[75]

Moving into the future, more decentralized and transparent systems are likely to be developed. We are already seeing the emergence of "alternative" social media sites that, like the alternative news outlets discussed in chapter 6, promote themselves as not commercially driven and open up their systems to user input.[76] Moreover, the distributed nature of blockchain technology holds a lot of promise for increasing the transparency and accountability not only of public discourse platforms,[77] but also other systems of civic participation that are meant to be public and open, such as elections,[78] bill referendums,[79] campaign financing,[80] and other forms of e-governance.[81] If the people have the knowledge and the passion to support systems that more readily empower citizens through dialogue, openness, and personal privacy protection, these are the systems that will prevail. Moreover, whenever we recognize insidious mechanisms of control being utilized or incentivized within *any* systems of public or political import, we can capitalize on the decentralized and networked nature of interactive media to help bring attention to, and circumvent, them.

## AS WORKERS

Just as we need to ensure a degree of balance with respect to our own personal uses of interactive media, we need to ensure that businesses and schools allow their employees and students to maintain such a balance when it comes to their work. As we move to more distributed and flexible models not requiring our presence in designated physical spaces in order to get things done, we must be also wary of the uses of surveillance for the purposes of work or education.[82] Having just completed an entirely online streaming semester due to the COVID-19 pandemic, it strikes me that I just spent sixteen weeks unquestioningly allowing a live camera feed into my home for hours on end each weekday, as did a large chunk of the workforce and students. Had I been asked under any non-work-related circumstance if I would be okay with this, I would have emphatically said no. During this period, we have seen students being invasively monitored while taking online exams[83] and the introduction of new tools that allow employers to more closely track what their employees are doing.[84] We must more seriously think through the consequences of allowing such intrusions into our private spaces moving forward, and ask ourselves how much we are willing to accept. We are also still working to fully understand the long-term effects of daily virtual work as it relates to productivity, morale, creativity, inspiration, and professionalism, as well as burnout, fatigue, and other psychological and physical maladies.[85]

The nature of work, even the "workday" itself, will look very different in the future. We will be freed up in many ways, not only with respect to when and where we can do our work, but also in what we are able to do and how we are able to accomplish it. For one, artificially intelligent machines will be developed that are capable of doing many of the tasks that are currently done by people, such as driving, building, and retail work.[86] Though this shift of labor to machines may be painful for us in the short term, in the long run it could actually be quite beneficial.[87] It is important to keep in mind that AI is most useful for carrying out tasks that have already been standardized in society, things for which we have established rules and protocols.[88] With these standardized and tedious aspects of our work outsourced to AI, we will be free to focus our efforts more on the innovative, progressive, spontaneous, novel, and unpredictable efforts that humans are uniquely designed for—innovation, imagination, design, philosophy, empathy, critique, advocacy, mentorship, leadership, community betterment, and asking the right questions.[89] As companies find more and more ways to profit off of non-human labor,[90] we humans can also find ways to create value by spending more of our time on social goods like community, creativity, and citizenship.[91] Meanwhile, done with thoughtfulness and balance, these networked learning machines can be employed in ways that help us to pool and benefit from our collective knowledge,[92] collaborate across sectors,[93] incorporate more perspectives when finding solutions to problems,[94] and open up institutions and systems with transparency.[95]

In addition, empowered by these tools of innovation, automation, and collaborative work, entrepreneurial ideas have more freedom to flourish.[96] We may even begin to see that everyone gains the potential to create their own entrepreneurship in the same way that these first few decades of interactive media gave everyone their own potential to be a media outlet.[97] The future of work could look much more independent and distributed as people move in and out of professional networks and interests, each individual creating their own career imprint as they cross disciplines and boundaries, as opposed to the limited set of siloed institutional options that we have today.[98]

## AS CONSUMERS

As consumers, we should be wary of the costs of the increased customization, recommendation, and predictive anticipation technologies that rely on the gathering and processing of massive amounts of personal data. It is important to recognize the ways in which these corporations commodify our behavior, using their products to capitalize off of their ability to watch us live our everyday lives, as another kind of exploited labor.[99] We need to also consider carefully the ways in which these devices can change the nature of our relationships to products, which are no longer fully "ours."[100] We will be ever subject to a state of constant updates and change, "endless newbies" to the latest and greatest improvements in technology.[101] The increasing Internet of Things (IoT) promises that we will rarely be more than five feet away from a "smart" device collecting information, sending it across the broader network, and using it in varying ways, most commonly to provide us with a more convenient or customized user experience.[102] Our homes, vehicles, and offices will be equipped with AI to predict and service our needs, and ultimately it could become very difficult, even penalizing, for those who wish to opt out of using such "smart" tools.[103] Although our consumer networks have tipped the power relations between consumers and companies to some degree in our favor,[104] these customized and updatable products have also put us increasingly at the mercy of those corporations that provide them. Thus we will want to use our collective voice to ensure that we as consumers have options, by encouraging competitive compatibility and interoperability not only amongst the new gatekeeper companies, but also the companies that make the cars, watches, home appliances, toothbrushes,[105] and other "things" that are becoming increasingly "smart" as time goes on.[106]

As with our roles as citizens and workers, we will need to be vigilant against the dangers of surveillance in the realm of consumerism.[107] At the very least, we need to utilize our role as consumers to show companies what we are and are not willing to accept and to demand accountability. When it comes to our personal data, we need to draw lines, be aware of abuses, and stand against them. Some have suggested an even more radical approach that involves reconsidering our stance on consumer data entirely, with proposals to heavily tax its collection and use[108] or outlaw human data trafficking altogether.[109] Since companies are not allowed to buy and sell human organs for profit, perhaps human data should be considered just as worthy of protection from corporate exploitation.[110] Although it doesn't always seem like it due to the fast pace of change, we are still in the early stages of this new world and only just beginning to understand what it should look like.

## AS HUMANS

When I was about five years old, I saw a scene in the movie *Superman III* that terrified me to the core and has stuck with me ever since. In it, a giant super-computer captured one of the villain's lab assistants and turned her into a robot.[111] I googled this scene to see if it was online, and (of course) it was.[112] Interestingly, the user who uploaded it, "TheChopperTube," specifically stated that they posted the clip because it "used to freak me out," and most of the comments on the video expressed similar sentiments, noting our collective trauma.[113] The fact that so many of us had such a memorable experience with this scene from our childhoods in 1983 is striking. More than three and a half decades later, I think I finally understand what it was that was ultimately so disturbing: the idea that technology could dehumanize a person. In her 2011 book, *Alone Together: Why We Expect More from Technology and Less from Each Other*, Sherry Turkle explains that "we are changed as technology offers us substitutes for connecting with each other face-to-face . . . as we distribute ourselves, we may abandon ourselves."[114] With every step we take into the mediated world, we become more dependent on it to function, to relate, and thus risk losing a part of our humanity.[115] It is not only the challenge of machines taking over humanity that we need to be concerned about; it is also humans entering into technology.

As we move into the future, we will be offered and enticed by ever more opportunities to give over those things about us that are uniquely human—our bodies, senses, knowledge, information, thoughts, identities, relationships, and spirituality—to mediated experiences that might seem preferable to real ones, somehow better, more efficient, stimulating, or satisfying.[116] But, like the false high of addictive substances, the fun is short-lived, and too much of it can do physical and mental damage to us by dulling our senses to the real world and diminishing our care for one another.[117] In the end, the experiences we have with and through our devices are only illusions, copies striving to be something like lived reality.[118] Just as robots are merely performing human-ness, machines are merely performing functions, and artificially intelligent tools are merely performing tasks, we, via interactive media, are frequently merely performing aspects of our lives, our relationships, and our selves.[119] But without proper perspective or balance, the fantasies of the screen can begin to creep into our understanding of reality.[120] Therefore it is of the upmost importance that we mindfully recognize interactive media for what they are—a proxy to authenticity that can help us to connect, communicate, or collaborate, but can also have negative consequences for us, both individu-ally and societally, when we make them too real.

## CONCLUSION

Throughout the generations, the tools of media, technology, and even com-munication itself have never been either inherently good or inherently evil; they have all had, and will continue to have, the potential for both.[121] As we have witnessed over the last few decades, it is the increasingly commercial forces behind interactive media systems that have replicated the economy of attention that also plagued those of the old media, in both cases pushing them away from the benefits that they could bring to society.[122] For the media of both the twentieth and twenty-first centuries, the underlying potential for good has been undermined by an increasingly monopolized and proprietary landscape, dominated by corporations through a concentration of power, and inevitably attracting the attention of those who would exploit that concen-trated power in order to manipulate and control others.[123] Yet, when the mass media of the twentieth century got out of hand, we emerged from that disem-powered darkness with a new option: interactive media, more participatory, more our own.[124] This reopening of increasingly closed systems is actually a cycle that can be observed throughout history, and today, something similar could happen again.[125]

As evidenced throughout this book, there is real danger here, but there is also reason for hope. Interactive media is an amplifier of humanity, neither the solution to all of our problems nor the cause of them.[126] Yet as we pro-mote its use in ways that lean toward decentralization, openness, balance, transparency, and human connection and away from closed systems of consolidation, control, surveillance, censorship, and divisiveness, the technologies, laws, and cultural norms that we accept and support could work to break down the structures of domination that well up within it.[127] And if we can do that continually, we could propagate an enduring and collective vision that, like those "kids" on the *Starship Enterprise*, recognizes how to enlist technology in such a way that its potential for good triumphs over its capacity for evil.

## NOTES

1. *Star Trek: The Next Generation*, season 5, episode 6, "The Game," directed by Corey Allen, written by Gene Roddenberry, Brannon Braga, Susan Sackett, and Fred Bronson. Aired October 26, 1991, in syndication.

2. "The Game," 23:11–24:57.

3. Bijker, Hughes, and Pinch, *Social Construction*, 50.

4. Almgren and Olsen, "'Let's Get Them Involved,'" 2; Isin and Ruppert, *Being Digital Citizens*, ix–x; Kirschenbaum and Werner, "Digital Scholarship," 406–7; Zollman, "Corporate-Market Power," 223–24.

5. Pangrazio, "Reconceptualising Critical Digital Literacy," 164.

6. Hobbs, "Propaganda in an Age," 521.

7. Hobbs, 528; Pangrazio, 170–71.

8. Buckingham, "Media Education," 115.

9. Pandya, "Exploring Critical Digital Literacy," 32.

10. Manovich, *Software Takes Command*, 237–38, Lessig, *Code*, 32; Zittrain, *The Future of the Internet*, 70.

11. Lessig, *Code*, 123; Solove, *The Future of Reputation*, 196; Tene and Polonetsky, "Theory of Creepy," 73.

12. Cialdini, Kallgren, and Reno, "Theory of Normative Conduct," 203.

13. Deuze, "Media Life"; Goffman, "The Interaction Order"; Shirky, *Here Comes Everybody*, 105.

14. Lanier, *Ten Arguments*, 31.

15. Aral, *The Hype Machine*, 97.

16. Lessig, *Code*, 32; Morozov, *To Save Everything*, 221.

17. Lanier, *Dawn of the New Everything*, 324.

18. Kranzberg, "Technology and History," 545–46.

19. Schaller, "Moore's Law," 53.

20. Tucker, "The Naked Future," 240.

21. Tucker, 238–39; Morozov, *To Save Everything*, 12–13.

22. Kelly, *The Inevitable,* 86.

23. Kelly, 225–26.

24. Kelly, 229.

25. Kelly, 112–13.

26. Kelly, 120; Johnson, "Bitcoin Bubble."

27. Kelly, 121; Bel, "Marketing Industry"; Russo, "Blockchain-Powered Rivals"; Crypto Briefing, "What Is Steem?"

28. Zuboff, *Surveillance Capitalism*, 524.

29. Kelly, 5.

30. Twenge, *iGen*, 95–112.

31. Twenge, 2.

32. Xiao et al., "Are We in Crisis," 407–08.

33. Toscano, *Automating Humanity*, 26; Turkle, *Alone Together*; Twenge, *iGen*, 3.

34. Carr, *The Shallows*, 222.

35. Kelly, *The Inevitable,* 229.

36. Holmes et al., "Access to High-Speed Internet."

37. Bimber, *Information and American Democracy*, 61; Czitrom, *Media and the American Mind*; de Sola Pool, *Technologies without Boundaries*, 60; Gilmor, *We the Media*, 2.

38. Socolow, "Substack Isn't a New."

39. Guiltinan, "Creative Destruction," 21.

40. Kuntsman and Rattle, "Environmental (Un)sustainability," 567.

41. Farrell, "Big Tech Benefitting"; Jemielnuak and Przegalinska, *Collaborative Society*, 192.

42. Kelly, *The Inevitable*, 53–55.

43. Turkle, *Alone Together*, 121.

44. Doctorow, "All Complex Ecosystems"; Kumar, "The Algorithmic Dance," 7.

45. Zittrain, *The Future of the Internet*, 2.

46. Wu, *The Master Switch*, 11–12; Zuboff, *Surveillance Capitalism*, 105.

47. Doctorow, "Bust 'Em All."

48. Lessig, *Free Culture*, 192.

49. Balkin, "Free Speech," 1177–78. Graber, "Internet Creativity, Communicative Freedom," 22.

50. Graber, 11–12.

51. Kelly, *The Inevitable*, 209–10; Thayer, "Corporate Monopolies Hurt Creative."

52. Cyphers and Doctorow, "Privacy without Monopoly," 32.

53. Doctorow, "Competitive Compatibility."

54. Zittrain, *The Future of the Internet*, 156.

55. Kelly, *The Inevitable*, 34.

56. Kelly, 113–14.

57. Brody, "The No-Code Movement."

58. Hatch, *The Maker Revolution*, 25.

59. Tolosana et al., "Deepfakes and Beyond," 131.

60. Stoycheff et al., "Privacy and the Panopticon," 611–12.

61. Verbeek, "Designing the Public Sphere," 225.

62. Mann and Smith, "Automated Facial Recognition Technology," 121.

63. Lyon, *Electronic Eye*, 30.

64. Lynch and Sobel, "New Federal Court Rulings."

65. Electronic Frontier Foundation, "EFF's Comments," 2.

66. Thierer, *Permissionless Innovation*, 20.

67. O'Hair and Eadie, "Communication as an Idea," 6–7.

68. Castells, *Communication Power*, 371.

69. Keller, "Who Do You Sue?" 8.

70. Doctorow and Schmon, "The EU's Digital Markets."

71. Braman and Roberts, "Advantage ISP," 444.

72. Keller, "Who Do You Sue?" 26–27.

73. Cyphers and Doctorow, 29–30; Keller, 24.

74. Donovan and boyd, "Stop the Presses?" 346.

75. Cyphers and Doctorow, "Privacy without Monopoly," 14, 32; Zittrain, *The Future of*, 163.

76. Gehl, "The Case for Alternative," 6.

77. Crypto Briefing, "What Is Steem?"

78. Hossain et al., "E-voting System Using Blockchain."

79. Allen et al., *Cryptodemocracy*, 11.

80. Serdült, "Reconnecting Citizens to Politics,"188.

81. Grover et al., "Blockchain and Governance," 136.

82. Blumenfeld et al., "Covid-19 and Employee," 43; Collier and Ross, "Higher Education after Surveillance?" 276; Monokha, "The Implications of Digital," 541.

83. Feathers, "Students Are Rebelling Against"; Chin, "Exam Anxiety."

84. Hartmans and Taylor, "Amazon Drivers"; Sandler, "Microsoft's New 'Productivity Score.'"

85. Tavares, "Telework and Health Effects," 33–34.

86. West, *The Future of Work*, 68.

87. West, 85.

88. Levy and Murmane, *The New Division*, 111.

89. Gilder, *Life After Google*, 98–100; Kelly, *The Inevitable*, 57; West, *The Future of Work*, 63.

90. West, 64–65.

91. Shirky, *Cognitive Surplus*, 118–19, 174–75.

92. Levy, *Collective Intelligence.*

93. Rainie and Wellman, *Networked*, 177.

94. Surowecki, *The Wisdom of Crowds*, 29.

95. Kelly, *The Inevitable*, 260–61.

96. Richards, *The Human Advantage*, 102.

97. Schwartz and Russ, *Work Disrupted*, 129.

98. Rainie and Wellman, *Networked*, 177.

99. Andrejevic, "Work of Being Watched," 233.

100. Gillmor, "The Facebook Template."

101. Kelly, *The Inevitable*, 11.

102. Andrejevic, "Work of Being Watched," 237.

103. Andrejevic, 238; Rainie and Anderson, "The Internet of Things."

104. Quinton, "The Community Brand Paradigm," 913–14.

105. Morozov, *To Save Everything*, 227.

106. Cyphers and Doctorow, "Privacy without Monopoly," 13.

107. Doctorow, "How to Destroy Surveillance."

108. Toscano, *Automating Humanity*, 222.

109. Zuboff, "It's Not That We've."

110. Zuboff.

111. *Superman III*, directed by Richard Lester, written by David Newman and Leslie Newman, 1983, Warner Bros.

112. TheChopperTube, "SUPERMAN 3—Computer Turns Ugly Woman Into Freaky Robot," March 12, 2011, Video, 1:31, https://youtu.be/fpTHrdemfQo.

113. TheChopperTube (Comments).

114. Turkle, *Alone Together*, 11–12.

115. Carr, *The Shallows*, 224; Lanier, *Not a Gadget*, 4.

116. Carr, 224; Kittler, *Gramophone, Film, Typewriter*, 17.

117. Turkle, *Reclaiming Conversation*, 40–41.

118. Lanier, *Not a Gadget*, 20, 134; Turkle, *Alone Together*, 6–10.

119. Turkle, 12.

120. Dill-Shackleford, *How Fantasy Becomes Reality*, 16.

121. Kranzberg, "Kranzberg's Laws," 545–46.

122. Webster, *The Marketplace of Attention*, 49–50.

123. Andrejevic, "Work of Being Watched," 245; Lessing, *The Future of Ideas*, 134; Vaidhyanathan, "Open Source as Culture," 24; McLintock, "The Destruction of Media," 602.

124. Jenkins, *Convergence Culture*, 136–38.

125. Wu, *The Master Switch*, 6.

126. Shirky, *Here Comes Everybody*, 11–12.

127. Doctorow, "How to Destroy Surveillance."

# Bibliography

Aakhus, Mark. "Communication as Design." *Communication Monographs* 74 (2007): 112–17.

Abad-Santos, Alex. "Plane Bae: How an In-Flight Matchmaker Broke the Internet." Vox, July 9, 2018. https://www.vox.com/2018/7/6/17537656/plane-bae-privacy -explained.

Aboujaoude, Elias. *Virtually You: The Dangerous Powers of the E-Personality.* New York: W. W. Norton & Company, 2011.

Agence French-Presse. "UN Agency Calls for Global Cyberwarfare Treaty, 'Driver's License' for Web Users." RawStory, January 30, 2010. https://www.rawstory.com /2010/01/agency-calls-global-cyberwarfare-treaty-drivers-license-web-users/.

Aguiar, Luis, Jörg Claussen, and Christian Peukert. "Catch Me if You Can: Effectiveness and Consequences of Online Copyright Enforcement." *Information Systems Research* 29, no. 3 (2018): 656–78.

Alcorn, Chauncey. "Left-Wing News Sites Censored on Facebook Aren't in Favor of Banning Alex Jones Either." Mic, August 9, 2018. https://www.mic.com/articles /190621/left-wing-news-sites-censored-on-facebook-arent-in-favor-of-banning -alex-jones-either#.pEYnJhB5r.

Alfonso, Fernando. "After 4chan Manhunt, Cat-Kicker Slapped with Animal Cruelty Charges," *Daily Dot,* March 2, 2020. https://www.dailydot.com/unclick/walter -easley-cat-kicker-animal-cruelty/.

Allen, Darcy W. E., Chris Berg, and Aaron M. Lane. *Cryptodemocracy: How Blockchain Can Radically Expand Democratic Choice.* Lanham, MD: Rowman & Littlefield, 2019.

Almeida, Paul D. and Mark Irving Lichbach. "To the Internet, From the Internet: Comparative Media Coverage of Transnational Protests." *Mobilization: An International Journal* 8, no. 3 (2003): 249–72.

Almgren, Susanne M. and Tobia Olsson. (2015). "'Let's Get Them Involved' . . . to Some Extent: Analyzing Online News Participation." *Social Media + Society* 1, no. 2 (2015): 1–11.

Amine, Abdelmajid and Lionel Sitz. "How Does a Virtual Brand Community Emerge ? Some Implications for Marketing Research." Paper Presented at the Esomar Conference, Marketing: Where Science Meets Practice, Warsaw, Poland, 2004.

Amusa, Malena. "Bold New Media Mogul—Cenk Uygur, CEO of The Young Turks." *Forefront Magazine*, September/October 2012. http://www.forefrontmag.com/2012/09/bold-new-media-mogul-cenk-uygur-ceo-of-the-young-turks/.

An, Sojung and Jason J. Jung. "A Heuristic Approach on Metadata Recommendation for Search Engine Optomization." *Concurrency and Computation: Practice and Experience* 33, no. 3 (2019): 1–10.

Anderson, Jack and Sille Obelitz Søe. "Communicative Actions We Live By: The Problem with Fact-Checking, Tagging, or Flagging Fake News." *European Journal of Communication* 35, no. 2 (2020): 126–39.

Anderson, Philip W. "More Is Different." *Science* 177, no. 4047 (1972): 393–96.

Anderson, Monica, Paul Hitlin, and Michelle Atkinson. "Wikipedia at 15: Millions of Readers in Scores of Languages." Pew Research Center. January 14, 2016. https://www.pewresearch.org/fact-tank/2016/01/14/wikipedia-at-15/.

Andrejevic, Mark. "The Kinder, Gentler Gaze of Big Brother: Reality TV in the Era of Digital Capitalism." *New Media & Society* 4 (2002): 251–70.

Andrejevic, Mark. "The Work of Being Watched: Interactive Media and the Exploitation of Self-Disclosure," *Critical Studies in Media Communication* 19, no. 2 (2002): 230–48.

Aral, Sinan. *The Hype Machine.* New York: Currency, 2020.

Arroyo Nieto, Carmen and Josep Valor. "How The Guardian Capitalized Its Membership Model." IESE Business School Media Matters Blog, May 29, 2019. https://blog.iese.edu/the-media-industry/2019/05/29/how-the-guardian-capitalized-its-membership-model/.

Arroyo Nieto, Carmen and Josep Valor. "The NYT Proves that Media Can Live Off Digital Revenues." IESE Business School Media Matters Blog, February 13, 2019. https://blog.iese.edu/the-media-industry/2019/02/13/the-nyt-proves-that-media-can-live-off-digital-revenues/.

Arulanantham, Rekha. "Free Speech and BART Cell Phone Censorship." American Civil Liberties Union blog, August 17, 2011. https://www.aclu.org/blog/national-security/free-speech-and-bart-cell-phone-censorship.

Asarch, Steven. "Steven Crowder Incites Homophobic Harrassment of Vox Reporter, YouTube Slow to React." *Newsweek*, May 31, 2019. https://www.newsweek.com/vox-carlos-maza-steven-crowder-twitter-youtube-1441076.

Ashby, LeRoy. *With Amusement for All: A History of American Popular Culture Since 1830.* Lexington, KY: University Press of Kentucky, 2006.

Asher-Schapiro, Avi and Ban Barkawi. "'Lost Memories': War Crimes Evidence Threatened by AI Moderation." *Reuters*, June 19, 2020. https://www.reuters.com/article/us-global-socialmedia-rights-trfn/lost-memories-war-crimes-evidence-threatened-by-ai-moderation-idUSKBN23Q2TO.

Atton, Chris. "Separate, Supplementary or Seamless? Alternative News and Professional Journalism." In *Rethinking Journalism: Trust and Participation in a Transformed News Landscape,* edited by Chris Peters and Marcel Jeroen Broersma, 131–43. New York: Routledge, 2013.

Atton, Chris and James F. Hamilton. *Alternative Journalism.* Thousand Oaks, CA: Sage, 2008.

Aubert, Paul. "Mike Cernovich's Documentary 'Hoaxed' Surges to #1 on iTunes After Being Removed by Amazon." *The Scoop,* April 12, 2020. https://thescoop.us/mike-cernovichs-documentary-hoaxed-surges-to-1-on-itunes-after-being-banned-by-amazon/.

Averian, Alexandru. "Digital Ecosystems Software Modeling from a Niche Perspective." *Annals of Spiru Haret University (Mathematics-Informatics Series)* 10 (2014): 37–47.

Axelrod, Robert. *The Evolution of Cooperation.* Cambridge, MA: Basic Books, 1984.

Ayden, Nursen. "Social Network Analysis: Literature Review." *Online Academic Journal of Information Technology* 9, no. 34 (2018).

Balasubramian, Siva K., James A. Karrh, and Hemant Patwardhan. "Audience Response to Product Placements: An Integrative Framework and Research Agenda." *Journal of Advertising* 35, no. 3 (2006): 115–41.

Ballono, Sonia, Ana Cynthia Uribe, and Rosa-Àuria Munté-Ramos. "Young Users and the Digital Divide: Readers, Participants, or Creators on Internet?" *Communication & Society* 27 (2014): 147–55.

Bakare, Lanre and Caroline Davies. "Blackout Tuesday: Black Squares Dominate Social Media and Spark Debate." *The Guardian,* June 2, 2020. https://www.theguardian.com/us-news/2020/jun/02/blackout-tuesday-dominates-social-media-millions-show-solidarity-george-floyd.

Bakeman, Roger and Stephen Beck. "The Size of Informal Groups in Public." *Environment and Behavior* 6, no 3 (1974): 378–90.

Baker, C. Edwin. "Media Concentration: Giving Up on Democracy." *Florida Law Review* 54, no 5 (2002): 843–919.

Baker, Marsha Lee, Eric Dieter, and Zachary Dobbins. "The Art of Being Persuaded: Wayne Booth's Mutual Inquiry." *Composition Studies* 42, no. 1 (2014): 13–34.

Balkin, Jack M. "Free Speech in the Algorithmic Society: Big Data, Private Governance, and New School Speech Regulation." *UC Davis Law Review* 51, no. 3 (2018): 1149–210.

Bambauer, Derek E. "What Does the Day After Section 230 Reform Look Like?" TechStream, January 22, 2021. https://www.brookings.edu/techstream/what-does-the-day-after-section-230-reform-look-like/.

Barberá, Pablo, Ning Wang, Richard Bonneau, John T. Jost, Jonathan Nagler, Joshua Tucker, Sandra González-Bailón. "The Critical Periphery in the Growth of Social Protests." *PLoS ONE* 10, no. 11 (2015). https://doi.org/10.1371/journal.pone.0143611.

Barlow, John Perry. "A Declaration of the Independence of Cyberspace." Electronic Frontier Foundation. February 8, 1996. https://www.eff.org/cyberspace-independence.

Barlow, John Perry. "The Economy of Ideas." *Wired Magazine,* March 1, 1994. https://www.wired.com/1994/03/economy-ideas/.

Barnes, Susan B. "A Privacy Paradox: Social Networking in the United States." *First Monday* 11, no. 9 (2006). https://firstmonday.org/ojs/index.php/fm/article/view/1394.

Barnhurst, Kevin G. "'Trust Me, I'm an Innovative Journalist,' and Other Fictions." In *Rethinking Journalism: Trust and Participation in a Transformed News Landscape,* edited by Chris Peters and Marcel Jeroen Broersma, 29–220. New York: Routledge, 2013.

Barratt, Neil and Leslie Regan Shade. "Net Neutrality: Telecom Policy and the Public Interest." *Canadian Journal of Communication* 32 (2007): 295–305.

Barrett, Brian. "You're About to Drown in Streaming Subscriptions." *Wired Magazine*, October 14, 2018. https://www.wired.com/story/streaming-subscriptions -competition-netflix-amazon-disney/.

Barrett, Michael, Sam Cappleman, Gamila Shob, and Geoff Walsham. "Learning in Knowledge Communities: Managing Technology and Context." *European Management Journal* 22, no 1 (2004): 1–11.

Baruh, Lemi and Hayley Watson. "Social Media Use During Political Crises: The Case of the Gezi Protests in Turkey." In *The Routledge Companion to Social Media and Politics*, edited by Axel Bruns, Gunn Enli, Eli Skogerbø, Anders Olaf Larsson, and Christian Christensen, 198–210. New York: Routledge, 2018.

Batsell, Jake. *Engaged Journalism: Connecting with Digitally Empowered News Audiences.* New York: Columbia University Press, 2015.

Baym, Nancy. *Personal Connections in the Digital Age.* Malden, MA: Polity Press, 2011.

BBC, "18 Revelations from Wikileaks Hacked Clinton Emails." US & Canada, October 27, 2016. https://www.bbc.com/news/world-us-canada-37639370.

BBC, "Esports 'Set for £1bn Revenue and 600 Million Audiences by 2020.'" Sport, March 21, 2017. https://www.bbc.com/sport/39119995.

BBC, "Julian Assange: Wikileaks Co-Founder Arrested in London." UK, April 12, 2019. https://www.bbc.com/news/uk-47891737.

BBC, "Reddit Apologises For Online Boston 'Witch Hunt.'" Tech, April 23, 2013. https://www.bbc.com/news/technology-22263020.

BBC, "Shia LaBeouf's Anti-Trump Exhibit Shut Down Over Violence." US & Canada, February 10, 2017. https://www.bbc.com/news/world-us-canada -38937476.

BBC, "Twitter-ban Feminist Defends Transgender Views Ahead of Holyrood Meeting." News, May 22, 2019. https://www.bbc.com/news/uk-scotland-48366184.

BBC. "Why Did This Song About A Family Of Sharks Go Viral?" NewsRound, September 1, 2018. https://www.bbc.co.uk/newsround/45195096.

BBC, "Why Joe Rogan's Exclusive Spotify Deal Matters." Entertainment & Arts, May 20, 2020. https://www.bbc.com/news/entertainment-arts-52736364.

Bee, Vanessa. "I Like Cenk Uygur, but Bernie Was Right to Retract His Endorsement." *Politico,* December 20, 2019. https://www.politico.com/news/magazine/2019/12 /20/opinion-cenk-uygur-bernie-sanders-endorsement-strategy-088566.

Beer, Jeff. "One Year Later, What Did We Learn from Nike's Blockbuster Colin Kaepernick Ad?" Fast Company, September 5, 2019. https://www.fastcompany. com/90399316/one-year-later-what-did-we-learn-from-nikes-blockbuster-colin -kaepernick-ad.

Bel, Nick. "How Blockchain Technology will Change the Marketing Industry," *Cointelgraph.* July 8, 2020. https://cointelegraph.com/news/how-blockchain -technology-will-change-the-marketing-industry.

Beltzer, Lindsay. "Why Brand Relatability Matters to Millenials and Gen Z." Financial Communications Society, April 12, 2019. https://thefcs.org/news/ relatability-recap/.

Benkler, Yochai. *The Wealth of Networks: How Social Production Transforms Markets and Freedom.* New Haven, CT: Yale University Press, 2006.

Benkler, Yochai, Robert Faris, and Hal Roberts. *Network Propaganda: Manipulation, Disinformation, and Radicalization in American Politics.* New York: Oxford University Press, 2018.

Benkler, Yochai and Helen Nissenbaum. "Commons-Based Peer Production and Virtue." *Journal of Political Philosophy* 14, no. 4 (2006): 394–419.

Benkler, Yochai, Hal Roberts, Robert Faris, Alicia-Solow-Niederman, and Bruce Etling. "Social Mobilization and the Networked Public Sphere: Mapping the SOPA -PIPA Debate." Berkman Center Research Publication No. 2013–16 (2013). http:// papers.ssrn.com/sol3/papers.cfm?abstract_id=2295953.

Bennett, W. Lance. "New Media Power: The Internet and Global Activism." In *Contesting Media Power: Alternative Media in a Networked World* edited by Nick Couldry and James Curran, 17–38. Lanham, MD: Rowman & Littlefield, 2003.

Bennett, W. Lance and Alexandra Segerberg. "The Logic of Connective Action." *Information, Communication & Society* 15, no. 5 (2012): 739–68.

Berkowitz, Dan and Zhengia Michelle Liu. "Media Errors and the 'Nutty Professor': Riding the Journalistic Boundaries of the Sandy Hook Shootings." *Journalism* 17, no. 2 (2016): 155–72.

Bhagat, Smirti, Maria Burke, Carlos Diuk, and Ismail Onur Filiz. "Three and a Half Degrees of Separation." Facebook Research Blog, February 4, 2016. https:// research.fb.com/three-and-a-half-degrees-of-separation/.

Bickford, Susan. "Emotion Talk and Political Judgement." *Journal of Politics* 73, no. 4 (2011): 1025–36.

Bijker, Wiebe E., Thomas P. Hughes and Trevor Pinch. *The Social Construction of Technological Systems.* Cambridge, MA: MIT Press, 2012.

Bimber, Bruce. *Information and American Democracy.* New York: Cambridge University Press, 2003.

Binns, Amy. "DON'T FEED THE TROLLS!: Managing Troublemakers in Magazines' Online Communities. *Journalism Practice* 6, no. 4 (2006): 547–62.

Bishop, Bryan. "How HBO's Westworld Installation Made Fans 'The Center of the Universe.'" *The Verge*, August 16, 2017. https://www.theverge.com/2017/8/16 /16156852/westworld-experience-immersive-theater-marketing-sdcc-2017.

Bishop, Katrina. "How 'Serial' Is Making Podcasts Mainstream." CNBC, November 21, 2014. https://www.cnbc.com/2014/11/21/podcasts-are-going-mainstreamheres -why.html.

Björn, Michael. "Why Targeted Advertising Is Becoming Creepy." Ericcson Blog, January 17, 2019. https://www.ericsson.com/en/blog/2019/1/why-targeted -advertising-is-becoming-creepy.

Blaagaard, Bolette B. "Situated, Embodied, and Political: Expressions of Citizen Journalism." In *Cosmopolitanism and the New News Media* edited by Lilie Chouliaraki and Bolette Blaagaard, 40–53. New York: Routledge, 2014.

Blair, Elizabeth. "A Song Called 'Quiet' Struck a Chord with Women. Two Years Later, It's Still Ringing." NPR Music: American Anthem, January 14, 2019. https://www.npr.org/2019/01/14/683694934/milck-quiet-womens-march-american -anthem.

Bleier, Alexander, Arne De Keyser, and Katrien Verleye. "Customer Engagement Through Personalization and Customization." In *Customer Engagement Marketing,* edited by Robert W. Palmatier, V. Kumar and Colleen M. Harmeling, 75–94. Cham, Switzerland: Palgrave MacMillan, 2018.

Blumenfeld, Stephen, Gordon Anderson, and Val Hooper. "Covid-19 and Employee Surveillance." *New Zealand Journal of Employment Relations*, 45, no 2 (2021): 42–56.

Blunt, Katherine. "Apple Fans Keep Up a Tradition by Camping Out for a New Device." *Houston Chronicle*, September 15, 2016. https://www.houstonchronicle. com /business /article /Apple -fans -keep -up -a -tradition -by -camping -out -for -9226495.php.

Bode, Karl. "The Rise of Netflix Competitors Has Pushed Consumers Back Toward Piracy." *Vice*, October 2, 2018. https://www.vice.com/en/article/d3q45v/bittorrent -usage-increases-netflix-streaming-sites.

Bogaerts, Jo and Nico Carpentier. "The Postmodern Challenge to Journalism: Strategies for Constructing a Trustworthy Identity." In *Rethinking Journalism: Trust and Participation in a Transformed News Landscape,* edited by Chris Peters and Marcel Jeroen Broersma, 60–71. New York: Routledge, 2013.

Booth, Wayne C. *Modern Dogma and the Rhetoric of Assent*. Chicago: University of Chicago Press, 1974.

Bond, Paul. "Largest-Ever Crowdfunding Campaign for a TV Show Issues Equity to Investors." *Hollywood Reporter,* January 5, 2019. https://www.hollywoodreporter. com /news /largest -ever -tv -crowdfunding -campaign -issues -equity -investors -1173422.

Borchardt, Alexandra, Julia Lück, Sabine Kieslich, Tanjev Schultz, and Felix M. Simon. *Are Journalists Today's Coal Miners?* Reuters Institute for the Study of Journalism, University of Oxford/Johannes Gutenberg University Mainz, 2019. https:// reutersinstitute.politics.ox.ac.uk/our-research/are-journalists-todays-coal -miners-struggle-talent-and-diversity-modern-newsrooms.

Borgatti, Stephen P., Ajay Mehra, Daniel J. Brass, and Giuseppe Labianca. "Network Analysis in the Social Sciences." *Science* 323 (2009): 892–95.

Bourdieu, Pierre. "On Television." In *Media and Cultural Studies: KeyWorks*, edited by Gigi Durham and Douglas M. Kellner, 328–36. Malden, MA: Blackwell Publishing, 2001.

Bouvier, Gwen. "Racist Call-Outs and Cancel Culture on Twitter: The Limitations of the Platform's Ability to Define Issues of Social Justice." *Discourse, Context & Media* 38 (2020): 1–11.

boyd, danah. "You Think You Want Media Literacy . . . Do You?" *Data & Society*, SXSW Edu Keynote (2018). https://points.datasociety.net/you-think-you-want -media-literacy-do-you-7cad6af18ec2.

boyd, danah and Nicole B. Ellison. "Social Network Sites: Definition, History, and Scholarship." *Journal of Computer-Mediated Communication* 13 (2008): 210–30.

Boyle, Emma. "Apple Has Patented iPhone Technology That Could Stop You Filming at Concerts." *Independent*, June 30, 2016. https://www.independent.co.uk/life-style /gadgets-and-tech/iphone-apple-patent-filming-concerts-a7111166.html.

Brabham, Daren C. *Crowdsourcing*. Cambridge, MA: MIT Press, 2013.

Braman, Sandra and Stephanie Roberts. "Advantage ISP: Terms of Service as Media Law." *New Media & Society* 5, no. 3 (2003): 422–48.

Brandel, Jennifer. "Questions Are the New Comments." Medium.com, August 29, 2015. https://medium.com/we-are-hearken/questions-are-the-new-comments -5169d0b2c66f.

Brennan, Bernie and Lori Schafer. *Branded!: How Retailers Engage Consumers with Social Media and Mobility*. Hoboken, NJ: John Wiley & Sons, 2010.

Brin, David. "The Transparent Society." *Wired Magazine*, December 1, 1996. https:/ /www.wired.com/1996/12/fftransparent/.

Brin, David. *The Transparent Society: Will Technology Force Us to Choose between Privacy and Freedom?* Cambridge, MA: Perseus Books Group, 1998.

Briquelet, Kate. "Jeffrey Epstein, Alan Dershowitz, and Pals Accused of Sex -Trafficking Ring." *The Daily Beast*, August 19, 2019. https://www.thedailybeast. com/jeffrey-epstein-alan-dershowitz-and-pals-accused-of-sex-trafficking-ring.

Britt, Lawrence. "Game of Thrones Ending: 6 Things I Still Can't Get Over." *Cinema Blend*, May 27, 2020. https://www.cinemablend.com/television/2547047/game-of -thrones-ending-6-things-i-still-cant-get-over.

Brockes, Emma. "#MeToo Founder Tarana Burke: 'You Have to Use Your Privilege to Serve Other People.'" *The Guardian*, January 15, 2018. https://www.theguardian. com/world/2018/jan/15/me-too-founder-tarana-burke-women-sexual-assault.

Brodkin, Jon. "To Kill Net Neutrality Rules, FCC Says Broadband Isn't 'Telecommunications.'" *ArsTechnica*, June 1, 2017. https://arstechnica.com/ information-technology/2017/06/to-kill-net-neutrality-rules-fcc-says-broadband -isnt-telecommunications/.

Brody, Liz. "The No-Code Movement Means Anyone Can Be a Tech Founder." *Entrepreneur*, December 3, 2020. https://www.entrepreneur.com/article/359949.

Broersma, Marcel. "A Refractured Paradigm: Journalism, Hoaxes, and the Challenge of Trust." In *Rethinking Journalism: Trust and Participation in a Transformed News Landscape,* edited by Chris Peters and Marcel Jeroen Broersma, 29–44. New York: Routledge, 2013.

Broersma, Marcel and Chris Peters. "Introduction: Rethinking Journalism: The Structural Transformation of a Public Good." In *Rethinking Journalism: Trust and Participation in a Transformed News Landscape,* edited by Chris Peters and Marcel Jeroen Broersma, 1–12. New York: Routledge, 2013.

Brown, Aaron. "Is 'Mumble Rap' the New Punk?" Medium.com, May 12, 2017. https:/ /medium.com/@aaronbrown_13097/is-mumble-rap-the-new-punk-93f80550593b.

Browning, Larry and Keri K. Stephens. "Giddens' Structuration Theory and ICTs." In *Information & Communication Technology in Action: Linking Theory and Narratives of Practice, r*evised ed., edited by Larry Browning, Alf Steinar Saætre, Keri K. Stephens, and Jan-Odvar Sørnes, 85–92. New York: Routledge, 2008.

Brownlee, Shannon. "Amateurism and the Aesthetics of Lego Stop-Motion on YouTube." *Film Criticism* 40, no. 2 (2016). https://doi.org/10.3998/fc.13761232.0040.204.

Bruns, Axel. *Blogs, Wikipedia, SecondLife and Beyond: From Production to Produsage.* New York: Peter Lang Publishing, 2008.

Bruns, Axel. *Gatewatching and News Curation: Journalism, Social Media, and the Public Sphere.* New York: Peter Lang Publishing, 2018.

Buckingham, David. "Media Education Goes Digital: An Introduction." *Learning, Media and Technology* 32, no. 2 (2008): 111–19.

Buffenstein, Alyssa. "Shia LaBeouf's 'He Will Not Divide Us' Is Temporarily Shut Down—Again," *Artnet,* February 24, 2017. https://news.artnet.com/art-world/shia-labeouf-livestream-gunshots-871238.

Burns, John F. and Ravi Somaiya. "Confidential Swedish Police Report Details Allegations Against Wikileaks Founder: Foreign Desk." *New York Times*, December 19, 2010. https://www.nytimes.com/2010/12/19/world/europe/19assange.html.

Burt, Ronald. "The Social Capital of Opinion Leaders." *Annals of the American Academy* 566 (1999): 37–54.

Burt, Ronald. "Structural Holes and Good Ideas." *American Journal of Sociology* 110, no. 2 (2004): 349–99.

Bush, Vannevar. "As We May Think," *Atlantic Monthly*, July 1, 1945. http://www.theatlantic.com/magazine/archive/1945/07/as-we-may-think/303881/.

Butovsky, Jonah. "Phony Populism: The Misuse of Opinion Polls in the *National Post.*" *Canadian Journal of Communication* 32 (2007): 91–102.

Calder, Bobby J., Linda D. Hollebeek, and Edward C. Malthouse. "Creating Stronger Brands Through Consumer Experience and Engagement." In *Customer Engagement Marketing,* edited by Robert W. Palmatier, V. Kumar, and Colleen M. Harmeling, 221–42. Cham, Switzerland: Palgrave MacMillan, 2018.

Campbell, Graeme. "KFC's Cheetos Sandwich Is a God-Level Stoner Snack." *HighSnobiety*, 2018. https://www.highsnobiety.com/p/kfc-cheetos-sandwich/.

Canan, Mustafa and Andres Sousa-Poza. "Pragmatic Idealism: Towards a Probabilistic Framework of Shared Awareness in Complex Situations." *Proceedings of the 2019 IEEE Conference on Cognitive and Computational Aspects of Situation Management (CogSIMA)*, Las Vegas, NV (2019): 114–21. http://doi.org/10.1109/COGSIMA.2019.8724208.

Carey, James. "The Press, Public Opinion, and Public Discourse: On the Edge of the Postmodern." In *James Carey: A Critical Reader*, edited by Eve Stryker Munson and Catherine A. Warren, 228–60. Minneapolis: University of Minnesota Press, 1997.

Carly, Kathleen. "A Theory of Group Stability." *American Sociological Review* 56, no. 3 (1991): 331–54.

Carr, Nicholas. "The Amorality of Web 2.0," Rough Type (blog), October 3, 2005. http://www.roughtype.com/?p=110.

Carr, Nicholas. *The Shallows: What the Internet Is Doing to Our Brains.* New York: W.W. Norton & Company, Inc., 2010.

Carson, Andrea. *Investigative Journalism, Democracy and the Digital Age.* New York: Routledge, 2020.

Carty, Victoria. *Social Movements and New Technology.* Boulder: Westview Press, 2015.

Castells, Manuel. *Communication Power.* New York: Oxford University Press, 2009.

Castells, Manuel. "Communication, Power, and Counter-Power in the Network Society." *International Journal of Communication,* 1 (2007): 238–66.

Castells, Manuel. *Networks of Outrage and Hope: Social Movements in the Internet Age.* Malden, MA: Polity Press, 2012.

Catapooolt. "Top 10 Highest Crowdfunded Movie Projects You Can Not Afford to Miss." Medium.com, February 19, 2019. https://medium.com/@catapooolt/top-10 -highest-crowdfunded-movie-projects-you-can-not-afford-to-miss-354ffa2853ff.

CBS News. "Ed Sheeran: Reinventing Pop Music." March 5, 2017. https://www. cbsnews.com/news/ed-sheeran-reinventing-pop-music/.

Cernovich, Mike. "CNN Caught in a Hoax About Trump, Google, and Coronavirus." Cernovich.com, March 14, 2020. https://www.cernovich.com/cnn-jake-tapper -trump-google-coronavirus/.

Cernovich, Mike. "Jeffrey Epstein Arrested Due to Mike Cernovich Court Win." Cernovich.com, July 7, 2019. https://www.cernovich.com/jeff-epstein-arrested-due -to-mike-cernovich-court-win/.

Chafin, Chris. "San Diego Comic-Con: The Untold History." *Rolling Stone*, July 19, 2017. https://www.rollingstone.com/culture/culture-features/san-diego-comic-con -the-untold-history-194401/.

Chandler, Justin. "MILCK: A Candid Q&A about Trauma, Silence, Activism and the Power of Sisterhood." CBC, March 7, 2018. https://www.cbc.ca/music/ milck-a-candid-q-a-about-trauma-silence-activism-and-the-power-of-sisterhood -1.5081372.

Chandler, Simon. "Social Media Is Fostering a Big Rise in Real-World Stalking." *Forbes*, October 11, 2019. https://www.forbes.com/sites/simonchandler/2019/10/11 /social-media-proves-itself-to-be-the-perfect-tool-for-stalkers/?sh=353c5ad63d79.

Chansanchai, Athima. "Twitter: More than 2.4 Million SOPA Tweets." Technolog on MSNBC, January 19, 2012. https://web.archive.org/web/20120119194334/ http://technolog.msnbc.msn.com/_news/2012/01/19/10190155-twitter-more-than -24-million-sopa-tweets.

Chen, Yuyu. "Hold My Meme: Brands Are Often Hijacking Digital Trends Too Often." *Digiday*, May 4, 2017. https://digiday.com/marketing/brands-use-memes/.

Chiarito, Robert. "This Woman's Unplanned Anthem United the Women's March in Song." *Vice,* January 24, 2017. https://www.vice.com/en_us/article/j5d747/milck -song-quiet-goes-viral-after-womens-march.

Chien, Eugenia. "4 Ways Muni Diaries Readers Document San Francisco Bus Riding." *Poynter*, December 27, 2011. https://www.poynter.org/reporting-editing

/2011/4-ways-to-cultivate-an-audience-that-contributes-to-conversations-shares
-tips/.

Chin, Monica. "Exam Anxiety: How Remote Test-Proctoring Is Creeping Students Out." *The Verge*, April 29, 2020. https://www.theverge.com/2020/4/29/21232777/ examity-remote-test-proctoring-online-class-education.

Choi-Fitzpatrick, Austin. "Drones for Good: Technological Innovations, Social Movements, and the State." *Journal of International Affairs* 68, no. 1 (2014): 19–36.

Chui, Michael, Markus Löffler, and Roger Roberts. "The Internet of Things," *McKinsey Quarterly*, March 1, 2010. http://www.mckinsey.com/insights/high_tech _telecoms_internet/the_internet_of_things.

Cialdini, Robert B., Carl A. Kallgren, and Raymond R. Reno. "A Focus Theory of Normative Conduct: A Theoretical Refinement and Reevaluation of the Role of Norms in Human Behavior." *Advances in Experimental Social Psychology* 24 (1991): 201–34.

Cicalese, Carmen. "Toxic Persuasion—The Worst a Buyer Can Get." *Cyber Cic*, March 18, 2019. https://cybercic.com/info-ops/toxic-persuasion-the-worst-a-buyer -can-get/.

Citron, Danielle Keats. "Extremist Speech, Compelled Conformity, and Censorship Creep." *Notre Dame Law Review* 93, no. 3 (2018): 1035–71.

Clark, Kate. "Joseph Gordon-Levitt's Artist-Collaboration Platform HitRecord Raises $6.4M." *TechCrunch*, January 31, 2019. https://techcrunch.com/2019/01/31/joseph -gordon-levitts-artist-collaboration-platform-hitrecord-raises-6-4m/.

Cochran, Eric. "I Blew the Whistle on Pinterest Censorship | Opinion." *Newsweek*, June 24, 2019. https://www.newsweek.com/i-blew-whistle-pinterest-censorship -opinion-1445496.

Coleman, E. Gabriella. *Coding Freedom: The Ethics and Aesthetics of Hacking*. Princeton, NJ: Princeton University Press, 2012.

Coleman, James S. "Social Capital and the Creation of Human Capital." *American Journal of Sociology* 94, supplement (1988): S95-S120.

Collier, Amy and Jen Ross. "Higher Education after Surveillance?" *Postdigital Science and Education* 2 (2020): 275–79.

Conger, Kate, Mike Isaac and Sheera Frenkel. "Violence on Capitol Hill Is a Day of Reckoning for Social Media." *New York Times*, January 6, 2021. https://www. nytimes.com/2021/01/06/technology/capitol-twitter-facebook-trump.html.

Cook, John. "AT&T and Time Warner to Merge in Massive $85B Media-Telecom Tie-Up." *GeekWire*, October 22, 2016. https://www.geekwire.com/2016/att-time -warner-merge-massive-85b-media-telecom-tie/.

Cope, Sophia and David Greene. "Ninth Circuit: Private Social Media Platforms Are Not Bound by the First Amendment." Electronic Frontier Foundation, March 4, 2020. https://www.eff.org/deeplinks/2020/03/ninth-circuit-private-social-media -platforms-are-not-bound-first-amendment.

Corzine, Ian. "Permission to Use Movie Clips—Have YOU Violated the LAW???" Video, 7:10. August 1, 2018. https://youtu.be/usQSaZ1mnwU.

Couch, Danielle L., Priscilla Robinson, and Paul A. Komesaroff. "COVID-19—Extending Surveillance and the Panopticon." *Journal of Bioethical Inquiry* 17 (2020): 809–14.

Couldry, Nick. "Beyond the Hall of Mirrors? Some Theoretical Reflections on the Global Contestation of Media Power." In *Contesting Media Power: Alternative Media in a Networked World,* edited by Nick Couldry and James Curran, 39–56. Lanham, MD: Rowman & Littlefield, 2003.

Couldry, Nick and Andreas Hepp. *The Mediated Construction of Reality.* Malden, MA: Polity Press, 2017.

CNN. "'Digg Dialogg': House Minority Leader John Boehner." Politics, January 23, 2009. https://www.cnn.com/2009/POLITICS/01/23/digg.dialogue.irpt/index.html.

CNN. "Protests Across the Globe After George Floyd's Death." June 13, 2020. https://www.cnn.com/2020/06/06/world/gallery/intl-george-floyd-protests/index.html.

Cross, Katherine. "The Dark Side of 'Plane Bae' and Turning Strangers into Social Media Content." *The Verge,* July 9, 2018. https://www.theverge.com/2018/7/9/17544354/plane-bae-rosey-beeme-euan-holden-sousveillance-livetweeting.

Crossley, Nick and Mario Diani. "Networks and Fields." In *The Wiley Blackwell Companion to Social Movements,* 2nd ed., edited by David A. Snow, Sarah A. Soule, Hanspeter Kriesi, and Holly J. McCammon, 151–66. Hoboken, NJ: John Wiley & Sons, 2019.

Crowston, Kevin, Qing Li, Kangning Wei, U. Yeliz Eseryel, and James Howison. "Self-Organization of Teams for Free/Libre Open Source Software Development." *Information and Software Technology* 49 (2007): 564–75.

Crypto Briefing (The Analyst Team). "What Is Steem? Introduction to Steemit." May 2, 2018. https://cryptobriefing.com/what-is-steem-introduction-to-steemit/.

Crystal, David. *Language and the Internet.* New York: Cambridge University Press, 2006.

Curran, James. "Rethinking Internet History." In *Misunderstanding the Internet,* edited by James Curran, Natalie Fenton, and Des Freedman, 34–65. New York: Routledge, 2012.

Curtis, Ramona. "Person Doxxed by Mayor Krewson Arrested in Florissant." *St. Louis American,* June 28, 2020. http://www.stlamerican.com/news/local_news/person-doxxed-by-mayor-krewson-arrested-in-florissant/article_6db6ded4-b978-11ea-a46f-97a3e62ee5dc.html.

Cyphers, Bennett and Cory Doctorow. "Privacy without Monopoly: Data Protection and Interoperability." Electronic Frontier Foundation, February 12, 2021. https://www.eff.org/wp/interoperability-and-privacy.

Czitrom, Daniel J. *Media and the American Mind: From Morse to McLuhan.* The University of North Carolina Press, 1982.

da Silva, Patrícia Dias and José Luís Garcia. "YouTubers as Satirists: Humor and Remix in Online Video." *eJournal of eDemocracy & Open Government* 4, no. 1 (2012): 89–114.

Dahlberg, Lincoln. "The Habermasian Public Sphere: A Specification of the Idealized Conditions of Democratic Communication." *Studies in Social and Political Thought* (2005): 1–18.

Dahlgren, Peter. "Professional and Citizen Journalism: Tensions and Complements." In *The Crisis of Journalism Reconsidered*, edited by Jeffrey C. Alexander, Elizabeth Butler Breese, and María Luengo, 247–63. New York: Cambridge University Press, 2016.

Dalelio, Corinne. "A Design Framework of Interactive Media." *Journal of Digital and Media Literacy* 3, no. 1 (2015).

Dalelio, Corinne. "The Development of a Structural Approach to the Study of Computer-Mediated Communication via Online Discussion Boards." PhD diss., Rutgers, the State University of New Jersey, 2010. RUCore: Rutgers University Community Repository. https://rucore.libraries.rutgers.edu/rutgers-lib/26519/.

Dalelio, Corinne and Wendy M. Weinhold. "'I Know From Personal Experience': Citizen News Discussions and Knowledge Sharing on Reddit." *International Journal of Technology, Knowledge, and Society* 16, no. 1 (2020): 13–34. https://doi.org/10.18848/1832-3669/CGP/v16i01/13-34.

Damon, Andre. "Google Intensifies Censorship of Left-Wing Websites." World Socialist Web Site, September 19, 2017. https://www.wsws.org/en/articles/2017/09/19/goog-s19.html.

Darcy, Oliver. "Right-Wing Troll Mike Cernovich Goes Professional With New Hosting Gig at InfoWars." CNN Business, May 3, 2017. https://money.cnn.com/2017/05/03/media/mike-cernovich-infowars-alex-jones/index.html.

Darden, Jenee. "What It Means to Rise." *Triton Magazine*, April 24, 2019. https://tritonmag.com/what-it-means-to-rise/.

Davis, Chelsea. "Maui Woman Starts What Could Be Largest Trump Inauguration Movement." *Hawaii News Now,* January 6, 2017. https://www.hawaiinewsnow.com/story/34198283/maui-woman-starts-what-could-be-largest-trump-inauguration-movement/.

Davison, Patrick. "The Language of Internet Memes." In *The Social Media Reader,* edited by Michael Mandiberg, 120–34. New York: NYU Press, 2012.

Dawkins, Richard. *The Selfish Gene.* Oxford University Press, 1989.

Dawson, Ella. "The Dark Side of Going Viral." *Vox*, July 10, 2018. https://www.vox.com/first-person/2018/7/10/17553796/plane-bae-viral-airplane-romance.

De Kosnick, Abigail. "Fandom as Free Labor." In *Digital Labor: The Internet as Playground and Factory* ,edited by Trebor Scholz, 98–111. New York: Routledge, 2013.

de Mooij, Marieke. *Global Marketing and Advertising: Understanding Cultural Paradoxes,* 4th ed. Thousand Oaks, CA: Sage, 2014.

de Sola Pool, Ithiel. *Technologies without Boundaries: On Telecommunications in a Global Age.* Cambridge, MA: Harvard University Press, 1990.

De Vierman, Marijke, Veroline Cauberghe, and Liselot Hudders. "Marketing through Instagram Influencers: The Impact of Number of Followers and Product Divergence on Brand Attitude." *International Journal of Advertising* 36, no. 5 (2017): 798–828.

Democracynow.org. "Rejecting Lucrative Offer, Cenk Uygur Leaves MSNBC After Being Told to 'Act Like an Insider.'" *Democracy Now!,* July 22, 2011. https://www.democracynow.org/2011/7/22/rejecting_lucrative_offer_cenk_uygur_leaves.

Denning, Stephanie. "Why Jeff Bezos Bought *The Washington Post.*" *Forbes*, September 19, 2018. https://www.forbes.com/sites/stephaniedenning/2018/09/19/why-jeff-bezos-bought-the-washington-post/?sh=a41aa923aabd.

Denniston, Michael S. "International Copyright Protection: How Does It Work?" *Bradley*, https://www.bradley.com/insights/publications/2012/03/international-copyright-protection-how-does-it-w__.

Dill-Shackelford, Karen. *How Fantasy Becomes Reality: Seeing through Media Influence.* Revised and Expanded Ed. New York: Oxford University Press, 2016.

Doctorow, Cory. "Adversarial Interoperability." Electronic Frontier Foundation, October 9, 2019. https://www.eff.org/deeplinks/2019/10/adversarial-interoperability.

Doctorow, Cory. "All Complex Ecosystems Have Parasites." Paper delivered at the O'Reilly Emerging Technology Conference, San Diego, CA, March 2005. https://craphound.com/content/Cory_Doctorow_-_Content.html.

Doctorow, Cory. "Bust 'Em All: Let's De-Monopolize Tech, Telecoms AND Entertainment." Electronic Frontier Foundation, September 28, 2020. https://www.eff.org/deeplinks/2020/09/bust-em-all-lets-de-monopolize-tech-telecoms-and-entertainment.

Doctorow, Cory. "Competitive Compatibility: Year in Review 2020." Electronic Frontier Foundation, December 30, 2020. https://www.eff.org/deeplinks/2020/12/competitive-compatibility-year-review.

Doctorow, Cory. "How to Destroy Surveillance Capitalism (e-book)." Medium.com (OneZero), August 26, 2020. https://onezero.medium.com/how-to-destroy-surveillance-capitalism-8135e6744d59.

Doctorow, Cory and Christoph Schmon. "The EU's Digital Markets Act: There Is a Lot to Like, but Room for Improvement." Electronic Frontier Foundation, December 15, 2020. https://www.eff.org/deeplinks/2020/12/eus-digital-markets-act-there-lot-room-improvement.

Donovan, Joan and danah boyd. "Stop the Presses? Moving from Strategic Silence to Strategic Amplification in a Networked Media Ecosystem." *American Behavioral Scientist* 65, no. 2 (2019): 333–50.

Douglas, David M. "Doxing: A Conceptual Analysis." *Ethics and Information Technology* 18 (2016): 199–210.

Douglas, Nick. "'It's Supposed to Look Like Shit': The Internet Ugly Aesthetic." *Journal of Visual Culture* 13, no. 3 (2014): 314–39. https://journals.sagepub.com/doi/10.1177/1470412914544516.

Draughton, Andrew T. "The 3-Act 'Cliffhanger' Formula for Crafting a Wickedly-Effective Call-to-Action." Elite Marketing Pro Blog. https://elitemarketingpro.com/blog/cliffhanger-formula-for-crafting-a-wickedly-effective-call-to-action/.

Dry, Jude. "Brad Neely's Adult Swim Show: How an Internet Pioneer Found New Audiences on Vine and TV." *IndieWire*, July 7, 2016. https://www.indiewire.com/2016/07/brad-neely-new-adult-swim-vine-early-internet-artist-1201703204/.

Duarte, José L., Jarret T. Crawford, Charlotta Stern, Jonathan Haidt, Lee Jussim, and Philip E. Tetlock. "Political Diversity Will Improve Social Psychological Science." *Behavioral and Brain Sciences* 38 (2015): e130. doi:10.1017/S0140525X14000430.

Dubois, Elizabeth and Grant Blank. "The Echo Chamber Is Overstated: The Moderating Effect of Political Interest and Diverse Media." *Information, Communication, & Society* 21, no. 5 (2018): 729–45.

Duribe, Jazmin. "Kim Kardashian Urged to Pay Fan Who Came Up with the Name of Her Shapewear Line Skims." *PopBuzz*, October 14, 2019. https://www.popbuzz.com/style/fashion/kim-kardashian-skims-shapewear-kimono/.

Dvir-Gvirsman, Shira. "One-Track Minds? Cognitive Needs, Media Diet, and Overestimation of Public Support for One's Views." *Media Psychology* 18 (2015): 475–98.

Dynel, Marta. "'I Has Seen Image Macros!' Advice Animal Memes as Visual-Verbal Jokes." *International Journal of Communication* 10 (2016): 660–88.

Eadie, William F. and Robin Goret. "Theories and Models of Communication: Foundations and Heritage." In *Theories and Models of Communication,* edited by Paul Cobley and Peter J. Shulz, 17–38. Berlin: De Gruyter, 2013.

Edelman, Gilad. "Stop Saying Facebook Is 'Too Big to Moderate." *Wired Magazine*, July 28, 2020. https://www.wired.com/story/stop-saying-facebook-too-big-to-moderate/.

Eisenstat, Yaël. "How to Hold Social Media Accountable for Undermining Democracy." *Harvard Business Review*, January 11, 2021. https://hbr.org/2021/01/how-to-hold-social-media-accountable-for-undermining-democracy.

Electronic Frontier Foundation. "EFF's Comments to the White House on Big Data." RFI OSTP-2014–0003–0001, April 8, 2014. https://www.eff.org/document/effs-comments-white-house-big-data.

Ellison, Nicole B. and danah m. boyd. "Sociality through Social Network Sites." In *The Oxford Handbook of Internet Studies,* edited by William H. Dutton, 151–72. New York: Oxford University Press, 2013.

Empson, Rip. "Jeff Jarvis: When It Comes to New Journalism, 'Transparency Is the New Objectivity.'" *TechCrunch*, May 23, 2011. https://techcrunch.com/2011/05/23/jeff-jarvis-when-it-comes-to-new-journalism-transparency-is-the-new-objectivity/.

Engleman, Eric. "Google Protest of Piracy Bills Upends Traditional Lobbying." *Bloomberg*, January 19, 2012. https://www.bloomberg.com/news/articles/2012-01-19/google-protest-of-anti-piracy-bills-upends-traditional-lobbying-process.

Entman, Robert M. "Framing: Toward Clarification of a Fractured Paradigm." *Journal of Communication* 43, no. 4 (1993): 51–58.

Erickson, Bonnie H. "Some Problems of Inference from Chain Data." *Sociological Methodoloy* 10 (1979): 276–302.

Esguerra, Richard. "Google CEO Eric Schmidt Dismisses the Importance of Privacy." Electronic Frontier Foundation, December 9, 2009. https://www.eff.org/deeplinks/2009/12/google-ceo-eric-schmidt-dismisses-privacy.

Eslinger, Tom. *Mobile Magic: The Saatchi and Saatchi Guide to Mobile Marketing and Design.* Hoboken, NJ: John Wiley & Sons, 2014.

Event Marketer. "Coachella Roundup: Heineken, Instagram, HP and More Activate in the Desert." *Event Marketer*, April 19, 2019. https://www.eventmarketer.com/article/inside-the-biggest-experiential-marketing-programs-at-coachella-2019/.

Farrell, James. "Big Tech Benefitting from Forced Labor in China, According to Report," *Silicon Angle*. March 2, 2020. https://siliconangle.com/2020/03/02/big-tech-benefiting-forced-labor-china-according-report/.

Fass, Craig. *Six Degrees of Kevin Bacon*. New York: Penguin, 1996.

Feathers, Todd. "Students Are Rebelling Against Eye-Tracking Exam Surveillance Tools." Vice, September 24, 2020. https://www.vice.com/en/article/n7wxvd/students-are-rebelling-against-eye-tracking-exam-surveillance-tools.

Finn, Greg. "#BlackoutSOPA: A Look at the Social Media Movement That Helped Stall the SOPA Legislation." *MarketingLand*, January 16, 2012. https://marketingland.com/blackoutsopa-a-look-at-the-social-media-movement-that-helped-stall-the-sopa-legislation-3453.

Fischer, Will. "'Ad Models Break Everyone's Brains': How Patreon and Substack are Trying to Make the Internet a Better Place with Membership and Subscriptions." *Business Insider*, August 11, 2019. https://www.businessinsider.com/subscription-platforms-patreon-substack-quality-alternative-to-social-media-2019-8.

Fleshman, Cu. "Got MILCK? Meet the Voice of the 2017 Women's March, Connie Lim." *Character Media,* September 12, 2019. https://charactermedia.com/got-milck-meet-the-voice-of-the-2017-womens-march-connie-lim/.

Fletcher, Anton. "Review of *Hoaxed: A Documentary*—Produced by Mike Cernovich." Medium.com, October 22, 2018. https://medium.com/@anton.fletcher.3/review-of-hoaxed-a-documentary-produced-by-mike-cernovich-41b96f0421bc.

Floridi, Luciano. "Four Challenges for a Theory of Informational Privacy." *Ethics and Information Technology* 8 (2006): 109–19.

Floridi, Luciano. "On Human Dignity as a Foundation for the Right to Privacy." *Philosophy & Technology* 29 (2016): 307–12.

Folberg, Effy. "Search Warrants for Digital Speech." *Yale Journal of Law & Technology* 22 (2020): 318–90.

Fornäs, Johan, Kajsa Klein, Martina Landendorf, Jenny Sundén, and Malin Sveningsson. *Digital Borderlands: Cultural Studies of Identity and Interactivity on the Internet.* New York: Peter Lang Publishing, 2002.

Fornier, Susan and Jill Avery. "The Uninvited Brand." *Business Horizons* 54 (2011): 193–207.

Fowler, Jim. "Why Minecraft Predicts the Future of Collaborative Work." TechCrunch, August 1, 2016. https://techcrunch.com/2016/08/01/why-minecraft-predicts-the-future-of-collaborative-work/.

Fowler, Tara. "Google Introduces 'Bacon Number' Search." *Entertainment Weekly.* September 14, 2012. https://ew.com/article/2012/09/14/google-introduces-bacon-number/.

Frankin, Bob. *Social Policy, the Media and Misrepresentation*. New York: Routledge, 1999.

Freeman, Linton C. *The Development of Social Network Analysis*. North Charleston, SC: BookSurge, LLC, 2004.

Freeman, Linton C., Douglas R. White, and A. Kimball Romney. *Research Methods in Social Network Analysis.* Fairfax, VA: George Mason University, 1989.

Fuchs, Christian. "Propaganda 2.0: Herman and Chomsky's Propaganda Model in the Age of the Internet, Big Data and Social Media." In *The Propaganda Model Today: Filtering Perception and Awareness*, edited by Joan Pedro-Carañana, Daniel Broudy, and Jeffrey Klaehn, 71–92. London: University of Westminster Press, 2018.

Fuchs, Christian. *Social Media: A Critical Introduction*. Thousand Oaks, CA: Sage, 2014.

Galloway, Alexander F. *Protocol: How Control Exists After Decentralization*. Cambridge, MA: MIT Press, 2006.

Galperin, Eva. "Want Public Safety? Don't Disable Cell Phones." Electronic Frontier Foundation, August 19, 2011. https://www.eff.org/deeplinks/2011/08/want-public-safety-dont-disable-cell-phones.

Gaming Street Staff. "How Baskin-Robbins Built a *Stranger Things* Alternate Reality Game Using 1985 Tech." *Gaming Street*, August 13, 2019. https://gamingstreet.com/baskin-robbins-stranger-things-arg/.

Ganz, Marshall and Elizabeth McKenna. "Bringing Leadership Back In." In *The Wiley Blackwell Companion to Social Movements*, 2nd ed. Edited by David A. Snow, Sarah A. Soule, Hanspeter Kriesi, and Holly J. McCammon, 185–202. Hoboken, NJ: John Wiley & Sons, 2019.

Garber, Megan. "Two Strangers Met on a Plane—and the Internet Ruined It." *Atlantic*, July 6, 2018. https://www.theatlantic.com/entertainment/archive/2018/07/planebae-and-the-slow-death-of-whimsy/564473/.

Garfinkel, Simson. *Database Nation: The Death of Privacy in the 21st Century*. Cambridge, MA: O'Reilly Media, 2000.

Gauntlett, David. *Making Is Connecting*, 2nd ed. Medford, MA: Polity Press, 2018.

Gehl, Robert W. "The Case for Alternative Social Media." *Social Media + Society* (July 2015): 1–12.

Gelderblom, Derik. "The Limits to Bridging Social Capital: Power, Social Context and the Theory of Robert Putnam." *Sociological Review* 66, no. 6 (2018): 1309–24.

George, Anita. "The Most-Viewed YouTube Videos of All Time," *Digital Trends*, December 1, 2020. https://www.digitaltrends.com/web/most-viewed-youtube-videos/.

Gen, Charo. "Read This Before You Even Think About Crowdfunding." Medium.com, August 6, 2018. https://medium.com/swlh/read-this-before-you-even-think-about-crowdfunding-9dede644cf09.

Gerbaudo, Paolo. "The 'Kill Switch' as 'Suicide Switch': Mobilizing Side Effects of Mubarak's Communication Blackout." *Westminster Papers* 9, no. 2 (2013): 25–43.

Gerbaudo, Paolo. "Social Media Teams as Digital Vanguards: The Question of Leadership in the Management of Key Facebook and Twitter Accounts of Occupy Wall Street, Indignados and UK Uncut." *Information, Communication & Society* 20, no. 2 (2017): 185–202.

Gerstein, Josh. "The One Weird Court Case Linking Trump, Clinton, and a Billionaire Pedophile." *Politico*, May 4, 2017. https://www.politico.com/story/2017/05/04/jeffrey-epstein-trump-lawsuit-sex-trafficking-237983.

Ghoshal, Abimanyu. "Why We Should Collectively Worry About Facebook and Google Owning Our Data." *The Next Web*, April 25, 2018. https://thenextweb.com/insights/2018/04/25/why-should-you-care-if-google-and-facebook-own-your-data/.

Gibson, William, *Neuromancer*. New York: Ace Books, 1984.

Giebelhausen, Michael D., Stacy G. Robinson, and J. Joseph Cronin Jr. "Worth Waiting For: Increasing Satisfaction by Making Consumers Wait." *Journal of the Academy of Marketing Science* 39 (2011): 889–905.

Gilbert, David. "Anonymous Declared War on Trump, and Then Disappeared." *Vice*, November 28, 2016. https://www.vice.com/en/article/ywna4w/anonymous-declared-war-on-trump-and-then-disappeared.

Gilder, George. *Life After Google: The Fall of Big Data and the Rise of the Blockchain Economy*. Washington, DC: Regenery, 2018.

Giles, Jim. "Internet Encyclopedias Go Head to Head." *Nature* 438 (2005): 900–01. https://www.nature.com/articles/438900a.

Gillespie, Tarleton. "The Relevance of Algorithms." In *Media Technologies: Essays on Communication, Materiality, and Society*, edited by Tarleton Gillespie, Pablo J. Boczowski, and Kirsten A. Foot, 167–93. Cambridge, MA: MIT Press, 2014.

Gillmor, Dan. "The Facebook Template: When Net Freedom Meets Market Forces." *The Guardian*, September 23, 2011. https://www.theguardian.com/commentisfree/cifamerica/2011/sep/23/internet-freedom-market-forces.

Gillmor, Dan. *Mediactive*. Dan Gillmor, 2010.

Gillmor, Dan. *We the Media: Grassroots Journalism by the People, for the People.* Sebastopol, CA: O'Reilly Media, 2004.

Gilkerson, Nathan and Kati Tusinski Berg. "Social Media, Hashtag Hijacking, and the Evolution of an Activist Group Strategy." In *Social Media and Crisis Communication*, edited by Lucinda Austin and Yan Jin, 141–55. New York: Routledge, 2018.t

Gitelman, Lisa. *Always Already New: Media, History and the Data of Culture.* Cambridge: MIT Press, 2006.

Gitlin, Todd. "Public Sphere or Public Sphericles?" In *Media, Ritual and Identity,* edited by Tamar Liebes and James Curran, 168–74. New York: Routledge, 1998.

Givetash, Linda. "Laura Loomer Banned from Twitter After Criticizing Ilhan Omar." NBC News, November 22, 2018. https://www.nbcnews.com/tech/security/laura-loomer-banned-twitter-after-criticizing-ilhan-omar-n939256.

Gladwell, Hattie. "Burger King Has Launched Flamin' Hot Mac 'n' Cheetos And They Sound Amazing." *Metro,* November 30, 2017. https://metro.co.uk/2017/11/30/burger-king-has-launched-flamin-hot-mac-n-cheetos-and-they-sound-amazing-7121317/.

Gleason, Tim. "If We Are All Journalists, Can Journalistic Privilege Survive?" *Jovnost: The Public* 22, no. 4 (2015): 375–86. http://dx.doi.org/10.1080/13183222.2015.1091625.

Gobé, Marc. *Emotional Branding: The New Paradigm for Connecting Brands to People*. Updated and revised ed. New York: Allworth Press, 2009.

Goffman, Erving. "The Interaction Order." *American Sociological Review* 48, no. 1 (1983): 1–17.

Goggin, Benjamin. "7,800 People Lost Their Media Jobs in a 2019 Landslide." *Business Insider*, December 10, 2019. https://www.businessinsider.com/2019-media-layoffs-job-cuts-at-buzzfeed-huffpost-vice-details-2019-2.

Goldhill, Olivia. "Wondering What Trolls Will Do in 2020? Watch the Misogynists." *Quartz,* November 9, 2019. https://qz.com/1744947/todays-sexist-weapon-is-tomorrows-political-tool/.

Gong, Taeshik. "Customer Brand Engagement Behavior in Online Brand Communities." *Journal of Services Marketing* 32, no. 3 (2018): 286–99.

Gordon-Levitt, Joseph. "Community Collaboration vs. Spec Work." Medium.com, June 14, 2018. https://medium.com/@hitRECordJoe/community-collaboration-vs-spec-work-8592692a875e.

Graber, Christoph B. "Internet Creativity, Communicative Freedom and a Constitutional Rights Theory Response to 'Code Is Law.'" *i-call Working Paper* no. 3 (2010): 1–26.

Grady, Constance. "Some Say the Me Too Movement Has Gone Too Far. The Harvey Weinstein Verdict Proves That's False." *Vox*, February 24, 2020. https://www.vox.com/culture/2020/2/24/21150966/harvey-weinstein-rape-conviction-sexual-predatory-assault-me-too-too-far.

Graham, Paul. "How to Disagree." Paulgraham.com, March 2008. http://www.paulgraham.com/disagree.html.

Graham, Todd. "Talking Back, But Is Anyone Listening? Journalism and Comment Fields." In *Rethinking Journalism: Trust and Participation in a Transformed News Landscape,* edited by Chris Peters and Marcel Jeroen Broersma, 114–27. New York: Routledge, 2013.

Graham, Todd and Scott Wright. "Discursive Equality and Everyday Talk Online: The Impact of 'Superparticipants'." *Journal of Computer-Mediated Communication* 19 (2014): 625–42.

Granka, Laura A. "The Politics of Search: A Decade Retrospective." *Information Society* 26 (2010): 364–74.

Grassini, Simone and Karin Laumann. "Evaluating the Use of Virtual Reality in Work Safety: A Literature Review." (2020). doi: 10.3850/978-981-14-8593-0_3975-cd.

Gray, Tyler. "Pop Goes Perez: How a Pudgy Miami Poseur Became Gossip's New Queen." *Radar Online,* September 28, 2006. https://web.archive.org/web/20070209022056/http:/www.radaronline.com/features/2006/09/perez_hilton_blogger_baron.php.

Grebb, Micheal. "Rejected TV Pilot Thrives on P2P." *Wired Magazine*, June 17, 2005. https://www.wired.com/2005/06/rejected-tv-pilot-thrives-on-p2p/.

Greenberg, Andy. "Researchers Say *WSJ*'s Wikileaks Copycat Is Full of Holes." *Forbes*, May 5, 2011. https://www.forbes.com/sites/andygreenberg/2011/05/05/researchers-say-wsjs-wikileaks-copycat-is-full-of-holes/?sh=5627e6584680.

Greenberg, Andy. "Wikileaks Reveals the Biggest Classified Data Breach in History." *Forbes*, October 22, 2010. https://www.forbes.com/sites/andygreenberg

/2010/10/22/wikileaks-reveals-the-biggest-classified-data-breach-in-history/?sh =16c3f9a86353.

Greenfield, Joshua. "[Music Discovery] An Exploration of the Lo-Fi Aesthetic." Medium.com, September 25, 2018. https://medium.com/@johngreenfield/music -discovery-an-exploration-of-the-lo-fi-aesthetic-487c4dbfc3fc.

Greenwald, Glenn. "Revealed: How US and UK Spy Agencies Defeat Internet Privacy and Security." *The Guardian*, September 6, 2013. https://www.theguardian.com/ world/2013/sep/05/nsa-gchq-encryption-codes-security.

Greenwald, Michelle. "What's Really Driving the Limitless Growth of Podcasts." *Forbes*, October 4, 2018. https://www.forbes.com/sites/michellegreenwald /2018/10/04/why-podcasts-will-continue-to-grow-why-its-great-for-brands/?sh =5343777b205f.

Greico, Elizabeth. "U.S. Newspapers Have Shed Half of Their Newsroom Employees Since 2008." Pew Research Center, April 20, 2020. https://www.pewresearch.org/ fact-tank/2020/04/20/u-s-newsroom-employment-has-dropped-by-a-quarter-since -2008/.

Griffin, Andrew. "Cheeto That Looks Like Harambe Sells for 100,000 on Ebay." *The Independent,* February 7, 2017. https://www.independent.co.uk/life-style/gadgets -and-tech/news/harambe-cheeto-ebay-flamin-hot-cincinnati-zoo-dead-slain-gorilla -ape-tree-a7567241.html.

Griffiths, James. "Internet Shutdowns Cost the Global Economy $8 Billion Last Year, Report Says." CNN Business, January 9, 2020. https://www.cnn.com/2020/01/09/ tech/internet-shutdowns-cost-intl-hnk/index.html.

Grind, Kirsten, Sam Schechner, Robert McMillan, and John West. "How Google Interferes with Its Search Algorithms and Changes Your Results." *Wall Street Journal*, November 15, 2019. https://www.wsj.com/articles/how-google-interferes -with-its-search-algorithms-and-changes-your-results-11573823753.

Groening, Stephen. "Introduction: Aesthetics of Online Videos." *Film Criticism* 40, no. 2 (2016). https://doi.org/10.3998/fc.13761232.0040.201.

Grossberg, Lawrence. *Cultural Studies in the Future Tense.* Durham, NC: Duke University Press, 2010.

Grover, Bhavya Ahuja, Bhawna Chaudhary, Nikhil Kumar Rajput, and Om Dukiya. "Blockchain and Governance: Theory, Applications, and Challenges." In *Blockchain for Business: How It Works and Creates Value,* edited by S.S. Tyagi and Shaveta Bhatia, 113–39. Hoboken, NJ: Wiley, 2021.

Gu, Xian, P. K. Kannan, and Liye Ma. "Selling the Premium in Freemium." *Journal of Marketing* 82, no. 6 (2018): 10–27.

Guare, John. *Six Degrees of Separation.* New York: Vintage, 1990.

Gui, March and Gianluca Argentin. "Digital Skills of Internet Natives: Different Forms of Digital Literacy in a Random Sample of Northern Italian High School Students." *New Media & Society* 13, no 6 (2011): 963–80. https://doi.org/10.1177 /1461444810389751.

Guiltinan, Joseph. "Creative Destruction and Destructive Creations: Environmental Ethics and Planned Obsolescence." *Journal of Business Ethics* 89 (2009): 19–28.

Gulbrandsen, Ib Tunby and Sine Nørholm Just. "Collaborative Constructed Contradictory Accounts: Online Organizational Narratives." *Media, Culture & Society* 35, no. 5 (2013): 565–85.

Gurevitch, Michael. "The Social Structure of Acquaintenceship Networks." PhD diss., Massachusetts Institute of Technology, 1961. DSpace@MIT. http://hdl.handle.net/1721.1/11312.

Guynn, Jessica. "Facebook While Black: Users Call It Getting 'Zucked,' Say Talking About Racism il Censored as Hate Speech." *USA Today,* July 9, 2020. https://www.usatoday.com/story/news/2019/04/24/facebook-while-black-zucked-users-say-they-get-blocked-racism-discussion/2859593002/.

Guynn, Jessica. "These Are Facebook's Secret Rules for Removing Posts." *USA Today,* April 24, 2018. https://www.usatoday.com/story/tech/news/2018/04/24/facebook-discloses-secret-guidelines-policing-content-introduces-appeals/544046002/.

Haas, Eric. "False Equivalency: Think Tank References on Education in the News Media." *Peabody Journal of Education* 82, no. 1 (2007): 63–102.

Habermas, Jürgen. "The Public Sphere: An Encyclopedia Article." In *Media and Cultural Studies: KeyWorks,* edited by Gigi Durham and Douglas M. Kellner, 73–78. Malden, MA: Blackwell Publishing, 2001.

Habernal, Ivan, Henning Wachsmuth, Iryna Gurevych, and Benno Stein. "Before Name-Calling: Dynamics and Triggers of Ad Hominem Fallacies in Web Argumentation." In *Proceedings of the 2018 Conference of the North American Chapter of the Association for Computational Linguistics: Human Language Technologies,* New Orleans, LA (2018): 386–96.

Hall, Mark A. "Common Carriers Under the Communications Act." *University of Chicago Law Review* 48, no. 2 (1981): 409–38.

Hamelink, Cees J. *The Ethics of Cyberspace.* Thousand Oaks, CA: Sage, 2000.

Hanitzch, Thomas. "Journalism, Participative Media and Trust in a Comparative Context." In *Rethinking Journalism: Trust and Participation in a Transformed News Landscape,* edited by Chris Peters and Marcel Jeroen Broersma, 200–09. New York: Routledge, 2013.

Hanna, Robin. "Amazon on a Positive Note: The End of Downvoting." Sellics Blog, May 26, 2020. https://sellics.com/blog-amazon-on-a-positive-note-the-end-of-downvoting/.

Hargittai, Eszter. "Second-Level Digital Divide: Differences in People's Online Skills." *First Monday* 7, no. 4 (2002). https://doi.org/10.5210/fm.v7i4.942.

Harper, Adam. "Lo-Fi Aesthetics in Popular Music Discourse." PhD thesis, University of Oxford, 2014. ORA: Oxford University Research Archive. https://ora.ox.ac.uk/objects/uuid:cc84039c-3d30-484e-84b4-8535ba4a54f8.

Hartmans, Avery and Kate Taylor. "Amazon Drivers Describe the Paranoia of Working Under the Watchful Eyes of New Truck Cameras That Monitor Them Constantly and Fire Off 'Rage-Inducing' Alerts If They Make a Wrong Move." *Business Insider,* April 12, 2021. https://www.businessinsider.com/amazon-delivery-cameras-tech-track-drivers-bezos-2021-4.

Hatch, Mark R. *The Maker Revolution: Building a Future on Creativity and Innovation in an Exponential World.* Hobooken, NJ: Wiley & Sons, Inc., 2018.

Havel, Vaclev. "Dear Dr. Husák." In *Open Letters: Selected Writings 1965–1990*, selected and edited by Paul Wilson, 50–83. New York: Vintage Books, 1991.

Havrilesky, Heather. "'Top Chef' Just Improves with Age." *Salon*, July 15, 2010. https://www.salon.com/2010/07/15/top_chef_dc_cranky_cheftestants/.

Hayes, Molly. "COLUMN: In Hindsight, The End of *Game of Thrones Is* Even Worse." *Indiana Daily Student,* May 17, 2020. https://www.idsnews.com/article /2020/05/column-game-of-thrones-ending-worse-in-hindsight.

Haynes, Marie. "Is Google Suppressing Alternative Health Sites? How Google Could Measure Scientific Consensus." MHC, August 6, 2020. https://www.mariehaynes. com/resources/scientific-consensus/.

Heaton, Alex. "Myrtle Beach police opening investigation into 'Grateful Doe,'" *ABC15NEWS,* January 14, 2015. https://abcnews.go.com/Health/girl-diagnosed -rare-genetic-disorder-reddit-years-inconclusive/story?id=38876898.

Hebdige, Dick. "(i) From Culture to Hegemony; (ii) Subculture: The Unnatural Break." In *Media and Cultural Studies: KeyWorks*, edited by Gigi Durham and Douglas M. Kellner, 144–62. Malden, MA: Blackwell Publishing, 2001.

Heim, Bec. "'Game of Thrones' Producers Benioff and Weiss Leave 'Star Wars' Film Series." *Film Daily*, November 5, 2019. https://filmdaily.co/news/benioff-and -weiss/.

Helmond, Anne. "The Algorithmization of the Hyperlink." *Computational Culture* 3 (2013). http://computationalculture.net/the-algorithmization-of-the-hyperlink/.

Herbert, Daniel and Amanda D. Lotz. "Approaching Media Industries Comparatively: A Case Study of Streaming." *International Journal of Cultural Studies* 22, no. 3 (2018): 349–66.

Herman, Edward S. and Noam Chomsky. *Manufacturing Consent: The Political Economy of Mass Media*. New York: Pantheon Books, 1988.

Hickman, Blair. "How We Used Facebook to Power Our Investigation into Patient Harm." ProPublica, December 19, 2012. https://www.propublica.org/article/how -we-used-facebook-to-power-our-investigation-into-patient-harm.

Hiebert, Paul. "America's Favorite Snack for the Third Year in a Row Is Flamin' Hot Cheetos." *Adweek,* December 10, 2019. https://www.adweek.com/retail/americas -favorite-snack-for-the-third-year-in-a-row-is-flamin-hot-cheetos/.

Higgins, Parker. "BART's Cell Phone Shutdown, One Year Later." Electronic Frontier Foundation, August 13, 2012. https://www.eff.org/deeplinks/2012/08/barts-cell -phone-shutdown-one-year-later.

Higgins, Tucker. "The Bizarre Political Rise and Fall of Infowars' Alex Jones." CNBC, September 14, 2018. https://www.cnbc.com/2018/09/14/alex-jones-rise -and-fall-of-infowars-conspiracy-pusher.html.

Hill, Evan, Ainara Tiefenthäler, Christiaan Triebert, Drew Jordan, Haley Willis, and Robin Stein. "How George Floyd Was Killed in Police Custody." *New York Times*, Video, 9:44, May 31, 2020. https://www.nytimes.com/video/us/100000007159353 /george-floyd-arrest-death-video.html.

Hill, Mark. "Write for Cracked and Get Paid: Here's How." *Cracked*, December 27, 2018. https://www.cracked.com/article_26097_write-cracked-get-paid-heres -how.html.

Hilton, Robin. "A Flash Mob Choir at the Women's March Turned This Unknown Song into an Anthem." WJCT-FM, January 22, 2018. https://news.wjct.org/post/flash-mob-choir-womens-march-turned-unknown-song-anthem.

Ho, Shannon. "A Social Media 'Blackout' Enthralled Instagram. But Did It do Anything?" NBCNews, June 13, 2020. https://www.nbcnews.com/tech/social-media/social-media-blackout-enthralled-instagram-did-it-do-anything-n1230181.

Hobbs, Renee. *Digital and Media Literacy: A Plan of Action.* Washington DC: The Aspen Institute, 2010.

Hobbs, Renee. "Propaganda in an Age of Algorithmic Personalization: Expanding Literacy Research and Practice." *Reading Research Quarterly* 55, no. 3 (2020): 521–33.

Hodgson Russ Media Law. "Assange Indictment Highlights Importance of Shield Laws for Protecting Press Freedoms." First Amendment Alert, May 3, 2019. https://www.hodgsonruss.com/newsroom-publications-11005.html.

Holiday, Ryan. "We Don't Have a Fake News Problem—We Are the Fake News Problem." *Observer*, November 29, 2016. https://observer.com/2016/11/we-dont-have-a-fake-news-problem-we-are-the-fake-news-problem/.

Holmes, Allan, Eleanor Bell Fox, Ben Weider, and Chris Zubak-Skees. "Rich People Have Access to High-Speed Internet; Many Poor People Still Don't," *The Center for Public Integrity.* May 12, 2016. https://publicintegrity.org/inequality-poverty-opportunity/rich-people-have-access-to-high-speed-internet-many-poor-people-still-dont/.

Hooks, Austin Michael. "Cancel Culture: Posthuman Hauntologies in Digital Rhetoric and the Latent Values of Virtual Community Networks." Master's thesis, University of Tennessee Chattnooga, 2020. UTC Scholar.

Hooton, Christopher. "Justin Bieber Arrested: MSNBC Interrupts Congresswoman During NSA Interview for Important Bieber News." *Independent*, January 24, 2014. https://www.independent.co.uk/news/people/news/congresswoman-interrupted-during-nsa-interview-report-justin-bieber-9082109.html.

Hore-Thorburn, Isabelle. "Cheetos Brings Its 'House of Flamin' Haute' Couture to NYFW." HighSnobiety, 2019. https://www.highsnobiety.com/p/cheetos-flamin-haute-couture-nyfw-19/.

Horkheimer, Max and Theodor W. Adorno. "The Culture Industry: Enlightenment as Mass Deception." In *Media and Cultural Studies: KeyWorks*, edited by Gigi Durham and Douglas M. Kellner, 41–72. Malden, MA: Blackwell Publishing, 2001.

Hossain, Syeda Sumbul, Samen Anjum Arani, Tanvir Rahman, Touhid Bhuiyan, Delwar Alam, and Moniruz Zaman. "E-voting Systems Using Blockchain Technology." *Proceedings of the 2019 ACM Conference*, Xian, China, December 9–11, 2019. https://doi.org/10.1145/3376044.3376062.

Hough, Q. V. "*Game of Thrones* Fan Rewrites Season 8 & Gives Viewers the End They Want." *Screen Rant,* June 18, 2019. https://screenrant.com/game-thrones-season-8-rewrite-ending-fan-video/.

Howard, Rob. "Three Reasons Why Journalism Paywalls Still Don't Work." *Quartz*, January 5, 2018. https://qz.com/1173033/the-psychology-behind-why-journalism -paywalls-still-dont-work/.

Huffington Post. "Cheerios' Facebook Hijacked by Anti-GMO Protestors." *HuffPost*, December 12, 2012. https://www.huffpost.com/entry/cheerios-gmo-facebook_n _2284387.

Hultgren, Kaylee. "Big Bets in Experiential at SXSW 2019, from Netflix to Sony to Lululemon." *Event Marketer*, March 19, 2019. https://www.eventmarketer.com/ article/experiential-sxsw-netflix-sony-lululemon/.

Hutchins, Brett. "The Acceleration of Media Sport Culture: Twitter, Telepresence and Online Messaging." *Information, Communication & Society* 14, no. 2 (2011): 237–57. https://doi.org/10.1080/1369118X.2010.508534.

Hutchins, Brett and David Rowe. "From Broadcast Scarcity to Digital Plentitude: The Changing Dynamics of the Media Sport Content Economy." *Television & New Media* 10, no. 4 (2009): 354–70.

Hyde, Adam, Mike Linksvayer, Kanarinka, Michael Mandiberg, Marta Peirano, Sissu Tarka, Astra Taylor, Alan Toner, and Mushon Zer-Aviv. "What Is Collaboration Anyway?" In *The Social Media Reader,* edited by Michael Mandiberg, 53–67. New York: NYU Press, 2012.

Immersely. "The Good, the Bad, the Ugly: Product Placements." Medium.com, https://medium.com/@immersely/the-good-the-bad-the-ugly-product-placements -4cdf6e0808bc.

Innes, Judith E. and Judith Gruber. "Planning Styles in Conflict: The Metropolitan Transportation Commission." *Journal of the American Planning Association* 71, no. 2 (2005): 177–88.

Isin, Engin and Evelyn Ruppert. *Being Digital Citizens,* 2nd ed. New York: Rowman & Littlefield, 2020.

Iyengar, Shanto and Sean J. Westwood. "Fear and Loathing Across Party Lines: New Evidence on Group Polarization." *American Journal of Political Science* 59, no. 3 (2015): 690–707.

Jackson, Rebecca. "The Glitch Aesthetic." Master's thesis, Georgia State University, 2011. ScholarWorks @ Georgia State University. https://scholarworks.gsu.edu/cgi/ viewcontent.cgi?article=1081&context=communication_theses.

James, John. "A Preliminary Study of the Size Determinant in Small Group Interaction." *American Sociological Review* 16, no. 4 (1951): 474–77.

Jemielniak, Dariusz and Aleksandra Przegalinska. *Collaborative Society*. Cambridge, MA: MIT Press, 2020.

Jenkins, Henry. *Convergence Culture: Where Old and New Media Collide.* New York: NYU Press, 2006.

Jenkins, Henry. "Quentin Tarantino's *Star Wars*? Grassroots Creativity Meets the Media Industry." In *The Social Media Reader* edited by Michael Mandiberg, 203–35. New York: NYU Press, 2012.

Jenkins, Henry, Katie Clinton, Ravi Purushotma, Alice J. Robison, and Margaret Wiegel. *Confronting the Challenges of Participatory Culture: Media Education for the 21st Century.* Chicago, IL: The John D. and Catherine T. MacArthur Foundation, 2006.

Jenkins, Henry and Mark Deuze. "Editorial: Convergence Culture." *Convergence* 14, no. 1 (2008): 5–12.

Jenkins, Henry, Sam Ford, and Joshua Green. *Spreadable Media: Creating Value and Meaning in a Networked Culture.* New York: NYU Press, 2013.

Jensen Schau, Hope, Alber M. Muñiz Jr., and Eric J. Arnould. "How Brand Community Practices Create Value." *Journal of Marketing,* 73 (2009): 30–51.

Johnson, Stephen. "Beyond the Bitcoin Bubble," *New York Times,* January 16, 2018. https://www.nytimes.com/2018/01/16/magazine/beyond-the-bitcoin-bubble.html.

Johnson, Steven. *Where Good Ideas Come fFom: The Natural History of Innovation.* New York: Riverhead Books, 2010.

Johnson, Ted. "Keith Olbermann Exits MSNBC." *Variety,* January 21, 2011. https://variety.com/2011/tv/news/keith-olbermann-exits-msnbc-1118030694/.

Johnstone, Caitlin. "Twitter Shut Down My Account for 'Abusing' John McCain." Medium.com, August 17, 2018. https://caityjohnstone.medium.com/twitter-has-shut-down-my-account-for-abusing-john-mccain-25e7be909f4d.

Jones, Stephen G. *Cybersociety 2.0: Revisiting Computer-Mediated Communication and Community.* Thousand Oaks, CA: Sage, 1998.

Jurkowitz, Mark. "The Losses in Legacy." Pew Research Center, March 26, 2014. https://www.journalism.org/2014/03/26/the-losses-in-legacy/.

Kahn, Gabriel. "Transparency Is the New Objectivity." *MediaShift,* September 27, 2017. http://mediashift.org/2017/09/transparency-new-objectivity/.

Kaplan, Andreas M. and Michael Haenlein. "Two Hearts in Three-Quarter Time: How to Waltz the Social Media/Viral Marketing Dance." *Business Horizons* 54 (2011): 253–63.

Karlberg, Tim. "The State of Technology in 1994." *DKY News,* June 25, 2019. https://dkyinc.com/2019/06/the-state-of-technology-in-1994.

Karpf, David. "Online Political Mobilization from the Advocacy Group's Perspective: Looking Beyond Clicktivism." *Policy Studies Organization* 4, no. 2 (2010): 7–41.

Kastrenakes, Jacob. "Verizon Now Officially Owns Yahoo, Marissa Mayer Resigns." *The Verge,* June 13, 2017. https://www.theverge.com/2017/6/13/15791784/verizon-yahoo-acquisition-complete-marissa-mayer-leaves.

Kearny, Laila. "Hawaii Grandma's Plea Launches Women's March in Washington." *Reuters,* December 5, 2016. https://uk.reuters.com/article/uk-usa-trump-women-idUKKBN13U0H9.

Keating, Joshua. "The George Floyd Protests Show Leaderless Movements Are the Future of Politics." *Slate,* June 9, 2020. https://slate.com/news-and-politics/2020/06/george-floyd-global-leaderless-movements.html.

Keats Citron, Danielle and Jonathan W. Penney. "When Law Frees Us to Speak." *Fordham Law Review* 87, no. 6 (2019): 2317–35.

Keen, Andrew. *The Cult of the Amateur: How Today's Internet Is Killing Our Culture.* New York: Currency, 2007.

Keller, Daphne. "Who Do You Sue?" A Hoover Institution Essay, Aegis Series, Paper no. 1902 (2019).

Kelley, Jason. "The CASE Act Is Just the Beginning of the Next Copyright Battle." Electronic Frontier Foundation, December 22, 2020. https://www.eff.org/deeplinks /2020/12/case-act-hidden-coronavirus-relief-bill-just-beginning-next-copyright -battle.

Kellner, Douglas M. and Meenakshi Gigi Durham. "Adventures in Media and Cultural Studies: Introducing the KeyWorks." In *Media and Cultural Studies: KeyWorks*, edited by Gigi Durham and Douglas M. Kellner, *ix-xxxviii*. Malden, MA: Blackwell Publishing, 2001.

Kelly, Caroline. "Founder of the Women's March Calls for Co-Chairs to Step Down." CNN Politics, November 20, 2018. https://www.cnn.com/2018/11/19/politics/ womens-march-founder-calls-leaders-to-resign/index.html.

Kelly, Kevin. *The Inevitable: Understanding the 12 Technological Forces That Will Shape Our Future.* New York: Viking, 2016.

Kelly, Kevin. "The New Socialism: Global Collectivist Society Is Coming Online." *Wired Magazine*, May 22, 2009. https://www.wired.com/2009/05/nep -newsocialism/.

Kelly, Kevin. "We Are the Web." *Wired Magazine,* August 1, 2005. http://www.wired. com/wired/archive/13.08/tech.html.

Kenix, Linda Jean. *Alternative and Mainstream Media: The Converging Spectrum.* New York: Bloomsbury Academic, 2011.

Kerr, Orin S. "Applying the Fourth Amendment to the Internet: A General Approach." *Stanford Law Review* 62, no. 4 (2010). 1005–50.

Kessler, Sarah. "*Wall Street Journal* Launches Wikileaks-Style Site for Whistle -Blowers." *Mashable,* May 5, 2011. https://mashable.com/2011/05/05/wsj -safehouse/.

Keyes, Ken Jr. *The Hundredth Monkey.* Coos Bay, OR: Vision Books, 1986.

Khadim, Riswan Ali, Mian Ahmad Hanan, Arooj Arshad, Noshina Saleem, and Noman Ali Kahdim. "Revisiting Antecedents of Brand Loyalty: Impact of Percieved Social Media Communication with Brand Trust and Brand Equity as Mediators." *Academy of Strategic Management Journal* 17, no. 1 (2018). https: //www.abacademies.org/articles/revisiting-antecedents-of-brand-loyalty-impact -of-perceived-social-media-communication-with-brand-trust-and-brand-equity-as -mediat-6968.html.

Khamitov, Mansur, Xin (Shane) Wang, and Matthew Thomson. "How Well Do Consumer-Brand Relationships Drive Customer Brand Loyalty? Generalizations from Meta-Analysis of Brand Relationship Elasticities." *Journal of Consumer Research* 46, no. 3 (2019). 435–59. https://doi.org/10.1093/jcr/ucz006.

Kim, Victoria. "K-Pop Fans, Maestros of Social Media, Bring Their Powers to Bear on #BlackLivesMatter Activism." *Los Angeles Times*, June 4, 2020. https://www. latimes.com/world-nation/story/2020-06-04/k-pop-fans-maestros-of-social-media -bring-their-powers-to-bear-on-blacklivesmatter-protests.

Kimmel, Allan J. *Marketing Communication: New Approaches, Technologies, and Styles.* New York: Oxford University Press, 2005.

Kiousis, Spiro. "Interactivity: A Concept Explication." *New Media & Society* 4 (2002): 355–56.

Kirschenbaum, Matthew and Sarah Werner. "Digital Scholarship and Digital Studies: The State of the Discipline." *Book History* 17 (2014): 406–58.

Kittler, Friedrich A. *Gramophone, Film, Typewriter.* Stanford, CA: Stanford University Press, 1999.

Klarreich, Erica. "How an Anonymous 4chan Post Helped Solve a 25-Year-Old Math Puzzle," *Wired Magazine,* November 11, 2018. https://www.wired.com/story/how-an-anonymous-4chan-post-helped-solve-a-25-year-old-math-puzzle/.

Klein, Roger D. and Stacy Naccarato. "Broadcast News Portrayal of Minorities." *American Behavioral Scientist* 46, no. 12 (2003): 1611–16.

Kleinman, Alexis. "Feb. 11 Is 'The Day We Fight Back' against NSA Surveillance." *Huffington Post,* December 6, 2017. https://www.huffpost.com/entry/the-day-we-fight-back_n_4759693.

Kligler-Vilenchik, Neta and Tenenboim, Ori. "Sustained Journalist-Audience Reciprocity in a Meso News-Space: The Case of a Journalistic WhatsApp Group." *New Media & Society* 22, no. 2 (2019): 264–82.

Kranzberg, Melvin. "Technology and History: 'Kranzberg's Laws.'" *Technology and Culture* 27, no 3 (1986): 544–60.

Kravets, David. "School District Pays $615,000 to Settle Webcam Spying Lawsuits." *Wired Magazine,* October 12, 2010. https://www.wired.com/2010/10/webcam-spy-settlement/.

Kumar, Sangeet. "The Algorithmic Dance: YouTube's Adpocalypse and the Gatekeeping of Cultural Content on Digital Platforms." *Internet Policy Review* 8 no. 2 (2019): 1–21.

Kuntsman, Adi and Imogen Rattle. "Towards a Paradigmatic Shift in Sustainability Studies: A Systematic Review of Peer Reviewed Literature and Future Agenda Setting to Consider Environmental (Un)sustainability of Digital Communication." *Environmental Communication* 13, no. 5 (2019): 567–81. https://doi.org/10.1080/17524032.2019.1596144.

Kurtzleben, Danielle. "Do Dove and Axe Sell the Same Message?" *U.S. News & World Report,* April 18, 2013. https://www.usnews.com/news/articles/2013/04/18/unilever-faces-criticism-for-real-beauty-ad-campaign.

Lai, Chih-Hui. "Can Our Group Survive? An Investigation of the Evolution of Mixed-Mode Groups." *Journal of Computer Mediated Communication* 19, no. 4 (2014): 839–54.

Lakshmanan, Indira A. R. "Why Off-the-Record Is a Trap Reporters Should Avoid." *Poynter,* March 19, 2018. https://www.poynter.org/ethics-trust/2018/why-off-the-record-is-a-trap-reporters-should-avoid/.

Lam, Katherine. "'Game of Thrones' Ending Could Mean Decrease in HBO Subscribers." *Fox Business,* May 21, 2019. https://www.foxbusiness.com/features/game-of-thrones-ending-hbo-subscribers.

Lamoureux, Mack. "How 4Chan's Worst Trolls Pulled Off the Heist of the Century," *Vice,* March 11, 2017. https://www.vice.com/en/article/d7eddj/4chan-does-first-good-thing-pulls-off-the-heist-of-the-century1.

Landemore, Hélène and Scott E. Page. "Deliberation and Disagreement: Problem Solving, Prediction, and Positive Dissensus." *Politics, Philosophy, and Economics* 14, no. 3 (2015): 229–54.

Landes, Jennifer. "Koenig's 'Serial' Wins Peabody." *East Hampton Star*, April 20, 2015. https://www.easthamptonstar.com/see-monster/2019-05-24/koenigs-serial -wins-peabody.

Langenderfer, Jeff and Don Lloyd Cook. "Copyright Policies and Issues Raised by *A & M Records v. Napster*: 'The Shot Heard 'Round the World' or 'Not with a Bang but a Whimper?'" *Journal of Public Policy and Marketing* 20, no. 2 (2001): 280–88.

Langvardt, Arlen W. "'I Have a [Fair Use] Dream': Historic Copyrighted Works and the Recognition of Meaningful Rights for the Public." *Fordham Intellectual Property, Media and Entertainment Law Journal* 25, no. 4 (2015): 939–1006.

Lanier, Jaron. *Dawn of the New Everything*. New York: Henry Holt and Company, 2017.

Lanier, Jaron. *Ten Arguments for Deleting Your Social Media Accounts Right Now.* New York: Picador, 2018.

Lanier, Jaron. *You Are Not a Gadget*. New York: Vintage Books, 2011.

Lankes, R. David. "Trusting the Internet: New Approaches to Credibility Tools." In *Digital Media, Youth, and Credibility,* edited by Miriam J. Metzger and Andrew J. Flanagin, 101–22. Cambridge, MA: MIT Press, 2008.

Laouris, Yiannis. "Reengineering and Reinventing Both Democracy and the Concept of Life in the Digital Era." In *The Onlife Manifesto: Being Human in a Hyperconnected Era,* edited by Luciano Floridi, 125–42. New York: Springer, 2015.

Lapowsky, Issie. "The Year Women Reclaimed the Web." *Wired Magazine,* December 26, 2017. https://www.wired.com/story/year-women-reclaimed-the-web/.

Lawardorn, Damien. "Is the Mainstream Ready for Transmedia Storytelling?" *Escapist Magazine*, January 12, 2020. https://www.escapistmagazine.com/v2/is -the-mainstream-ready-for-transmedia-storytelling/.

Lawson, Mark, Lyn Gardner, Peter Bradshaw, Stuart Hertiage, Andrew Dickson, Brian Logan, Jonathan Jones, and Judith Mackerell. "Arts Preview 2014: Comebacks." *The Guardian*, January 1, 2014. https://www.theguardian.com/culture/2014/jan/01 /arts-preview-2014-comebacks.

Leavitt, Alex and John J. Robinson. "Upvote My News: The Practices of Peer Information Aggregation for Breaking News on Reddit.com." *Proceedings of the Association for Computing Machinery on Human-Computer Interaction* 1, article no. 65 (2017). https://doi.org/10.1145/3134700.

Ledbetter, Andrew M. "An Introduction to the Special Issue on Social Media, or Why This Isn't a Special Issue on Social Networking Sites." *Communication Monographs* 88, no. 1 (2021): 1–4.

Lee, Timothy B. "Why Mickey Mouse's 1998 Copyright Extension Probably Won't Happen Again." *Ars Technica*, January 8, 2018. https://arstechnica.com/tech-policy /2018/01/hollywood-says-its-not-planning-another-copyright-extension-push/.

Leetaru, Kalev. "The Daily Mail Snopes Story and Fact Checking the Fact Checkers." *Forbes*, December 22, 2016. https://www.forbes.com/sites/kalevleetaru/2016/12 /22/the-daily-mail-snopes-story-and-fact-checking-the-fact-checkers/.

Lessig, Lawrence. *Code: Version 2.0.* New York: Basic Books, 2006.

Lessig, Lawrence. *Free Culture: How Big Media Uses Technology and the Law to Lock Down Culture and Control Creativity*. New York: Penguin, 2004.

Lessig, Lawrence. *The Future of Ideas: The Fate of the Commons in a Connected World*. New York: Random House, 2001.

Lessig, Lawrence. "Remix: How Creativity Is Being Strangled by the Law." In *The Social Media Reader,* edited by Michael Mandiberg, 155–69. New York: NYU Press, 2012.

Lessig, Lawrence. *Remix: Making Art and Commerce Thrive in the Hybrid Economy.* New York, NY: Penguin, 2008.

Levin, Josh. "*Serial* Wasn't a Satisfying Story: It Was a Master Class in Investigative Journalism." *Slate*, December 18, 2014. https://slate.com/culture/2014/12/serial -as-investigative-journalism-the-hit-podcast-was-a-master-class-in-reporting.html.

Levin, Sam. "Facebook Removed Post by Ex-Manager Who Said Site 'Failed' Black People." *The Guardian,* December 4, 2018. https://www.theguardian.com/ technology/2018/dec/04/facebook-mark-s-luckie-african-american-workers-users.

Levine, Sheen S. and Michael J. Prietula. "Open Collaboration for Innovation: Principles and Performance." *Organization Science* 25, no. 5 (2014): 1414–33. https://doi.org/10.1287/orsc.2013.0872.

Levy, Frank and Richard J. Murnane. *The New Division of Labor: How Computers Are Creating the Next Job Market*. Princeton, NJ: Princeton University Press, 2004.

Lévy, Pierre. *Collective Intelligence: Mankind's Emerging World in Cyberspace*. Cambridge, MA: Perseus, 1997.

Lewis, Rhyd. "Who Is the Centre of the Movie Universe? Using Python and NetworkX to Analyse the Social Network of Movie Stars." *The Conversation,* February 20, 2020. https://arxiv.org/pdf/2002.11103.pdf.

Lhooq, Michelle. "How Did the Pirate Bay, the World's Biggest Illegal Downloading Site, Stay Online for So Long?" *Vice*, December 11, 2014. https://www.vice.com/ en/article/ypk9xg/how-did-the-pirate-bay-the-worlds-biggest-illegal-downloading -site-stay-online-for-so-long.

Liebowitz, Matt. "Social Media Status Updates Tip Off Burglars, Study Shows." NBC News, November 7, 2011. https://www.nbcnews.com/id/wbna45195926.

Lima, Manuel. *Visual Complexity: Mapping Patterns of Information.* New York: Princeton Architectural Press, 2011.

Lin, Hui, Weiguo Fan, and Zhongju Zhang. "A Qualitative Study of Web-Based Knowledge Communities: Examining Success Factors." *International Journal of e -Collaboration* 5, no. 3 (2009): 39–57.

Lindgren, Simon. *Digital Media & Society*. Thousand Oaks, CA: Sage, 2017.

Lindgren, Simon and Jessica Linde. "The Subpolitcs of Online Piracy: A Swedish Case Study." *Convergence* 18, no. 2 (2012): 143–64.

Lindgren, Simon and Ragnar Lundström. "Pirate Culture and Hacktivist Mobilization: The Cultural and Social Protocols of #Wikileaks on Twitter." *New Media & Society* 13 (2011): 999–1018.

Liptak, Andrew. "Facebook Says That It Removed 1.5 Million Videos of the New Zealand Mass Shooting." *The Verge*, March 17, 2019. https://www.theverge.com /2019/3/17/18269453/facebook-new-zealand-attack-removed-1-5-million-videos -content-moderation.

Liptak, Andrew. "Verizon Blocks Messages of Abortion Rights Group." *New York Times*, September 27, 2007. https://www.nytimes.com/2007/09/27/us/27verizon. html.

Lister, Mary. "37 Staggering Video Marketing Statistics for 2018." The WorldStream Blog, last updated June 30, 2020. https://www.wordstream.com/blog/ws/2017/03 /08/video-marketing-statistics.

Lohmann, Susan. "The Dynamics of Informational Cascades: The Monday Demonstrations in Leipzig, East Germany, 1989–91." *World Politics* 47, no. 1 (1994): 42–101.

Loosen, Wiebke, Julius Reimer, and Fenja De Silva-Schmidt. "Data-Driven Reporting: An On-going (R)evolution? An Analysis of Projects Nominated for the *Data Journalism Awards* 2013–2016." *Journalism* 21, no. 9 (2020): 1246–63.

López, Cristina, Brendan Karet, and John Kerr. "Mike Cernovich's Far-Right Conspiracy Theories, Bigotry, and Association with White Supremacists." *Media Matters,* August 21, 2018. https://www.mediamatters.org/maga-trolls/mike -cernovichs-far-right-conspiracy-theories-bigotry-and-association-white.

Lorenz, Taylor. "Unidentified Plane-Bae Woman's Statement Confirms the Worst." *The Atlantic,* July 13, 2018. https://www.theatlantic.com/technology/archive/2018 /07/unidentified-plane-bae-womans-statement-confirms-the-worst/565139/.

Lubin, Gus. "McDonald's Twitter Campaign Goes Horribly Wrong #McDStories." *Business Insider*, January 24, 2012. https://www.businessinsider.com/mcdonalds -twitter-campaign-goes-horribly-wrong-mcdstories-2012-1.

Luckerson, Victor. "A Decade Ago, Google Bought YouTube—and It Was the Best Tech Deal Ever." *The Ringer*, October 10, 2016. https://www.theringer.com/2016 /10/10/16042354/google-youtube-acquisition-10-years-tech-deals-69fdbe1c8a06.

Luckie, Mark S. "Facebook is failing its black employees and its black users." Facebook, November 27, 2018. https://www.facebook.com/notes/mark-s-luckie/ facebook-is-failing-its-black-employees-and-its-black-users/1931075116975013.

Ludlow, Peter. "Wikileaks and Hacktivist Culture." *The Nation,* October 4, 2010. http://www.thenation.com/article/154780/wikileaks-and-hacktivist-culture.

Luong, Ashely. "All That Glitters Is Gold: The Regulation of Hidden Advertisements and Undisclosed Sponsorships in the World of Beauty Social Media Influencers." *William and Mary Business Law Review* 11, no. 2 (2020): 565–607.

Lynch, Jennifer and Nathaniel Sobel. "New Federal Court Rulings Find Geofence Warrants Unconstitutional." Electronic Frontier Foundation, August 31, 2020. https://www.eff.org/deeplinks/2020/08/new-federal-court-rulings-find-geofence -warrants-unconstitutional-0.

Lyon, David. *The Electronic Eye: The Rise of Surveillance Society.* Minneapolis: University of Minnesota Press, 1994.

Lyon, David. "Surveillance Culture: Engagement, Exposure, and Ethics in Digital Modernity." *International Journal of Communication* 11 (2017): 824–42.

Maddaus, Gene. "VidAngel Hit with $62.4 Million Judgment for Pirating Movies." *Variety,* June 17, 2019. https://variety.com/2019/biz/news/vidangel-jury-verdict -damages1203245947/.

Madlena, Chavala. "Cenk Uygur on the Success of The Young Turks." *The Guardian,* April 26, 2010. https://www.theguardian.com/media/2010/apr/26/cenk -uygur-young-turks.

Makalintal, Bettina. "Inside the Dazzling, Incredibly Orange Cheetos Fashion Show." *Vice,* September 6, 2019. https://www.vice.com/en/article/d3a3zw/inside -the-dazzling-incredibly-orange-cheetos-fashion-show.

Mandelbaum, Michael. "The Age of the Whistleblower." *American Interest,* October 19, 2019. https://www.the-american-interest.com/2019/10/29/the-age-of-the -whistleblower/.

Mandiberg, Michael. "Introduction." In *The Social Media Reader,* edited by Michael Mandiberg, 10. New York: NYU Press, 2012.

Mangan, Dan. "'Don't Touch Me Again, Man': Sen. Marco Rubio Faces Off Against Alex Jones in Hallway Heckle Spat." CNBC, September 5, 2018. https://www. cnbc.com/2018/09/05/infowars-alex-jones-rants-as-social-media-giants-testify-at -congress.html.

Mann, Monique and Marcus Smith. "Automated Facial Recognition Technology: Recent Developments and Approaches to Oversight." *UNSW Law Journal* 40, no. 1 (2017): 121–45.

Mann, Steve, Jason Nolan, and Barry Wellman. "Sousveillance: Inventing and Using Wearable Computing Devices for Data Collection in Surveillance Environments." *Surveillance & Society* 1, no. 3 (2003): 331–55.

Manokha, Ivan. "The Implications of Digital Employee Monitoring and People Analytics for Power Relations in the Workplace." *Surveillance & Society* 18, no. 4 (2020): 540–54.

Manovich, Lev. *Software Takes Command.* New York: Bloomsbury, 2013. https:// www.bloomsburycollections.com/book/software-takes-command/.

Manovich, Lev. *The Language of New Media.* New York: MIT Press, 2001.

Mansfield-Devine, Steve. "Hacktivism: Assessing the Damage." *Network Security* 8 (2011): 5–13.

Marantz, Andrew. "Free Speech Is Killing Us." *New York Times,* October 4, 2019. https://www.nytimes.com/2019/10/04/opinion/sunday/free-speech-social-media -violence.html.

Marantz, Andrew. "Reddit and the Struggle to De-Toxify the Internet." *New Yorker,* March 18, 2018. https://www.newyorker.com/magazine/2018/03/19/reddit-and-the -struggle-to-detoxify-the-internet.

Marwick, Alice E. and danah boyd. "I Tweet Honestly, I Tweet Passionately: Twitter Users, Context Collapse, and the Imagined Audience." *New Media & Society* 13, no. 1 (2010): 114–33.

Mattes, Andrew. "Techniques for Communicating with the Public Where Hazard Is Low, but Public Concern Is High." *Air Quality and Climate Change* 54, no. 1 (2020): 13–16.

McCall, Leslie. "The Complexity of Intersectionality." *Signs* 30, no. 3 (2005): 1771–800.

McCarthy, Tyler. "Kathy Griffin Calls for Doxing Student's Identities After Viral Video at Native American March: 'Shame Them.'" Fox News, January 21, 2019. https://www.foxnews.com/entertainment/kathy-griffin-calls-for-doxing-students -in-viral-video-shame-them.

McChesney, Robert. *Digital Disconnect: How Capitalism Is Turning the Internet against Democracy*. New York: The New Press, 2013.

McClure Haughey, Melinda, Meena Devii Muralikumar, Cameron A. Wood, and Kate Starbird. "On the Misinformation Beat: Understanding the Work of Investigative Journalists Reporting on Problematic Information Online." *Proceedings of the ACM on Human-Computer Interaction*, article no. 33 (2020): 1–22. https://doi.org /10.1145/3415204.

McCormick, Rich. "PewDiePie and Other YouTubers Took Money from Warner Bros. for Positive Game Reviews." *The Verge*, July 12, 2016. https://www.theverge.com /2016/7/12/12157310/pewdiepie-youtubers-sponsored-videos-ftc-warner-bros.

McCoy, Kevin. "Cyber Hack Got Access to Over 700,000 IRS Accounts." *USA Today*, Feburary 26, 2016. https://www.usatoday.com/story/money/2016/02/26/ cyber-hack-gained-access-more-than-700000-irs-accounts/80992822/.

McGlynn, Clare, Erika Rackley, and Ruth Houghton. "Beyond 'Revenge Porn': The Continuum of Image-Based Sexual Abuse." *Feminist Legal Studies* 25 (2017): 25–46.

McGonigal, Jane. "'This Is Not a Game': Immersive Aesthetics and Collective Play." In *Proceedings of the Streamingworlds Conference*, Melborne, Australia (2003).

McIntyre, Douglas A. "Over 2000 American Newspapers Have Closed in Past 15 Years." 24/7 Wall St., July 23, 2019. https://247wallst.com/media/2019/07/23/over -2000-american-newspapers-have-closed-in-past-15-years/.

McLaughlin, Caitlin and Jessica Vitak. "Norm Evolution and Violation on Facebook." *New Media & Society* 14, no. 2 (2011): 299–315.

McLintock, Christa Corrine. "The Destruction of Media Diversity, or: How the FCC Learned to Stop Regulating and Love Corporate Dominated Media." *Journal of Computer & Information Law* 22 (2004): 569–623.

McNair, Brian. "Journalism and Democracy in Contemporary Britain." In *Political Journalism: New Challenges, New Practices*, 397–425. New York: Routledge, 2002.

McNair, Brian. "Trust, Truth and Objectivity: Sustaining Quality Journalism in the Era of the Content-Generating User." In *Rethinking Journalism: Trust and Participation in a Transformed News Landscape,* edited by Chris Peters and Marcel Jeroen Broersma, 78–88. New York: Routledge, 2013.

McNeill, J. R. and William H. McNeill. *The Human Web: A Bird's Eye View of World History*. New York: W. W. Norton & Company, 2003.

McSherry, Corynne. "When Academic Freedom Depends on the Internet, Tech Infrastructure Companies Must Find the Courage to Remain Neutral." Electronic Frontier Foundation, November 2, 2020. https://www.eff.org/deeplinks/2020/11/when-academic-expression-depends-internet-tech-infrastructure-companies-must-find.

Meisner, Colten and Andrew Ledbetter. "Participatory Branding on Social Media: The Affordances of Live Streaming for Creative Labor." *New Media & Society* (2020): 1–17. https://doi.org/10.1177/1461444820972392.

Meyrowitz, Joshua. *No Sense of Place: The Impact of Electronic Media on Social Behavior*. New York: Oxford University Press, 1985.

Miège, Bernard. "Theorizing the Cultural Industries: Persistent Specificities and Reconsiderations." In *The Handbook of Political Economy of Communication*, edited by Janet Wasko, Graham Murdock, and Helena Sousa, 83–108. Malden, MA: John Wiley & Sons, 2014.

Mihailidis, Paul. *Civic Media Literacies: Re-Imagining Human Connection in an Age of Digital Abundance*. New York: Routledge, 2019.

Mihailidis, Paul and Samantha Viotty. "Spreadable Spectacle in Digital Culture: Civic Expression, Fake News, and the Role of Media Literacies in 'Post-Fact' Society." *American Behavioral Scientist* (2017): 1–14.

Milgram, Stanley. "The Small World Problem." *Psychology Today* 2 (1967): 60–67.

Miller, Vincent. *Understanding Digital Culture*. Thousand Oaks, CA: Sage, 2011.

Mironenko, Irina A. and Pavel S. Sorokin. "Seeking for the Definition of 'Culture': Current Concerns and their Implications. A Comment on Gustav Jahoda's Article, 'Critical Reflections on Some Recent Definitions of 'Culture.'" *Integrative Psychological and Behavioral Science* 52 (2018): 331–40.

Mitchell, Gail. "Usher Introduces Teen Singer Justin Bieber." *Billboard*, April 28, 2009. https://www.billboard.com/articles/news/268791/usher-introduces-teen-singer-justin-bieber/.

Mohney, Gillian. "Girl Diagnosed With Rare Genetic Disorder Thanks to Reddit After Years of Inconclusive Testing," ABC, May 4, 2016. https://abcnews.go.com/Health/girl-diagnosed-rare-genetic-disorder-reddit-years-inconclusive/story?id=38876898.

Mollick, Ethan. "The Dynamics of Crowdfunding: An Exploratory Study." *Journal of Business Venturing* 29 (2014): 1–16.

Montfort, Nick and Ian Bogost. *Racing the Beam: The Atari Video Computer System*. Cambridge, MA: MIT Press, 2009.

Moore, Evan. "Elgin Filmmaker Wants People to #Bingejesus Through a Streaming App." *Chicago Sun-Times*, March 18, 2020. https://chicago.suntimes.com/2020/3/18/21185293/dallas-jenkins-chosen-jesus-vidangel-christ-bible-streaming-app.

Moradi, Bonnie. "(Re)focusing Intersectionality: From Social Identities Back to Systems of Oppression and Privilege." In *Handbook of Sexual Orientation and Gender Diversity in Counseling and Psychology*, edited by Kurt A. DeBord, Ann R. Fischer, Kathleen J. Bieschke, and Ruperto M. Perez, 105–28. Washington, DC: American Psychological Association, 2017.

Morgan, Bronwen. "Welcome to the New Era of Crowdsourced Creativity." CampaignUS, March 26, 2019. https://www.campaignlive.com/article/welcome-new-era-crowdsourced-creativity/1579994.

Moritz, Brian P. "Newspapers: Don't Lecture Your Audience, and Don't Blame Them Either." *Sports Media Guy*, June 22, 2020. https://www.sportsmediaguy.com/blog/2020/6/22/newspapers-dont-lecture-your-audience-and-dont-blame-them-either.

Morozov, Evengy. *The Net Delusion: The Dark Side of Internet Freedom*. New York: Public Affairs, 2012.

Morozov, Evengy. *To Save Everything, Click Here*. New York: Perseus Books Group, 2013.

Mott, Meg. "Don't Dismiss Debate." Heterodox: The Blog, November 30, 2020. https://heterodoxacademy.org/blog/dont-dismiss-debate/.

Mulligan, Deirdre K. and Daniel S. Griffin. "If Google Goes to China, Will It Tell the Truth about Tiananmen Square?" *The Guardian*, August 21, 2018. https://www.theguardian.com/commentisfree/2018/aug/21/google-china-search-tiananmen-square-massacre.

Muñiz, Albert M. Jr. and Thomas C. O'Guinn. "Brand Community." *Journal of Consumer Research* 27 (2001): 412–32.

Muñiz, Albert M. Jr. and Thomas C. O'Guinn. "Marketing Communications in a World of Consumption and Brand Communities." In *Marketing Communication: New Approaches, Technologies, and Styles*, edited by Allan J. Kimmel, 63–85. New York: Oxford University Press, 2005.

Munro, Cait. "Why Are Flamin' Hot Cheetos Everywhere Right Now?" *UrbanDaddy*, March 7, 2018. https://www.urbandaddy.com/articles/41847/why-are-flamin-hot-cheetos-everywhere-right-now/.

Murawski, Bartosz. "Marvel Makes Films. The *Shared Universe* as a New Trend in Hollywood Cinema." *Ars Educandi* 12 (2015): 31–40.

Murdock, Jason. "Arizona Senate Candidate Kelli Ward Wants to Reach Mike Cernovich's Pizzagate Audience." *Newsweek*, August 10, 2018. https://www.newsweek.com/video-arizona-senate-candidate-kelli-ward-wants-reach-mike-cernovichs-1080137.

Myers, Fraser, "Patreon Is a Threat to the Free Internet." *Spiked*, January 7, 2019. https://www.spiked-online.com/2019/01/07/patreon-is-a-threat-to-the-free-internet/.

Nadler, Anthony, Matthew Crain, and Joan Donovan. *Weaponizing the Digital Influence Machine: The Political Perils of Ad Tech*. New York: Data & Society Research Institute, 2018. Accessed April 27, 2021. https://datasociety.net/wp-content/uploads/2018/10/DS_Digital_Influence_Machine.pdf.

Nadler, Tony. "For Every Citizen Journalist, a Flock of User-Editors: Digg and the Social News Challenge to Professional Journalism." *Flow*, May 29, 2009. https://www.flowjournal.org/2009/05/for-every-citizen-journalist-a-flock-of-user-editors-digg-and-the-social-news-challenge-to-professional-journalism-tony-nadler-university-of-minnesota/.

Nansen, Bjorn, Michael Arnold, Marcus Carter, Rowen Wilken, Jerry Kennedy, and Martin Gibbs. "Proxy Users, Use by Proxy: Mapping Forms of Intermediary

Interaction." *Proceedings of the Annual Meeting of the Australian Special Interest Group for Computer Human Interaction.* (2015): 294–98. https://doi.org/10.1145 /2838739.2838789.

N'Duka, Amanda. "Eva Longoria to Direct Cheetos Movie 'Flamin' Hot' For Fox Searchlight & Franklin Entertainment." *Deadline,* August 26, 2019. https: //deadline.com/2019/08/eva-longoria-directing-flamin-hot-cheetos-movie-fox -searchlight-1202704372/.

Neier, Aryeh. *Dossier: The Secret Files They Keep on You.* Briarcliff Manor, NY: Scarborough House, 1975.

Netenel, Neil Weinstock. *Copyright: What Everyone Needs to Know.* New York: Oxford University Press, 2018.

Neumayer, Christina. "Nationalist and Antifascist Movements in Social Media." In *The Routledge Companion to Social Media and Politics*, edited by Axel Bruns, Gunn Enli, Eli Skogerbø, Anders Olaf Larsson, and Christian Christensen, 296– 307. New York: Routledge, 2018.

Neumayer, Christina and Gitte Stald. "The Mobile Phone in Street Protest: Texting, Tweeting, Tracking, and Tracing." *Mobile Media & Communication* 2, no. 2 (2014): 117–33.

Nevue, Erik. "Four Generations of Political Journalism." In *Political Journalism: New Challenges, New Practices*, edited by Raymond Kuhn and Erik Nevue, 72–116. New York: Routledge, 2002.

Norris, Rebecca. "Hot Cheetos Hair Is the Most Dangerously Cheesy Dye Job on Instagram." *Allure,* March 20, 2018. https://www.allure.com/story/hot-cheetos-hair -color-instagram.

Nunez, Vivian. "12 Flamin' Hot Cheetos Memes You'll Understand Perhaps a Little Too Well." *PopSugar*, December 6, 2017. https://www.popsugar.com/latina/Flamin -Hot-Cheetos-Memes-44029019?stream_view=1#photo-44107803.

Ochigame, Rodrigo and James Holston. "Filtering Dissent: Social Media and Land Struggles in Brazil." *New Left Review* 99 (2016): 85–108.

O'Hair, H. Dan and William F. Eadie. "Communication as an Idea and as an Ideal." In *21st Century Communication: A Reference Handbook,* edited by William F. Eadie, 3–11. Thousand Oaks, CA: Sage, 2009.

O'Hara, Kieron and David Stevens. "Echo Chambers and Online Radicalism: Assessing the Internet's Complicity in Violent Extremism." *Policy & Internet* 7, no. 4 (2015): 401–22.

Ohlheiser, Abby. "How K-Pop Fans Became Celebrated Online Vigilantes." *MIT Technology Review*, June 5, 2020. https://www.technologyreview.com/2020/06/05 /1002781/kpop-fans-and-black-lives-matter/.

Olenski, Steve. "3 Reasons Why CMOs Should Embrace Experiential Marketing." *Forbes*, August 15, 2018. https://www.forbes.com/sites/steveolenski/2018/08/15 /3-reasons-why-cmos-should-embrace-experiential-marketing/?sh=d49eb597da6e.

Olson, Shad. "After Man Hating TV Spot, Gillette Caught Using Hot Female Ass to Sell Razors." *The Shad Olson Show*, January 19, 2019. http://www.shadolsonshow. com/2019/01/19/after-man-hating-tv-spot-gillette-caught-using-hot-female-ass-to -sell-razors/.

Ong, Walter J. "The Writer's Audience Is Always a Fiction." *Publications of the Modern Language Association* 90, no. 1 (1975): 9–21.

O'Reilly, Tim. "What Is Web 2.0?" In *The Social Media Reader,* edited by Michael Mandiberg, 32–52. New York: NYU Press, 2012.

Orend, Angela and Patricia Gagné. "Corporate Logo Tattoos and the Commondifcation of the Body." *Journal of Contemporary Ethnography* 38, no. 4 (2009): 493–517.

Orlikowski, Wanda J. "Using Technology and Constituting Structures: A Practice Lens for Studying Technology in Organizations." *Organization Science* 11, no. 4(2000): 404–28.

Orlitzky, Marc. "Virtue Signaling: Oversocialized 'Integrity' in a Politically Correct World." In *Integrity in Business and Management: Cases and Theory,* edited by Marc Orlitzky and Majit Manga, 172–88. New York: Routledge, 2018.

Ortegon, Mira. "The Danger of Branding Social Activism." *Brown Political Review*, April 19, 2019. https://brownpoliticalreview.org/2019/04/danger-branding-social -activism/.

Osborne, Charlie. "FTC Finalizes Charges Against Snapchat Over User Privacy," *ZDNet*, January 2, 2015. http://www.zdnet.com/article/ftc-finalizes-charges-against -snapchat-over-user-privacy/.

Ostergren, Cassidy. "Revisiting the 'Game of Thrones' Ending One Year Later." *Our Community Now,* May 1, 2020. https://ourcommunitynow.com/tv/revisiting-the -game-of-thrones-ending-one-year-later.

O'Sullivan, Donie and Dylan Byers. "Exclusive: Fake Black Activist Accounts Linked to Russian Government." CNN Business, September 28, 2017. https:// money.cnn.com/2017/09/28/media/blacktivist-russia-facebook-twitter/index.html.

Palfrey, John. "Four Phases of Internet Regulation." *Social Research* 77, no. 3 (2010): 981–96.

Pallotta, Frank. "'Game of Thrones' Finale Sets New Viewership Record." *CNN Business,* May 20, 2019. https://www.cnn.com/2019/05/20/media/game-of-thrones -finale-ratings/index.html.

Pandya, Jessica Zacher. *Exploring Critical Digital Literacy Practices.* New York: Routledge, 2018.

Pangrazio, Luciana. "Reconceptualising Critical Digital Literacy." *Discourse: Studies in the Cultural Politics of Education* 37, no. 2 (2016): 163–74. http://dx.doi.org /10.1080/01596306.2014.942836

Pansari, Anita and V. Kumar. "Customer Engagement Marketing." In *Customer Engagement Marketing ,* edited by Robert W. Palmatier, V. Kumar, and Colleen M. Harmeling, 1–27. Cham, Switzerland: Palgrave MacMillan, 2018.

Pappacharissi, Zizi. *Affective Publics: Sentiment, Technology, and Politics.* New York: Oxford University Press, 2015.

Pappacharissi, Zizi. *A Private Sphere: Democracy in a Digital Age.* Malden, MA: Polity Press, 2010.

Pareen, Alex. "How Political Fact-Checkers Distort the Truth." *New Republic*, January 8, 2020. https://newrepublic.com/article/156039/political-fact-checkers -distort-truth.

Pariser, Eli. *The Filter Bubble: What the Internet Is Hiding from You.* New York, NY: Penguin, 2011.

Parke, Caleb. "Story About Life of Jesus Emerges as Largest Crowdfunded Entertainment Project in History." Fox News, January 7, 2019. https://www.foxnews.com/entertainment/story-about-the-life-of-jesus-largest-ever-crowdfunding-campaign-for-a-tv-show.

Pasquale, Frank. *The Black Box Society: The Secret Algorithms That Control Money and Information.* Cambridge, MA: Harvard University Press, 2015.

Pedro-Carañana, Joan, Daniel Broudy, and Jeffrey Klaehn. "Introduction." In *The Propaganda Model Today: Filtering Perception and Awareness*, edited by Joan Pedro-Carañana, Daniel Broudy, and Jeffrey Klaehn, 1–18. London: University of Westminster Press, 2018.

Pela, Roebrt L. "I Hate Crowdfunding. Here's Why." *Phoenix New Times*, October 13, 2015. https://www.phoenixnewtimes.com/arts/i-hate-crowdfunding-heres-why-7724723.

Pelling, Rowan. "Why Do Today's Feminists Hate *Sex and the City?*" *Stuff*, June 1, 2018. https://www.stuff.co.nz/life-style/life/104387851/why-do-todays-feminists-hate-sex-and-the-city.

Peters, Jonathan. "Shield Laws and Journalistic Privilege: The Basics Every Reporter Should Know." *Columbia Journalism Review*, August 22, 2016. https://www.cjr.org/united_states_project/journalists_privilege_shield_law_primer.php.

Petri, Alexandra. "#WhyIStayed, Digiorno, and Other Corporate Disasters." *Washington Post*, September 9, 2014. https://www.washingtonpost.com/blogs/compost/wp/2014/09/09/whyistayed-digiorno-and-other-corporate-disasters/.

Petronio, Sandra. "Communication Boundary Management: A Theoretical Model of Managing Disclosure of Private Information Between Marital Couples." *Communication Theory* 1, no. 4 (1991): 311–35.

Petronio, Sandra and Jeffrey T. Child. "Conceptualization and Operationalization: Utility of Communication Privacy Management Theory." *Current Opinion in Psychology* 31 (2020): 76–82.

Piell Wexler, Joyce. *Who Paid for Modernism?: Art, Money, and Fiction of Conrad, Joyce, and Lawrence.* Fayetteville, AK: University of Arkansas Press, 1997.

Pierpoint, George. "Reddit Sleuth Identifies Car Part, Leading To Hit-And-Run Arrest," BBCNEWS, August 15, 2018. https://www.bbc.com/news/blogs-trending-45194123.

Pinsker, Joe. "The Covert World of People Trying to Edit Wikipedia—for Pay." *Atlantic*, August 11, 2015. https://www.theatlantic.com/business/archive/2015/08/wikipedia-editors-for-pay/393926/.

Pomerleau, Colette. "Glitch Art Design: An Inside Look at the History and Best Uses of a Modern Trend." 99designs, 2018. https://99designs.com/blog/design-history-movements/glitch-art-design/.

Poole, Marshall Scott and Gerardine DeSanctis. "Understanding the Use of Group Decision Support Systems: The Theory of Adaptive Structuration." In *Organizations and Communication Technology*, edited by Janet Fulk & Charles W. Steinfeld, 173–93. Thousand Oaks, CA: Sage Publications, 1990.

Porges, Seth. "4 Trends That Could Define Immersive Entertainment in 2020." *Forbes*, December 16, 2019. https://www.forbes.com/sites/sethporges/2019/12/16/4-trends-that-could-define-immersive-entertainment-in-2020/?sh=1884d2924c4a.

Porter, Constance Elise. "A Typology of Virtual Communities: A Multi-Disciplinary Foundation for Future Research." *Journal of Computer-Mediated Communication* 10, no. 1 (2004). https://doi.org/10.1111/j.1083-6101.2004.tb00228.x.

Porter, Constance Elise. "Virtual Communities and Social Networks." In *Communication and Technology*, edited by Lorenzo Cantoni and James A. Danowski, 161–79. Boston: De Gruyter, 2015.

Postigo, Hector, Laura DeNardis, and Michael Zimmer. *The Digital Rights Movement: The Role of Technology in Subverting Digital Copyright*. Cambridge, MA: MIT Press, 2012.

Poulson, Kevin. "Pentagon Demands Wikileaks 'Return' All Classified Documents." *Wired Magazine*, August 5, 2010. https://www.wired.com/2010/08/pentagon-demands-wikileaks/.

Powazek, Derek. "Death to User-Generated Content." *Lab Zine* 0.5 (2006): 97–98.

Prensky, Marc. "Digital Natives, Digital Immigrants." *On the Horizon* 9, no. 5 (2001). http://www.marcprensky.com/writing/Prensky%20-%20Digital%20Natives,%20Digital%20Immigrants%20-%20Part1.pdf.

Price, John. "How to Feed the Ferret: Understanding Subscribers in the Search for a Sustainable Model of Investigative Journalism." *Journalism* 21, no. 9 (2020): 1320–37.

Protalinski, Emil. "Joseph Gordon-Levitt: HitRecord Is 'GitHub for Creativity.'" *VentureBeat,* May 30, 2019. https://venturebeat.com/2019/05/30/joseph-gordon-levitt-hitrecord-is-github-for-creativity/.

Putnam, Robert. *Bowling Alone: The Collapse and Revival of American Community*. New York: Simon & Schuster, 2000.

Quintais, João Pedro and Joost Poort. "The Decline of Online Piracy: How Markets—Not Enforcement—Drive Down Copyright Enforcement." *American University International Law Review* 34, no. 4 (2019): 807–76.

Quintero Rivera, Angel G. "Migration, Ethnicity, and Interactions between the United States and Hispanic Carribean Popular Culture." *Latin American Perspectives* 34, no. 1 (2007): 83–93.

Quinton, Sarah. "The Community Brand Paradigm: A Response to Brand Management's Dilemma in the Digital Era." *Journal of Marketing Management* 29, nos. 7–8 (2013): 912–32.

Rainey, James. "On the Media: For Young Turk Cenk Uygur, TV is the Next Frontier." *Los Angeles Times,* September 8, 2010. https://www.latimes.com/archives/la-xpm-2010-sep-08-la-et-onthemedia-20100908-story.html.

Rainie, Lee and Janna Anderson. "The Internet of Things Connectivity Binge: What Are the Implications?" Pew Research Center, June 6 2017. https://www.pewresearch.org/internet/2017/06/06/the-internet-of-things-connectivity-binge-what-are-the-implications/.

Rainie, Lee and Barry Wellman. *Networked: The New Social Operating System*. Cambridge, MA: MIT Press, 2012.

Ramirez, Elaine. "How This 'Baby Shark' Video Went Insanely Viral in Indonesia." *Forbes,* September 1, 2017. https://www.forbes.com/sites/elaineramirez/2017/09/01/smartstudy-pinkfong-baby-shark-video-indonesia/#deb813b73e19.

Raustiala, Kal and Chris Sprigman. "Copying Is Not Theft." Freakonomics Blog, April 2, 2012. https://freakonomics.com/2012/04/02/copying-is-not-theft/.

Raymond, Eric. "The Cathedral and the Bazaar." *Knowledge, Technology & Policy* 12, no. 3 (1999): 23–49.

Reese, Stephen D. "Setting the Media's Agenda: A Power Balance Perspective." *Communication Yearbook* 14 (1991): 309–40.

Reitman, Rainey. "3 Years Later, the Snowden Leaks Have Changed How the World Sees NSA Surveillance." Electronic Frontier Foundation, June 5, 2016. https://www.eff.org/deeplinks/2016/06/3-years-later-snowden-leaks-have-changed-how-world-sees-nsa-surveillance.

Rheingold, Howard. *Smart Mobs.* Cambridge, MA: Perseus Publishing, 2002.

Rheingold, Howard. *The Virtual Community.* Reading, MA: Addison-Wesley, 1993.

Rheingold, Howard. *The Virtual Community,* 2nd ed. Cambridge, MA: MIT Press, 2000.

Richards, Jay W. *The Human Advantage: The Future of American Work in an Age of Smart Machines.* New York: Crown Forum, 2018.

Ritschel, Chelsea. "What Is the 'Baby Shark Song,' Where Did It Come from and Why Do Children Love it?" *Independent,* September 7, 2018. https://www.independent.co.uk/life-style/baby-shark-song-baby-shark-challenge-pinkfong-youtube-instagram-a8507036.html.

Rizzo, Lillian and Drew FitzGerald. "Cord-Cutting Accelerated in 2019, Raising Pressure on Cable Providers." *Wall Street Journal*, February 20, 2020. https://www.wsj.com/articles/cord-cutting-accelerates-raising-pressure-on-cable-providers-11582149209.

Roberts, Kevin. *Lovemarks: The Future Beyond Brands.* New York: powerHouse Books, 2005.

Robertson, Adi. "Social Media Bias Lawsuits Keep Failing in Court." The Verge, May 27, 2020. https://www.theverge.com/2020/5/27/21272066/social-media-bias-laura-loomer-larry-klayman-twitter-google-facebook-loss.

Robertson, David G. *UFOs, Conspiracy Theories and the New Age.* New York: Bloomsbury, 2016.

Roesner, Franziska, Brian T. Gill, and Tadayoshi Kohno. "Sex, Lies, or Kittens? Investigating the Use of Snapchat's Self-Destructing Messages." Paper presented at the *Financial Cryptography and Data Security Conference*, March 2014. https://homes.cs.washington.edu/~yoshi/papers/snapchat-FC2014.pdf.

Rohlinger, Deana A. "American Media and Deliberative Democractic Processes." *American Sociological Association* 25, no. 2 (2007): 122–48.

Rosell Llorens, Mariona. "eSport Gaming: The Rise of a New Sports Practice." *Sports, Ethics and Philosophy* 11, no. 4 (2017): 464–76. https://doi.org/10.1080/17511321.2017.1318947.

Rosen, Jay. "Show Your Work: The New Terms for Trust in Journalism." PressThink, December 31, 2017, https://pressthink.org/2017/12/show-work-new-terms-trust -journalism/.

Rosenzweig, Roy. "Can History Be Open Source? *Wikipedia* and the Future of the Past." *Journal of American History* 93, no. 1 (2006): 117–46. https://doi.org /10.2307/4486062.

Rosoff, Matt. "Congress Grills Tech CEOs Amid Backdrop of Coronavirus and Economic Struggles." CNBC, July 29, 2020. https://www.cnbc.com/2020/07/29/ tech-ceos-testify-before-house-antitrust-subcommittee-recap.html.

Rowley, Jennifer, Beata Kupiec-Teahan, and Edward Leeming. "Customer Community and Co-Creation: A Case Study." *Marketing Intelligence & Planning* 25, no. 2 (2007): 136–46.

Rozenshtein, Alan Z. "Surveillance Intermediaries." *Stanford Law Review* 70 (2018): 99–189.

Rushkoff, Douglas. "Think Occupy Wall St. Is a Phase? You Don't Get it." CNN Opinion, October 5, 2011. https://www.cnn.com/2011/10/05/opinion/rushkoff -occupy-wall-street/index.html.

Russo, Camilla. "YouTube and FaceBook Are Losing Creators to Blockchain-Powered Rivals," *Bloomberg Businessweek*, April 10, 2018. https://www.bloomberg.com/ news/articles/2018-04-10/youtube-and-facebook-are-losing-creators-to-blockchain -powered-rivals.

Ryfe, David M. and Donica Mensing. "Citizen Journalism in a Historical Frame." In *Public Journalism 2.0: The Promise and Reality of a Citizen-Engaged Press,* edited by Jack Rosenberry and Burton St. John III, 32–44. New York: Routledge, 2010.

Sahms, Jacob. "*The Chosen*'s Dallas Jenkins: Get Used to Different." Dove.org, accessed January 1, 2021. https://dove.org/the-chosens-dallas-jenkins-get-used-to -different/.

Salamon, Errol. "E-lancer Resistance." *Digital Journalism* 4, no. 8 (2016): 980–1000. http://dx.doi.org/10.1080/21670811.2015.1116953.

Salazar, Eduardo. "Hashtags 2.0—An Annotated History of the Hashtag and a Window into Its Future." *Icono 14* 15, no. 2 (2017): 16–54.

Salmon, Felix. "Media Trust Hits New Low." *Axios*, January 21, 2021. https://www. axios.com/media-trust-crisis-2bf0ec1c-00c0-4901-9069-e26b21c283a9.html.

San Miguel, Renay. "Taking Back the Tweet: ABC, Obama and the Jackass." *TechNewsWorld*, September 16, 2009. https://www.technewsworld.com/story /68138.html.

Sanders, Rachel. "How to Pitch Essays to Buzzfeed Reader." BuzzFeed, January 17, 2017. https://www.buzzfeednews.com/article/rachelysanders/how-to-pitch-essays -to-buzzfeed-reader.

Sandler, Rachel. "Microsoft's New 'Productivity Score' Lets Your Boss Monitor How Often You Use Email and Attend Video Meetings." *Forbes*, November 25, 2020. https://www.forbes.com/sites/rachelsandler/2020/11/25/microsofts-new -productivity-score-lets-your-boss-monitor-how-often-you-use-email-and-attend -video-meetings/?sh=15537f891a46.

Savigny, Heather. "Public Opinion, Political Communication and the Internet." *Politics* 22, no. 1 (2002): 1–8.

Schaffhauser, Dian. "Esports Joining Olympics in 2024." *Steam Universe*, July 20, 2019. https://steamuniverse.com/articles/2019/07/30/esports-joining-olympics-in -2024.aspx.

Schaller, George. "Moore's Law: Past, Present, and Future," *IEEE Spectrum*, June 1997, https://ieeexplore.ieee.org/stamp/stamp.jsp?tp=&arnumber=591665.

Schmidt, Christine. "It's Not 'Citizen Journalism,' But It Is 'Citizens Taking Notes at Public Meetings with No Reporters Around." NiemanLab, January 11, 2018. https: //www.niemanlab.org/2018/01/its-not-citizen-journalism-but-it-is-citizens-taking -notes-at-public-meetings-with-no-reporters-around/.

Schneier, Bruce. "Google and Facebook's Privacy Illusion." *Forbes*, April 6, 2010. https://www.forbes.com/2010/04/05/google-facebook-twitter-technology-security -10-privacy.html?sh=646c77ba3f34.

Scholz, Joachim and Andrew N. Smith. "Augmented Reality: Designing Immersive Experiences That Maximize Consumer Engagement." *Business Horizons* 59 (2016): 149–61.

Schudson, Michael. *The Good Citizen: A History of American Civic Life*. New York: The Free Press, 1998.

Schulman, Marc. "YouTube Wants to Fight Hate Speech. So It Censored My Educational Video about the Holocaust." *Newsweek*, June 14, 2019. https:// www.newsweek.com/youtube-holocaust-censorship-hate-speech-google-facebook -1444090.

Schwartz, Jeff and Suzanne Riss. *Work Disrupted: Opportunity, Resilience, and Growth in the Accelerated Future of Work*. Hoboken, NJ: John Wiley & Sons, 2021.

Schwier, Richard A. "Shaping the Metaphor of Community in Online Learning Environments." In *Video for Education: Volume 1*, edited by Gayle Calver, Mark Childs, and Lori Schnieders, 68–76. Headington, Oxford: Association for Learning Technology, 2007.

Scott, Kimberly. "Cheetos and Ripley's Believe It or Not! Bring an Unbelievable Cheetos Museum to Life." *Multivu,* June 8, 2017. https://www.multivu.com/ players/English/8117651-cheetos-museum-unique-shapes-contest/.

Seabough, Julie. "The Woman Behind Miranda, One of the Strangest and Most Beloved Characters on YouTube." *LA Weekly*, July 23, 2015. https://www. laweekly.com/the-woman-behind-miranda-one-of-the-strangest-and-most-beloved -characters-on-youtube/.

Seemayer, Zach. "Music Industry Calls for 'Blackout Tuesday' in Response to George Floyd's Death." ETOnline, June 1, 2020. https://www.etonline.com/music-industry -calls-for-blackout-tuesday-in-response-to-george-floyds-death-147499.

Sen, Indrani. "'Baby Shark': A Viral Earworm for Kids That Is Eating the World," *Quartz,* September 7, 2018. https://qz.com/quartzy/1364335/the-story-behind-the -astonishingly-viral-baby-shark-youtube-video/.

Serdült, Uwe. "Reconnecting Citizens to Politics via Blockchain—Starting the Debate." *Proceedings of Ongoing Research, Practitioners, Posters, Workshops, and Projects of the International EGOV-CeDEM-ePart* (2019): 185–90.

Shafto, Patrick. "Why Big Tech Companies Are Open-Sourcing Their AI Systems." , Feburary 22, 2016. https://www.govtech.com/computing/Why-Big-Tech -Companies-are-Open-Sourcing-Their-AI-Systems.html.

Shaw, Lucas. "President Obama Misses LAPD Officer's Marijuana Question as Google Skips It." *Reuters*, The Wrap, January 30, 2012. https://www.reuters.com/ article/idUS61868057620120131.

Shead, Sam. "Facebook Owns the Four Most Downloaded Apps of the Decade." BBC News, December 18, 2019. https://www.bbc.com/news/technology-50838013.

Sheehan, Matt. "How Google Took on China—and Lost." *MIT Technology Review*, December 19, 2018. https://www.technologyreview.com/2018/12/19/138307/how -google-took-on-china-and-lost/.

Sheffield, Matthew. "'Fake News' or Free Speech: Is Google Cracking Down on Left Media?" *Salon*, October 18, 2017. https://www.salon.com/2017/10/18/fake-news -or-free-speech-is-google-cracking-down-on-left-media/.

Shein, Esther. "Ephemeral Data." *Communications of the ACM* 56, no. 9 (2013): 20–22. https://doi.org/10.1145/2500468.2500474.

Shemkus, Sarah. "Why Are Food Activists Targeting Honey Nut Cheerios?" *The Guardian*, February 19, 2014. https://www.theguardian.com/sustainable-business/ cheerios-general-mills-gmo-genetically-modified-food.

Shensa, Ariel, Jaime E. Sidani, Mary Amanda Dew, César G. Escobar-Viera, and Brian A. Pimrack. "Social Media Use and Depression and Anxiety Symptoms: A Cluster Analysis." *Americal Journal of Health Behavior* 42, no. 2 (2018): 116–28.

Shirky, Clay. *Cognitive Surplus: How Technology Makes Consumers into Collaborators*. New York: Penguin, 2010.

Shirky, Clay. *Here Comes Everybody: The Power of Organizing without Organizations*. New York: Penguin, 2008.

Shirky, Clay. "Why We Need the New News Environment to Be Chaotic," *Clay Shirky Weblog*, July 9, 2011. http://www.shirky.com/weblog/2011/07/we-need-the -new-news-environment-to-be-chaotic/.

Shoemaker, Pamela J. and Tim P. Vos. *Gatekeeping Theory*. New York: Routledge, 2009.

Shontell, Alyson. "What It's Like When Reddit Wrongly Accuses Your Loved One of Murder." *Business Insider*, July 26, 2013. https://www.businessinsider.com/reddit -falsely-accuses-sunil-tripathi-of-boston-bombing-2013-7.

Short Takes. "Lena Dunham's YouTube Beginnings." *Criterion*, April 14, 2012. https: //www.criterion.com/current/posts/2254-lena-dunham-s-youtube-beginnings.

Sickels, Robert. "'The Future, Mr. Gittes. The Future.': Next Wave Filmmaking and Beyond, Part 1.*" *Flow*, August 13, 2010. http://www.flowjournal.org/2010/08/the -future-mr-gittes-the-future/.

Sill, Melanie. "How to Begin Practicing Open Journalism." Poynter, January 9, 2012. https://www.poynter.org/reporting-editing/2012/how-to-begin-practicing-open -journalism/.

Silver, Nate. "How Trump Hacked the Media." *FiveThirtyEight*, March 30, 2016. https://fivethirtyeight.com/features/how-donald-trump-hacked-the-media/.

Silverman, Craig. "Black Lives Matter Activists Say They're Being Silenced by Facebook." BuzzFeed, June 19, 2020. https://www.buzzfeednews.com/article/craigsilverman/facebook-silencing-black-lives-matter-activists.

Silverman, Craig. "Show the Reporting and Sources That Support Your Work." American Press Institute, September 24, 2014. https://www.americanpressinstitute.org/publications/reports/strategy-studies/show-sources/.

Singh, Karan Deep. "Twitter Blocks Accounts in India as Modi Pressures Social Media." *New York Times*, February 10, 2021. https://www.nytimes.com/2021/02/10/technology/india-twitter.html.

Smalls, Bernard Beanz. "Run Willy Run: Outrageously Woke Moments From The Season 2 Premiere of 'Atlanta.'" *Hip-Hop Wired*, March 2, 2018. https://hiphopwired.com/745848/run-willy-run-outrageously-woke-moments-from-the-season-2-premiere-of-atlanta/3/.

Smith, Aaron C. T., Constantino Stavros, and Kate Westberg. *Brand Fans: Lessons from the World's Greatest Sporting Brands.* Cham, Switzerland: Palgrave Macmillan, 2017.

Smith, Phillip. "Push Journalism vs. Pull Journalism." Philipadsmith.com, February 19, 2019. https://phillipadsmith.com/2019/02/push-journalism-vs-pull-journalism.html.

Socolow, Michael J. "Substack Isn't a New Model for Journalism—It's a Very Old One." NiemanLab, December 7, 2020. https://www.niemanlab.org/2020/12/substack-isnt-a-new-model-for-journalism-its-a-very-old-one/.

Solis, Brian. *Engage! The Complete Guide for Brands and Businesses to Build, Cultivate, and Measure Success in the New Web.* Hoboken, NJ: John Wiley & Sons, 2010.

Solomon, Leron. "Fair Users or Content Abusers: The Automatic Flagging of Non-Infringing Videos by Content ID on YouTube." *Hofstra Law Review* 44, no. 1 (215): 237–68.

Solove, Daniel J. *The Future of Reputation: Gossip, Rumor, and Privacy on the Internet.* New Haven, CT: Yale University Press, 2007.

Spohr, Dominic. "Fake News and Ideological Polarization: Filter Bubbles and Selective Exposure on Social Media." *Business Information Review* 34, no. 3 (2017): 150–60.

Stack, Liam. "Who Is Mike Cernovich? A Guide." *New York Times,* April 5, 2017. https://www.nytimes.com/2017/04/05/us/politics/mike-cernovich-bio-who.html.

Stadler, Felix. "Between Democracy and Spectacle." In *The Social Media Reader,* edited by Michael Mandiberg, 242–56. New York: NYU Press, 2012.

Statista Research Department. "Percentage of Households with a Computer at Home in the United States from 1984 to 2010." *Statista*, February 1, 2010. https://www.statista.com/statistics/184685/percentage-of-households-with-computer-in-the-united-states-since-1984/.

Steele, Bill. "Kevin Bacon Shows the Way to a Much Smaller World Than We Thought, Cornell Mathematicians Find." *Cornell Chronicle,* June 5, 1998. https://news.cornell.edu/stories/1998/06/networks-become-small-very-quickly.

Stengel, Richard. *Information Wars: How We Lost the Global Battle Against Disinformation and What We Can Do About It.* New York: Grove Press, 2019.

Stock, Axel and Subramanian Balachander. "The Making of a 'Hot Product': A Signaling Explanation of Marketers' Scarcity Strategy." *Management Science* 51, no. 8 (2005): 1181–92.

Stokel-Walker, Chris. "To Compete with Netflix, Online Piracy Is Upping Its Game." *Wired Magazine*, March 26, 2019. https://www.wired.co.uk/article/online-video-piracy-is-on-the-rise.

Stone, Brad. "Amazon Erases Orwell Books from Kindle." *New York Times*, July 17, 2009. https://www.nytimes.com/2009/07/18/technology/companies/18amazon.html.

Stork, Benedict. "Aesthetics, Politics, and the Police Hermeneutic: Online Videos of Police Violence Beyond the Evidentiary Function." *Film Criticism* 40, no. 2 (2016). https://doi.org/10.3998/fc.13761232.0040.210.

Stoycheff, Elizabeth, Juan Liu, Kai Xu, and Kunto Wibowo. "Privacy and the Panopticon: Online Mass Surveillance's Deterrence and Chilling Effects." *New Media & Society* 21, no. 3 (2019): 602–19.

Stroud, Natalie Jomini. "Media Use and Political Predispositions: Revisiting the Concept of Selective Exposure." *Political Behavior* 30 (2008): 341–66.

Surowiecki, James. *The Wisdom of Crowds.* New York, NY: Anchor, 2005.

Sweeney, Latanya. "Simple Demographics Often Identify People Uniquely." Carnegie Mellon University, Data Privacy Working Paper 3, 2000.

Tandoc, Edson C. Jr., Zheng Wei Lim, and Richard Ling. "Defining 'Fake News.'" *Digital Journalism* 6, no. 2 (2017): 137–53. https://doi.org/10.1080/21670811.2017.1360143.

Tapscott, Don and Anthony D. Williams. *Wikinomics: How Mass Collaboration Changes Everything.* New York: Portfolio/Penguin, 2008.

Tavares, Aida Isabel. "Telework and Health Effects Review." *International Journal of Healthcare* 3, no. 2 (2017): 30–36.

Taylor, Derek Bryson. "George Floyd Protests: A Timeline." *New York Times*, May 30, 2020. https://www.nytimes.com/article/george-floyd-protests-timeline.html.

Taylor, Emily, Stacie Walsh, and Samantha Bradshaw. "Industry Responses to the Malicious Use of Social Media." Riga, Latvia: Oxford Information Labs, 2018.

Tene, Omer and Jules Polonetsky. "A Theory of Creepy: Technology, Privacy, and Shifting Social Norms." *Yale Journal of Law & Technology* 16 (2013): 59–102. https://yjolt.org/theory-creepy-technology-privacy-and-shifting-social-norms.

Teotonio, Isabel. "Google Adds Six Degrees of Kevin Bacon to Search Engine." *Toronto Star,* September 13, 2012. https://www.thestar.com/entertainment/2012/09/13/google_adds_six_degrees_of_kevin_bacon_to_search_engine.html.

Tewksbury, David and Jason Rittenburg. *News on the Internet: Information and Citizenship in the 21st Century.* New York: Oxford University Press, 2012.

Thacker, Eugene. "Foreword: Protocol Is as Protocol Does." In *Protocol: How Control Exists after Decentralization* by Alexander Galloway, *xi–xxii.* Cambridge, MA: MIT Press, 2006.

Thayer, Katheryn. "Corporate Monopolies Hurt Creative Expression; Cory Doctorow's New Audiobook Challenges Them." *Kickstarter*, September 22, 2020. https://www.kickstarter.com/articles/corporate-monopolies-hurt-creative-expression-cory -doctorow-s-new-audiobook-challenges-them.

*The Economist*. "The World's Most Valuable Resource Is No Longer Oil, but Data." May 6, 2017. https://www.economist.com/leaders/2017/05/06/the-worlds-most -valuable-resource-is-no-longer-oil-but-data.

The Marketing Arm. "House of Flamin' Haute." News, September 10, 2019. https:// share.themarketingarm.com/cheetos-house-of-flamin-haute.

The Mentor. "The Conscience of a Hacker." *Phrack*, January 8, 1986. http://phrack. org/issues/7/3.html.

Thierer, Adam. *Permissionless Innovation and Public Policy: A 10-Point Blueprint*. Arlington, VA: The Mercatus Center at George Mason University, 2016.

Thompson, Matt. "6 Reasons Journalists Should 'Show Your Work' While Learning & Creating." *Poynter*, October 24, 2011. https://www.poynter.org/reporting-editing /2011/6-reasons-journalists-should-show-your-work-while-learning-creating/.

Thornburn, Elise Danielle. "Social Media, Subjectivity, and Surveillance: Moving on from Occupy, the Rise of Live Streaming Video." *Communication and Critical/ Cultural Studies* 11, no. 1 (2014): 52–63.

Tiffany, Kaitlyn. "Why K-Pop Fans Are No Longer Posting About K-Pop." *The Atlantic*, June 6, 2020. https://www.theatlantic.com/technology/archive/2020/06/ twitter-k-pop-protest-black-lives-matter/612742/.

Tocano, Joe. *Automating Humanity*. New York: powerHouse Books, 2018.

Toffler, Alvin. *The Third Wave*. New York: Bantam Books, 1980.

Tolosana, Ruben, Ruben Vera-Rodriguez, Julian Fierrez, Aythami Morales, and Javier Ortega-Garcia. "Deepfakes and Beyond: A Survey of Face Manipulation and Fake Detection." *Information Fusion* 64 (2020): 131–48.

Toto, Christian. "Cernovich's 'Hoaxed' Torches Media Bias." Hollywood in Toto, February 1, 2019. https://www.hollywoodintoto.com/hoaxed-mike-cernovich/.

Toto, Christian. "Toto: 'Hoaxed' Doc Cancelled By Amazon, but the Story Doesn't End There." *Daily Wire*, April 11, 2020. https://www.dailywire.com/news/toto -hoaxed-doc-canceled-by-amazon-but-the-story-doesnt-end-there.

Tracy, Ryan and John D. McKinnon. "Tech CEOs Square Off with Senators in Hearing over Online Speech." *Wall Street Journal*, October 28, 2020. https://www. wsj.com/articles/senate-tech-hearing-facebook-twitter-google-11603849274.

Trendacosta, Katharine. "The FCC Has Made the Same Mistake for Text Messaging That It Did for Net Neutrality." Electronic Frontier Foundation, December 12, 2018. https://www.eff.org/deeplinks/2018/12/fcc-has-made-same-mistake-text -messaging-it-did-net-neutrality.

Trendacosta, Katharine. "Unfiltered: How YouTube's ContentID Discourages Fair Use and Dictates What We See Online." Electronic Frontier Foundation, December 10, 2020. https://www.eff.org/wp/unfiltered-how-youtubes-content-id-discourages -fair-use-and-dictates-what-we-see-online#Introduction.

Tredennick, John. "Wikipedia: An Open Source Encyclopedia." Merlin Foundation, accessed December 27, 2020. https://www.merlinfoundation.org/wikipedia-an -open-source-encyclopedia/.

Tucker, Patrick. *The Naked Future: What Happens in a World That Anticipates Your Every Move?* New York: Penguin Group, 2014.

Turkle, Sherry. *Alone Together: Why We Expect More from Technology and Less from Each Other.* New York: Basic Books, 2011.

Turkle, Sherry. *Reclaiming Conversation: The Power of Talk in a Digital Age.* New York: Penguin, 2015.

Turner-Zwinkles, Felicity M. and Martijn van Zomeren. "Identity Expression Through Collective Action: How Identification with a Politicized Group and Its Identity Contents Differently Motivated Identity-Expressive Collective Action in the U.S. 2016 Presidential Elections." *Personal and Social Psychology Bulletin* (2020): 1–15.

Twenge, Jean M. *iGen: Why Today's Super-Connected Kids Are Growing Up Less Rebellious, More Tolerant, Less Happy—And Completely Unprepared for Adulthood—And What That Means for the Rest of Us.* New York: Simon & Schuster, Inc., 2017.

U.S. Bureau of Labor Statistics. "Job Market Remains Tight in 2019, as the Unemployment Rate Falls to Its Lowest Level Since 1969." *Monthly Labor Review,* April 2020. https://www.bls.gov/opub/mlr/2020/article/job-market-remains-tight -in-2019-as-the-unemployment-rate-falls-to-its-lowest-level-since-1969.htm.

Vaidhyanathan, Siva. "Open Source as Culture/Culture as Open Source." In *The Social Media Reader,* edited by Michael Mandiberg, 24–31. New York: NYU Press, 2012.

Vankatesan, Rajkumar, J. Andrew Peterson, and Leonardo Guissoni. "Measuring and Managing Customer Engagement Value Through the Customer Journey." In *Customer Engagement Marketing,* edited by Robert W. Palmatier, V. Kumar, and Colleen M. Harmeling, 53–74. Cham, Switzerland: Palgrave MacMillan, 2018.

Verbeek, Peter-Paul. "Designing the Public Sphere: Information Technologies and the Politics of Mediation." In *The Onlife Manifesto: Being Human in a Hyperconnected Era,* edited by Luciano Floridi, 217–27. New York: Springer, 2015.

Victor, Daniel. "An Egg, Just a Regular Egg, Is Instagram's Most-Liked Post Ever." *New York Times,* January 13, 2019. https://www.nytimes.com/2019/01/13/style/egg -instagram-most-liked.html.

Viner, Katharine. "A Mission for Journalism in a Time of Crisis." *The Guardian,* November 16, 2017. https://www.theguardian.com/news/2017/nov/16/a-mission -for-journalism-in-a-time-of-crisis.

Vitak, Jessica, Paul Zube, Andrew Smock, Caleb T. Carr, Nicole Ellison, and Cliff Lampe. "It's Complicated: Facebook Users' Political Participation in the 2008 Election." *Cyberpsychology, Behavior, and Social Networks* 14, no. 3 (2011): 107–14.

Volkmer, Ingrid and Amira Firdaus. "Between Networks and 'Hierarchies of Credibility': Navigating Journalistic Practice in a Sea of User-Generated Content." In *Rethinking Journalism: Trust and Participation in a Transformed News*

*Landscape,* edited by Chris Peters and Marcel Jeroen Broersma, 101–13. New York: Routledge, 2013.

Vrendenburg, Jessica, Sommer Kapitan, Amanda Spry, and Joya A. Kemper. "Brands Taking a Stand: Authentic Brand Activism or Woke Washing?" *Journal of Public Policy & Marketing* 39, no. 4 (2020): 444–60.

Waites, Rosie. "*V for Vendetta* Masks: Who's Behind Them?" BBC News, October 20, 2011. https://www.bbc.com/news/magazine-15359735.

Wallance, Gregory. "A Journalist Brought Epstein to Justice and Acosta's Resignation—So Stop Demonizing the Press." The Hill, July 12, 2019. https://thehill.com/opinion/judiciary/452808-a-journalist-brought-epstein-to-justice-and-acostas-resignation-stop.

Wang, Emily. "Chromat Had Cheetos as Accessories for Their NYFW Runway Show." *Teen Vogue,* February 12, 2018. https://www.teenvogue.com/story/chromat-new-york-fashion-week-flamin-hot-cheetos.

Warschauer, Mark, Tamara Tate, Melissa Niiya, Soobin Yim, and Youngmin Park. *Supporting Digital Literacy in Educational Contexts: Emerging Pedagogies and Technologies.* Irvine, CA: International Baccalaureate Program, 2014.

Watercutter, Angela. "Instagram Users Post Black Squares After Trump Wins US Presidency." *Wired Magazine*, November 9, 2016. https://www.wired.com/2016/11/instagram-trump-win/.

Watson, Chloe. "The Key Moments from Mark Zuckerberg's Testimony to Congress." *The Guardian*, April 11, 2018. https://www.theguardian.com/technology/2018/apr/11/mark-zuckerbergs-testimony-to-congress-the-key-moments.

Watts, Duncan J. and Steven H. Strogatz. "Collective Dynamics of 'Small-World' Networks." *Nature* 393 (1998): 440–42.

Webster, James G. *The Marketplace of Attention: How Audiences Take Shape in the Digital Age.* Cambridge, MA: MIT Press, 2014.

Weekes, Julia. "Warhol's Pop Politics." *Smithsonian Magazine*, October 30, 2008. https://www.smithsonianmag.com/arts-culture/warhols-pop-politics-89185734/.

Weger, Harry Jr. and Mark Aakhus. "Arguing in Internet Chat Rooms: Argumentative Adaptations to Chat Room Design and Some Consequences for Public Deliberation at a Distance." *Argumentation and Advocacy* 40 (2003): 23–38.

Weinhold, Wendy Marie. "Watching the Watchdogs: Defining Journalists in the United States." PhD diss., Southern Illinois University Carbondale, 2013. OpenSIUC Dissertations, Paper 707. http://opensiuc.lib.siu.edu/dissertations.

Weiss, Suzannah. "Cheetos Designed a Line of Clothing & Accessories That Make Snacking Easier." *Refinery29,* March 21, 2017. https://www.refinery29.com/en-us/2017/03/146442/cheetos-clothing-accessories.

Wellman, Barry and Milena Gulia. "Virtual Communities as Communities." In *Communities in Cyberspace,* edited by Peter Kollock and Marc Smith, 167–93. New York: Routledge, 1999.

Wells, Georgia and Shan Li. "How TikTok Users Targeted Trump Rally." *Wall Street Journal*, June 21, 2020. https://www.wsj.com/articles/how-tiktok-users-targeted-trump-rally-11592795368.

West, Darrell M. *The Future of Work: Robots, AI, and Automation.* Washington, DC: Brookings Institution Press, 2018.

Western, Simon. "Autonomous Leadership in Leaderless Movements." *Ephemera: Theory in Politics & Organizaiton* 14, no. 4 (2014): 673–98.

Whittaker, Zack. "Five Years On, Snowden Inspired Tech Giants to Change, Even If Governments Wouldn't." ZDNet, June 6, 2018. https://www.zdnet.com/article/edward-snowden-five-years-on-tech-giants-change/.

Wihbey, John and Bud Ward. "Communication about Climate Change with Journalists and Media Producers." *Climate Science*, December 22, 2016. https://doi.org/10.1093/acrefore/9780190228620.013.407.

Willens, Max. "Once Dominant, Amazon-Owned Gaming Platform Twitch Has More Competition and More Problems." *Digiday*, August 14, 2019. https://digiday.com/future-of-tv/dominant-amazon-owned-gaming-platform-twitch-competition/.

Williams, Kyann-Sian. "'It Might Become as Big as Hip-Hop': The Rise and Rise of Hyperactive Subgenre Glitchcore." *NME*, December 18, 2020. https://www.nme.com/features/glitchcore-hyperpop-charli-xcx-100-gecs-rico-nasty-hip-hop-2841348.

Williams, Trey. "Women in Hollywood Are Fighting to Change the Culture of Sexual Harrassment." *MarketWatch*, January 3, 2018. https://www.marketwatch.com/story/how-hollywood-is-aiming-to-change-its-culture-of-sexual-harassment-2017-12-28.

Wikileaks. "Press Release: Wikileaks Releases Fifth Estate Challenger: Mediastan—A Wikileaks Road Movie." News, October 11, 2013. https://wikileaks.org/Press-Release-WikiLeaks-Releases.html.

Witchge, Tamara. "Transforming Journalistic Practice: A Profession Caught between Change and Tradition." In *Rethinking Journalism: Trust and Participation in a Transformed News Landscape,* edited by Chris Peters and Marcel Jeroen Broersma, 160–72. New York: Routledge, 2013.

Wojcicki, Susan. "YouTube at 15: My Personal Journey and the Road Ahead." YouTube Official Blog, February 14, 2020. https://blog.youtube/news-and-events/youtube-at-15-my-personal-journey.

Wolchover, Nicole. "How Did BART Kill Cellphone Service?" *Scientific American*, August 16, 2011. https://www.scientificamerican.com/article/how-did-bart-kill-cellpho/.

Woolley, Samuel. "We're Fighting Fake News AI Bots by Using More AI. That's a Mistake." *MIT Technology Review*, January 9, 2020. https://www.technologyreview.com/2020/01/08/130983/were-fighting-fake-news-ai-bots-by-using-more-ai-thats-a-mistake/.

Workman, Robert. "Coke Launches Interactive Billboard in Times Square." *AList Daily*, July 8, 2015. https://www.alistdaily.com/media/coke-launches-interactive-billboard-in-times-square/.

Wortham, Jenna. "A Political Coming of Age for the Tech Industry." *New York Times*, January 17, 2012. https://www.nytimes.com/2012/01/18/technology/web-wide-protest-over-two-antipiracy-bills.html.

Wright, Scott. "From 'Third Place' to 'Third Space': Everyday Political Talk in Non-Political Online Spaces," *Javnost—The Public* 19, no. 3 (2012): 5–20.

Wu, Sarah. "YouTuber Curls Her Hair Using Cheetos." *Teen Vogue,* September 8, 2016. https://www.teenvogue.com/story/youtuber-curls-hair-with-cheetos-challenge.

Wu, Tim. *The Master Switch.* New York: Vintage Books, 2010.

Wu, Tim. "Network Neutrality, Broadband Discrimination." *Journal of Telecommunications and High Technology Law* 2 (2003): 141–79.

Xiao, Henry, Dever M. Carney, Soo Jeong Youn, Rebecca A. Janis, Louis G. Castonguay, Jeffrey A. Hayes, and Benjamin D. Locke. "Are We in Crisis? National Mental Health and Treatment Trends in College Counseling Centers." *Psychological Services* 14, no. 4 (2017): 407–15. http://dx.doi.org/10.1037/ser0000130.

Yang, Xin-She. "Fractals in Small-World Networks with Time-Delay." *Chaos, Solitions, and Fractals* 13 (2002): 215–19.

York, Eric J. and Johndan Johnson-Eilola. "Enduring Designs, Transient Designers: A Comparison of the Workspaces and Materials of Professionals and Novices." *Proceedings of the 38th ACM International Conference on Design of Communication,* article no. 40 (2020): 1–8. https://doi.org/10.1145/3380851.3416783.

York, Jillian C. "Reddit Banned a Pro-Trump Subreddit. Here's What That Means for Hate Speech." NBC News, July 2, 2020. https://www.nbcnews.com/think/opinion/reddit-banned-pro-trump-subreddit-here-s-what-means-hate-ncna1232797.

York, Jillian C. *Silicon Values: The Future of Free Speech Under Surveillance Capitalism.* New York: Verso, 2021.

York, Jillian C. and David Greene. "Facebook's Latest Proposed Policy Change Exemplifies the Trouble with Moderating Speech at Scale." Electronic Frontier Foundation. February 4, 2021. https://www.eff.org/deeplinks/2021/02/facebooks-latest-proposed-policy-change-exemplifies-trouble-moderating-speech-0.

York, Jillian C., Corynne McSherry, and Danny O'Brien. "Beyond Platforms: Private Censorship, Parler, and the Stack." Electronic Frontier Foundation, January 11, 2021. https://www.eff.org/deeplinks/2021/01/beyond-platforms-private-censorship-parler-and-stack.

Yoshida, Emily. "Shows About Nothing: Togetherness and HBO's Sunday Night Mumblecore Block." *The Verge*, January 12, 2015. https://www.theverge.com/2015/1/12/7531631/hbo-togetherness-girls-looking-mumblecore-sunday-night.

Young, Iris Marion. "Communication and the Other: Beyond Deliberative Democracy." In *Democracy and Difference: Contesting the Boundaries of the Political,* edited by Seyla Benhabib, 120–35. Princeton, NJ: Princeton University Press, 1996.

Younger, Jon. "Contra and Other Platforms Are Building a New Kind of Freelance Community." *Forbes*, April 10, 2020. https://www.forbes.com/sites/jonyounger/2020/04/10/contra-and-other-platforms-are-building-a-new-kind-of-freelance-community/?sh=616d0f8c6de7.

Yousman, Bill. "Challenging the Media/Incarceration Complex Through Media Education." In *Working for Justice: A Handbook of Prison Education and Activism,* edited by Stephen John Harnett, Eleanor Novek, and Jennifer K. Wood. Urbana, IL: University of Illinois Press, 2013.

Zeger, Eli. "How Corporations Try to Be More Human Than Humans." *Current Affairs*, June 24, 2020. https://www.currentaffairs.org/2020/06/how-corporations -try-to-be-more-human-than-humans.

Zittrain, Jonathan. *The Future of the Internet and How to Stop it*. New Haven: Yale University Press, 2008.

Zittrain, Jonathan, Robert Faris, Helmi Norman, Justin Clark, Casey Tilton, and Ryan Morrison-Westphal. "The Shifting Landscape of Global Internet Censorship." Cambridge, MA: Internet Monitor, a project of the Berkman Center for Internet & Society at Harvard University, 2017.

Zollman, Florian. "Corporate-Market Power and Ideological Domination: The Propaganda Model after 30 Years—Relevance and Further Application." In *The Propaganda Model Today: Filtering Perception and Awareness*, edited by Joan Pedro-Carañana, Daniel Broudy, and Jeffrey Klaehn, 223–36. London: University of Westminster Press, 2018.

Zoltany, Monika. "Shia LaBeouf Flag Capture Is Nothing—4Chan Once Called in an Airstrike." *Inquisitr*, March 12, 2017. https://www.inquisitr.com/4053076/shia -labeouf-flag-capture-is-nothing-4chan-once-called-in-an-airstrike/.

Zuboff, Shosana. "It's Not That We've Failed to Rein in Facebook and Google. We've Not Even Tried." *The Guardian*, July 2, 2019. https://www.theguardian. com/commentisfree/2019/jul/02/facebook-google-data-change-our-behaviour -democracy.

Zuboff, Shoshana. *The Age of Surveillance Capitalism*. London: Profile Books, 2019.

# Index

*Page references for figures are italicized*

# About the Author

**Corinne M. Dalelio**, PhD, is an assistant professor in the Department of Communication, Media, and Culture at Coastal Carolina University. Having worked professionally for eight years in education and outreach with a specialization in digital web design, her research focus is on the effects and impacts of interactive media and online communication. She developed an original method for mapping and visualizing informal, asynchronous, online discussions, which she has used for analyses in a variety of contexts, including fan communities, higher education, and citizen discussions of news. Her work has been published in the *International Journal on E-Learning*, the *Journal of Digital and Media Literacy*, *Communication Teacher*, and the *International Journal of Knowledge, Technology, and Society.*

Made in the USA
Columbia, SC
31 August 2023

22328922R00172